jBPM5 Developer Guide

A Java developer's guide to the JBoss Business Process Management framework

Mauricio Salatino

Esteban Aliverti

[PACKT] PUBLISHING open source community experience distilled

BIRMINGHAM - MUMBAI

jBPM5 Developer Guide

First published: December 2012

Production Reference: 1101212

Published by Packt Publishing Ltd.
Livery Place
35 Livery Street
Birmingham B3 2PB, UK.

ISBN 978-1-84951-644-0

www.packtpub.com

Cover Image by Asher Wishkerman (wishkerman@hotmail.com)

Credits

Authors
Mauricio Salatino
Esteban Aliverti

Reviewers
Mariano Nicolas De Maio
Maciej Swiderski
Demian Calcaprina

Acquisition Editor
Joanna Finchen

Lead Technical Editor
Susmita Panda

Technical Editors
Charmaine Pereira
Pooja Pande

Copy Editors
Aditya Nair
Brandt D'Mello
Alfida Paiva

Project Coordinator
Michelle Quadros

Proofreader
Stephen Silk

Indexer
Monica Ajmera

Graphics
Aditi Gajjar

Production Coordinator
Shantanu Zagade

Cover Work
Shantanu Zagade

Foreword

Business Process Management (BPM), in general, is not something you learn overnight. I personally consider it more like learning a new language, where you first have to spend some time getting familiar with the basics and gradually extend your vocabulary. Learning or staying up-to-date with some of the latest technology changes has never been easy. It might not always be easy to find a good overview, detailed information on the web, or examples that explain the concepts in detail. A book like this definitely helps a lot by starting with the basics and gradually diving more into the details.

The jBPM project—while it might have started as a simple, open source workflow engine—has grown significantly over the last few years. jBPM uses a lot of the same approaches and provides solutions similar to the way other BPM vendors are applying the BPM methodology. With the arrival of the BPMN 2.0 specification, which is being supported by many different vendors nowadays, there is even a (business user friendly) language for defining business processes that is shared across vendors. So, there is a huge amount of generic BPM knowledge for you to learn. But jBPM also has its own key characteristics (for example, how it integrates business processes with business rules and complex event processing in a unique way), and only on learning these will you be able to access the full power of the project.

I have known Mauricio and Esteban for quite a few years now, as they have been working in the jBPM and Drools community for a long time already. I met them a few times over the years, and recently had the privilege of being able to hire Mauricio as part of the core team. He's very enthusiastic, and combines this with a deep technical knowledge of all the internal details, which makes him one of the best evangelists in our project. For that reason, he received two JBoss Recognition Awards for his work on new features and bug fixing for the jBPM project in 2011. Esteban received a similar one in 2012 for his work on new features.

Mauricio and Esteban have done a great job in this book in starting from the basics; by first introducing BPM as a discipline, exploring the details on how to then start modeling your first few processes while learning the language, and then going deeper into specific features and tools that are built around that. Some of the chapters go into a lot of detail on specific components (for example, human task management), so there is a lot of information for those who are looking for some of these details as well.

Without a doubt, the authors have deep technical knowledge of all the internal technical details of the project. I believe they have made a great mix of first explaining some of the concepts in an abstract way and then jumping into details with real code and by using realistic examples. The emergency service example and many others had already made Mauricio famous in the jBPM community, before he joined the project full-time.

So I hope this book will help you in getting a better understanding of the concepts behind the jBPM project, although this might require a second read of some of the chapters, as is stated in the first chapter. But I believe it will also provide you with some of the answers when you're deep into the coding already and are looking for that example on exactly how to do that one thing you've been fighting with for several hours.

Kris Verlaenen
jBPM Project Lead
JBoss, by Red Hat

About the Authors

Mauricio Salatino (a.k.a. Salaboy) has been an active part of the Java and open source software community for more than eight years. He got heavily involved in the JBoss jBPM and Drools projects as a community contributor five years ago. After publishing his first book about jBPM for Packt Publishing, he was recognized as a valuable member of both projects at the JBoss Community Awards 2011.

During the last three years, Mauricio has being teaching and consulting on jBPM and Drools in America and Europe. In 2010, he co-founded Plugtree (`www.plugtree.com`), which is a company that provides consultancy and training around the world. Since then, he has participated in international conferences such as Java One, Rules Fest, Jazoon, JBoss In Bossa, and RuleML, as the main speaker. He is now a Drools and jBPM Senior Software Developer at Red Hat / JBoss, fully dedicated to moving these projects forward.

Mauricio is now based in London. In his free time, he passionately promotes the open source projects he is using, and he is very active in the community forums on these projects. He also runs his personal blog (`http://salaboy.com`) about jBPM, Drools, and artificial intelligence.

I would like to thank Esteban for joining me in writing this book; he is an invaluable friend and a skilled professional. I also want to thank a friend, Diego Naya from OSDE, for his constant support of the Drools and jBPM community. Last but not least, I would like to thank all my blog followers and the Drools and jBPM community members, who are always pushing the boundaries to make these projects better.

Esteban Aliverti is an independent IT Consultant and Software Developer with more than eight years of experience in the field. He is a fervent open source promoter and developer with meaningful contributions to JBoss Drools and jBPM5 frameworks. After he got his Software Engineer degree in Argentina, he started working at local IT companies fulfilling different roles ranging from Web Developer to Software Architect. In 2009, while working for Plugtree, he was introduced to the JBoss Drools and jBPM5 projects. Over the next three years, he became one of the lead consultants inside Plugtree, providing services to its most important clients all around the world.

A former Professor of Java and object-oriented programming at Universidad de Mendoza, Argentina, he decided to continue with his passion for education outside the academic field by co-authoring the jBPM5 Community Training and Drools 5 Community Training online courses. The urge to share his knowledge and experience led him to participate as a speaker and co-speaker at several international conferences, such as Java One Brazil, RuleML, October Rule Fest, and various Drools and jBPM summits.

In JUDCon 2012, Esteban was recognized as a JBoss Community Leader during the JBoss Community Recognition Awards, as a way to acknowledge his contributions to Drools framework.

Currently located in Germany, he works as an independent Drools/jBPM Consultant and Developer. During his free time, he enjoys contributing to Drools and jBPM projects and in helping other people to embrace these technologies. In addition, Esteban has a personal blog (`http://ilesteban.wordpress.com`), which he uses to publish his work and discoveries on his journey through the open source world.

My contributions to this book would not have been possible without all the "mentors" I have had in my life: professors, colleagues, friends, and family. Their support, knowledge, and experience have made this book possible in one way or another. I would also like to especially thank Diego Naya, an open source visionary who taught me that companies are not just about money.

The most important acknowledgment is to Mauricio for giving me the opportunity to help him during the amazing adventure that was the writing process of this book.

About the Reviewers

Mariano Nicolas De Maio is a Software Engineer who graduated from Argentinian Enterprise University (UADE, from its initials in Spanish). He has over eight years of experience in Java and open source frameworks. He has been working with Drools and jBPM for the past three years, and has collaborated with the Drools and jBPM projects by adding extensions to the Human Task API's jBPM implementation and an initial implementation of the jBPM Form Builder (it can currently be found at `https://github.com/droolsjbpm/jbpm-form-builder`). He is happily married and taking care of a beautiful baby daughter.

He is currently working at Plugtree (`http://www.plugtree.com`) as a Solutions Architect for all jBPM- and Drools-related projects.

I would like to thank Mauricio and Packt Publishing for their confidence in me to review this book, as well as my wife and baby girl for putting up with me during the overtime I took to do it.

Maciej Swiderski is a jBPM Core Developer and enthusiast of open source software, especially in the Business Process Management domain. He has over eight years of experience in software development, and over five in the BPM area. He has helped many companies ease their way into adopting BPM technologies. You can find the latest information on his blog at `http://mswiderski.blogspot.com`, and you can get in touch with him on the official jBPM IRC channel `#jbpm` at `irc.freenode.net`.

Demian Calcaprina is a software developer driven by passion. He has spent his last seven years learning new technologies and ways to build software. He has found the JBoss Community, specially the Drools and jBPM ones, a great place to learn about producing great results with the collaborative effort of everyone to be used by everyone!

He met Mauricio when working in Plugtree, offering Drools and jBPM consulting, and it has been the most challenging and important part of his career. Nowadays, he continues providing jBPM and Drools consulting services as well as Java development services. He always makes an effort to be up-to-date with the new open source technologies, to find more places to help with passion.

He is currently pursuing his Software Engineering course in the Universidad Nacional del Centro de la Provincia de Buenos Aires at Tandil, Argentina.

He also loves playing chess and being in contact with the nature. He is really crazy about San Lorenzo, his favourite Argentinian soccer team!

I would like to thank Mauricio Salatino and Esteban Aliverti, two of the most important people in my career. Their knowledge is infinite, and their personal values even more!

I would also like to thank my wife, Julia, my parents and brothers, and specially my precious daughter, Manuela, who is my reason to smile everyday!

www.PacktPub.com

Support files, eBooks, discount offers and more

You might want to visit www.PacktPub.com for support files and downloads related to your book.

Did you know that Packt offers eBook versions of every book published, with PDF and ePub files available? You can upgrade to the eBook version at www.PacktPub.com and as a print book customer, you are entitled to a discount on the eBook copy. Get in touch with us at service@packtpub.com for more details.

At www.PacktPub.com, you can also read a collection of free technical articles, sign up for a range of free newsletters and receive exclusive discounts and offers on Packt books and eBooks.

PACKTLIB™

http://PacktLib.PacktPub.com

Do you need instant solutions to your IT questions? PacktLib is Packt's online digital book library. Here, you can access, read and search across Packt's entire library of books.

Why Subscribe?

- Fully searchable across every book published by Packt
- Copy and paste, print and bookmark content
- On demand and accessible via web browser

Free Access for Packt account holders

If you have an account with Packt at www.PacktPub.com, you can use this to access PacktLib today and view nine entirely free books. Simply use your login credentials for immediate access.

Mauricio Salatino:

This book is dedicated to my lovely wife Mariela,
writing a book without her support would be an impossible task.

Esteban Aliverti:

To Florencia, my supporting and beloved wife.
She is the person who brings balance to my life.

Table of Contents

Preface **1**

Chapter 1: Why Do We Need Business Process Management? **7**

Theoretical background **9**
Standard specifications – introduction, analysis, and explanations 9
jBPM5 – technical details and common practices 10
BPM conceptual background **10**
Business processes 11
Sequence of business activities 12
Activities are performed by business users and business applications 13
Humans and systems/applications behave differently 14
Humans and systems/applications can be classified differently 14
Achieving a business goal 15
The Business Process Management (BPM) discipline **15**
BPM stage 1 – discovering your business processes 17
BPM stage 2 – formalizing your new processes 19
BPM stage 3 – implementing your technical assets 21
Business entity model 21
Coordinating and orchestrating activities 23
BPM stage 4 – runtime 23
BPM stage 5 – monitoring 24
BPM stage 6 – improvements 25
Applying BPM in the real world **26**
BPMS checklist 26
Summary **29**

Chapter 2: BPM Systems Structure 31
Key components in a BPMS 31
BPMS core 32
The semantic module 33
The process engine 33
Process instance structures 37
Process engine execution mechanisms 37
Facts about the two approaches 42
Transactions and persistence 42
Human Task Component 44
Human tasks – life cycle 44
Human tasks – APIs 45
The identity component 45
Audit/history logs 46
Process engine components summary 47
Components inside jBPM5 48
Knowledge-centric APIs 49
Knowledge Builder 50
Knowledge Base 51
Knowledge Session 51
BPM systems surrounding topics 52
Service-oriented architecture 53
WS-BPEL and service orchestration 54
Enterprise Service Bus 56
Rule engines 59
Classic BPM system and rule engine integration 60
Event-driven architecture and complex event processing 61
Summary 64
Chapter 3: Using BPMN 2.0 to Model Business Scenarios 65
BPMN 2.0 introduction 66
Process Modelling Conformance 66
BPMN elements 67
Flow objects 68
Connecting objects 71
Data 72
Grouping 73
Artifacts 74
Task types 74
BPMN 2.0 introduction summary 77
Modelling business scenarios with BPMN 2.0 77
Hospital emergency scenario 77
Technical perspective 81
Hospital emergency technical overview 81
Summary 91

Chapter 4: Knowing Your Toolbox **93**
Setting up our environment **94**
Downloading the jBPM5 installer 94
Running the jBPM5 installer 96
Installed tools' description 97
JBoss Application Server 97
Drools Guvnor 98
jBPM5 process server 99
jBPM5 GWT console 99
Web process designer 100
Eclipse IDE – evaluation sample project 101
jBPM GWT console – evaluation sample process 107
jBPM GWT console summary 113
Drools Guvnor and web process designer 114
Frequently asked questions **119**
Summary **120**
Chapter 5: The Process Designer **121**
An IDE for our processes **121**
So many jBPM Designers, which one should I use? 122
The JBPM5 Eclipse plugin 122
Web Process Designer 123
The Eclipse BPMN 2.0 plugin 125
Interacting with Web Process Editor 126
Creating new processes 126
Accessing an existing process 128
Modifying the existing processes 128
Deleting the existing processes 129
Implementing our first process **130**
The Web Process Designer sections 130
Toolbar 131
Shape Repository 131
Editing canvas 132
The Properties panel 133
Footer 133
Emergency Bed Request Process First Design **134**
Configuring the process properties 135
Configuring the Start Event node 137
Configuring sequence flow elements 138
Configuring task nodes 139
Testing the process definition 148
Emergency Bed Request Process V2 **149**
Configuring process properties 150
Configuring the Exclusive Gateway node 150
Configuring the Sequence Flow elements 151
Configuring task nodes 153

Configuring the End Event nodes 154
Testing the process definition 154
Emergency Bed Request Process V3 **154**
Configuring process properties 155
Configuring Intermediate Signal events 156
Configuring the Terminate End events 156
Testing the process definition 157
Process modeling summary 158
Web Process Designer advanced topics **158**
Importing process definitions 158
Visual process validation 159
Domain-specific tasks 160
Work Item definition editor 161
Using Work Item Definitions in the Web Process Designer 162
Service Repository 163
Web Process Designer integration with Service Repository 163
Summary **165**
Chapter 6: Domain-specific Processes **167**
BPMN 2.0 task **168**
Domain-specific behavior in jBPM5 **169**
The work item handler interface 171
Synchronous interactions 173
Asynchronous interactions 176
Executor component 178
External service interactions 186
Summary **198**
Chapter 7: Human Interactions **199**
Human interactions **199**
Human interactions inside our processes 200
Web Services Human Task specification 201
Human tasks service APIs 203
Human tasks life cycle 205
External identity component integration 207
Human tasks and business processes' interactions 207
jBPM5 human task component overview **208**
Human task service APIs example 210
The human task work item handler 214
The user/group callbacks 215
HT work item handler and UserGroupCallback example 215
Task list oriented user interfaces **217**
Task lists 217

Group task lists 219
Task forms 220
Building our own user interfaces **225**
Summary **228**
Chapter 8: Persistence and Transactions **229**
Why we need persistence mechanisms **229**
Persisting long-running processes 232
Persistence in jBPM5 **233**
But how does it work internally? 235
Why we need a transaction mechanism **237**
Simple jBPM5 persistence and transactions configuration 240
Advanced jBPM5 persistence and transactions configuration 248
How much robustness do we need? 250
Frequently asked questions **252**
Summary **256**
Chapter 9: Smart Processes Using Rules **257**
Good old integration patterns **258**
The Drools Rule Engine **259**
What Drools needs to work 264
The power of the rules applied to our processes **268**
Gateway conditions 269
Java-based conditions 269
Rule-based conditions 271
Multi-process instance evaluations 274
Rule-based process selection and creation 277
Summary **281**
Chapter 10: Reactive Processes Using Drools Fusion **283**
What is an event? **284**
Event characteristics 285
Event-driven architectures **287**
Complex event processing **289**
Drools Fusion **290**
Event definitions 290
System clocks 293
Temporal operators 294
The Coincides temporal operator 296
Temporal operators summary 297
Sliding window support 298
Events life cycle management 299

Drools Fusion in action **300**
Mixing processes and events **302**
Summary **307**
Chapter 11: Architectural and Integration Tips **309**
Defining our architecture **309**
Using multiple knowledge sessions **313**
Defining a knowledge context 314
One session per knowledge context level 316
One session per process instance 316
One session per process category 324
Multiple sessions' coordination 326
Summary **329**
Index **331**

Preface

The jBPM5 Developer Guide book was written with the main goal of providing a comprehensive guide to understanding the main principles used by the jBPM project to build smarter applications using the power of business processes. This book covers important topics such as the BPMN 2.0 specification, the WS-HT specification, domain-specific constructs, and integration patterns. All these topics are covered with a technical perspective, which will help developers to adopt these technologies. The second half of the book is targeted at topics that are not usually covered by BPM systems. Topics such as business rules and complex event processing are introduced to demonstrate the power of mixing different business knowledge descriptions into one smarter platform.

What this book covers

Chapter 1, Why Do We Need Business Process Management?, covers an introduction to the BPM discipline. The content inside this chapter will guide you throughout the rest of the book, allowing you to understand why and how the jBPM project has been designed, and its constant evolution.

Chapter 2, BPM Systems Structure, goes in depth into understanding what the main pieces and components inside a **Business Process Management System (BPMS)** are. In this chapter, once we understand the basic concepts behind the BPM discipline, the concept of BPMS is introduced. The reader will find a deep and technical explanation about how a BPM system core can be built from scratch and how it will interact with the rest of the components in the BPMS infrastructure. This chapter also describes the intimate relationship between the Drools and jBPM projects, which is one of the key advantages of jBPM in comparison with all the other BPMSs.

Chapter 3, Using BPMN 2.0 to Model Business Scenarios, covers the main constructs used to model our business processes, guiding the reader through a set of examples that illustrate the most common modeling patterns. The BPMN 2.0 specification has become the de facto standard for modeling executable business processes since it was released in early 2011.

Chapter 4, Knowing Your Toolbox, gives an overview of all the tooling provided with jBPM 5.4.0.Final. This chapter describes each project feature and enumerates each project responsibility. This chapter also shows that different setups can be created, or components replaced, to fit into different scenarios.

Chapter 5, The Process Designer, covers a step-by-step tutorial on how to use the Web Process Designer provided by jBPM. The main idea behind this chapter is to help the user get comfortable with the modeling phase, providing in-depth examples of how to model our own business processes.

Chapter 6, Domain-specific Processes, covers the mechanisms provided by jBPM to extend the process diagrams and execution with domain-specific constructs, allowing the business and technical users to simpler and more and meaningful processes. One very important part of business processes is the ability to reflect how a company is doing its work.

Chapter 7, Human Interactions, covers in depth the Human Task service component inside jBPM. A a big feature of BPMS is the capability to coordinate human and system interactions. It also describes how to build a user interface using the concepts of task lists and task forms.

Chapter 8, Persistence and Transactions, covers the shared mechanisms between the Drools and jBPM projects used to store information and define transaction boundaries. When we want to support processes that coordinate systems and people over long periods of time, we need to understand how the process information will be persisted.

Chapter 9, Smart Processes Using Rules, gives a quick introduction to the Drools Rule Engine, and how we can use the inference power provided by Drools in conjunction with our business processes. Mixing business processes with business rules gives us the ultimate power to define advanced and complex scenarios.

Chapter 10, Reactive Processes Using Drools Fusion, covers the most important features of Drools Fusion, and how these features can be used to improve, monitor, and cover business situations that require temporal inferences. Drools Fusion adds the ability of temporal reasoning to the Drools Rule Engine.

Chapter 11, Architectural and Integration Tips, describes what the internal structure of our applications will look like, depending on the number of scenarios that we want to cover. A set of patterns is described in order to give the reader a comprehensive way to deal with different situations.

What you need for this book

This is a developer guide, and for that reason it is highly recommended that you read this book with a computer beside you, where you can try the examples and open, compile, and test the provided projects. The main idea behind the book is to get you up to speed in the development of applications or tooling that use jBPM, and for that reason this book spends a lot of time with code examples and unit tests to run.

Good programming skills are required to easily understand the examples presented in this book. Most of the chapters complement the covered topics with a set of executable Maven projects. A basic understanding of Maven, Java, and JUnit is required.

Who this book is for

This book is intended for Java developers and architects who want to start developing applications using jBPM. jBPM 5 is a very flexible framework; but with this flexibility comes architectural and design decisions that we need to make when we start using it. This book offers a complete reference to all of the components distributed with jBPM 5.4.0.Final community version, and it can be used as reference material to guide a team of developers in building efficient solutions using business processes, business rules, and complex event processing.

After reading this book, you will have a good understanding of jBPM 5 architecture and components. jBPM5 is a Red Hat lead open source community project and is fully supported through JBoss BRMS product. If you are interested in the BRMS Product you can find more details here: `https://www.redhat.com/products/jbossenterprisemiddleware/business-rules/`.

Conventions

In this book, you will find a number of styles of text that distinguish between different kinds of information. Here are some examples of these styles, and an explanation of their meaning.

Code words in text are shown as follows: "We can include other contexts through the use of the `include` directive."

A block of code is set as follows:

```
public interface ProcessDefinition {
  public Map<Long, Task>getTasks();
  public void setTasks(Map<Long, Task> tasks);
  public void addTask(Long id, Task node);
}
```

When we wish to draw your attention to a particular part of a code block, the relevant lines or items are set in bold:

```
public interface ProcessDefinition {
  public Map<Long, Task>getTasks();
  public void setTasks(Map<Long, Task> tasks);
  public void addTask(Long id, Task node);
}
```

Any command-line input or output is written as follows:

```
# cp /usr/src/asterisk-addons/configs/cdr_mysql.conf.sample
    /etc/asterisk/cdr_mysql.conf
```

New terms and **important words** are shown in bold. Words that you see on the screen, in menus or dialog boxes for example, appear in the text like this: "clicking the **Next** button moves you to the next screen".

> Warnings or important notes appear in a box like this.

> Tips and tricks appear like this.

Reader feedback

Feedback from our readers is always welcome. Let us know what you think about this book—what you liked or may have disliked. Reader feedback is important for us to develop titles that you really get the most out of.

To send us general feedback, simply send an e-mail to `feedback@packtpub.com`, and mention the book title via the subject of your message.

If there is a topic that you have expertise in and you are interested in either writing or contributing to a book, see our author guide on `www.packtpub.com/authors`.

Customer support

Now that you are the proud owner of a Packt book, we have a number of things to help you to get the most from your purchase.

Downloading the example code

You can download the example code files for all Packt books you have purchased from your account at `http://www.PacktPub.com`. If you purchased this book elsewhere, you can visit `http://www.PacktPub.com/support` and register to have the files e-mailed directly to you.

Errata

Although we have taken every care to ensure the accuracy of our content, mistakes do happen. If you find a mistake in one of our books—maybe a mistake in the text or the code—we would be grateful if you would report this to us. By doing so, you can save other readers from frustration and help us improve subsequent versions of this book. If you find any errata, please report them by visiting `http://www.packtpub.com/support`, selecting your book, clicking on the **errata submission form** link, and entering the details of your errata. Once your errata are verified, your submission will be accepted and the errata will be uploaded on our website, or added to any list of existing errata, under the Errata section of that title. Any existing errata can be viewed by selecting your title from `http://www.packtpub.com/support`.

Piracy

Piracy of copyright material on the Internet is an ongoing problem across all media. At Packt, we take the protection of our copyright and licenses very seriously. If you come across any illegal copies of our works, in any form, on the Internet, please provide us with the location address or website name immediately so that we can pursue a remedy.

Please contact us at `copyright@packtpub.com` with a link to the suspected pirated material.

We appreciate your help in protecting our authors, and our ability to bring you valuable content.

Questions

You can contact us at `questions@packtpub.com` if you are having a problem with any aspect of the book, and we will do our best to address it.

1
Why Do We Need Business Process Management?

The adoption of new technologies, new concepts, and upgraded definitions often requires a change of mindset. The open mindedness to acquire a new vision is also fundamental to a successful experience with a new framework or platform. Moreover, new adoptions sometimes cause frustration, wasted time, wrong results, painful nights of coding, projects that never end, and <<*add your own experience here*>>. However, you will see that it is worth the effort. As you may have noticed, the software industry pushes you to continuously learn new tools that will improve the way you design and architect solutions. Nowadays, **Business Process Management** (**BPM**) is becoming something that every developer needs to understand.

BPM is not only about coding or application development, but also about improving how a company works. We, as developers, need to understand this in order to start using BPM-oriented tools and frameworks. The main goal of BPM is to provide visibility to the company's business processes and find ways to improve and speed them up to increase profit and reduce costs.

In this, the first chapter, you will find some of the most important topics that you need to understand in order to start creating solutions that have an impact on how a company drives its business. Most important is the fact that the solution you build will enable the company to adapt the software to its current business reality.

With every new discipline that we want to learn, we need to start with baby steps and we have to try to understand how the change of paradigm enriches what we already know about building solutions. This book's main goal is to help you with the adoption and integration of the most common conceptual and technical topics that are required to work with the latest version of jBPM. To achieve its main goal, this book attacks both conceptual topics that can be used to understand any BPMS (Business Process Management System) and technical topics required to build great applications using jBPM5. Important definitions and concepts are highlighted throughout this book, which makes it easier to find solutions to new problems when they arise.

As soon as you start adopting these important concepts, you will notice a change in the way you find solutions, model situations, and build applications. At this point, it is of great significance for developers to start teaching these concepts to partners/ co-workers. Not only to developers, but also managers, business analysts, end users, and anyone interested in a BPM talk. In doing so, you will get immediate attention for sharing your recently acquired knowledge. Disciplines like BPM require a mind shift from the entire company, though obviously the change starts with you. Your help in the process of adopting BPM is vital, because it needs to happen at the company level and not only in the IT department. This ambitious goal will guarantee the total success of your projects.

We really need BPM to improve the quality and the flexibility of software solutions that we build. BPM is one more tool that will allow us to build exactly what a company pays us to do, helping them to drive their business. You will notice that there are a lot of things that you need to learn in order to drive successful BPM implementations, so I strongly recommend to first get yourself involved in the BPM world. That is to say spread the word, open a blog to share your personal experiences, and read others' experiences to enrich yourself. Then preach what you have learned from this book and from your own experience. What is more, teaching and sharing what you have acquired develops your professional skills and helps you to gather different perspectives and visions from the topics that you find relevant. So be confident and proud of your own achievements. Now let's get down to work.

The content of this book is divided into three different facets:

- Theoretical background
- Introduction to standard specifications
- jBPM5 technical details

Each type of content requires you to change your way of perceiving the presented information.

Theoretical background

These sections are vital, so you have to read them carefully at least twice. Important definitions that you must adopt for your everyday work will be discussed, exemplified, and dissected. Moreover, you should discuss each of these definitions with your co-workers. That's the ultimate step to understand and apply these terms. It's important to focus your mind on getting the new concepts and trying to understand how each definition fits with all the things that you know from your previous experience. You really need to open your mind in order to understand the definitions and the context where we will use them. If you read a lot of different papers and studies, you will notice that nowadays a lot of buzz words are being introduced in the BPM field, and this fact can cause a lot of confusion. That's why I scope each definition to a particular context. I will first explain each concept in a very generic way, helping you to understand the reason and purpose of the concept without including any reference to implementation or technical details. In the more technical sections, I will map these concepts to more technical terms with concrete references to jBPM5.

Standard specifications – introduction, analysis, and explanations

Based on industry experience and the collaboration of different groups of companies, standard specifications are created to define a common baseline to be shared and applied in new developments.

This book introduces two of the main standard specifications behind jBPM5: the BPMN 2.0 specification and the Web Service Human Task specification. Both standards are introduced and analyzed because both contain core concepts needed to fully understand how to create industry-accepted and interoperable applications.

Keep in mind that some topics are only introduced here; but it's important to read all the specifications entirely to really understand the big picture. Gaining experience from reading specifications will give you a great and solid vision about common and standard practices adopted in a wide range of industries.

The content of these sections must be understood as "standards reflect good practices". Standardized data structures, APIs, and code conventions may or may not be adopted by a concrete implementation of the standard. If the implementation does not comply 100 percent with the whole specification (this usually happens), we need to know what those situations are and how to deal with them.

jBPM5 – technical details and common practices

Third, but no less important, this book will cover a complete list of the most important technical topics inside jBPM5, which will be discussed and demonstrated in practice.

A "simple-to-very-complex" approach will be used in the examples to reach real-life solutions with real-life complexity. The source code of these examples can be found in github: `https://github.com/Salaboy/jBPM5-Developer-Guide/archive/1.0.Final.zip`. Not all of the lines of code will be explained here.

The examples are created to show the common pitfalls that you often find during the first adoptions of the tool; so this will save you time.

As I have read in many of my first book reviews, the technical sections of this book should be read having the source code available. I strongly recommend you to look at the code reference in each section and open the provided projects in your favorite IDE. This will help you to practice and get used to real development tools, projects, and errors.

This chapter is focused on the whole conceptual background needed to get your hands on jBPM5. Most of the concepts that will be introduced in the next section are related to the Business Process Management discipline. You really need to have those concepts in your head when you start with your first project. Believe me, you will save a lot of time in the process of learning jBPM5 if you understand the concepts that make it the way it is.

BPM conceptual background

As you may know, BPM stands for Business Process Management. So, in this section we will go deeply into the conceptual cornerstone behind it and try to fully comprehend it. The first thing that we need to understand is the concept of process.

The broadest meaning of the term **process** is to transform an input to get a more useful outcome for a specific context.

Process or processing is about transformation, for which we usually need to have three things:

- An input to transform
- A set of steps to explicitly achieve the transformation
- A well-defined desired output

If we want to transform wood into paper, we obviously need to follow some steps depending on the wood we have and the outcome (type of paper) we want.

About four years ago, I read an incredibly good and concrete phrase that completely changed my way of proposing a solution to a problem:

> If you can't explain what you are doing, you don't know what you are doing.

If we want a transformation to happen, we need to define an input, the desired outcome, as well as the intermediate steps. If we can't do that, we really don't know what we need to make the transformation happen. That's a fact of life.

Summing up, for each transformation (process) we need to know all the steps required to achieve the required outcome (goal) giving a well-defined input.

The knowledge of how to achieve the goal, and the transformation steps required, is usually known by an expert in the context. This expert knows how to deal with normal processes and also how to deal with specific or exceptional situations for a wide range of different types of woods and papers.

I may possibly have a basic idea about how to make paper from wood, but for a real-life scenario, I may not be able to describe all the steps needed to make quality paper. If we really want to know about real-life processes, we need to talk to experts in that field.

Business processes

The word **business** highlights the relationship between transformations with a specific domain/context. Business processes need to be evaluated, analyzed, modeled, validated, and designed by people trained to understand the domain where they belong. The people related to business processes usually come from different places and/or different business units, and have different roles. Because of this, it's extremely important to understand the analysis and the point of view that comes from people with different skills and different backgrounds.

The terms business user and business role use the business prefix for exactly the same reason. In order to have a wider definition, we can say that business could also mean more than one domain / company / business unit.

Going back to business processes, it's important to note that the goal of a business process will be highly related to the business strategy and domain.

> Business processes are a sequence of business activities that are performed by business users and business applications (company systems or third party systems) to achieve a business goal.

If you hate the word "business" as much as I do, please feel free to mentally skip it or replace it with one of the following alternatives:

- Domain
- Company
- Company unit
- Field

The following sections dissect the proposed definition of business process into three parts. Let's analyze together the different sections in order to understand why it is extremely important to manage these concepts when we design and develop our business processes.

Sequence of business activities

You will see from the domain's perspective (manager, high-level company people) that a process is only composed of activities chained together. From the technical angle, we can say that our process will be composed of:

- Activities
- Events
- Gateways
- Sequence flows

Don't worry about these terms. All these technical concepts will be analyzed when the BPMN2 specification is introduced in *Chapter 3, Using BPMN 2.0 to Model Business Scenarios*.

The only thing you need to know right now is that an activity is just an "atomic" piece of work that contributes directly to achieving the business goal. I've used quotes in the previous sentence around atomic because an activity can be atomic in one context but composed of multiple subactivities in another lower-level (more specific) perspective. Here's a simple example: in a car factory, one activity inside a high-level process can be "build the car engine", but from a low-level perspective, this activity can be composed of many different activities and low-level processes.

The business perspective used to describe a business process should be maintained to describe all the activities inside that process. This will contribute to a better understanding of the different users and roles inside the company, which may probably raise the question in your mind, "How do I find the correct/right business perspective to describe and define a business process and all the activities inside it?"

Don't worry! This is a common question, and the answer is fairly simple: all the perspectives are right. A manager (high-level) perspective process will handle information that can be used for decision making or strategy analysis. On the other hand, if we describe a lower-level process, the audience will probably change to more specific business users who really know the low-level activities that need to be done in order to achieve the day-to-day goals that benefit the company.

The business user perspective is great for formalizing and guiding how the day-to-day work is done by the company members. The process execution will guide them throughout their daily activities. These low-level activities will be in charge of handling information related to many areas, including the following:

- Customer information
- Account information
- Document-specific meta information

In the end, all the processes will interact together in order to coordinate activities across all the company roles and business units. It is common to see that a low-level process triggers a high-level process and vice versa. Usually, high-level processes are interested in aggregating information about low-level processes to analyze the overall performance or to gather important information for decision making.

Activities are performed by business users and business applications

The title of this section is pretty clear. We will have people and systems working together to fulfill a goal. Let's go deeper into some related topics, such as the following:

- Humans and systems behave differently
- Humans and systems can be classified differently

Because processes are basically a sequence of interactions between systems and people, we need to clearly identify the main characteristics and differences between them.

Humans and systems/applications behave differently

Human activities (user tasks in the BPMN2 specification) will represent all the human interactions in our processes. In other words, we say that each time a person is involved in a business process, we will end up having a human activity to represent the interaction in our process definition.

If we want to automate our business process execution, knowing that a person or a group of people are involved in a set of activities will help us to clearly define how the interaction between the process and the person must be achieved.

On the other hand, when we talk about systems or applications we usually think in terms of remote procedure calls. We can assume that the company will have a set of external systems exposing well-defined interfaces that are waiting to be called to solve a very specific problem. Systems can be internal applications/services of the company that are in charge of doing internal calculations or specific procedures that are usually atomic. That means that if we want to obtain a piece of information or a calculation, we just call a service and get a response from the system.

Humans and systems/applications can be classified differently

It's important to notice that when we talk about people in a business process, we usually talk about different groups depending on the process context and perspective. The following groups/roles of people can be involved in a process definition:

- Business user: Managers and employees, internal to the company / business unit
- Customer / client / providers: external interaction with a person outside the company
- Third-party business users: external individuals that participate in specific activities providing knowledge that we don't have inside our company

Systems can be classified based on their technical behavior as synchronous or asynchronous. We can also classify them by their owners. Systems can be internal to the company or third-party applications. These external / third-party interactions are not a technical problem at all. From the perspective of the process, it's important to define the ownership of each application/system in order to understand how the interaction will be made. We usually create a dictionary containing a map of all the systems and functionalities that our processes will use. Most of the time we need to optimize third-party service consumption based on company regulations or requirements.

Achieving a business goal

The most important part of the business process definition is achieving goals. The goal of the process should never be forgotten. We can say that the goal of a business process is the soul that defines the activities and the process' existence.

The business goal shouldn't be in any way disruptive or impossible to accomplish in the selected business process perspective. Each business process definition must define a clear goal and all the activities must be defined in order to contribute to the goal achievement.

Mixing goals and perspectives is a common mistake that you need to avoid when you model your first business process. When this happens, it's recommended to split the business process definition into multiple well-scoped processes for the sake of understandability and maintainability.

One way of achieving this difficult task is to create a brief textual description about the process' main responsibility, ownership, and the concrete goal that was designed to be achieved. This brief description can be used to train new people to understand why the process is useful to the company. You also will end up with a self-documented process that can be used by the company to improve quality levels.

The Business Process Management (BPM) discipline

We already know what a business process is, so now it's time to take a look at the discipline that helps us to discover, model, formalize, execute, monitor, and improve our business processes.

BPM is an iterative discipline that defines multiple stages that are executed in repeated cycles, which provides us a path of continuous business process improvements. BPM can also be seen as a set of best practices with a lot of focus on improving the way the company does its job.

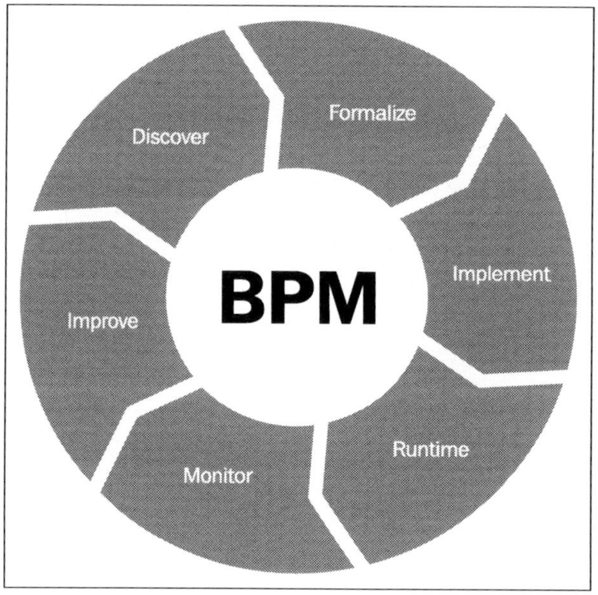

For the rest of this section we will analyze the main stages of the BPM discipline. We need to understand the proposed activities in depth in order to be able to put them into practice. You will see that the rest of the book is about how to create or integrate applications for implementing these stages with jBPM5.

Once again, BPM is not about coding Java or software development at all. You need to understand that BPM's focus is on how work is done inside a company / business / domain. The BPM discipline's scope and main goal is to improve the current business situation by planning iterations to solve well-defined problems. You may be wondering how BPM achieves such a difficult task and also how it is related to jBPM5.

After the first three chapters of this book, the content will be really technical. However, it will be clearly shown how all these concepts solve real situations. We will see that the jBPM5 project structure, APIs, and designs are backed up by these concepts, and you will understand the importance of knowing them for future designs.

The following sections describe the stages proposed by the BPM discipline. These stages highlight the most important points that need to be understood to start using a BPM system.

BPM stage 1 – discovering your business processes

This is probably the hardest stage inside the BPM discipline and the one that gives the company the most benefits. Obviously, we first need to identify how the company is doing the job. This task is usually done by business analysts, who need to understand the activities and the goals that different sectors of the company have. From a developer's perspective, we need to understand how they discover those tasks in order to understand the information that they will generate.

It's common practice in big companies to have a full department of business analysts, technical people, and a project leader solely dedicated to discovering and improving company business processes. This department is usually called the Process Improvement department.

To achieve such a level of maturity, it's important to explain and understand the advantages of adopting BPM as the entire company's way of working. BPM is not a change that can be made only at the developer's level or the IT department level. It needs to be made throughout the business units, and all the business roles of the company need to wholly agree with the change. That's why finding sponsors that really believe in BPM as a discipline will help you during technical implementations, because they know the challenges that you might find and they will understand the effort required to get the best results for the company.

Failing to communicate the advantages or the investment of applying BPM inside the company may cause frustration and project failures. A huge amount of collaboration among different roles in a company will be required to discover and correctly understand the best way to accommodate the BPM discipline to each company.

We, as developers, can promote BPM in our companies and help during the initial phases of adoption. To start a brand new BPM project, you can choose a small process that achieves a non-critical business goal. After identifying a concrete goal, a set of interviews is held with the people involved in that process. To achieve effective interviews, you have to prepare a questionnaire for each person/role involved in the process. It is also advisable to have a wide set of questions to ask each interviewee, as well as more specific questions in case complex activities arise.

Some questions that I've found useful for these interviews are:

- What's your role in the X process?
- Which systems/applications and screens do you use to complete the X activity?
- Are you doing paper work? What kind of forms are you filling out?

- Is the activity related to the review of information sent by another person or system?
- Are you an expert in a specific field? Are you the only one responsible for that activity? Are there other people trained for that specific activity?
- How many activities are you doing inside a specific business process?
- How many activities related to different business processes are you currently doing? (day / week / month)
- Do you need to move information from one place to another by moving paper forms to different departments or using the postal service?
- Do you use email/chat as a communication channel to send information to customers or to other business units?
- Do you interact directly with customers/clients, face-to-face?
- Are you aware of the BPM practice and why the company wants to adopt it?
- Do you understand the goals that your activities help to achieve? Can you provide an end-to-end (visibility) description about how your activities fit within the other activities in the same process?
- Are you handling duplicate or unnecessary information?
- What are the well-known flaws of your activities?
- How do you deal with exceptional situations, missing pieces of information, or new cases?

If they answer that they do paper work, you should get a scanned version of all the forms that they have to fill out. If they are using different systems / screens / applications, get those screenshots.

A questionnaire like this one should be introduced and explained to each person who participates in the interview. Explaining the objective of these questions will encourage collaboration and will reduce the stress generated by the feeling of being graded on their work performance.

The answers to these questions are extremely valuable pieces of information. They will give us a primary understanding of what is being done to achieve the business goal.

Once we finish all the interviews from the people involved in one process, we can mix all the answers to get an accurate description of your business process' main path, highlighting the most important activities.

The questions will be specifically targeted to the selected role in the company, but the answers will belong to a specific user. Each person involved in the interview process will receive a questionnaire tailored to his/her role in the company. This allows us to gather specific information for each role, facilitating the interview process.

Based on the answers from the interview process and the collaboration with the IT department, you can structure the information to recognize as well as describe systems and paper forms that are being used in current activities. There will be a process for the disambiguation of the gathered information, and a business dictionary will be created. The information gathered by the interview process will result in a tabular list of activities that each role in the company executes.

Each of these activities will contain the information that is used by a human actor or during a system interaction. This information is vital in order to be able to formalize how the process is done and to correctly understand how people and systems interact together.

Finally, you can try to find hidden or missing pieces about how the business goal is currently being achieved. Sometimes during the interview phase, we miss information related to company-wide procedures (for example, systems that execute periodic batch procedures that impact some processes' activities). Finding these missing pieces will give you a complete view of what is going on. To find these missing pieces, you will require a certain amount of expertise in the domain to decide how much information you need in order to start formalizing and putting together these activities' lists into business processes' definitions. At this point, it is extremely useful to check the results of the interview process with one of the domain experts. An expert will quickly point out the vocabulary inconsistencies, the missing activities, and the ambiguous terms.

BPM stage 2 – formalizing your new processes

Once we identify a new business process, and the owner and the business goal are well defined, we can create a formal representation of the process, without ambiguities.

A business process can be formalized using a predefined language. Using a common language will help us to share the process definition with different people who understand this language. For this formalization stage, several languages have been designed during the last 20 years. Most of these are usually graphical languages that express workflow-like diagrams to describe business situations. Using specific iconography, these charts represent different domains or industries. You can read about Petri nets and pi-calculus to understand where new languages come from. Using languages that can be graphically represented and easily understood really helps business professionals to understand the activities that need to be done in order to achieve the business goal.

Most languages are designed with these concepts in mind. It is always a problem to learn more than one language to express the same concepts in different areas of the company. Then, the problem shifts to picking ones that fit your company best.

In 2012, we can say that BPMN 2.0 is the de facto standard for process modeling. We will analyze this standard in depth in a chapter completely dedicated to it. In *Chapter 3, Using BPMN 2.0 to Model Business Scenarios*, we will learn about the BPMN 2.0 graphical representation and execution semantics proposed by the standard specification.

For us and for the project itself, it's really important to have a unified and standard language that is compatible with multiple vendors. These days, to learn standards like BPMN 2.0 is becoming really necessary. A thorough (widely practical) knowledge of a standard like BPMN 2.0 will help you to understand different systems' implementations, tooling, and common practices.

We will elaborate on the formalizing stage in *Chapter 3, Using BPMN 2.0 to Model Business Scenarios*, which is about the BPMN 2.0 Specification, where we'll do a complete analysis of the language and how to use it.

> Formalizing means creating an unambiguous model

At this stage, business analysts are usually in charge of modeling business processes. All those analysts will need to be trained in the BPMN 2.0 language to model business processes correctly.

Some important decisions need to be made at this stage. Business analysts will be in charge of the accuracy of the models. They will need to decide which types of activities are required to represent the current process situation.

Obviously, a deep knowledge of the selected language will be required. In other words, business analysts will be responsible for the process. It must be semantically correct and represented accurately. During the first iteration, the process should be modeled to represent the "as is" situation. During the more advanced iterations, improvements can be included towards the desired "to be" representation of the process.

The resulting artifacts from this stage will be the formalized processes using a graphical representation that can be shared and understood by the different roles in the company.

BPM stage 3 – implementing your technical assets

At this stage, with the already formalized process, the IT/technical team needs to work in collaboration with the business analysts' team in order to add all the technical details required to run the modeled process.

At this point we already have a very important business knowledge asset for the company. The business process' formalized model provides a detailed specification about how the work is done inside that process. We need to keep this business asset safe and versioned. We usually set up a knowledge repository to store all our business assets in a centralized location.

It's really important to review the process definition and add all the details about the information that the activity inside our business process will handle and manipulate. In order to do this we need to make a couple of decisions. The following sections analyze and describe the options that we have to define and implement how the information is maintained and manipulated inside our business processes.

Business entity model

At this stage we usually create, define, or select a business entity model to work with. We need to have an executable entity model in order to use it inside our runtime environment. If we are working in a Java environment, for example, our entity model will need to be translated to Java classes. This model will be created based on the discovery stage results and it will represent the information that the business process will handle.

Usually, you will find that the company already has an existing business entity model taken from legacy systems. In such situations you will have to choose between the following three options:

- Use the inherited entity model inside your process activities.
    - Pros: You don't need to define a new model using new concepts. If your developers are already trained to understand this model, you don't need to rethink it.
    - Cons: Inherited models are usually complex, hard to understand, not updated, and make the process more difficult, causing technical delays and complicated workarounds. Inherited models are usually mixed with old application code. Legacy applications don't have simple data structures without functionality. We can find weird structures that mix functionality and add a lot of confusion to the data that is really important.

- Store external keys to the real entities inside your business processes.
    - Pros: You can re-use your old model data structures and store just a business key to be able to find all the related information when you need it.
    - Cons: If you only have a key, you will need the external system or data source each time you want to query/preview or update information. You need to have access to modify external system information, if that's required. You need to have public APIs to modify external information and keep it consistent. You need to evaluate network traffic usage. If you have a large number of concurrent users, this could be a problem. This is because in every system we need to take some precautions to support stress situations, trading off between memory usage and I/O.
- Create a model to store the data that will be handled by the process. This model can abstract the data sources and communication strategies required to retrieve the information.
    - Pros: You can define a dictionary of meaningful terms and concepts that abstract old and non-updated data structures that contain technical names and were conceived for old and low-level systems. You can define the underlying strategies to fetch all the information from the external systems. You can maintain a hybrid strategy for storing process information in dedicated storage, and keep the most queried and accessed information there, to avoid extensive network usage. You can unify terms across multiple systems.
    - Cons: Sometimes, maintaining the integrity between the old model and the new model becomes painful and an expert needs to be in charge of keeping everything in sync.

Once you define and know how to get and update information from your business model, you will need to bind each bit of information with the corresponding activity in your process. We usually do this with an expression language that allows us to express in a declarative way the information we need, without saying where it can be obtained.

One example of this could be: `#{ambulance.doctor.speciality}`

This expression will be evaluated at runtime, and an internal mechanism will be used to retrieve the information.

Coordinating and orchestrating activities

We will end up with a sequence of activities to coordinate between people and systems. As technical developers, we will find some interesting challenges to solve. We will be in charge of gluing together all the system interactions and providing a neat user interface for human interactions. In *Chapter 7, Human Interactions*, we will analyze all the technical requirements to implement stunning user interfaces and in *Chapter 6, Domain-specific Processes*, we will review all the relevant details about system-to-system interactions and the mechanisms that we need to know in order to keep everything simple.

Having a clear vision of the components that we need to implement and having a standardized and conceptually coherent way of interaction will make our life easier and we will end up with simple applications that are easy to maintain.

As I have mentioned in the discovery stage, we will create software assets and business assets that are extremely important, self documented, and expressed in domain- or business-specific languages.

At the end of this stage, we will end up with running processes that will allow us to test, validate, and simulate process behavior. Once you have learned the basics, this stage becomes trivial and the only thing that changes between one implementation and another are the external systems' connectors as well as the technologies used to build frontends. All these topics will be covered in the jBPM5 technical sections, where the best practices and the technical details that need to be considered will be introduced.

BPM stage 4 – runtime

I call this stage "runtime", though for more technical people we can call it "production runtime". In this stage we execute our defined business processes in order to drive the company's real activities. This stage is where the real fun begins. We need to be sure of the process correctness and that all the process interactions with external systems are already tested and working as expected.

When we reach this point, we can deploy our business assets (processes, rules, and associated descriptions) to our production environment and start training users to learn how to interact with their activities.

Now all the people involved in a selected process will use the same **user interfaces (UI)** to do their activities. Most of the time the UI replaces two or more third-party screens for different systems, unifying the interactions and making it easier to learn and train new people.

A unified approach to building all our UI makes a lot of sense in the integration context. We will go deeper into some rules and structures to build these UIs for human interactions in *Chapter 7, Human Interactions*.

The first time we enter this stage, we will probably try the UI with a couple of simple processes, restricted to a well-known group of users, where they can do their daily activities using the provided tools. When we have tested the processes with a small group of users doing real work, we will be ready to handle larger processes, larger groups of people, and more critical tasks and business goals.

In this stage we can detect performance issues, minor modifications in the data model, improvements in user interfaces for better usability, and so on.

> Be ready to take notes about what can be improved for the next iteration!

Until we see real people doing real work while interacting with our processes, we won't know what is OK and what is not. Based on what we see and what we can measure, we will learn important lessons for future processes.

After running some processes in a production environment, you will gain a lot of experience, and deploying new processes will be very easy and trivial. The first time will always be a traumatic and stressful experience. In this book I will try to share a fair number of tips and tricks to reduce the first timer's stress.

BPM stage 5 – monitoring

When we are confident in the runtime stage and more and more processes are being executed, we can start monitoring the processes' execution and performance.

For this stage we usually build a dashboard-like tool that allows us to monitor process execution and performance metrics. These dashboards are really important for high-level professionals that want to see snapshots of how the company is working in order to make the right decisions. As you can imagine, knowing the number of processes and activities that are completed per hour can be really helpful for planning reasons, accepting new commitments of work with providers and customers, as well as measuring the company's growth rate. This is just one example of the things you can do if you have information available.

Another related branch of study is called **Business Activity Monitoring (BAM)**. BAM defines the best practices as well as the metrics that are usually important for different types of companies.

Monitoring is about real-time information analysis and display. Tools for BAM must be designed and made flexible to show information from different sources and different types of metrics. Managers are usually interested in seeing aggregated pieces of information such as "The average time of completion of one or a more processes related to a particular business unit in the last month".

We usually display this information using different widgets that are specially designed to show very simple values. These widgets provide an overview about what is happening in the company in just one screen.

Managers can quickly see a high-level snapshot of the whole company, with information updates every minute. You need to remember that the information generated by your company processes is extremely important, and this stage is about externalizing this information for different perspectives in order to maximize data utilization.

BPM stage 6 – improvements

The last stage of the BPM discipline is about continuous improvement of your processes. This stage is not about real-time analysis, but some of the tools built for this stage can quickly analyze real-time incoming information.

New improvements should be found by means of analyzing the history of process executions as well as the exceptional situations registered per process and their ad hoc solutions. Moreover, the process flaws must be taken into account.

This stage is also in charge of modifications based on business changes that need to be reflected in our business processes. Historical analysis is usually done by specific tooling designed to analyze large amounts of information. The tooling aggregates information based on different business rules and perspectives. Well-known data mining tools can be used at this stage in order to detect common patterns in process executions that are usually hidden.

The result of this stage is usually used as input for following iterations.

Applying BPM in the real world

After getting to know the basics of the BPM discipline, we need to apply it to a real-world scenario in order to gain experience. That's why we need to choose a tool that helps us with our BPM project. **Business Process Management System (BPMS)** helps us implement the stages specified in the previous sections.

BPM systems are middleware components (in the sense that they are software that allows us to create more software) that give us a set of functionality oriented to solving very specific tasks in each stage of the discipline. The following section describes what we need to have in mind in order to properly evaluate a BPM system.

BPMS checklist

Let's talk about the main features that a BPMS must provide to its users. First of all, a BPMS should provide the notion of the different stages and a set of different tools oriented to each particular stage. For each stage, you need to evaluate the strengths and the weaknesses of each project/tool that you are planning to adopt.

Starting with the first stage of the discipline (stage 1 – discovering your business processes), a BPMS should provide a way to gather business knowledge. As described earlier, this task of gathering knowledge will require a set of interviews in order to find out how the company is doing the work. All the information gathered from this stage needs to be stored and analyzed in order to understand how things are working. Most of the open source projects provide a modeling tool without giving us the appropriate analysis tools. This usually confuses new adopters because they start working without figuring out first what they need to model and solve. You should be aware of this situation and be prepared to spend some time asking questions and analyzing the results.

Nowadays stage 2 (formalizing your new processes) is achieved by tools that allow us to model business processes using the BPMN v2 language. Multiple editors from different vendors can accomplish this task. You should know that most of these editors are targeted at business analysts as the only requirement is to learn the BPMN v2 language in order to model and design coherent business processes. At this stage you need to be ready to train your people to correctly understand the BPMN v2 standard language. During the first iterations, most of the time, the first processes need to be modeled and designed by people who already know the language and who usually understand the technical implication of modeling an executable business process. In the later iterations, business analysts can start making changes to the existing business processes; and when they feel comfortable, they can start creating new ones.

In the open source community, we need to recognize the fact that we usually develop the most complicated and interesting tools first (from a developer's perspective). This is the reason why most of the OSS projects are focused on process execution engines and developers' tooling. This kind of tooling is commonly focused on in stage 3, implementing your technical assets , and stage 4, runtime, where high technical skills are required. From the software point of view, these two stages are well covered by the existing open source projects on the market. It's important to understand that a BPMS should allow the technical people of the company to directly interact with the process engine so that they can customize and extend the provided generic behavior.

For the last two stages (stage 5, monitoring, and stage 6, improvements), you should evaluate the tools and the APIs provided to extract and display information about the process executions. These tools usually offer you some analytics capabilities, real-time dashboard widgets, and reporting tools—all of which help you to understand how your processes are being executed and their respective performance.

Most of the problems right now are in stages 1, 5, and 6. Because there is no standard methodology to discover business processes and because this is usually a non-technical task, the maturity of the software related to these stages is not good enough. Notice that these stages (1, 5, and 6) are highly related to human interactions and data analysis based on the company domain. Besides the tooling, you will need to learn about the company in order to acquire the correct information about how things work inside that company.

A large percentage of the success ratio of your BPM project depends on your knowledge and comprehension of the company's domain. You need to understand the problems that you are trying to solve and the reasons behind them. The open source community is always trying to build software for these stages, so feedback from the users is highly appreciated and helps a lot in improving current tools. As you may know, most of the open source BPMS, like jBPM5, are generic enough to work in different industries and environments. It's very important for this type of project to have feedback, blog posts, and papers about how the users' communities customize them for different industries.

From a developer's perspective, most of the BPMS provide a set of APIs to easily integrate your applications with the process engine (no matter the technology or language that you use in your company applications). All the BPM systems also provide a clear description of the information that they store by default, and how to extend and customize that information for specific domain analysis.

It's truly important to understand that the mechanism exists and is usually designed to be generic and extensible. Most of the time, the differences between process engines are about:

- Standards that the project implements
- Flexible core to support custom services
- Documentation of the engine internals
- Integrations with other projects
- Support
- Release cycles
- Community engagement

We can say that this is a common checklist to evaluate, analyze, and compare different process engines' features.

The next step is to analyze the tooling available for each stage. Based on my experience with OSS projects and in particular with integration projects, the tooling is heavily evaluated during the first few phases of comparison between different projects. In other words, tooling is commonly just a tick in a checklist when you evaluate projects. In real implementations, tooling always needs to be extensively modified and adapted for particular usage. The tooling that companies will end up using is usually integrated with their existing applications and proprietary frameworks.

From the process engine's internal functionality perspective, you will find that it's pretty easy to build tools and integrate them with your existing applications using the process engine APIs. You need to make sure that the BPMS that you are evaluating provide those APIs, because most of the closed source products don't.

If tooling is extremely important for you and your company at project evaluation time, take a look at the project-specific tooling and choose based on the following criteria:

- The amount of tooling available
- The number of features
- The flexibility of the results generated by the tooling
- The technology that the project uses to build the tooling
- The skills that you have in those front-end technologies

Remember, you must be ready for changing each project's generic UI/tooling provided by the BPMS and you must know how they were built. If not, you will be stuck training a team in order to modify and extend the project-proposed tooling.

Last, but no less important, is the fact that you need to evaluate some specific features related to human interactions. There is a pretty interesting standard called **Web Service Human Tasks (WS-HT)** that defines two important features:

- A standard set of APIs (interfaces) to interact and manage human activities.
- A complete and flexible human-activities life cycle. This life cycle defines the states through which a human interaction will transit during its life.

Obviously, having a standard set of APIs gives you the freedom to choose different implementations without compromising the core process engine functionality. We will learn more about these human interactions and the proposed life cycle in *Chapter 7, Human Interactions*.

Summary

After this heavy introduction to a wide range of conceptual topics, we can start working with all of these concepts by applying them to real-life projects. I strongly recommend having all the introduced concepts in mind for the next chapters, as they will help you understand how and why the tools that will be introduced were created, and their design goals.

The next chapter focuses on explaining how Business Process Management Systems are structured to give us support to automate the BPM discipline stages. You will see how a BPMS gives us an environment to develop applications on top of, which will be able to guide your company work.

In the following chapters, we will analyze how to implement and use tools that are related to the BPM arena. The second part of the book will be focused on how we can leverage the power of rule engines and complex event processing to create solutions for real problems using a declarative approach.

2

BPM Systems Structure

If you want to provide solutions, you first need to know what you have available to create these solutions. This chapter will give you a detailed description of the structure, functionality, and internal components that are provided by Business Process Management Systems.

This chapter is divided into two main sections:

- Introduction to the common structure and functionality provided by a BPMS
- Technologies surrounding BPMS

The first section will cover some topics that you will need to have in mind before starting with a BPMS. The second section of this chapter introduces the relationship between a BPMS and other tools that provide complementary functionality. After completing this chapter, you will be able to:

- Understand the framework components
- Understand some of the low-level data structures and mechanisms commonly used in BPM systems
- Understand how the generic concepts are mapped to jBPM5
- Know about the technologies that are used in conjunction with BPM systems

Let's start with a description of the common structure and functionality that a BPMS should provide us with.

Key components in a BPMS

From a technical perspective, we will see how a BPMS project is internally structured. The goal of this analysis is to understand the functionality provided by each component inside the BPMS architecture.

The following figure shows us some of the most important and high-level components found inside a BPMS project:

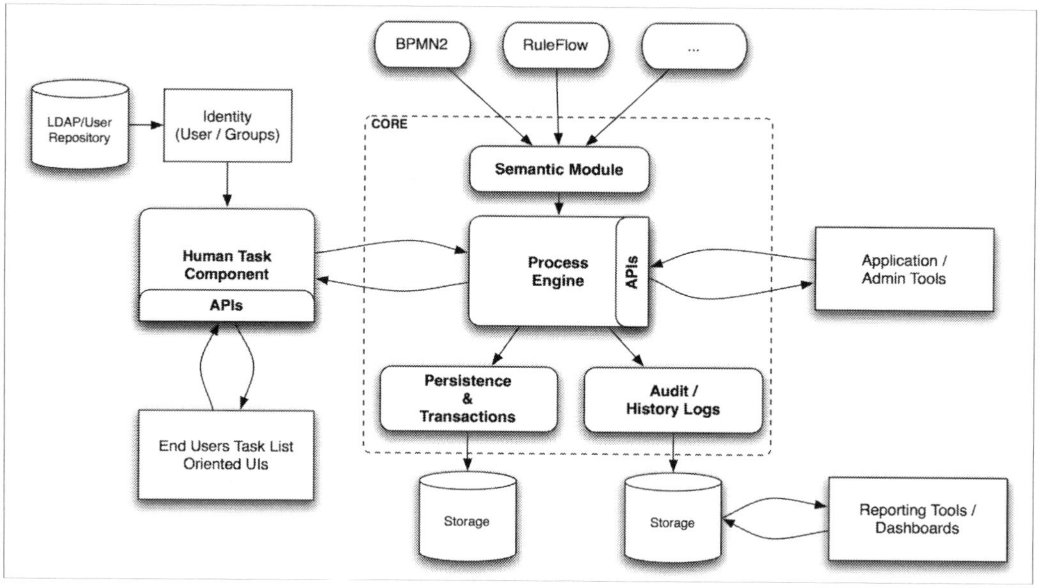

BPMS core

The BPMS core is composed of a set of low-level components that provide the main functionalities for parsing and executing our business processes' definitions. Let's take a look at the key pieces inside a BPMS core:

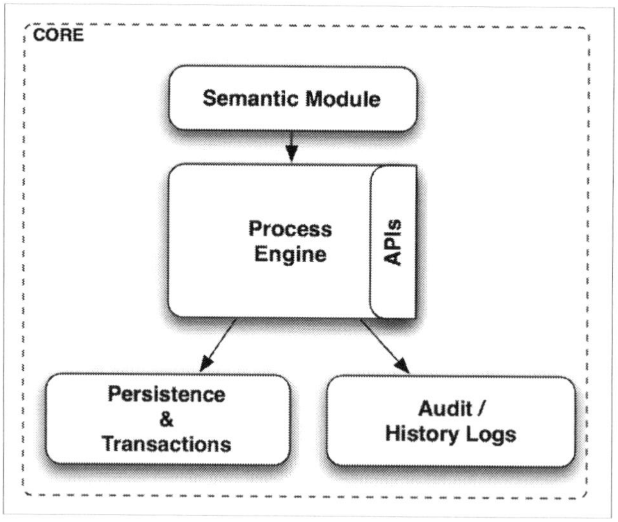

The semantic module

The semantic module is in charge of defining the language semantic (what each word means) and how it will be translated for the process engine's internal structures that are ready to be executed. This module basically contains the parsers to understand the BPMN2 language that will be introduced in *Chapter 3, Using BPMN 2.0 to Model Business Scenarios*.

The semantic module is usually fully pluggable and can be extended to support multiple languages. Changing the language or creating your own language is not a common requirement, but you can do it if you need to create your own domain-specific language that requires completely different structures.

You will find that most of the BPMS out there have this layer of abstraction and a generic process engine. This allows the vendors to migrate or update to a different language in the future without changing the process engine's core mechanisms.

The process engine

The process engine is the one responsible for actually executing our business processes. The process engine is in charge of creating new process instances and keeping the state for each of them. Inside the process engine code, the internal structures are defined to represent each activity that is in our process definitions. All the mechanisms that are being used to instantiate these process definitions and execute them are defined inside the process engine. Knowing about how the process engine works becomes really important for technical people involved in stage 4, runtime, where depending on the requirements, different tunings can be applied to improve performance.

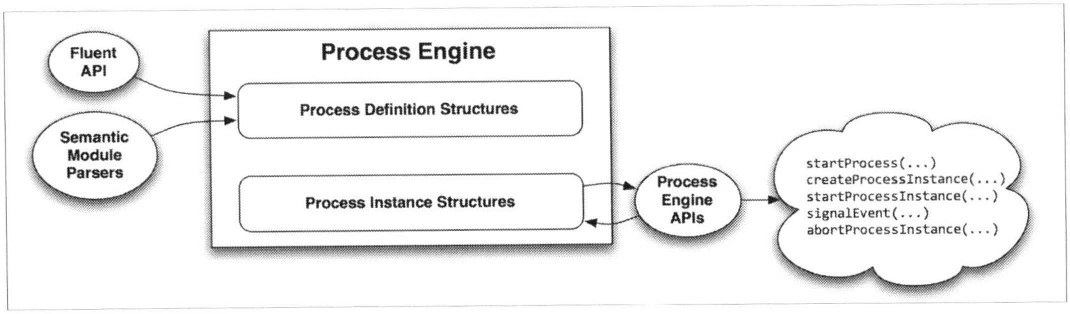

In almost every open source BPM system, we will find the process definition structures and the process instance structures. We need to understand how these structures interact in order to understand how the process engine behaves when it wants to execute one or multiple instances of our processes.

The following sections go deep into the technical details about how we can create a very simple process engine that demonstrates how these interactions happen. For this purpose, a set of complementary Java projects are provided. Feel free to open the project called `jBPM5-GOP-NodeInstance` provided inside the directory of *Chapter 2, BPM Systems Structure*. Just for completeness, I've also included the code provided in the previous version of the jBPM Developer guide. In the following sections I will make references to both approaches, but only the approach implemented by jBPM5 will be discussed.

Process definition structures

These structures are static representations of our business processes. They will represent each activity that is defined inside a graphical representation of our business process. We will see in *Chapter 3, Using BPMN 2.0 to Model Business Scenarios*, how we can create these graphical representations in a language called BPMN2. Usually, these graphical representations end up being stored in an XML file that can be parsed by the semantic module. As a result of this parsing process, we obtain a structure of objects that represent the graph.

The following figure shows how this parsing process happens and the resultant structures:

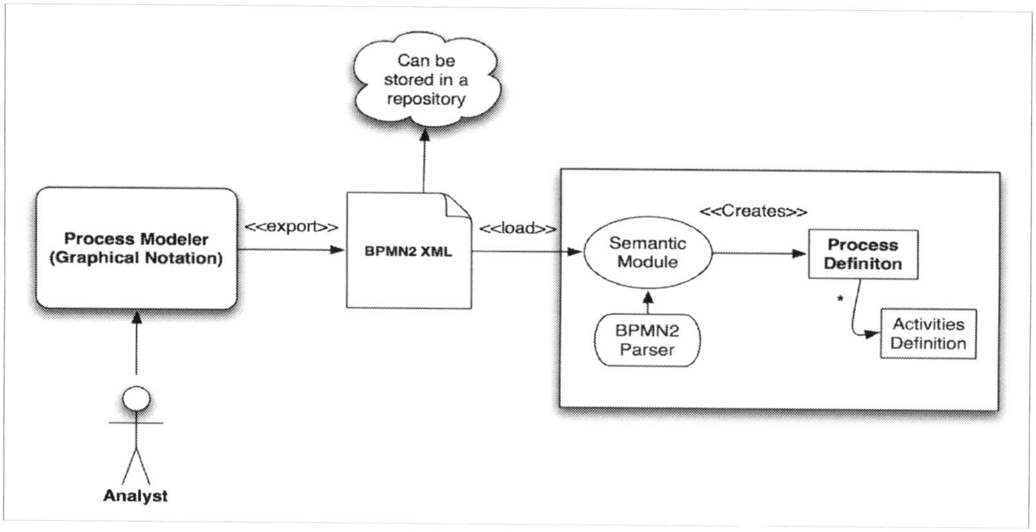

Using a graphical **Process Modeler**, business analysts can draw business processes by dragging and dropping different activities from the modeler palette. These graphical representations of our business processes are stored in an XML file compliant with the BPMN 2 specification.

Notice that any BPMN 2 compliant **Process Modeler** can be used to create the graphical representation of the process. Up to this point, there is nothing specific to jBPM5. When you want to start using your BPM system, the semantic module will load the XML file; then it will choose the right parser (in this case the **BPMN2 Parser**) and create the internal structures that the process engine will use.

Usually we get a root structure (in this case, it's called **Process Definition**) that will contain all the activities that are represented inside the graphical representation.

Inside the project called `jBPM5-GOP-NodeInstance`, you will find the `ProcessDefinition` interface. This interface looks like this:

```
public interface ProcessDefinition {
  public Map<Long, Task>getTasks();
  public void setTasks(Map<Long, Task> tasks);
  public void addTask(Long id, Task node);
}
```

This very simple interface defines that a process definition will be composed by tasks.

The `ProcessDefinitionImpl` class inside the package `com.salaboy.process.engine.structures.impl` provides a simple implementation for this interface. I recommend opening this implementation and taking a look at it.

The following code snippet located inside the method `createProcessDefinition()` inside the `SimpleProcessExecutionTest.java` class shows how to create a very simple process definition using the interface and the implementation:

```
//Process Definition
ProcessDefinition process = new ProcessDefinitionImpl();
//Start Task
StartTaskstartTask= new StartTask();
process.addTask(0L, startTask);

//Script Task
ScriptTaskscriptTask = new ScriptTask("java",new Action() {
  @Override
  public void execute() {
    System.out.println("Executing the Action!!");
  }
});

process.addTask(1L, scriptTask);
```

```
//End Task
EndTaskendTask= new EndTask();
process.addTask(2L, endTask);

//Adding the connections
startTask.addOutgoingFlow(
      SequenceFlow.FLOW_DEFAULT_TYPE,
      newSequenceFlowImpl(
        SequenceFlow.FLOW_DEFAULT_TYPE, scriptTask));

actionTask.addOutgoingFlow(
      SequenceFlow.FLOW_DEFAULT_TYPE,
      newSequenceFlowImpl(
        SequenceFlow.FLOW_DEFAULT_TYPE,
        endTask));
```

We just manually create the object structures that represent the following process:

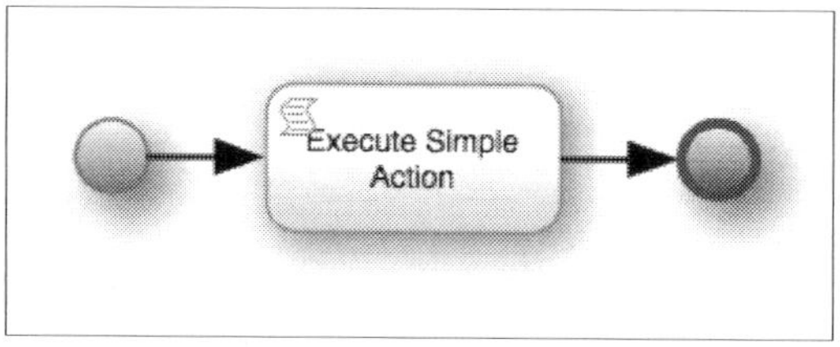

This process contains three tasks: start, script, and end. In this case, this simple process is in charge of just executing a simple action. The start and end tasks are used to specify sequence.

Technically, the process definition is correct and it can be used to create new process instances that will run, but we are missing one of the big advantages of using business processes. As you may have realized, we've just created a business process in Java but we will not be able to share this process definition with non-technical people.

We usually create these structures programmatically when we want to do low-level tests of functionality. For real-world implementations, using a graphical modeler and the provided BPMN2 parsers is the recommended way of working.

Up to this point we only have the process definition structures that this simple engine needs in order to create new process instances. Let's analyze how the process instance's structures are created and how the process executes them.

Process instance structures

The process instance structures represent our running processes and all the information that they are handling. For each process that we want to execute, the engine will create one instance of this structure. These structures will be in charge of keeping track of the activities that are being created by this process execution.

As for the process definition, we will have a root structure that will be in charge of keeping all the information for one process instance. The `ProcessInstance` interface represents the contract for this runtime structure:

```
public interface ProcessInstance extends
                        NodeInstanceContainer {
  public void setId(long id);
  public long getId();
  public void setProcessDefinition(ProcessDefinition process);
  public ProcessDefinition getProcessDefinition();
  public ContextInstance getContextInstance();
  public void start();
  public void start(Map<String, Object> variables);
  public void triggerCompleted();
  public void addService(String name, Service service);
  public Service getService(String name);
  public void setServices(Map<String, Service> services);
  public void setStatus(STATUS status);
  public STATUS getStatus();
}
```

How the engine creates these instances and how these instances keep track of the current execution depends on the engine implementation.

The following sections explain the most common implementations, contrasting jBPM3 with jBPM5.

Process engine execution mechanisms

The following quote has been extracted from the BPMN 2.0 standard specification:

> *Throughout this document, we discuss how Sequence Flows are used within a Process. To facilitate this discussion, we employ the concept of a token that will traverse the Sequence Flows and pass through the elements in the Process. A token is a theoretical concept that is used as an aid to define the behavior of a Process that is being performed. The behavior of Process elements can be defined by describing how they interact with a token as it "traverses" the structure of the Process. However, modeling and execution tools that implement BPMN are NOT REQUIRED to implement any form of token.*

The BPMN 2.0 specification uses the concept of a token to explain how a process behaves during its execution. Each activity inside the process, depending on its type, defines how to interact with a conceptual token and when to propagate the token to one or more sequence flows attached to it. As you may notice, the specification doesn't force the modeling and execution tools to implement the concept of a token.

This fact forces us to understand the two common approaches that are used to represent how a process is being executed:

- Token-based approach
- Node instance based approach

Token-based approach

For each process instance, we create a token that will transverse all the process activities. The token will be in charge of carrying information that is needed in each activity. When the token reaches the last activity (usually a specific activity that represents the end), the process instance dies and the process itself is marked as completed.

For a detailed description about the token-based approach and an example of how to build a very simple process engine from scratch, you can read my previous book, *jBPM Developer Guide*, which explains how the jBPM 3.X core engine internal was built. The project called `jBPM3-GOP-Token/simpleGOPExecution` inside the source code directory of *Chapter 2, BPM Systems Structure*, implements a simple example of how the token-based approach works.

Node instance based approach

In the node instance approach, obviously there is no token. In this case we will dynamically create a new instance of an object that represents the execution status of a specific task, which is defined in `ProcessDefinition`. Each time the process execution hits an activity, a node instance ready to be executed will be placed in the node instance collection. As soon as the activity is completed, the node instance is automatically removed from this collection. The collection of node instances will represent the running activities in each of our processes.

As you may have noticed, the `ProcessInstance` interface extends another interface called `NodeInstanceContainer`:

```
public interface NodeContainer {
  public List<NodeInstance> getNodeInstances();
  public void setNodeInstances(List<NodeInstance>
                                           nodeInstances);
  public void addNodeInstance(NodeInstancenodeInstance);
```

```
    public void removeNodeInstance(NodeInstancenodeInstance);
    public NodeInstance getNodeInstance(Task node);
    public void nodeInstanceCompleted(NodeInstance
                                nodeInstance, String outType);
}
```

The process instance will now contain a list of node instances that will represent the tasks that are being executed. The process engine instantiates, based on the defined task type, the required node instance and places it inside the process instance.

For this simple example, the `ProcessInstance` structure will be created by `ProcessInstanceFactory`, which contains the logic about how to create and initialize it. As we can see in the `ProcessInstance` interface, we have a reference to `ProcessDefinition` that will be used to create and direct the execution.

The process instance initialization will include, for this implementation, the initialization of different services that will be used for the execution, as well as the initialization of the internal structures that will be used to keep the runtime status of the process.

Once the `ProcessInstance` structure is created and correctly initialized, we can start the process by calling the method `start(...)`. This causes the first activity to be instantiated and executed. Another important concept that appears in the `ProcessInstance` interface is `ContextInstance`, which defines the methods to set and get the information related to a specific `ProcessInstance` structure.

```
public interface ContextInstance {
  public Map<String, Object>getVariables();
  public Object getVariable(String key);
  public void setVariables(Map<String, Object> variables);
  public void setVariable(String key, Object value);
}
```

Each process instance will have a unique `ContextInstance` instance that will differentiate one `ProcessInstance` from the others.

There are two ways of starting a `ProcessInstance` structure:

1. Without parameters.
2. With a map of parameters.

When a map of parameters is provided, they will be copied into the `ContextInstance` object for that specific `ProcessInstance` when the process is started. This means that the instance will use the information provided in that map, and all the activities inside that process will have access to that information to operate.

Finally, we need to know that a `ProcessInstance` instance will change its internal status over time. This implementation provides the available statuses in an `enum` instance called `STATUS` inside the `ProcessInstance` interface:

```
public enum STATUS {
   CREATED, ACTIVE, SUSPENDED, CANCELLED, ENDED
};
```

Let's analyze how the execution happens for our simple `ProcessDefinition` interface introduced earlier.

Once we have our `ProcessDefinition` instance ready, we can use the `ProcessInstanceFactory` helper class to get a new `ProcessInstance` object. The following code snippet shows a very simple test using a `ProcessDefinition` instance to create a new `ProcessInstance` object:

```
@Test
public void simpleProcessExecution() {
  ProcessDefinition processDefinition =
                                  createProcessDefinition();
  ProcessInstance processInstance =
                 ProcessInstanceFactory
                   .newProcessInstance(processDefinition);
  assertEquals(processInstance.getStatus(), STATUS.CREATED);
  processInstance.start();
  assertEquals(processInstance.getStatus(), STATUS.ENDED);
}
```

This test creates a `ProcessInstance` structure using the factory, checks that `ProcessInstance` has been initialized correctly, asserts that `processInstance.getStatus()` is STATUS.CREATED, and then it finally starts the `ProcessInstance` object. Inside the `start()` method is where the magic happens. When we call the method `start()`, the first activity inside our process is picked up and a new `NodeInstance` object is created. The first activity for all of our processes will be `StartTask`, and so the process engine will create a new `StartTaskNodeInstance` object and trigger the execution of it. At this point, the newly created `StartTaskNodeInstance` object will be placed inside the `NodeInstance` list inside `ProcessInstance`.

Because the example provides a very basic implementation of `StartTaskNodeInstance`, it just propagates the execution to the next task described inside `ProcessDefintion`. In this example, the next task in our process is `ScriptTask`, so a new `ScriptTaskNodeInstance` object is created and placed inside the `NodeInstance` list. The following code snippet shows the simple implementation provided for `ScriptTaskNodeInstance`:

```
public class ScriptTaskNodeInstance extends
                                   AbstractNodeInstance {

  private Action action;

  public ScriptTaskNodeInstance(ProcessInstancepI,
                              Task task, Action action) {
    super(pI, task);
    this.action = action;
  }
  @Override
  public void internalTrigger(NodeInstance from, String type){
    System.out.println("Executing Script Task ("
             +((ScriptTask)this.task).getDialect()+") !");
    action.execute();
    triggerCompleted(SequenceFlow.FLOW_DEFAULT_TYPE, true);
  }
  public Action getAction() {
    return action;
  }
}
```

As soon as this `NodeInstance` object is placed inside the `NodeInstance` list and its `internalTrigger()` method is executed, the associated action is executed using the command pattern. For more information about the command pattern, look at `http://en.wikipedia.org/wiki/Command_pattern`. After the action is executed, the sequence flow associated with the task is executed, causing the process to move to the `EndTask` task.

I strongly recommend you to debug this execution in order to understand the execution flow step-by-step. When debugging, notice how the `addService()` and `getService()` methods are used to provide contextual services to the execution. This project shows how services can be injected into each node execution for handling events, but any other service can be implemented and registered using the `addService()` method for similar purposes.

The *Knowledge-centric APIs* section will analyze and describe the process engine APIs proposed by jBPM5. A simple process execution inside jBPM5 is also analyzed.

Please remember that these examples show how a very simple version of a process engine works. These examples were designed only for learning purposes and not to be used in real applications.

Facts about the two approaches

As we saw in the previous section, the BPMN2 specification lets you choose any approach to implement your process engine as long as you provide the functionality defined in the spec. None of the previously introduced approaches are better than any other. They are just different. Both approaches:

- Contain structures that define the process model and the runtime behavior.
- Provide a flexible way of adding more activity structures and execution behavior. The engine will be smart enough to recognize new activity definitions and how they need to be executed at runtime.
- Can express unlimited business situations, providing you rock-solid platforms to execute your business processes. The exposed APIs usually don't reflect the internal mechanisms used by the process engine to execute its instances, but if you have low-level APIs, you will probably find the concept of a token or an accessor to the `NodeInstance` collection. None of the other components inside the BPM system will be affected by the internal implementation of the process engine core.
- Different approaches can also be used to define where and how all these pieces of information are connected and managed, in order to work correctly.

jBPM5 uses the `NodeInstance` approach, which provides a flexible mechanism to add dynamic nodes instances without adding unnecessary complexity. This is for checking all the sequence flow logic and conditions, and the token status.

The following sections describe in detail the components around the process engine core and give us an overview of how all the pieces fit together.

Transactions and persistence

Transactions and persistence of the runtime status of the process execution engine are two extremely important topics to understand. Remember that BPM systems are commonly used for integration purposes: multiple systems and people collaborating to achieve a common goal.

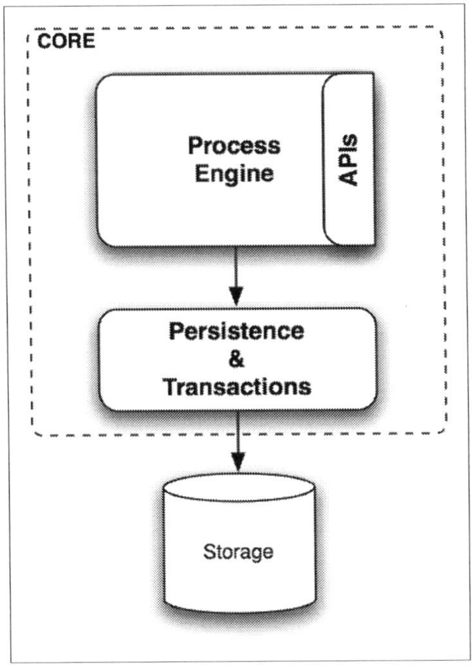

The previous figure shows how the **Persistence & Transaction** layer is in charge of defining the mechanisms to store the runtime information in a persistent storage.

In most enterprise applications all the interactions must run inside a transaction boundary, and we must deal with different systems, APIs, and designs. We must have a flexible mechanism to define:

- How to handle long-running processes
- How and when we can store information about the process status and the information that the process is handling
- How and when we need to create, commit, or roll back the process engine transactions
- Which business exceptions can roll back or compensate already executed business actions

All these topics and sample configuration files for these mechanisms will be discussed in depth in *Chapter 8, Persistence and Transactions*.

Human Task Component

As you may have noticed, the **Human Task Component** entity is a separate component that interacts with the process engine and two other external components:

- The **Identity** component will be used in order to have an internal reference to the company users
- The end users' interface

The **Human Task Component** entity will be responsible for the human task's life cycle as well as for exposing a set of APIs that will enable us to create user interfaces. You can notice the big difference in contrast to jBPM3, where the **Human Task Component** entity has been embedded in the process engine.

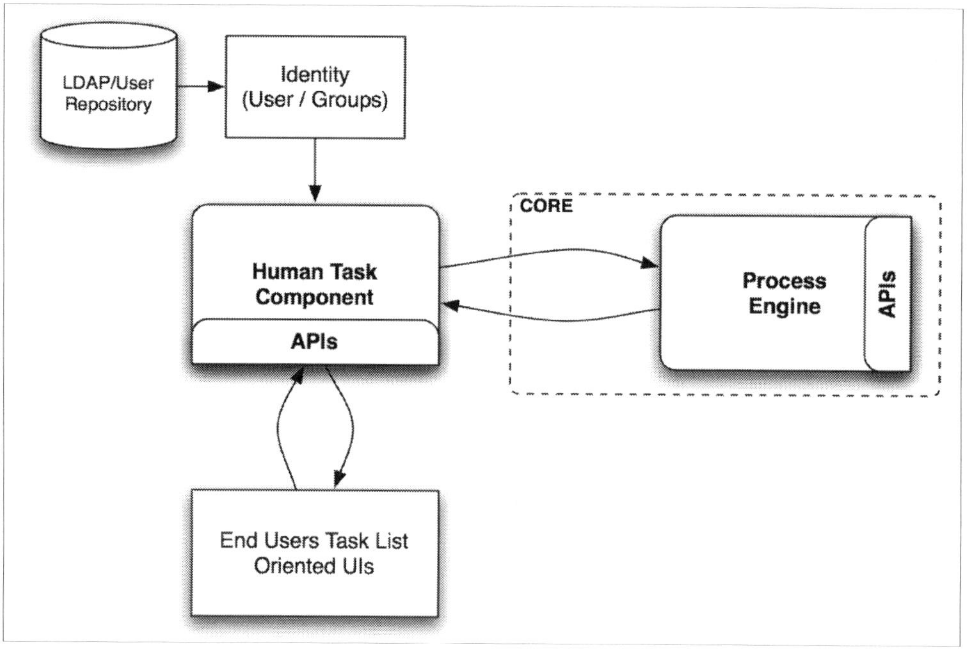

The following sections describe these internal responsibilities and each of these related components, so that you have a clear vision of how they interact with each other.

Human tasks – life cycle

The big box in the diagram (**Human Task Component**) represents the core functionality of the human task service, and it consists of a set of services that define how a human activity must be handled during its life cycle.

Just to give you some context (because these topics require a full chapter), a human task is created each time a running process hits a user-task activity. At that point, the person who is in charge of the task will see a new activity that needs to be completed in his/her task-list inbox. When the person in charge starts working on the activity, the task is assigned and the task status is changed to "in progress". A simple life cycle will include only the completed status. But there is a specification that defines a more robust, realistic, and industry-based life cycle. This standard is called the **Web Services Human Task** (**WS-HT**), and it provides core definitions to structure our activities and define the stages that can be assigned to each activity in our processes.

Human tasks – APIs

The **Human Task Component** entity exposes a set of APIs that are also defined by the WS-HT standard specification. The API's responsibility is to provide us a way to handle human tasks from the user interfaces in a task lists oriented way.

The APIs will provide us all the functionality to build end users' task lists and task forms using any rendering technology. Using the same APIs, the process engine will create tasks each time a process reaches a user task.

The identity component

This component is in charge of abstracting the source where you have stored the information and mappings of your business users. This module is in charge of interacting with the company repository where the users' and groups' information is being stored, in order to bind this information to the user tasks in our processes. This binding happens transparently inside the engine that only handles users'/groups' IDs, allowing us to change the backend storage or technology without affecting our business processes' definitions.

In each BPM system implementation, we will need to map the organizational structure of users and groups to the roles defined in our business processes. It's important to notice that BPM systems are independent of the way the company stores and manages their business' organizational entities. That's why a mapping will be required, allowing us to have different names or IDs for our users inside our business processes and the company's directory.

> *Chapter 7, Human Interactions*, goes deep into all these concepts and explains how we can use this component. It explains the key points of the WS-HT specification that is used to design and implement this component. Because the **Human Task Component** entity is a completely decoupled component from the process engine perspective, we can easily replace it, if necessary, without affecting our business processes. *Chapter 6, Domain Specific Processes*, analyzes the technical details required to achieve external interactions. All the necessary configurations and extension points will be described there.

Audit/history logs

This module is in charge of giving the user a way to query information about how our processes are being executed. This information includes historic information about processes that have already ended and the latest information about the processes that are being executed. **Business Activity Monitoring (BAM)** tools and information dashboards are some of the most common clients for the information generated by this module. The **Audit/History Logs** module is commonly used to extract useful information and metrics that will hydrate different tools designed to display this information accordingly. We need to understand that different roles—developers, business analysts, managers, and so on—need to see the information represented, aggregated, and/or composed in different ways to do their work.

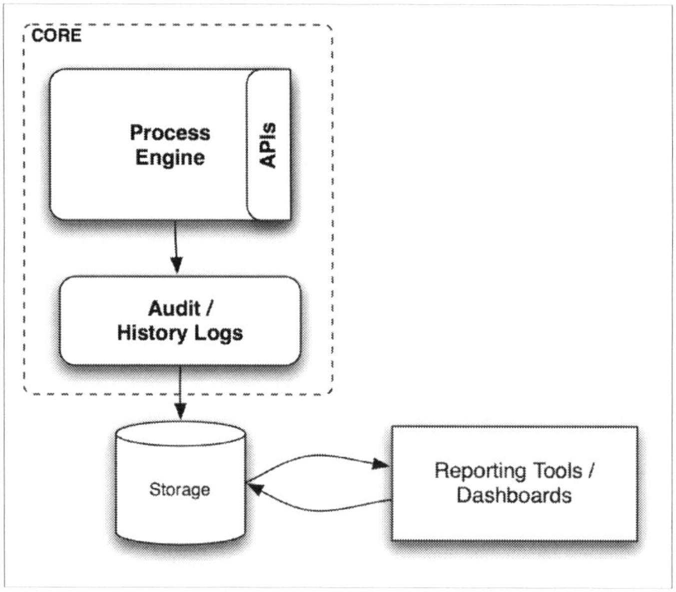

Some common applications that can be created using these components are:

- Real-time dashboards
- Data-mining or data-analysis tools

Real-time dashboards

Dashboards are usually composed of different widgets that we will choose depending on the type of information we need to display, as well as the audience. These widgets gather information about what is happening at a precise point in time. We can set different metrics and calculations that will define how the information will be aggregated and summarized for the end user.

Data mining and data analysis tools

These kinds of tools are designed to facilitate the analysis of huge amounts of information. As you can imagine, when we execute more than 10,000 processes per month, we are generating lots of history logs that can be very useful for understanding how the company is working. Data mining and data analysis tools help us identify patterns, find hidden or hard-to-discover situations, and also improve the way the information is being stored/generated.

These kinds of tools require that the provided information be unstructured, which is extremely useful for these scenarios.

Tools such as real-time widgets query the data storage too often, so they do a lot of in-memory calculations in order to present summarized information. In contrast, data mining tools query just once, in which a huge amount of information is queried, and then the analysis can be done offline.

It's usually a good practice to keep the audit/history logs separated from the runtime and human task storage. This is just to improve the performance of the different modules and keep them isolated.

Process engine components summary

As you may notice, a process engine is composed of a set of components with well-focused and decoupled functionality, as described in the previous sections. The following section gives an analysis on how the previously described components can be found in jBPM5.

As I mentioned in *Chapter 1, Why Do We Need Business Process Management?*, jBPM5 is not a common BPMS and most of the advantages that it gives you (in comparison to common BPMSs) depend on the tight integration with a rule engine. The next section shows us some concepts that have been upgraded for jBPM5, where the rule engine plays a major role in the design.

Components inside jBPM5

This section describes how jBPM5 provides the BPMS components previously introduced. This section explains some higher-level abstractions and integrations with other components that provide a unique set of features.

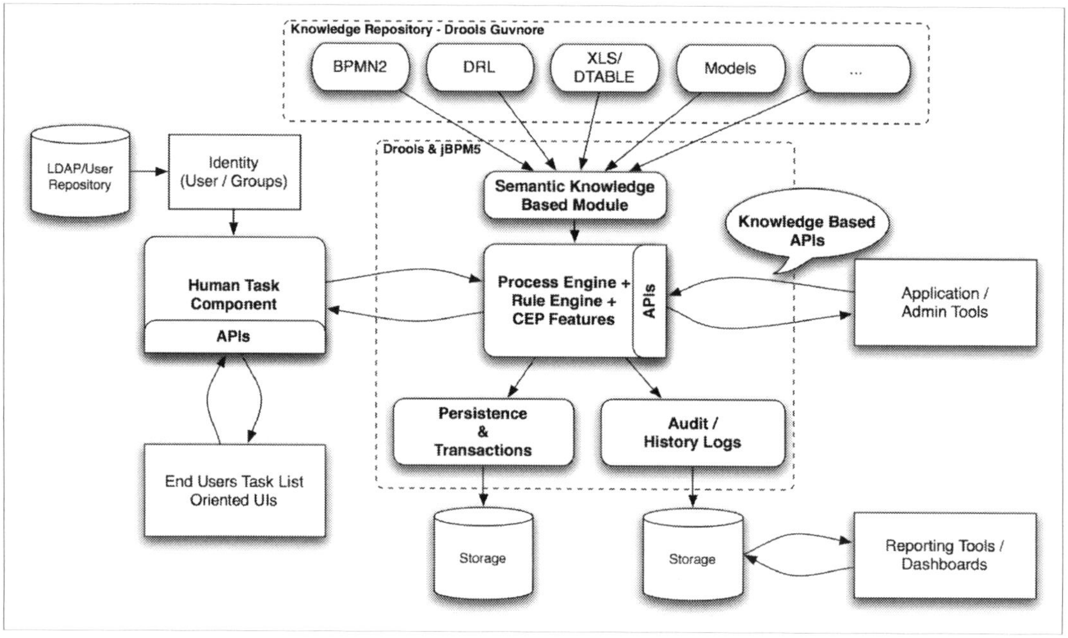

As you may notice, now the **Rule Engine** (Drools—`www.drools.org`), the **Process Engine**, and Complex Event Processing Features (**CEP Features**) are merged to work together. This merging forces us to define a higher-level concept to model and execute our business knowledge. This is why the concept of the business logic integration platform was created. **Drools & jBPM5** provide an integrated environment where we can represent our business knowledge using different metaphors to express different models. This platform allows us to execute in a uniform way business processes and business rules, and analyze and correlate complex events. In order to provide this unification, the APIs exposed by this platform are heavily based on the concept of knowledge.

Now the process and the rule engine will share the **Human Task Component** entity and **Persistence & Transactions** mechanisms, as well as the **Knowledge Repository** entity to store knowledge assets (process, rules, models, and so on).

Using this newly proposed architecture, rules and processes can co-exist and collaborate in the same context. In contrast to normal BPMSs, the unified Knowledge-Centric APIs will hide the parsers for each type of knowledge, allowing us to use the same APIs to load business processes and business rules. This is extremely useful because:

- No matter what the type of a particular knowledge representation is (a rule or a business process), it will be handled transparently by the engine.
- We will not lose time learning different APIs to interact with our rules and processes.

In order to start using jBPM5, we need to quickly review the knowledge-centric APIs and see how we can interact with the rules and process engine. The following section will cover the most important concepts that we have to understand in order to start using jBPM5/Drools APIs.

Knowledge-centric APIs

If you have worked with jBPM3 or the never-productized jBPM4 implementation, the new APIs may look strange at first. This section gives a quick overview of how the APIs reflect and expose the functional behavior provided by this platform.

In order to understand the jBPM5 APIs, we need to understand that the same APIs will be used to interact with the rule engine. For now, we will be focused on learning how to use the APIs to create and interact with our process instances. During the second half of the book, we will see how, by using the same APIs we can mix rules and processes without learning anything new.

In order to start on the right foot, we need to understand three main concepts:

- Knowledge Builder
- Knowledge Base
- Knowledge Session

Knowledge Builder

The Knowledge Builder encapsulates a set of semantic modules and parsers that know how to handle different types of resources. It is responsible for adding and creating a binary representation of our knowledge models that are ready to be executed. In order to create a Knowledge Builder, we will use a Knowledge Builder Factory. The following code shows how to obtain a new instance:

```
KnowledgeBuilder kbuilder =
              KnowledgeBuilderFactory.newKnowledgeBuilder();
kbuilder.add(
           newClassPathResource("simple/patientCheckIn.bpmn"),
           ResourceType.BPMN2);
if (kbuilder.hasErrors()) {
  for (KnowledgeBuilderError error : kbuilder.getErrors()) {
     System.out.println(">>> Error:" + error.getMessage());
  }
  throw new IllegalStateException(
              ">>> Knowledge couldn't be parsed! ");
}
```

The first line creates the Knowledge Builder using the `KnowledgeBuilderFactory` helper. This `KnowledgeBuilderFactory` helper provides a couple of methods to get the `KnowledgeBuilder` instance, which allows us to configure some parameters for the compiler mechanisms. The second line loads, for this example, the `patientCheckIn.bpmn` process file from the application classpath and specifies that the resource that is being added is a BPMN2 model. The `KnowledgeBuilder.add()` method is in charge of picking the right parser and compiler for the specified resource.

Notice that we can add multiple resources of different types by calling the `KnowledgeBuilder.add()` line multiple times. Also notice that the `KnowledgeBuilder.add()` method accepts a `Resource` and a `ResourceType` value each as arguments. The available `ResourceTypes` at the time of writing this book are:

- **DRL**: Drools Rule Language
- **XDRL**: XML Drools Rule Language
- **DSL**: Domain-specific Language Mapping
- **DSLR**: Rules using Domain-specific Languages
- **DRF**: Drools Flow (Proprietary Flow Language, not maintained)
- **BPMN2**: Business Process using the BPMN2 Standard
- **DTABLE**: Decision Table
- **PKG**: Compiled Package

- **BRL**: Drools Business Rule File
- **CHANGE_SET**: Bundle of Resources to load based on an XML file
- **PMML**: Predictive Model Markup Language (Experimental Support)

The last `if` block checks for errors during the compilation process, and it throws an `IllegalStateException` exception if something goes wrong.

Knowledge Base

The Knowledge Base contains all our binary packages, which contain the compiled knowledge assets such as business processes, business rules, and DSL mappings. We can say that the Knowledge Base is a static container for our compiled knowledge.

In order to obtain a new `KnowledgeBase` instance, we execute the following lines:

```
KnowledgeBasekbase = KnowledgeBaseFactory.newKnowledgeBase();
kbase.addKnowledgePackages(kbuilder.getKnowledgePackages());
```

The first line obtains a new instance of `KnowledgeBase` using `KnowledgeBaseFactory`. This helper also provides a couple of methods that receive configuration parameters that will be applied to the created instance. The second line fills the `KnowledgeBase` object by getting all the compiled knowledge packages from `KnowledgeBuilder`. Notice that the `kbuilder.getKnowledgePackages()` method can also be used to get the compiled version of our processes and business rules, and store that compiled representation into the database or filesystem so that we avoid recompilation of our knowledge assets.

Knowledge Session

Once we get our `KnowledgeBase` with all the compiled resources, we can start creating `KnowledgeSessions` based on this Knowledge Base. Our business processes and business rules will run inside an instance of `KnowledgeSession`. The `KnowledgeSession` instance will host our processes, providing them all the services that they need to run. We use the following line to obtain a new `KnowledgeSession` instance based on a particular `KnowledgeBase`:

```
StatefulKnowledgeSession ksession =
                        kbase.newStatefulKnowledgeSession();
```

As you may imagine at this point, the `newStatefulKnowledgeSession()` method also receives parameters to configure the instance of `KnowledgeSession` that will be created based on that particular `KnowledgeBase`. Notice that for this particular example we are obtaining a `StatefulKnowledgeSession` instance. There are two kinds of `KnowledgeSession` instances:

- **Stateless sessions**: This kind of session doesn't maintain the context between one interaction and the next one. Stateless sessions can be re-used multiple times and will not keep information from previous calls. This kind of session is useful for scenarios where we want to use the rule engine to evaluate a set of rules and obtain a result.
- **Stateful sessions**: This kind of session keeps the information from several calls and interactions. By keeping the context information, it provides a rich environment to work in, where previous calls can be used to add and enrich the information that we already have. Most of the examples in this book will be using stateful sessions, because business processes require keeping track of the context of the execution.

Once we have our `StatefulKnowledgeSession`, we can start interacting with it. It's important to notice that using the same `KnowledgeBase` instance, we can instantiate multiple `StatefulKnowledgeSessions` that keep completely separated contexts.

From the process perspective, we are interested in the following methods exposed by the `StatefulKnowledgeSession` interface:

```
public ProcessInstance startProcess (String processId)
public void signalEvent(String type, Object event)
```

We will use these methods to create and interact with our business processes.

The following section introduces some topics that are related to BPM systems.

BPM systems surrounding topics

This section is about the surrounding ecosystem that we can and will find around BPM systems technologies. It's highly recommended that you learn about some of them, and the rest are optional or for future reference. This section will also cover some architectural patterns that we can benefit from in our projects. Most of the topics that I've included here are related to building more robust, scalable, and better designed applications without reinventing the wheel.

Service-oriented architecture

Everybody has heard about SOA at least once these days. SOA is a practice that pushes you to change the way that you architect your systems, promoting highly decoupled and scoped services. The main idea behind SOA is that you can create different modules/services focused on specific pieces of functionality. These services will be able to live alone and work without external requirements such as black boxes that solve specific situations. Each of these services will expose a well-defined interface that will allow us to access specific functionality.

When you want to create a new application, you will need to wire up all these service definitions in order to achieve a high-level functionality and behavior. Some of the most visible advantages of this approach are:

1. Easy-to-maintain decoupled pieces of software.
2. Reusable components/services that can be used to build different systems.
3. A set of well-defined interfaces that makes it possible to switch implementations without interfering with applications that have already been created.

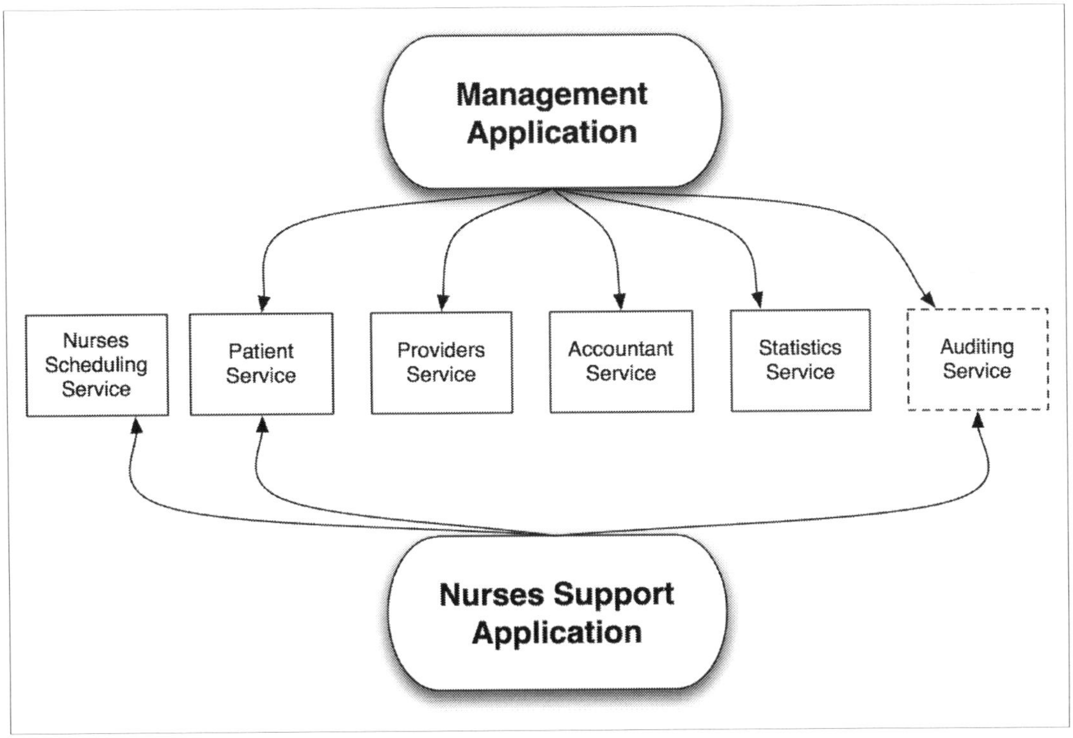

As you can see in the previous figure, we can create applications by composing a different set of services that can be shared and re-used. Each of our services will provide specific functionality according to the business requirement. In this example we can see how **Patient Service** and **Auditing Service** are being used by two different applications, which require the same business logic.

There is an intimate relationship between SOA and BPM systems. Most of our business processes will end up having interactions with our company systems and third-party services.

From the BPMS perspective, it's really important to have a list of services that have well-defined interfaces to interact with. When we have this clear list of services, the process implementations become less painful and more straightforward. In this type of scenario, external systems' connectors become easy to implement because we can implement the connector against the service interface, which allows us to easily change the service's implementation without affecting the business process performance.

We as developers need to understand SOA as a popular set of best-design practices and architectural patterns. You will see in many books that BPM systems are considered the business layer on top of the SOA infrastructure, because a business process can be used to orchestrate the services exposed by the SOA architecture.

WS-BPEL and service orchestration

As was mentioned in the previous section, there is a strong relationship between BPMS and SOA, but we need to know how to differentiate between a business process calling a service and the concept of service orchestration. BPEL is also known as **WS-BPEL (Web Services Business Process Execution Language)**, which usually confuses people. BPEL was created as a service orchestration language for services exposed using web services. BPEL allows us to have a flow chart defining how we want to coordinate different services in order to obtain a desired result.

In an SOA infrastructure, having a language to define the sequence in which our services will be called was a major milestone in the system integration field.

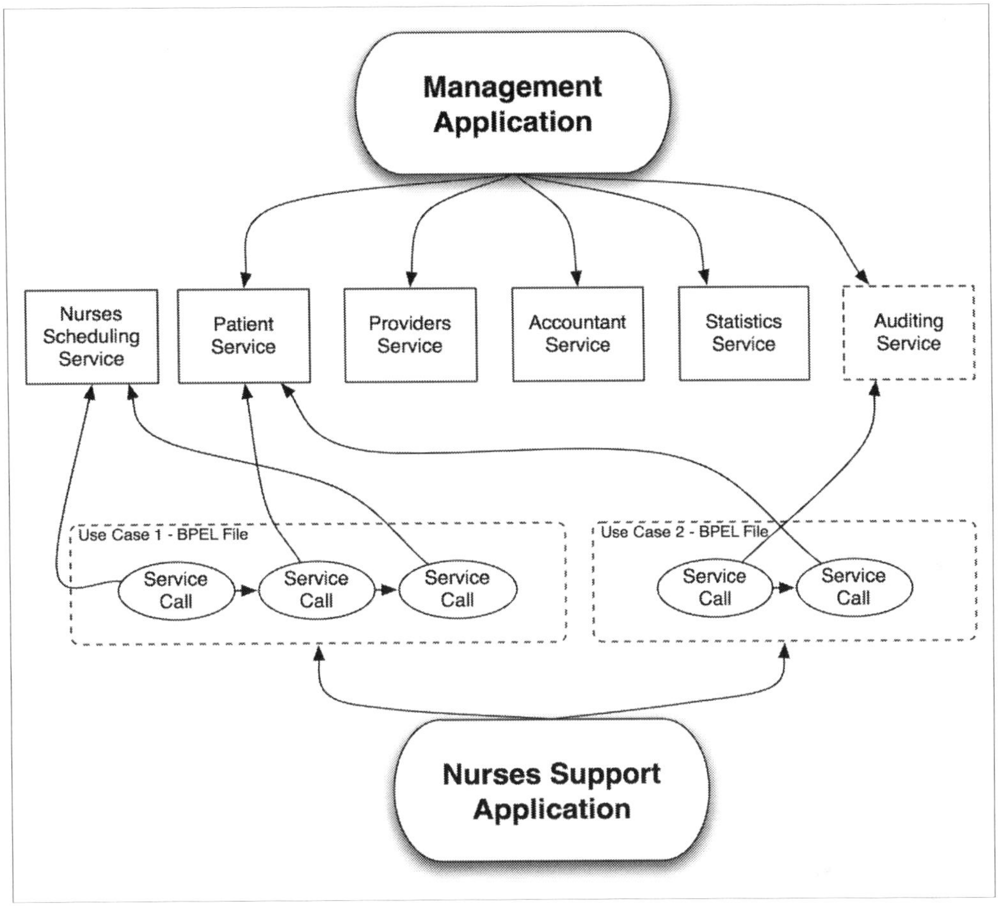

Looking at the previous figure, we can see that now our application can implement different use cases or scenarios defining a sequence of services to call using a BPEL definition file. The idea behind BPEL was great from the system integration and technical perspective, but it has some very well-known drawbacks.

WS-BPEL relies on the fact that all the services must be exposed by using web services. XPath is being used to move information from one service to another, which is technically correct but not business friendly. BPEL flow files tend to become extremely large and unmaintainable. WS-BPEL doesn't include support for modeling human interactions, making it difficult to be adopted by business analysts, who generally define high-level business processes. Nowadays BPEL is considered a very technical tool that can be used by system integrators; this is in contrast with a BPMS, which is oriented towards business users.

Even though BPEL and the BPMS process model have fundamental differences, there is still some overlap between these technologies. Both define a graph model that will represent a sequence of things to be done, but the semantics of these two models will be extremely different because of the design principles that were used.

Enterprise Service Bus

Enterprise Service Bus (ESB) is another technology closely related to SOA. At the infrastructural level, an ESB can also be used to coordinate different service calls and abstract the transport layer that needs to be used to interact with those services. An ESB provides a way to connect different services, hiding the low-level complexity of those interactions. Using an ESB to build a consistent SOA implementation is strongly recommended because it simplifies a lot of the integration problems that can arise from keeping those systems working together. In contrast to BPM systems, ESBs are technical solutions that don't accurately describe how the business works. Knowing how to use an ESB will obviously increase your knowledge of how to design your system integrations, but this will not expose useful information to the business professionals.

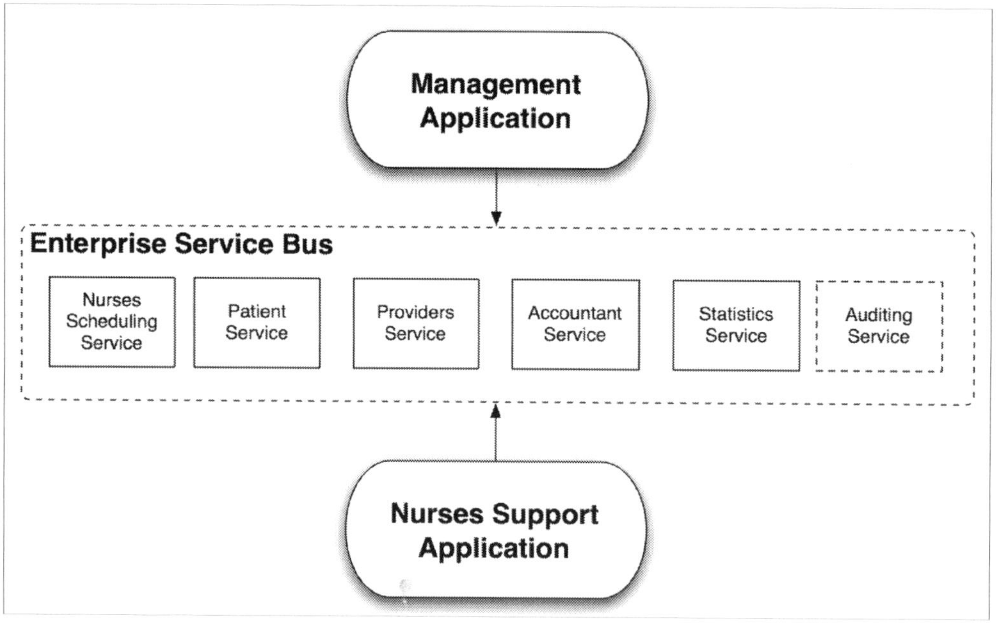

ESBs and BPMS are not exclusive tools—quite the opposite. Using an ESB to simplify the system interactions that happen inside a business process helps a lot during the implementation process. ESBs are used in the integration field; so several integrations with BPEL exist nowadays.

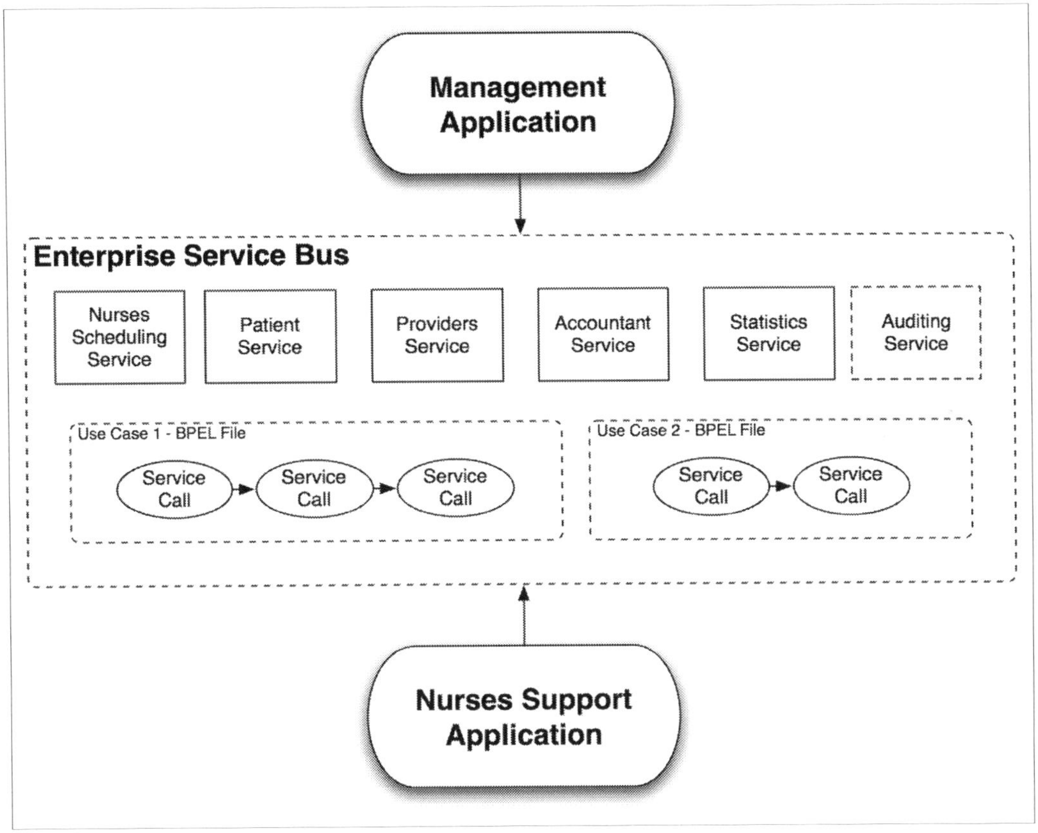

You will find ESBs that provide BPEL integration, allowing us to define BPEL flows that will be executed against the services configured inside our ESB. Using this kind of integration, we can avoid the need to use web services to trigger our BPEL flows; and we can leverage the power of the ESB, which will abstract the transport used for the interactions.

If we compare this BPEL integration with the BPMS integration, we notice that the BPMS will be outside the ESB. Our automated activities can contact the ESB in order to reach a specific service, but the business process definitions will be kept as a business asset instead of as a technical asset.

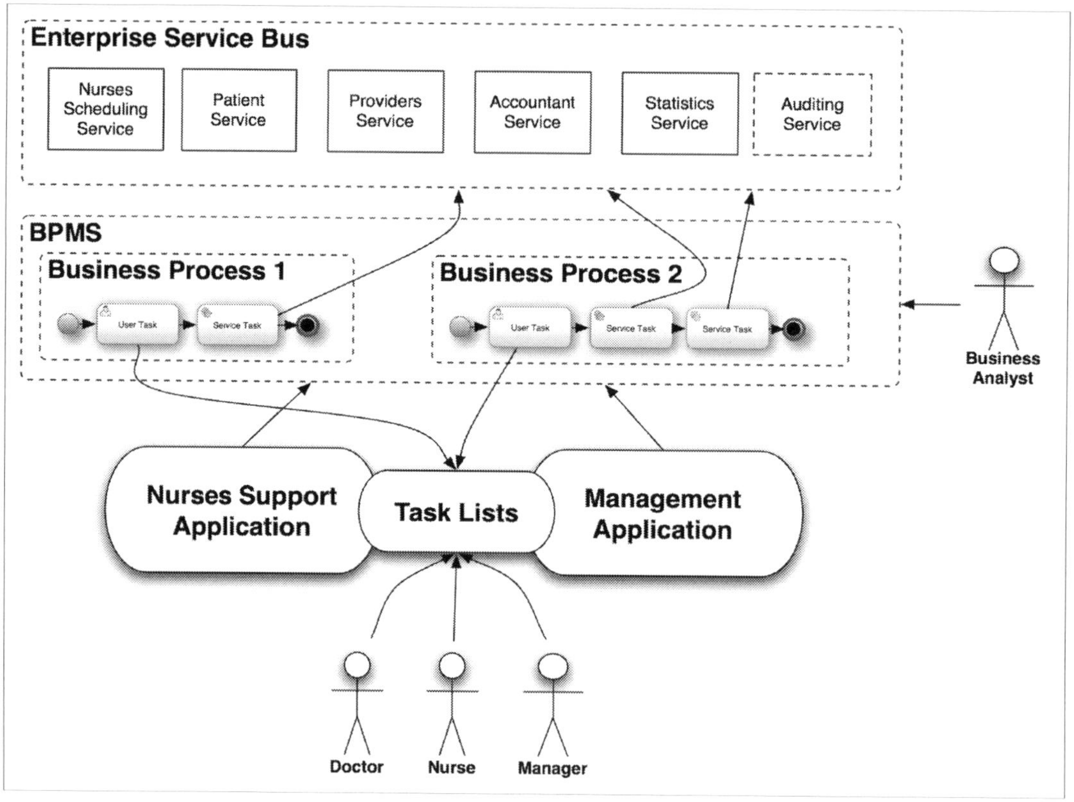

The business process flows will describe how the work is being done in the company and not the technical details required to move information from one place to another. As you can see, now the business users appear in the picture because this is not a technical solution. **Business Analyst** will now be able to understand, improve, and develop new business process definitions. All of these are possible because of the semantics proposed by business process modeling languages such as BPMN 2, which will be introduced in the next chapter.

Rule engines

When we decide to express our business processes declaratively in a modeling language such as BPMN 2, we start noticing the advantages and the importance of these business assets. When we define our business processes, we can share with non-technical people how the company's activities are done. Business processes expose the sequence of activities that need to be executed in order to achieve a business goal, but what about the business logic inside those activities? What about the business logic around our business processes? Can we expose that logic in a declarative way instead of burying it inside our application code? The answer is, of course, yes! One of the common approaches to defining business logic is using a rule engine, which allows us to create compact and atomic representations to identify business situations. The Drools Rule Engine, which will be introduced in *Chapter 9*, allows us to define business situations using the DRL language. This language allows us to express what the business situation looks like and how we want to react to it.

A business rule will look like this:

```
rule "Driver License only for persons over 18 years Old"
   when
     $applicant: Person(age > 18)
     $medicalRevision: MedicalRevision(
                                 person == $applicant,
                                 status == "Approved")
  then
     startProcess("driverLicenseTest", $applicant)
end
```

Rules are described using two main sections. The `When` part (also called **Left-Hand Side (LHS)** or conditional section) will wait until all the conditions are true in order to activate the rule. Then the consequence section of the rule (`then` part of the rule or **Right-Hand Side (RHS)**) contains the actions that need to be executed when the activated rule is chosen to be fired by the engine.

You can imagine that to solve complex problems, we can use many of these rules to describe multiple situations and the steps that need to be executed when those situations take place.

The rule engine will be in charge of matching all of these rules against the current state of the world in order to execute the activated set of rules.

Rule engines were specially designed to evaluate a huge number of these rules at the same time, so you don't need to be worried about performance issues for analyzing more complex situations. We are trying to describe in a declarative way our business situations (logic) in order to share with non-technical people how the company tools work.

BPM systems have an intimate relationship with business rule engines, which is why the following section explains the classic approach of integrating a BPM system (where our processes live) and a business rule engine (where our business logic is kept and executed from).

Classic BPM system and rule engine integration

When business processes want to leverage the power of a rule engine to execute business logic, a process activity must do an external call to the rule engine instance that contains the desired logic. In order to do this external call, we need to gather all the information required by the business rule engine, prepare it, and then send it.

A common scenario where we probably need to call a rule engine is when one activity in our business process requires the evaluation of a set of business rules to perform a complicated task, for example, Risk Calculations, Security Validations, Data Validations, and so on.

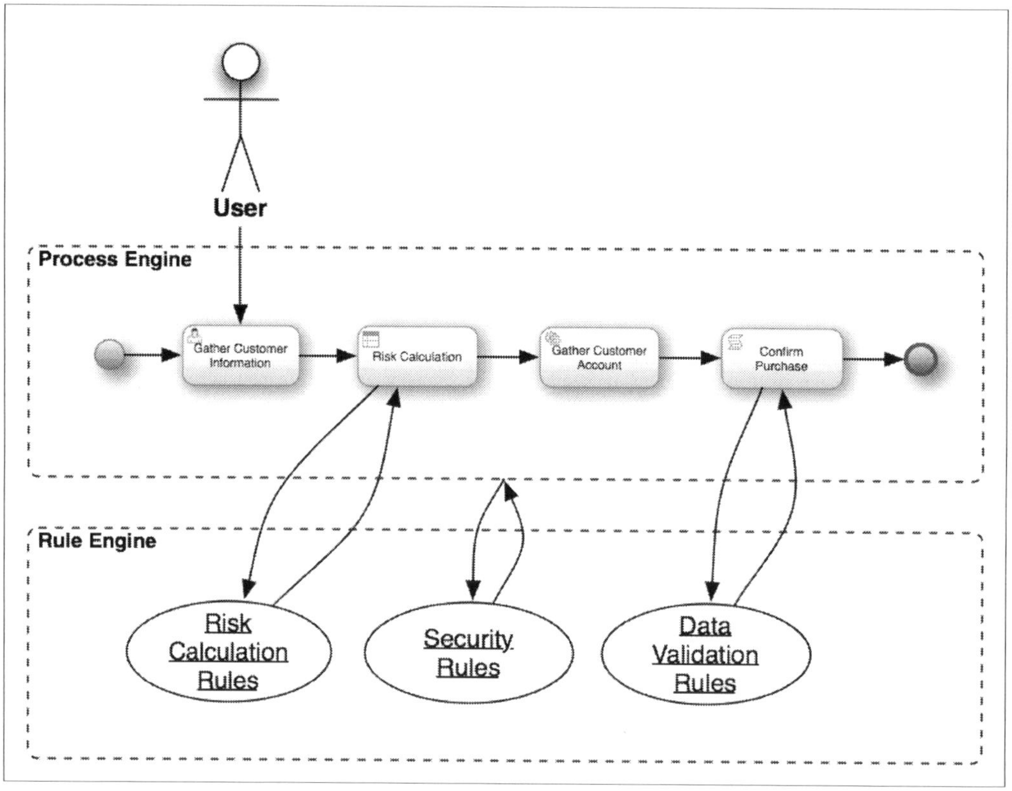

In such situations we will need to deal with some common issues, such as:

- Gathering the information that the rule engine requires
- Preparing the information to be sent to the rule engine
- Dealing with communication problems between the two different runtimes (process engine and rule engine)
- Adapting the data structures between those platforms

The classic integration between rules engines and process engines only leverage a very small percentage of the rule engine's capabilities and the interactions are commonly stateless. In other words, the processes just use the rule engine to solve small problems (most of them with a stateless nature).

This book will demonstrate how jBPM5 and the Drools Rule Engine integrate seamlessly. We will see how this integration allows us to enrich our business processes by using the rule engine to create more flexible and smarter processes.

Event-driven architecture and complex event processing

Event Driven Architecture (**EDA**) allows us to build highly decoupled systems based on the generation and consumption of events. Like SOA, EDA can be considered a reference architecture used to build scalable applications. Service Oriented Architecture and Event Driven Architecture can co-exist and complement each other very well.

EDA proposes a set of highly decoupled components to build our applications: **Event Producer**, **Event Processing Agent**, and **Event Consumer**. Event Producer is in charge of generating events that will be consumed, composed, aggregated, and analyzed by Event Processing Agents. Simultaneously, Event Processing Agents can generate high-level events based on compositions or aggregations of the events that they are processing. We can have any number of Event Consumers that are interested in the events that are being processed and generated by the Events Producers.

For example, we can consider a Patient Vital Sign Monitor as an Event Producer. The Vital Sign Monitor will generate different events based on the measurements that it makes periodically on the assigned patient. We can have an application that is in charge of acting as an Alert Dashboard. This application will be an Event Consumer that will display the information provided by the Event Processing Agents. One or more Event Processing Agents will receive the Heart Rate, Temperature, and Blood Pressure Events from the Monitor; analyze the patient status; and if something goes wrong, they will generate Alert Events that are then propagated/forwarded to the Alert Dashboard application.

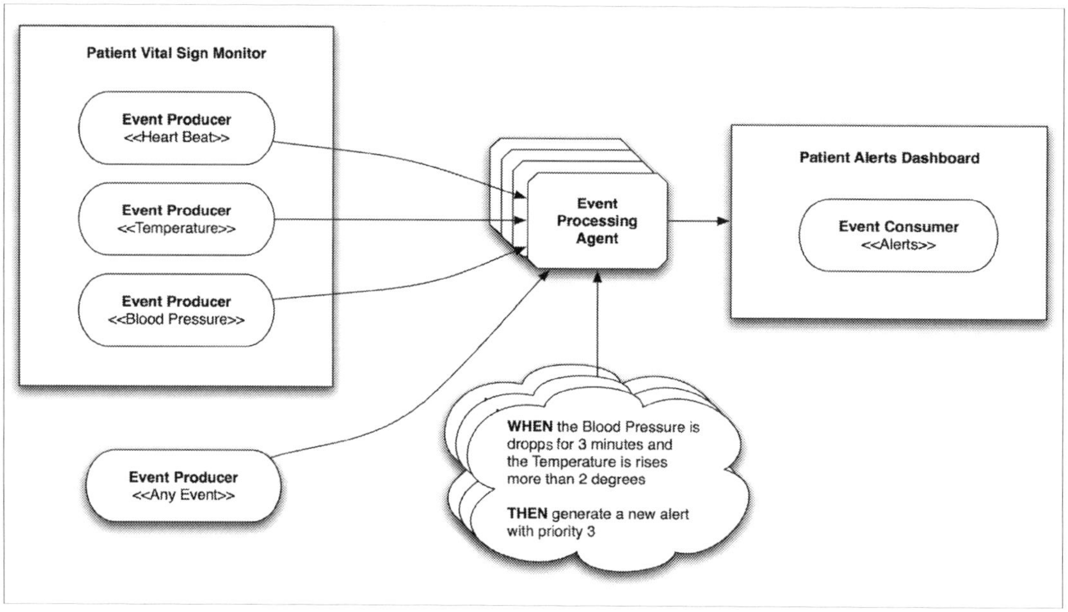

It's important to notice that **Event Producer**, **Event Processing Agent**, and **Event Consumer** are totally decoupled and don't know of the existence of each other. They all work and are able to exist separately, without any dependency.

As you can see, we can have very disparate Event Producers that can generate various types of events. The Event Processing Agents will have the knowledge to filter, compose, and aggregate different events that can come from multiple sources and route them to the different interested consumers.

The core of an EDA infrastructure are the Event Processing Agents, which are the ones in charge of aggregating, correlating, filtering, and composing events from different sources. These Event Processing Agents are usually built using a Complex Event Processing Framework, which gives us all the tools for handling different streams of events and define filters and conditions to identify higher-level situations.

All these concepts can be applied to events produced and consumed by business processes. We can easily integrate these concepts and components with a BPMS, which can produce and receive events.

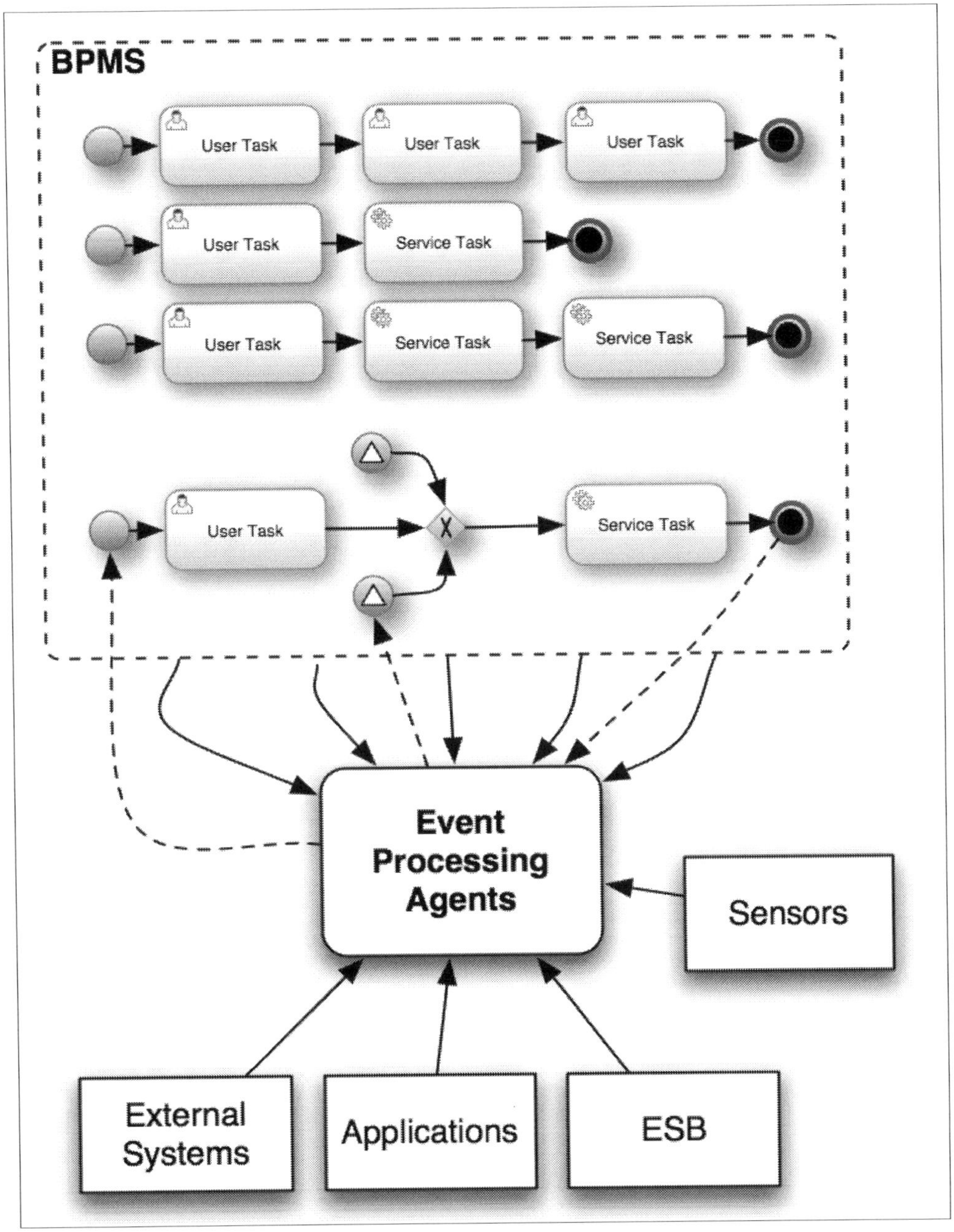

The previous image shows how the Process Engine and the Event Processing Agents can be combined to model and execute complex business scenarios.

We can leverage the power of the Event Processing Agent to influence our business processes execution, create new process instances based on the aggregation and correlation of events that are coming from different sources, or even notify external applications or actors about the completion of a business process under a set of specific circumstances. In *Chapter 10, Reactive Processes Using Drools Fusion*, Drools Fusion will be introduced to show how we integrate jBPM5 with the Complex Event Processing features.

Summary

In this chapter, we have covered all the internal components that a BPM system should provide, and how jBPM5 can be compared with a traditional BPMS.

As you may have noticed, a wide variety of design and architectural patterns can be applied to build applications, and different technologies can be mixed to simplify our software solutions. For the rest of this book, we will tackle different problems using these previously described tools and concepts. It's extremely important for you to learn about all the related technologies around BPM systems in depth in order to enrich your design and implementations.

The next chapter will introduce the BPMN 2 specification, which will enable us to understand and model more complex scenarios.

3

Using BPMN 2.0 to Model Business Scenarios

Once we understand the concepts related to the BPM discipline, we quickly recognize the need for a flexible and standard language to describe our business activities. This chapter is focused on showing the main constructs in the BPMN 2.0 language; it will introduce a real-life use case to demonstrate best practices and some design alternatives to break down a business scenario.

By introducing the Emergency Services use case, we will be able to learn the language and map real activities to artifacts that are specified in the BPMN 2.0 specification. Following the introduction, we will cover the modeling of the processes required to satisfy the described scenario.

This chapter will cover the following topics:

- Introduction to the BPMN 2.0 standard specification
- Modeling elements
- Modeling examples

If you are reading this book and you already have a relevant scenario defined by you, try to abstract the behaviors and map the modeling decisions to your own use case. The examples in this chapter will be covering most of the common constructs required to model and build real-life business processes.

Let's begin the BPMN 2.0 journey with a quick introduction to the standard.

BPMN 2.0 introduction

The BPMN 2.0 standard specification was formally released in January 2011. This specification is the result of collaboration between companies such as Oracle, IBM, Red Hat, Intalio, and many others within the Object Management Group, to conform a unified language to model and execute business processes.

The specification aims to reduce/eliminate the gap between technical business process representations and the fact that a lot of business analysts use flow chart representations to define how a company works. This gap can be eliminated using a standardized mapping between the visual notation of the business process and the execution semantic of the model. A business processes modeled using the BPMN notation defines the flow of data (messages) and the association of the data artifacts to business activities.

This version of the BPMN specification (Version 2.0) covers more than just the notation that needs to be used to draw our business processes, and the complete specification is divided into four sections that allow different vendors to be compliant with one or more of these four conformance types:

- Process Modeling
- Process Execution
- Collaboration Modeling
- Choreography Modeling

For the scope of this book we will be focusing on the analysis of only the Process Modeling and Execution types because jBPM5 is focused only on those areas.

Process Modelling Conformance

We need to be sure that we understand what kind of things need to be covered by a tool that claims to implement the Process Modeling Conformance type of the BPMN 2.0 specification. Usually, Process Modeling Conformance is targeted at graphical tools that allow us to draw/model our business processes and collaboration diagrams. The specification defines two types of business processes:

- Non-executable
- Executable

The modeling tools can be used to only model non-executable processes, or they can also add all the details to get executable versions of our business processes. Depending on the modeling tool, we choose the amount of detail and features that we will be able to add in our process definitions. If our tool is only focused on modeling non-executable processes then the only requirement is the visual appearance of our processes. In other words, the icon and the artifact representations should be the ones proposed by the specification. These non-executable processes can be very useful for documentation and sketching purposes, where the final objective of the diagram is to only show how the company is doing its work.

If we are interested in a tool for modeling an executable process, the specification creates a subcategory (like a subclass) of this conformance type, called Common Executable Conformance, that covers the following requirements:

- The data types and data models that will be related with our business processes must be XML schemas
- The default service interfaces must be WSDL service definitions
- The default data access language must be XPATH

Different vendors can decide how to cover these requirements and be conformant or not with what the specification states. It's always useful to understand which features each vendor is implementing, in order to compare them.

BPMN elements

This section will cover only the basic categorization of the BPMN elements proposed by the standard. For the full specification document, you can visit the following URL: `http://www.omg.org/spec/BPMN/2.0/`

The specification provides a classification of the elements that can be used in our diagrams in order to simplify the recognition of each type of element. Five basic categories are provided:

- Flow objects
- Connecting objects
- Data
- Grouping
- Artifacts

Flow objects

Flow objects are in charge of defining behavior. These are the main set of elements that we need to learn. Inside this category, the specification defines three flow objects: **events, activities**, and **gateways**. We need to know them all in order to have a good understanding of the tools that we will use to define our business processes.

Events

Events will represent that something of interest has happened, usually having a cause or an external trigger and a result/impact. They are represented using a circle. The graphical representation and the border of the circle will vary depending on the type of the event that we need to use.

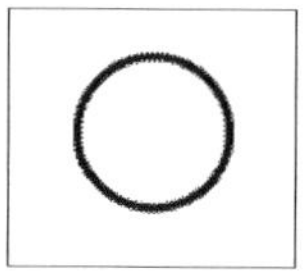

We can clearly differentiate three different types of events:

- Start events
- Intermediate events
- End events

Start events will be used to represent the beginning of a business process. Because we can have different ways to initiate a business process, different types of start events are defined inside the specification. A generic start event is denoted with the same icon of a generic event:

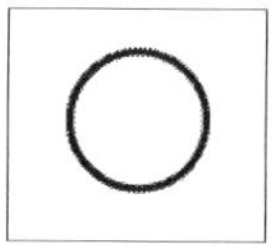

Intermediate events are in charge of throw or catch events that can happen after the process has started and before the process has ended. This type of event will be able to influence the flow of the business process, but it will not be able to start or terminate the process instance by itself.

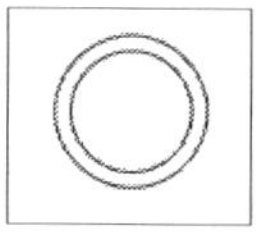

End events will be used to denote the end of a process instance or execution path inside a process instance. End events are not received from the outside world; quite the opposite, in fact. We need to see an end event as a notification from the business process letting us know that it ends.

Activities

Activities define a piece of work that is being done within a company. We can define atomic and non-atomic activities. For this purpose, the specification defines three types of activities: subprocesses, tasks, and call activities. We use tasks when the work that is being done cannot be broken down (atomic). We use subprocesses when we have a set of activities that it makes sense to execute in their own context (non-atomic). We use call activities to invoke reusable definitions.

The following icon represents a generic activity:

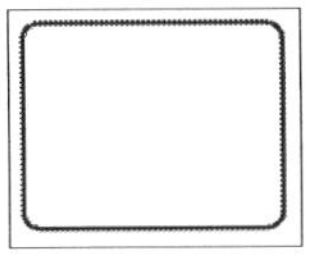

If a **task** is represented using this rounded rectangle, we consider the task an atomic task. If a **+** sign is added to the rounded rectangle, the activity is considered a subprocess, meaning that it can be decomposed into multiple activities.

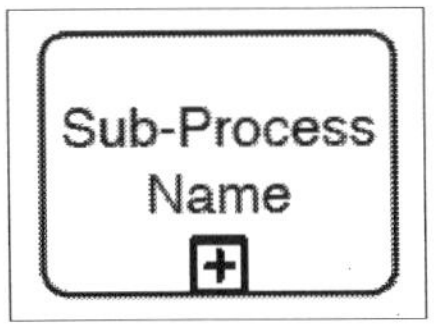

A **subprocess** activity can be used to represent composition when we draw several layers of business processes with different perspectives. In this case, subprocesses can be used to describe a set of low-level activities that are not relevant in the current abstraction level that we are describing.

Call activities allow us to invoke a process definition from within a task in our processes. This encourages reutilization and transfers the control of the execution to the activity that is being called.

Gateways

Gateways control the divergence and convergence of sequence flows in a business process. The internal markers define the behavior of the gateways. The different types of gateways that are commonly used are: **Parallel gateway, Exclusive gateway, Inclusive gateway**, and **Complex gateway**.

The Parallel gateway allows us to define concurrent paths that need to be created or synchronized inside our business processes. We will use Parallel gateways when we want to represent activities that can be executed in parallel. When a Parallel gateway is used to synchronize different paths of execution, it will wait for all the paths to finish before propagating the execution to the next activity.

The Exclusive gateway allows us to define a decision point where the process flow will choose only one path to continue. When an Exclusive gateway is used to join multiple paths, it will wait until the first path is completed to propagate the execution to the next activity. Expressions in the gateway's outgoing flow are used to decide which execution path should be followed.

The Inclusive gateway is a less restrictive version of an Exclusive gateway where the process execution could continue through more than one of its outgoing paths. Whether the execution continues through a path depends on a condition held by the path. All the conditions of the outgoing paths are evaluated by the gateway, and the execution will continue only through those expressions evaluating to true. In the case of the converging version of this node, it will wait until all the active paths connected to it arrive before it continues with the execution.

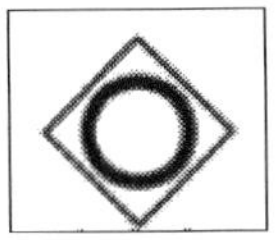

The Complex gateway allows us to define a complex path selection mechanism for branching or joining concurrent paths. We will be able to define from *1* to *n* branches to continue. When we are using a Complex gateway to join concurrent branches, we will be able to define whether we will wait for 1 or more branches before propagating the execution to the next activity in the process.

Connecting objects

Sequence flows define the sequence between flow objects. The specification defines three kinds of sequence flows to specify different behaviors to propagate the execution: **uncontrolled sequence flow**, **conditional sequence flow**, and **default sequence flow**.

The uncontrolled sequence flow is the most common sequence flow. It is the one that we will use to connect two activities, representing a sequence between them.

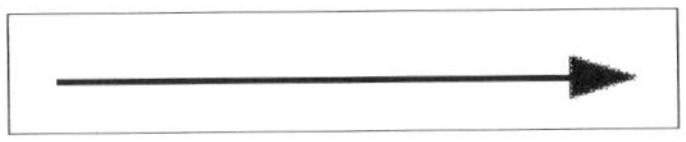

The conditional sequence flow evaluates an expression in order to decide whether it can propagate the execution to the next activity or not. The expression is evaluated in runtime when the process is being executed, usually evaluating a process variable.

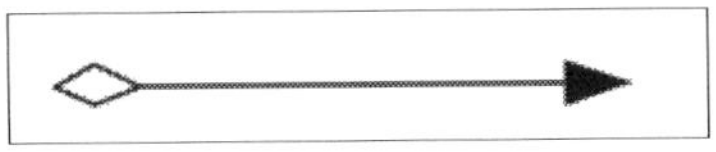

The default sequence flow will be used in Exclusive/Inclusive/Complex gateways where data is evaluated to decide which path(s) will continue the execution. The default sequence flow will be selected if no other sequence flow matches with the specified criteria.

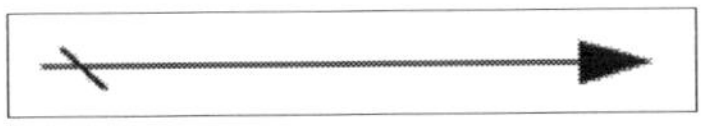

Data

Data objects represent data that will be handled and manipulated during the process execution. In BPMN 2.0, we can define the information that will be used by our process, inside the process graphically, diagram, and specify where the data will be used. The following elements are defined to specify different information sources and how this information will be used:

- Data objects
- Data stores
- Properties (no visual representation)
- Data inputs & Data outputs

Data objects are the most basic representations of a piece of information that will be used by our process. We can add data objects to processes and subprocesses. Data objects have an associated life cycle that will depend on the process or subprocess where they belong. This means that when our process gets instantiated, the data objects specified inside it will be instantiated as well. We can mark our data object to be a single instance.

We can also mark our data object to be a collection.

Data stores allow us to interact with information that is outside the scope of the process. We will use data stores to represent external sources of information that can be accessed by the process but are not being handled or instantiated by the process execution. The most common example of a data store is an external service that lets us query and update information from a database.

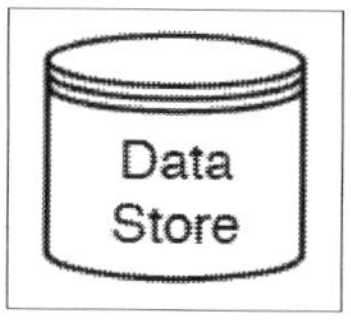

Properties include data objects, pieces of information that can be associated to processes, and flow objects. In contrast to data objects, properties will not be visually displayed inside our process diagram. Processes/subprocesses, activities, and events can define internal properties that are tied to each object life cycle. Process properties will be accessible by all the activities inside that process. Activity properties will only be accessible by the same activity. Process properties are usually known as process variables.

Data inputs will be used to specify information that will be needed to execute a process or an activity. **Data outputs** will represent the information that will be generated by the process or by the activity as a result of adding information or modifying the information that was provided as input.

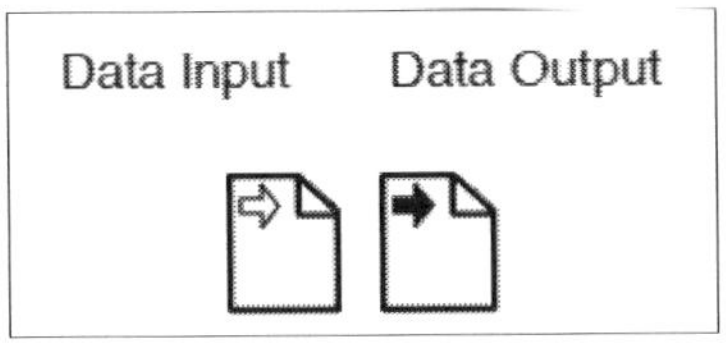

Finally, **data associations** will be used to represent the relationship of a data object with a flow object. Data associations can also be considered as a mechanism to share information between the source and the target property. The specification also defines that, during this process of moving information from one flow object to another, we can also apply transformations by using expressions. Data associations don't affect the process execution flow, meaning that a data association can never propagate process execution.

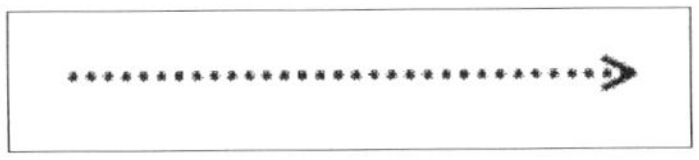

Grouping

Grouping elements are defined to organize and categorize the activities that belong to a process. Using pools and lanes, we can denote responsibility from a role or a business unit to a set of activities. The specification doesn't impose the use of pools and lanes. Most of the time, pools and lanes are used to improve process readability.

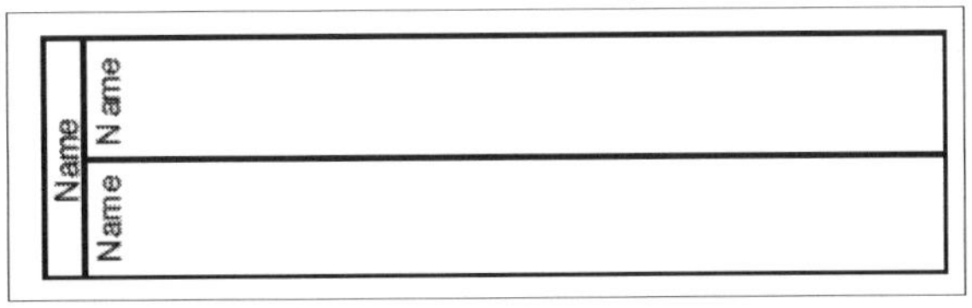

The preceding figure shows a pool with two lanes where the pool can represent a business unit and each lane can represent different departments inside that business unit.

Artifacts

Artifacts elements help us to add additional information to our business process diagrams. Artifacts are always used to improve the documentation aspects of our diagrams. The specification defines two types of artifacts: **Groups** and **Text Annotations**.

Groups are used to encapsulate a group of tasks together, with the sole purpose of demarcating a logical relationship between them. Groups don't affect the process flow and are commonly used for documentation purposes.

Text Annotations allow us to add notes to our process diagrams to clarify different aspects. It is strongly suggested that Text Annotations be used to clarify complex activities or to add information that can be useful to explain the business process to non-technical people.

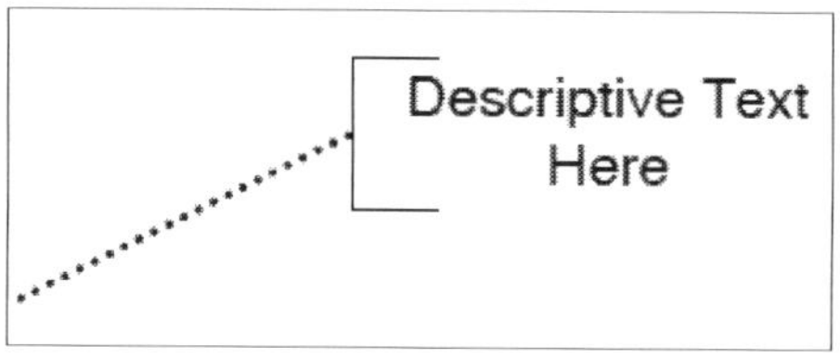

Task types

As we previously mentioned, one of the most important types of flow objects is the activity. Each activity will represent a task related with our business scenario. The specification provides a set of specific tasks that can be used to define different behaviors. This section covers the most commonly-used tasks that we need to know in order to start modeling business scenarios.

The following task types will be described in this section:

- Abstract task
- Service task
- User task
- Business rule task
- Script task

The **Abstract task** is the base type of all the other tasks in BPMN 2.0. Even if, according to the specification, this task is abstract and we should never use it in our processes, jBPM5 uses it as an extension point where we can define different behavior during runtime. We will see more about this in *Chapter 6, Domain-specific Processes*.

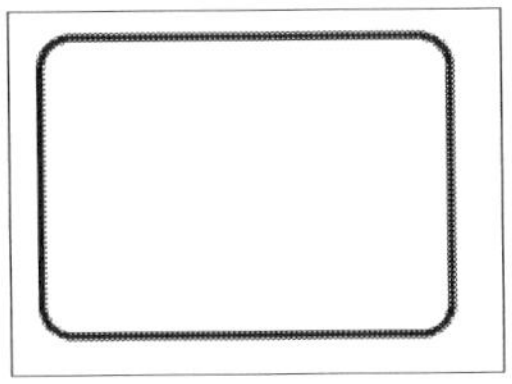

The **Service task** allows us to represent interactions with external automated systems. Each time that our business process needs to interact with a service or procedure, we will use a Service task. The Service task element defines an attribute called `implementation` that looks like this:

```
implementation: string = ##webService
```

This attribute is used to specify the underlying implementation of the service that we are calling.

The **User task** represents a human interaction. Each time that we want to represent a person doing an activity, we use a User task to model this situation. Because User tasks represent a human interaction, we need to provide a way to assist the performer during this interaction. Most of the time, we end up with a task list-oriented user interface that assists each user during these interactions. We will take a close look at this approach in *Chapter 7, Human Interactions*.

The **Business rule task** allows us to interact with a **Business Rule Engine** (**BRE**) to do some business logic evaluation. The interaction with the Business Rule Engine usually involves sending information to the Engine, which will be evaluated by a set of business rules, and a result will be returned.

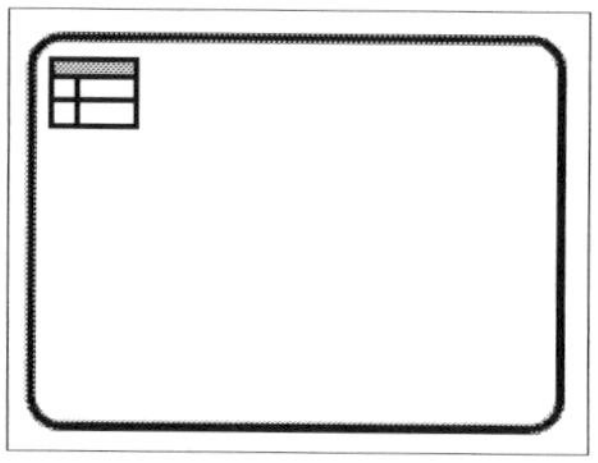

The **Script task** allows us to execute a script that can be specified in various languages. A script basically represents a set of actions that we can code using a scripting language with business-friendly syntax.

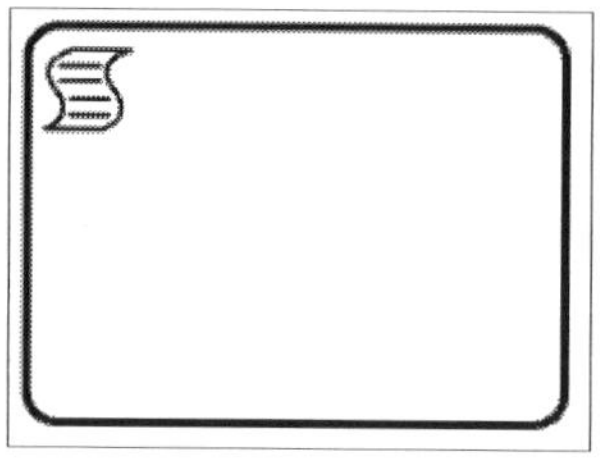

BPMN 2.0 introduction summary

Now that we have a high-level overview of the main elements defined in the specification, we need to see them in action. The following section proposes a set of simple processes to analyze the functional and technical aspects of each of these elements. We will analyze some scenarios and the possible options that we will have for modeling them. For the moment, we are not going to see how we can execute these scenarios, but we will analyze them and take a look at the XML files generated by the modeler tool.

Modelling business scenarios with BPMN 2.0

Translating our business scenarios into business processes modeled with BPMN 2.0 is a very sensitive task. Modeling our business processes using the correct elements sounds simple, but we really need to understand the technical implications that our decisions at the modeling stage will have when we want to execute our process definitions.

So, let's get started with a real example.

Hospital emergency scenario

The first scenario that we will be covering describes the activities that need to be executed in order to accept an ambulance request to transport a patient to hospital. The business goal of the following process is to speed up the response, and if possible, accept the patient as quickly and efficiently as possible.

If we agree to accept the ambulance request, we will need to coordinate the hospital's internal resources to receive the patient. The following business process description describes this scenario:

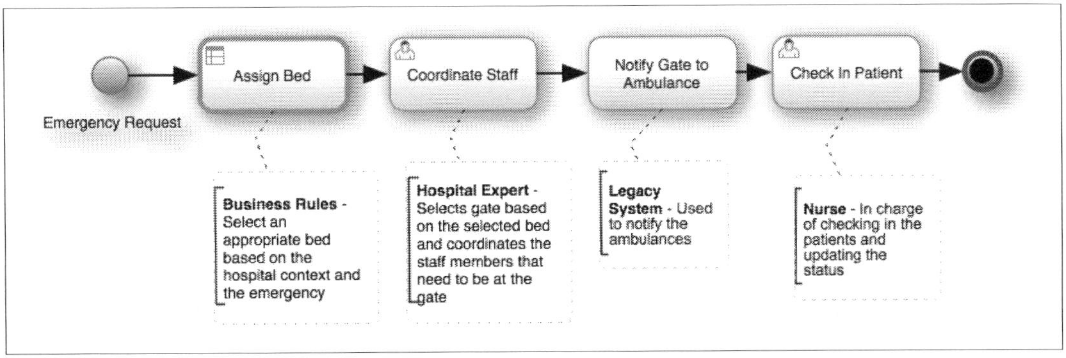

This process describes the standard activities defined in the hospital's happy path to handle the situation. As you may imagine, the activities inside this process will be executed each time a new emergency request arrives at the hospital. As you can see, the process ends when the assigned nurse checks the patient in and updates his/her status.

As you can see in the process diagram, the first flow object that will be executed is a start event. This start event will contain information about the emergency request that we will use to understand the context and complete the following activities accordingly. Once we receive the start event, we will use the information to execute a Business rule task that will be in charge of assigning a bed based on the emergency information and on the hospital context. Once we get the assigned bed, we will notify a hospital resource planning expert about the situation and the already assigned bed. The expert will be in charge of selecting the best way to receive the ambulance and which members of staff will be in charge of going to the specified gate to receive the patient. Once this coordination is done and the gate is selected, we will use a legacy system that the hospital has to send a notification to the ambulance of the gate that was selected and how to proceed with the emergency. As soon as the ambulance arrives, a nurse will be waiting for the patient to check his/her status at arrival and fill in all the information that is required by the hospital to check the patient in.

This is a very simplistic representation of the proposed business scenario, but we need to start simply. We need to be sure that we gather the correct information about the activities that are being executed. We need to be sure that we represent the activities that really matter from the hospital's perspective. Modeling these scenarios is not about how the process will be executed but about which activities are relevant for modeling within the business processes. We will use this simple representation as a kick-start process to represent the situation more accurately.

At this point, we can create a brief description, in tabular form, of the resources that our business processes are using.

At this point, we can say that our process requires the interaction of two human roles: a nurse and a hospital resource planner expert. We are interacting with the rule engine to carry out the bed assignment; this means that we will need to have a set of business rules that evaluate the emergency situation and the hospital context in order to assign a bed. We are also sending notifications to the ambulance using a connector to a legacy system that was being used by the hospital before the business process was designed. Using this information, we can easily define the business requirements in terms of resources and system interactions. Defining these requirements, when the processes get executed we can quickly define the metrics to understand how the process works in the hospital context.

We will be able to analyze whether we will need to hire more nurses or whether we need to improve our old notification system to accept more requests because the old one is introducing too much delay into hospital operations.

The second version of our process could look like the following figure:

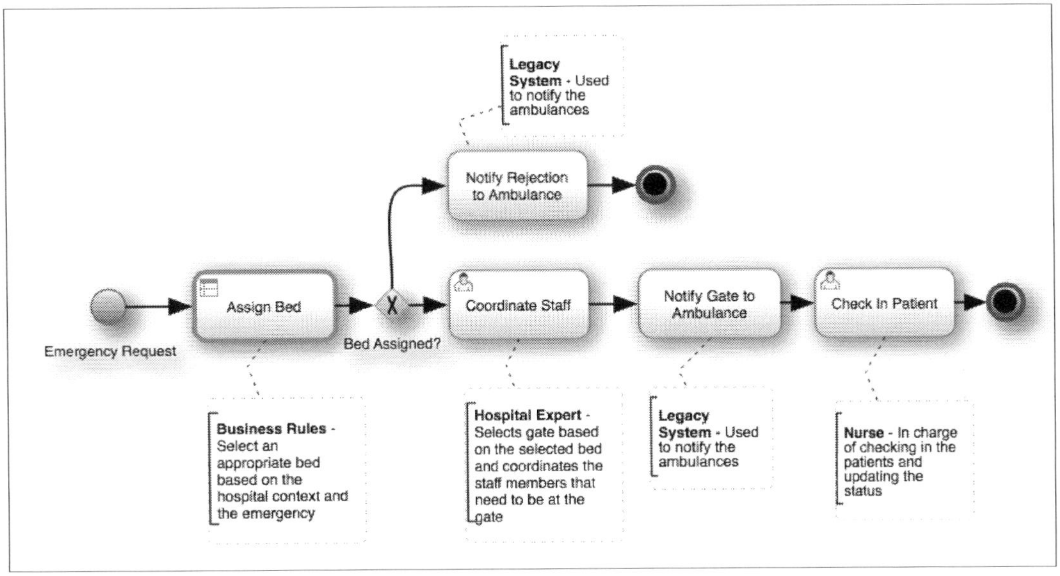

Here, we are adding an Exclusive gateway to evaluate whether a bed was correctly assigned or not. Based on this evaluation, we will continue with the happy path or send a rejection notification to the ambulance, so they can request a bed authorization from another hospital. We need to evaluate whether this gateway will add unnecessary complexity to our model or whether it will help us to better reflect what is happening. Once again, we need to be able to decouple how we are representing the business scenario and the technical implications that our model will have when we want to run it. We will see that these kinds of exceptional paths can also be solved technically without adding more flow objects to our business process diagram. We need to find the right balance between the technical decisions and what the process diagram represents for the business scenario.

A third option for our business process could be the following:

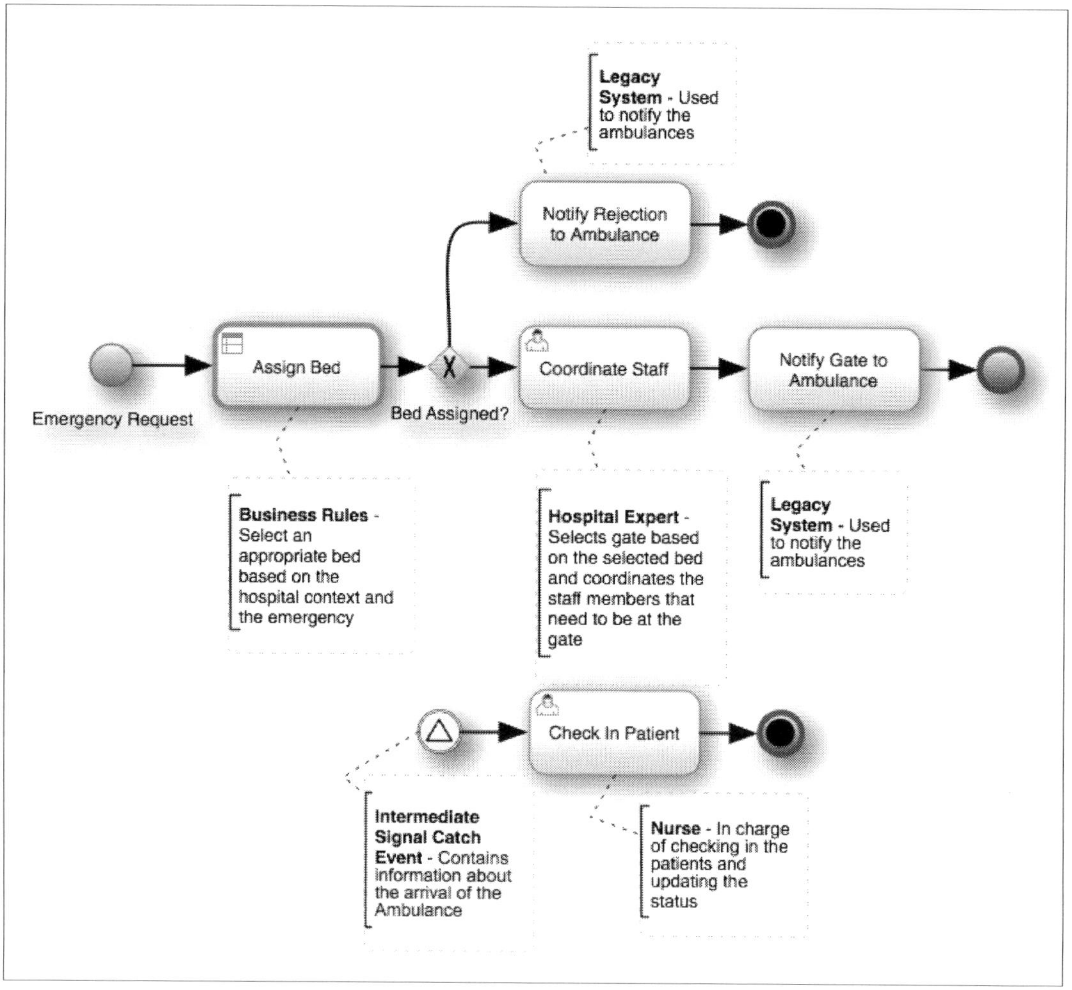

This third option includes an Intermediate Signal Catch event that is going to be notified when the ambulance reaches the gate. We are supposing, for this situation, that we will receive an external stimulus notifying us when the ambulance arrives at the hospital. The notification will contain information about this arrival event, for example the time of arrival. Only at that point will the `Check In Patient` activity for the nurse be created. Once again, we need to properly identify whether this event addition adds too much complexity to the process diagram. A sensor located at the gate can be in charge of generating the external notification, or the ambulance can send an automated notification when it's approaching the selected gate.

A good practice is to validate each of these improvements with the business users executing the activities. As a rule of thumb, we need to keep the process diagram as clean and simple as possible.

Technical perspective

Once we understand each scenario, we can start thinking about the technical implications that our models will have. We can start analyzing which technical details we need to add in order to automate our business processes. In this section, we will start analyzing the technical assets that will be generated when we model our business process diagram in a BPMN2 tool that allows us to export the model as an XML file.

Let's start modeling the first version of the hospital emergency scenario.

Hospital emergency technical overview

Having the initial description of our business process, we can go ahead and model it inside our Business Process Designer tool. If we do that in jBPM5 Web Designer (introduced in *Chapter 4, Knowing Your Toolbox*, and developed in depth in *Chapter 5, The Process Designer*) or in any other BPMN2 tool, we will get something like this:

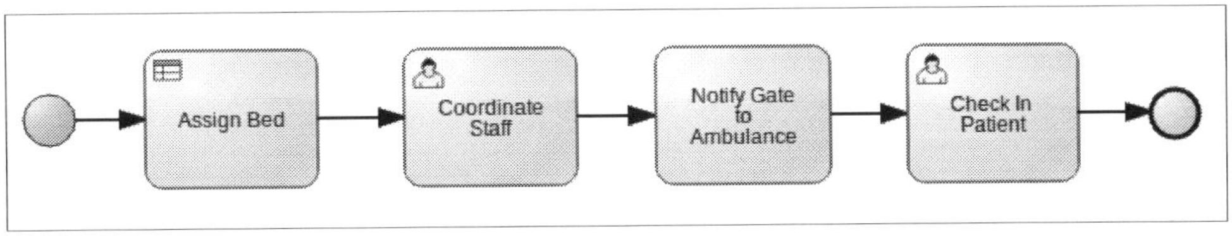

This process definition only contains the activities and flow objects as we described them previously. We haven't added any technical detail or data mappings yet. We first need to work on the completion of the model and reach a state where we are satisfied with what the process represents, in this case, for the hospital.

If we analyze the XML generated by this simple model, we will see how each task is being represented inside the XML file:

```
<bpmn2:definitions
  xmlns:xsi="http://www.w3.org/2001/XMLSchema-instance"
  xmlns="http://www.omg.org/bpmn20"
  xmlns:bpmn2="http://www.omg.org/spec/BPMN/20100524/MODEL"
  xmlns:bpmndi="http://www.omg.org/spec/BPMN/20100524/DI"
  xmlns:dc="http://www.omg.org/spec/DD/20100524/DC"
  xmlns:di="http://www.omg.org/spec/DD/20100524/DI"
  xmlns:drools="http://www.jboss.org/drools"
```

```
    id="_yxaVMDUxEeGuKd61boWk5A"
    xsi:schemaLocation="http://www.omg.org/spec/BPMN/20100524/MODEL
            BPMN20.xsd" targetNamespace="http://www.omg.org/bpmn20">
...
<bpmn2:process id="hospitalEmergencyV1" name="Emergency Process"
                                        isExecutable="true">
  <bpmn2:startEvent id="_1" name="">
    <bpmn2:outgoing>_2</bpmn2:outgoing>
  </bpmn2:startEvent>
  <bpmn2:businessRuleTask id="_3" name="Assign Bed">
    <bpmn2:incoming>_2</bpmn2:incoming>
    <bpmn2:outgoing>_4</bpmn2:outgoing>
  </bpmn2:businessRuleTask>
  <bpmn2:userTask id="_5" name="Coordinate Staff">
    <bpmn2:incoming>_4</bpmn2:incoming>
    <bpmn2:outgoing>_6</bpmn2:outgoing>
  </bpmn2:userTask>
  <bpmn2:task id="_7" name="Notify Gate to Ambulance"
          drools:taskName="Notify Gate to Ambulance">
     <bpmn2:incoming>_6</bpmn2:incoming>
     <bpmn2:outgoing>_8</bpmn2:outgoing>
  </bpmn2:task>
  <bpmn2:userTask id="_9" name="Check In Patient">
    <bpmn2:incoming>_8</bpmn2:incoming>
    <bpmn2:outgoing>_10</bpmn2:outgoing>
  </bpmn2:userTask>
  <bpmn2:endEvent id="_11" name="">
    <bpmn2:incoming>_10</bpmn2:incoming>
  </bpmn2:endEvent>

  <bpmn2:sequenceFlow id="_2" sourceRef="_1" targetRef="_3"/>
  <bpmn2:sequenceFlow id="_4" sourceRef="_3" targetRef="_5"/>
  <bpmn2:sequenceFlow id="_6" sourceRef="_5" targetRef="_7"/>
  <bpmn2:sequenceFlow id="_8" sourceRef="_7" targetRef="_9"/>
  <bpmn2:sequenceFlow id="_10" sourceRef="_9" targetRef="_11"/>
</bpmn2:process>

</bpmn2:definitions>
```

After cleaning up the XML code a little bit to remove autogenerated IDs (from something like `_DA2EDFB2-D539-4244-A66A-585C7496A7BA` to `_1`), and after removing the graphical layout information, we get a clean description of the activities contained inside our process.

We can clearly see that the XML file structure begins with a `<bpmn2:definitions>` tag. This tag is in charge of containing our process definitions. As you may notice, inside this tag a lot of references to the OMG BPMN2 schemas are included. These schemas will be used to validate that our BPMN2 file is compliant with the BPMN2 specification. I've cleaned up some global definitions that can be included outside of the process definitions because we don't need them right now. As I previously mentioned, inside the `definitions` tag we will include our process definition tags.

The `<bpmn2:process>` tag requires us to assign an ID to the process, and depending on the tooling, it will either let us create an executable process or won't. In this case, the attribute `isExecutable` is set to `true` by the tooling, by default.

Once we are inside the `process` tag we can start defining our flow objects. Keep in mind that sometimes we may find that our activities are defined out of order inside the XML file. We don't need to worry about this, but it's good to understand how the activities are correlated. For this example, I've ordered the XML file so we can easily identify the activity sequence.

The first flow object that we find inside our process is `<bpmn2:startEvent>`. This is a very simple tag that represents the start event in our process. Notice that within the `startEvent` tag we will find a reference to the outgoing sequence flow that will be in charge of propagating the execution to the `businessRuleTask` tag.

The `<bpmn2:businessRuleTask>` tag represents the interaction with a rule engine. As you may notice, inside this tag, there is no reference at all to how this interaction will happen or what information needs to be sent to the rule engine to be evaluated. As you can see, this tag also allows us to assign a name to this activity, which in this case is `Assign Bed`.

The next activity in the process is the `<bpmn2:userTask>` tag, which contains the attribute name set to `Coordinate Staff`. Until this point, we are only saying that there will be a human interaction. But the process definition doesn't include any reference to any role in charge of performing the task, or to any information that needs to be exchanged in order to complete the activity. We will need to include all this information in order to have a fully executable process. The same situation occurs with the activity called `Check In Patient`, where there is no reference to the performer who will be in charge of this activity.

The `<bpmn2:task>` tag represents the interaction with an external system (external from the process engine perspective). In this case, the service task named `Notify Gate to Ambulance`, will be in charge of contacting a specific service that the hospital uses to send notifications to the ambulances.

Next, the `<bpmn2:endEvent>` tag is defined, and it represents the end of our business process.

Finally, we find all the sequence flows; they join all the activities in a sequence. Note that each `sequenceFlow` element specifies its `id`, `sourceRef` and `targetRef` values.

Once again, until this point we have a very basic XML representation of our activities. Now, it's not just a diagram. We have a formalized description of the activities that we have included in our process and that can be used by technical people to add all the technical details needed to execute this process.

Once we reach this state, the business analyst can start adding information about data that will flow throughout the activities. Technical roles will be in charge of adding the information about the external systems that will be contacted.

Version 2 of this process will include an **XOR Exclusive Diverging gateway** that will be in charge of analyzing whether a bed was correctly assigned. If not, a rejection notification will be sent to the ambulance that requested authorization to go to this hospital.

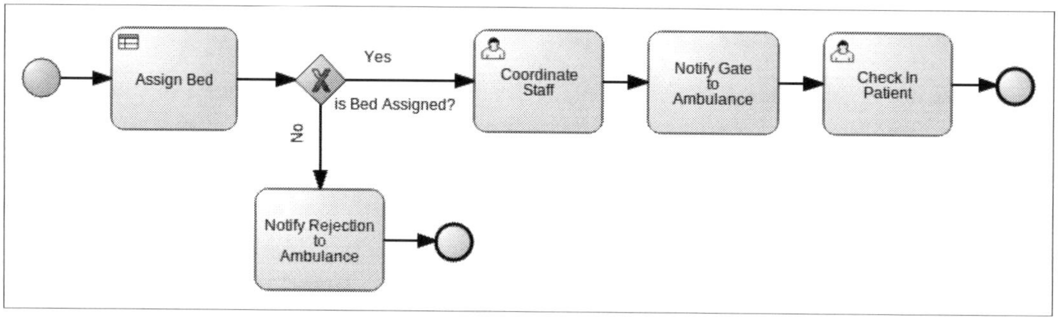

The following XML snippet shows how this flow object is represented in the XML syntax:

```
<bpmn2:exclusiveGateway
    id="_F3BA0E13-33CD-48D3-A8B6-6CF5642849BF"
    name="Is Bed Assigned?" gatewayDirection="Diverging">
<bpmn2:incoming>
        _AD663BD1-0132-4DCB-9714-697E54C75A78
</bpmn2:incoming>
<bpmn2:outgoing>
        _6A7F9148-E9C4-4F36-BA2A-4DBB30FEDCD3
</bpmn2:outgoing>
<bpmn2:outgoing>
        _98172B69-DD90-4BEA-B16D-6E1F276FF9D7
</bpmn2:outgoing>
</bpmn2:exclusiveGateway>
```

As we can see, two outgoing sequence flows are referenced from this diverging flow object.

Version 3 of the process also includes an **Intermediate Signal Catch event** definition that is used to wait for an external notification that will be generated when the ambulance is approaching the gate.

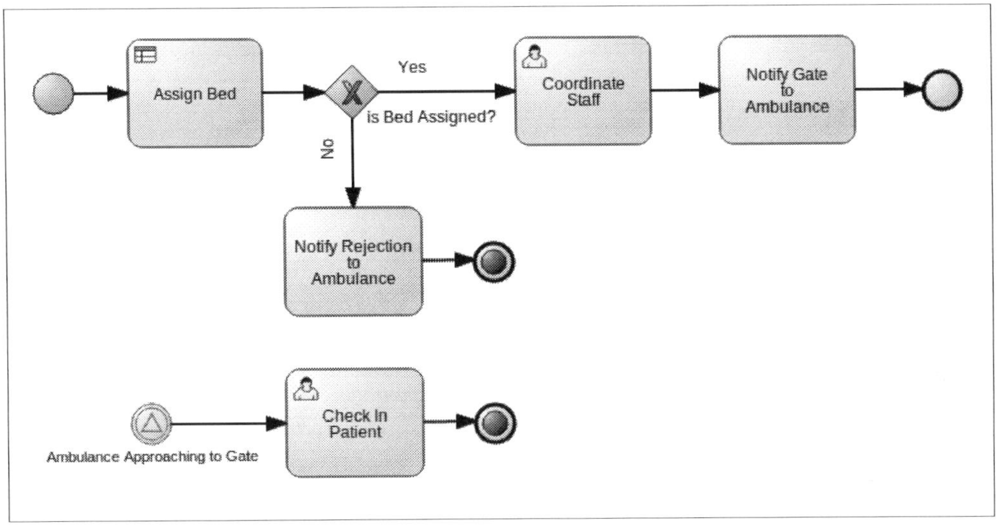

The Intermediate Signal Catch event is represented by the following XML snippet:

```
<bpmn2:intermediateCatchEvent id="_4" name="Ambulance
                                        Approaching Gate">
  <bpmn2:outgoing>_5</bpmn2:outgoing>
  <bpmn2:signalEventDefinition id="_6" signalRef="Ambulance
                                                 Arrived"/>
</bpmn2:intermediateCatchEvent>
```

As you can see, this event flow object doesn't have any information about the event type. It doesn't have the information that this event will contain (and that needs to be propagated to the process context), either.

Adding simple process data

In this section, we will add more information to our process diagram so as to be able to execute it. We will need to specify the information that will be required by the process to start, the information that will be required and generated by the human interactions, and the information that will be sent to the external services that will be used by the process.

We will use the first and simplest version of the process to easily understand how we can technically define the information exchange that will be required to accomplish the process' business goal.

This information will be provided to the start event and will represent the information sent by the ambulance to the hospital. Because this information needs to be stored inside our process, we will define what we call process variables. These process variables (or process properties) are defined within the `<bpmn2:process>` tag, but outside any other task.

```
<bpmn2:property id="bedrequest_id"
    itemSubjectRef="_bedrequest_idItem"/>
<bpmn2:property id="bedrequest_date"
    itemSubjectRef="_bedrequest_dateItem"/>
<bpmn2:property id="bedrequest_entity"
    itemSubjectRef="_bedrequest_entityItem"/>
<bpmn2:property id="bedrequest_patientage"
    itemSubjectRef="_bedrequest_patientageItem"/>
<bpmn2:property id="bedrequest_patientname"
    itemSubjectRef="_bedrequest_patientnameItem"/>
<bpmn2:property id="bedrequest_patientgender"
    itemSubjectRef="_bedrequest_patientgenderItem"/>
<bpmn2:property id="bedrequest_patientstatus"
    itemSubjectRef="_bedrequest_patientstatusItem"/>
<bpmn2:property id="bedrequest_selectedBed"
    itemSubjectRef="_bedrequest_selectedBedItem"/>
<bpmn2:property id="checkinresults_gate"
    itemSubjectRef="_checkinresults_gateItem"/>
<bpmn2:property id="checkinresults_checkedin"
    itemSubjectRef="_checkinresults_checkedinItem"/>
<bpmn2:property id="checkinresults_notified"
    itemSubjectRef="_checkinresults_notifiedItem"/>
<bpmn2:property id="checkinresults_time"
    itemSubjectRef="_checkinresults_timeItem"/>
```

These process variables represent the information that will be carried out by the process activities. We need to define all the information that we want to handle at the process level. These properties will not have any visual representation in our diagram, but we can usually define them in our modeling tool, within a property panel.

Note that a process variable is composed of an `id` and an `itemSubjectRef` reference. The `id` parameter represents the name of the variable. We will use the value of `id` to reference the process variable in different activities of our process. The `itemSubjectRef` parameter is used to reference a type of information that was externally defined. Given that BPMN2 is language-independent, we cannot make direct references to Java types. For this reason we use the following item definitions:

```
<bpmn2:itemDefinition id="_bedrequest_idItem"
                      structureRef="String"/>
<bpmn2:itemDefinition id="_bedrequest_dateItem"
                      structureRef="String"/>
<bpmn2:itemDefinition id="_bedrequest_entityItem"
                      structureRef="String"/>
<bpmn2:itemDefinition id="_bedrequest_patientageItem"
                      structureRef="String"/>
<bpmn2:itemDefinition id="_bedrequest_patientnameItem"
                      structureRef="String"/>
<bpmn2:itemDefinition id="_bedrequest_patientgenderItem"
                      structureRef="String"/>
<bpmn2:itemDefinition id="_bedrequest_patientstatusItem"
                      structureRef="String"/>
<bpmn2:itemDefinition id="_bedrequest_selectedBedItem"
                      structureRef="String"/>
<bpmn2:itemDefinition id="_checkinresults_gateItem"
                      structureRef="String"/>
<bpmn2:itemDefinition id="_checkinresults_checkedinItem"
                      structureRef="String"/>
<bpmn2:itemDefinition id="_checkinresults_notifiedItem"
                      structureRef="String"/>
<bpmn2:itemDefinition id="_checkinresults_timeItem"
                      structureRef="String"/>
```

These item definition tags can be understood as type imports in Java. We are defining with a name, all the items of type `String` in this case. We are using `String` for our first executable version, but these item definitions can be of any type.

With these two steps, defining the `itemDefinition` parameters and our process variables, we have defined placeholders for information. Now when we start our process, we can fill some of these buckets that will be accessible for all the activities inside our process. Let's analyze what exactly we have defined. The process will maintain the following information:

- Request ID
- Request date (timestamp)

- Entity that made the request (ambulance, 911, firefighters department, and so on)
- Patient age
- Patient name
- Patient gender
- Patient status
- Selected bed
- Selected gate
- Ambulance notified (true/false)
- Patient checked in (true/false)
- Patient status at checkin
- Check-in time (timestamp)

Some of these variables will be filled when the process starts. The request ID, request date, request entity, patient age, name, gender, and status will be provided when a new instance of the process needs to be created. The rest of the activities in the process will generate all the other information.

After the execution of the first activity in our process, the rule engine will fill the process variable called selected bed. We will see how this happens later on.

The first `userTask` instance in our process, called `Coordinate Staff`, will require us to map information from the process scope to the `userTask` scope. We will be narrowing down the process information to just the information required by this task to work. This `userTask` instance will be in charge of designating the gate where the hospital staff will receive the ambulance. This `userTask` instance will be the responsibility of the hospital resource planner expert, who will assign (based on the assigned bed and his/her expert knowledge) the staff and the gate to deal with this emergency.

For this simple example, and to get the first version of this process working, we will do the data assignments inside this `userTask` object. To see the complete mapping, open the process definition called `HospitalEmergencyScenarioV1-data.bpmn` and look for the `userTask` called `Coordinate Staff`.

```
<bpmn2:userTask id="_5" name="Coordinate Staff">
        ...
</bpmn2:userTask>
```

To understand—without all the visual clutter—what is going on inside the variable mappings, let's analyze the following XML structure:

```
<userTask id="_10">
  <incoming/>
  <outgoing/>
  <ioSpecification>
<dataInput id="_10_varXInput" name="varX"/>
<dataOutput id="_10_varYOutput" name="varY"/>
    <inputSet>
      <dataInputRefs>_10_varXInput</dataInputRefs>
    </inputSet>
    <outputSet>
      <dataOutputRefs>_10_varYOutput<dataOutputRefs>
    </outputSet>
  </ioSpecification>
<dataInputAssociation>
<sourceRef>varX</sourceRef>
  <targetRef>_10_varXInput</targetRef>
</dataInputAssociation>
  <dataOutputAssociation id="_A">
  <sourceRef>_10_varYOutput</sourceRef>
  <targetRef>varY</ targetRef>
</dataOutputAssociation>
  <potentialOwner id="_A">
  <resourceAssignmentExpression id="_A">
    <formalExpression id="_A">
        hospital_resource_planner
      </formalExpression>
  </resourceAssignmentExpression>
</potentialOwner>
</userTask>
```

Inside the `<ioSpecification>` tag, we will define the information that will be injected and generated inside our `userTask` object. Using the `dataInput` and `dataOutput` tags, we define the variables that will be available in the `userTask` context. From a business perspective, we can say that the `ioSpecification` tag represents the information that will be required to execute the interaction. If we are taking about a `userTask` object, this information will be probably displayed to the user so he/she can work with it.

The `inputSet` and `outputSet` tags represent the list of variables that will be expected inside the `userTask` context. This looks redundant, but don't worry; most of the time, all of this XML code will be generated automatically by the tooling. We as developers need to know its structure.

The `dataInputAssociation` and `dataOutputAssociation` tags are where the magic happens. In this section we will map the information from our process scope to the `userTask` internal variables. In this case, the `dataInputAssociation` tag is copying the information from the variable called `varX` to the internal variable called `10_varXInput`. Note that the information will be copied and not moved. Now, inside the `userTask` object , we will be able to modify this information without affecting the process scope information. If we want to modify or add more information to our process scope variables, we need to create a `dataOutputAssociation` tag that will be in charge of copying information from inside the `userTask` scope to the process scope. In this case we are copying the content of the `10_varYOutput` variable to a variable called `varY` in the process scope. This action will override the value of the `varY` variable with the content generated inside the `userTask` object.

The last section of the structure is in charge of defining the resource that will be in charge of executing the activity. In this case, `hospital resource planner` is defined as potential owner, which means that a user with that ID will be responsible for executing this task. Note that `hospital resource planner` can also be a role. From the process perspective, it's only a string that needs to be resolved in runtime, probably by an external component that is in charge of knowing the company's identity structures.

When we want to map information for an Abstract task (or any other task type), we use the same XML structures and rules. You can take a look at the complete process and how all of the variables are mapped looking at the file called `HospitalEmergencyScenarioV1-data.bpmn`.

The following figure shows where the data is generated or moved:

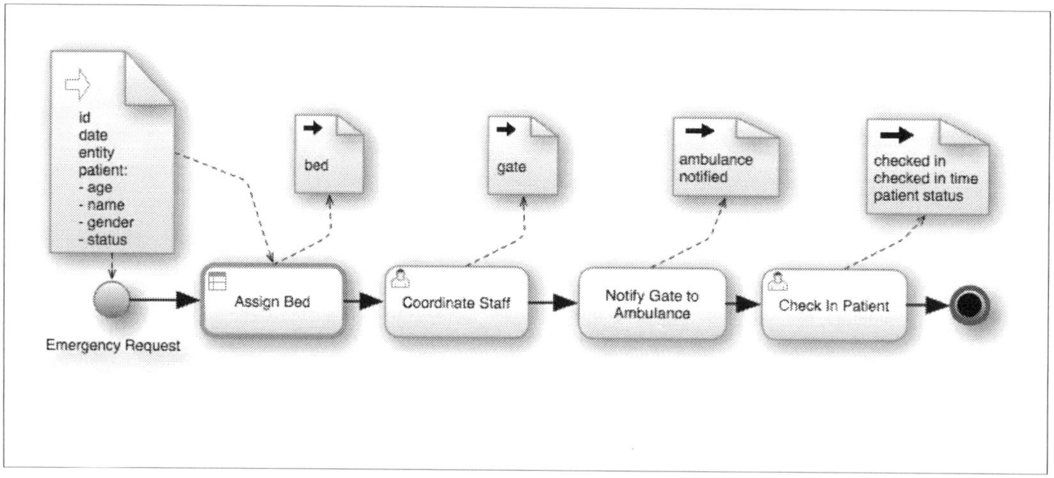

The data inputs are omitted in all the activities, and only the necessary information is copied for each task.

At this point, don't worry if you feel a little bit confused by all the XML elements we have to use in order to define a business process. Most of the times, these processes are designed using a designing tool. *Chapter 5, The Process Designer*, will cover one of these tools, and it will introduce a step-by-step tutorial on how we can model this process (all three different versions) in it.

Summary

In this chapter we have learned the basic flow objects that we can use to model our process diagrams. We have also covered an introduction on how to add the initial technical details required for defining the information that our process definition will need in order to define the data interchange required by this business situation.

The next two chapters will introduce the tooling provided by jBPM5 to model and execute our business processes. Knowing the tooling that the project provides will help us to get a complete overview of how we can implement the BPM discipline in our own business domains.

4
Knowing Your Toolbox

By now you must have a clear understanding of the BPM system structure, the language that we will use to define our business processes, and we have already had a sneak preview of the jBPM5 project APIs.

Now it's time to take a look at the tooling provided by the jBPM5 project. As introduced previously, jBPM5 can be considered as a module inside **Business Logic integration Platform (BLiP)**, and for this reason jBPM5 shares a set of common mechanisms with the rest of the components in the suite. One of the things that jBPM5 has in common with the rest of the components is the tooling. In this chapter we will study these tools and their relationship with jBPM5.

This chapter starts by describing the tooling projects related to BLiP and describes how to adapt, re-use, or implement from scratch your own domain-specific tooling, keeping in mind the important concepts that were used to design and develop the project tooling.

Most of the time, commercial products provide you tooling that you cannot change or update to your needs. Here is quite the opposite; you will find tooling that is continuously being improved, and continuously adapting towards covering new scenarios. Knowing each of these tooling projects will enable you and your company to choose wisely which of them to use and when it's time to adapt them to fit your needs.

In this chapter we will cover the following topics:

- Setting up our environment to start working with jBPM5
- Installed tooling description
- Evaluation Example Project inside Eclipse
- Evaluation Example Process inside the jBPM5 Console
- Frequently asked questions

Setting up our environment

Before starting with the descriptions of each specific component, I would like to mention the fact that in order to install and use the tooling, we need to have basic knowledge of how to work with Java. The installation procedure requires us to know some tools that are commonly used in the Java environment, and for that reason the method of installing those tools is out of the scope of this section. The prerequisites for working with all of the tooling projects provided by jBPM5 and Drools are as follows:

- JDK 6, which can be found at `http://www.oracle.com/technetwork/java/javase/downloads/index.html`
- Apache Ant 1.8.X, which can be found at `http://ant.apache.org/bindownload.cgi`
- `JAVA_HOME` and `<ANT_HOME>/bin` added to the `PATH` system variable

Once we have these tools installed and ready to be used, we will download the jBPM5 installer that will help us to download all of the different projects, plugins, and configurations that we need to start using these tools. This section will cover the following steps:

- Downloading the jBPM5 installer
- Running the jBPM5 installer
- Installed tools description
- Opening and testing the evaluation example inside the Eclipse IDE
- Testing the evaluation example inside the jBPM console

Downloading the jBPM5 installer

jBPM5 provides an installer that contains a set of scripts to download and install all of the tools that you commonly use in your BPM project. As previously mentioned, some of the tools will be shared with the rule engine, for example, the common repository.

You can direct your browser to the jBPM5 official page at `http://www.jbpm.org`.

On the home page you will find an introduction to the framework and some very useful links related to the project. Consider this page as the central resource for helpful tips, information, and answers to questions that you may have about the project. The **Community** section provides very useful links to get in touch with the team members, ask questions in the forums, and, as in every community project, how to contribute to the project.

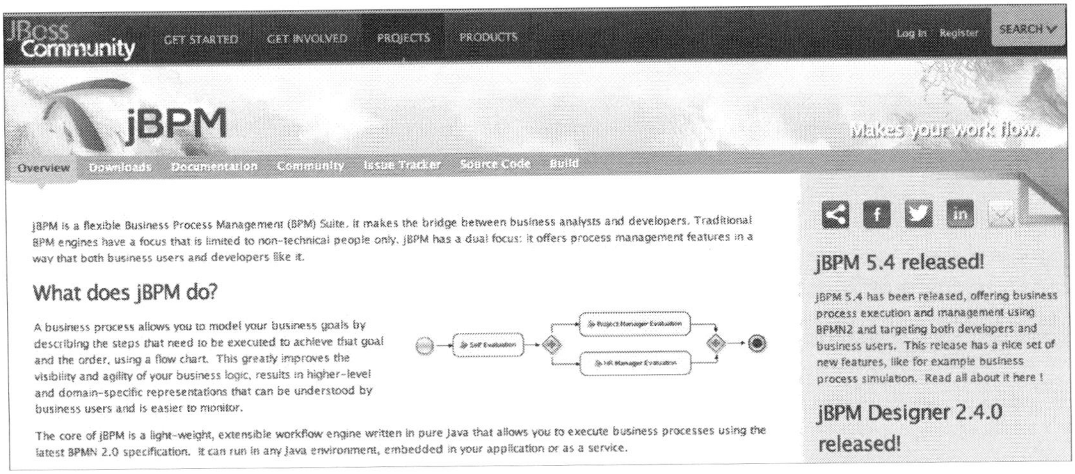

Don't forget to bookmark this page for quick access to the documentation and to the community sites.

If you go to the **Downloads** section you will be redirected to `http://sourceforge.net/`, where jBPM5 stores its releases.

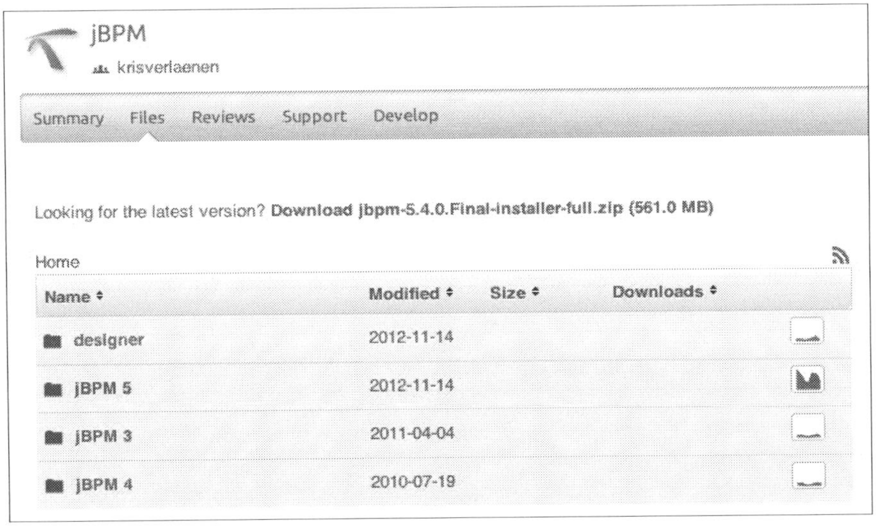

Inside the **jBPM 5** directory you will find different flavors of the jBPM5 installer. Each time a new release is published, you can find it in on `sourceforge.net`. I recommend that you download the one tagged with *installer-full*, which contains most of the tooling in a ready-to-be-used state. Once we download the installer and have Ant installed, we can unzip the downloaded file and continue with the next section.

Running the jBPM5 installer

The ZIP file that you downloaded contains an Ant script that will download from the Internet all the jBPM5 tooling that is platform-dependent (Windows, Linux, or Mac OSX). Once the script downloads all the required binaries, you can start all of the provided tooling to test that everything is working properly.

For this section I strongly recommend that you work with your computer next to you, to follow the proposed steps.

To begin the installation process, we need to run the following commands from the console/terminal:

```
cd <JBPM_HOME >
antinstall.demo
```

`JBPM_HOME` from now on will be the uncompressed directory that you obtained from the downloaded installer file. Running the `antinstall.demo` command will start the installation process and a collection of projects will be configured and set up for you.

> This operation may take a while if you are not using the full installer, because it will need to download all the projects from the Internet.

As you will notice, Eclipse is the only tool that depends on the platform, so you will need to wait until it is downloaded:

```
download.eclipse:
     [echo] Getting Eclipse ...
      [get] Getting: http://download.eclipse.org/technology/epp/downloads/release/helios/SR2/eclipse-java-helios-SR2-macosx-cocoa.tar.g
      [get] To: /Users/salaboy/MyApplications/jbpm-installer-5.4.0.Final/lib/eclipse-java-helios-SR2-macosx-cocoa.tar.gz
```

By changing the `build.properties` file that's located in the `JBPM_HOME` directory, we can configure the URLs and parameters that this script is using to download the tooling. The `build.xml` file contains all the Ant goals that will be executed.

Installed tools' description

By default, the installer will download and install the following software:

- JBoss Application Server 7.x
- Drools Guvnor
- jBPM5 GWT process server
- jBPM5 GWT console
- Web process designer
- Eclipse + jBPM5 plugin

Because you have some time to wait until the installer finishes the installation, let's see a brief description of the modules that are being installed by this script.

JBoss Application Server

The **JBoss Application Server** will be responsible for hosting all the web tooling provided by the project. We will need to start an instance of the application server to be able to use and share the web applications provided to the author and interact with our business processes. **Drools Guvnor, jBPM5 process server, jBPM5 GWT console**, and **web process designer** will be automatically deployed inside the `standalone/deployments/` directory by the installation script.

Once everything is downloaded and installed, we can start the demo environment using the Ant goal:

```
ant start.demo
```

We can access the application server welcome screen by directing our browser to the following URL:

`http://localhost:8080/`

By default the application server will start locally, but if you want to enable access to people from different machines, you can parameterize how the application server is started by using the `(-b 192.168.0.X)` flag and binding the LAN/WAN address to the current instance. As was mentioned before, the jBPM5 installer comes with JBoss Application Server 7, but in no way is jBPM5 tied to a Java EE environment or application server vendor/version.

Drools Guvnor

Drools Guvnor is the knowledge-assets repository where we can store and keep centralized all of our knowledge assets: business processes, business rules, and so on. Drools Guvnor also provides an entry point to a set of tools that help us during the authoring phase of our business assets. Behind the Drools Guvnor user interface, a **Java Content Repository** (**JCR**) is responsible for storing and managing all our business assets, allowing different clients to access them. The internal repository structure is organized as a directory tree, allowing us to browse our assets as if they were plain directories. We can take advantage of the fact that the JCR repository can be exposed using WebDav (`http://webdav.org`) to browse our centralized repository using our operating system file browser.

This centralized repository is called Drools Guvnor because it was born within the Drools project but later it was extended and improved to host different types of knowledge assets, such as business processes, business rules, and business models. If we direct our browser to `http://localhost:8080/drools-guvnor`, we can access the business knowledge repository.

Nowadays, Drools Guvnor can be considered the access point to business analyst oriented tooling. You will see that all the process-oriented tooling is integrated with it. The following screenshot shows the start-up screen of Guvnor:

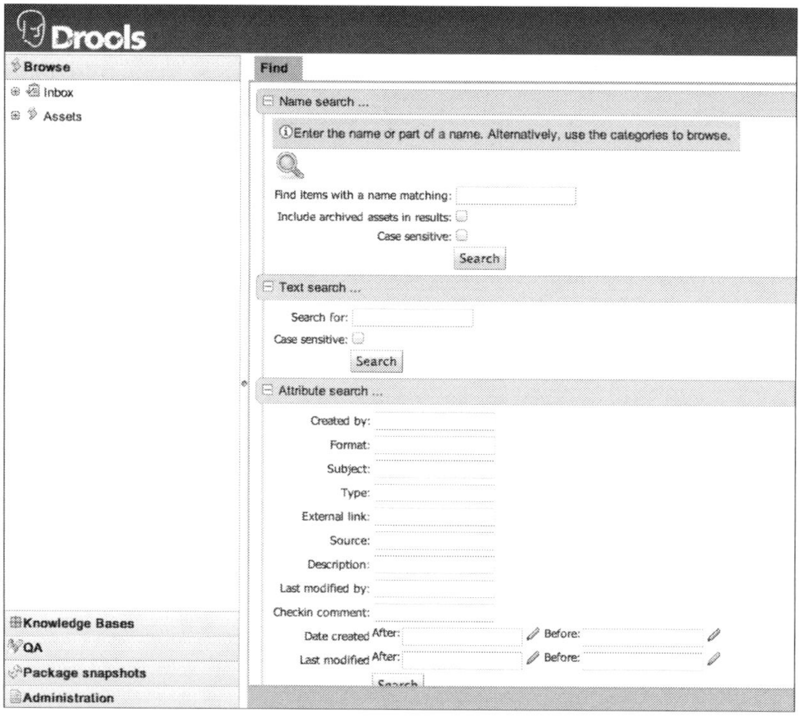

We will dive deeper into Guvnor's functionalities later in this chapter.

jBPM5 process server

The process server is a web application that exposes an instance of jBPM5 process engine using a REST interface, allowing us to have different clients written in different languages accessing and manipulating our business processes. You can find more information about the process server and how to interact with it in the jBPM5 official documentation (`http://docs.jboss.org/jbpm/v5.4/userguide/ch.console.html`).

If you direct your browser to the URL `http://localhost:8080/gwt-console-server/`, you should get the following screen showing that the server is up and running and also providing a link (`http://localhost:8080/gwt-console-server/rs/server/resources/jbpm`) to report issues with the server or provide feedback about its internal functionality:

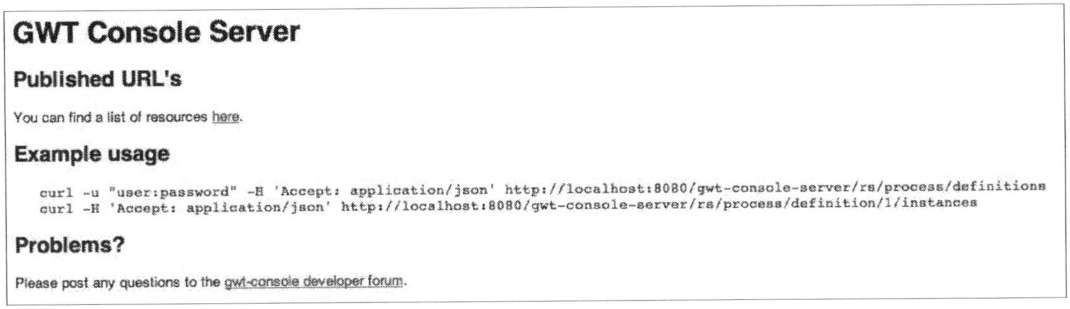

jBPM5 GWT console

The jBPM5 GWT console allows us to interact with our business processes, providing us a simple implementation of task list oriented user interfaces and management tooling. We can start new process instances and interact with the human activities that were defined in our processes using the task lists provided. In this chapter we will be covering a simple example showing how we can interact with this console.

Directing your browser to the URL `http://localhost:8080/jbpm-console` will allow you to access the jBPM console application; you can use the user `krisv` and the password `krisv` to test the console.

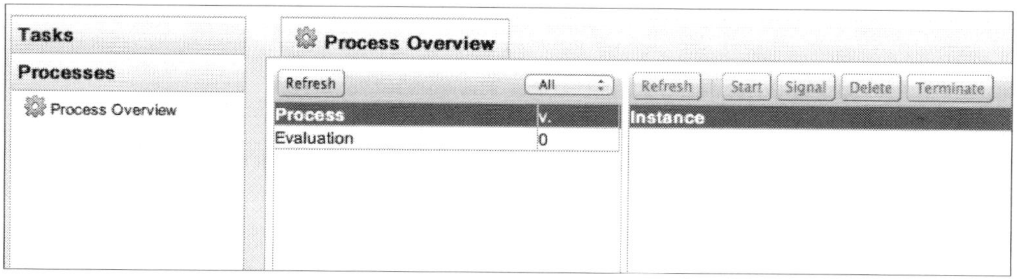

Web process designer

The web process designer is a web application that allows us to model our BPMN2 business processes by dragging and dropping activities from a palette. This process designer was created to enable non-technical people to analyze, maintain, and update the company's business processes. Because it's a web application, different roles and users inside the company can use the same installation. They will be able to access the same repository of business assets without needing a technical tool such as Eclipse IDE to be installed on their machines.

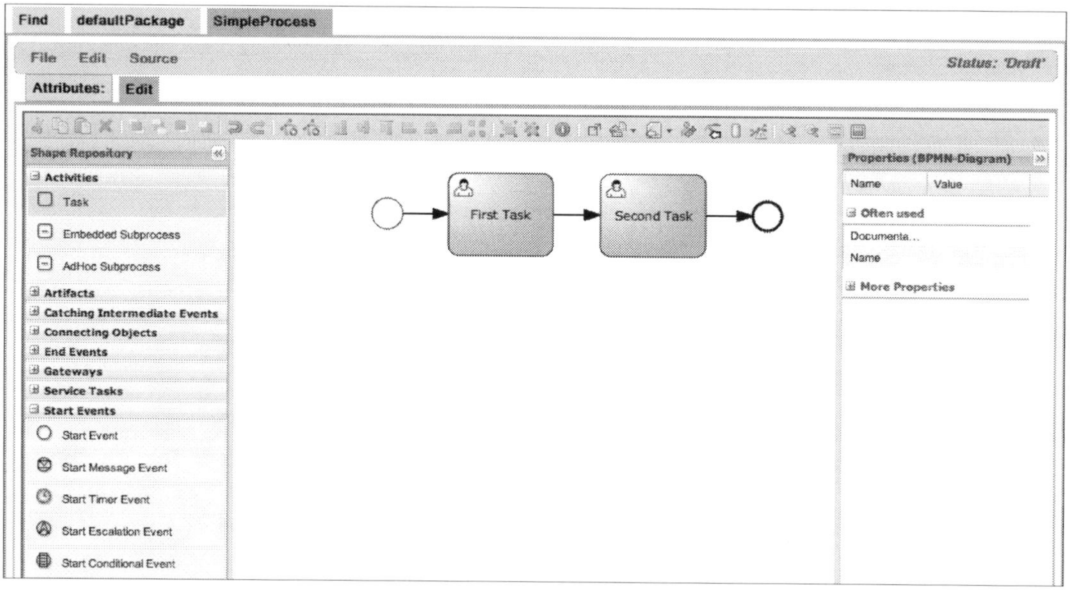

As soon as the user saves the process diagram, the process definition will be stored in Guvnor's repository, allowing us to version and keep metadata about our process diagrams. *Chapter 5, The Process Designer*, will go deeper into this very important tool by providing a step-by-step tutorial on creating and designing business processes using this editor.

Eclipse IDE – evaluation sample project

The Eclipse IDE provides us (developers) an **Integrated Development Environment (IDE)** to work with and create all the technical artifacts required to build our projects. Inside the Eclipse IDE, we will be able to create projects that use business processes and business rules to define the logic of our applications. For this reason, the jBPM5 installer downloads and installs some plugins that will help us to author and verify our business processes and business rules inside the same environment. Depending on the project and the technologies that you are planning to use in your projects, you can download specific plugins that will speed up development time. The jBPM installer downloads the latest version of Eclipse, the Drools and jBPM5 plugins, and installs them, allowing you to use them to create rules and processes.

Once the installation is complete you can run just Eclipse using the following command:

```
ant start.eclipse
```

This ant command will start the already installed Eclipse with all the plugins configured. When Eclipse opens you will see that now the IDE includes a **jBPM** perspective, which pops up the properties panel related to jBPM.

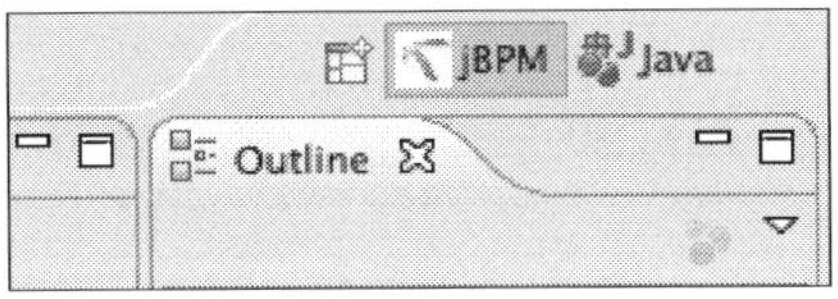

Notice that the jBPM5 installer is installing a fresh copy of the Eclipse IDE. At this point, you have two options:

- Use our own Eclipse installation
- Use the Eclipse provided by the jBPM5 installer

The first option will give us the freedom to install all the plugins by hand, having control of the versions and which plugins we want to have enabled. We will usually go with the first option when we already have an Eclipse IDE installed and we don't want to use another version of it.

If we are planning to set up multiple machines with all the tooling, the second option will do that for us. Remember that the jBPM5 installer can be considered as a default setup for our components, and it is in no way the only possible way of working. If we want to continue using the Eclipse IDE installed by the jBPM5 installer for the rest of the examples in this book, we will need to install a Maven plugin.

Once Eclipse starts, we can open the **evaluation** example to see if everything is working correctly.

To do that, we need to right-click inside the **Package Explorer** section and then go to **Import | Existing Project into Workspace**.

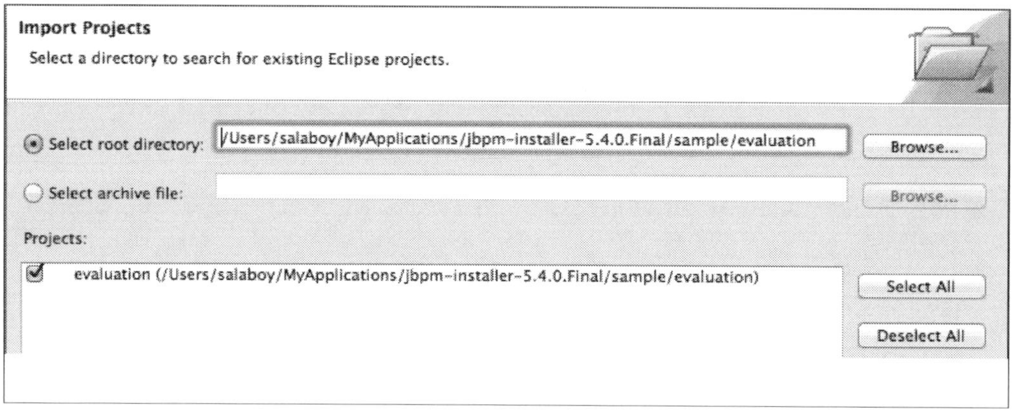

Here we are importing the sample project that comes inside `jbpm-installer.zip`. Notice that this is not a Maven project, and for this reason, in the Import wizard we have to choose **Existing Project into Workspace** instead of **Existing Maven Project**. This project includes a very simple process for evaluating the employee's performance at the end of the year.

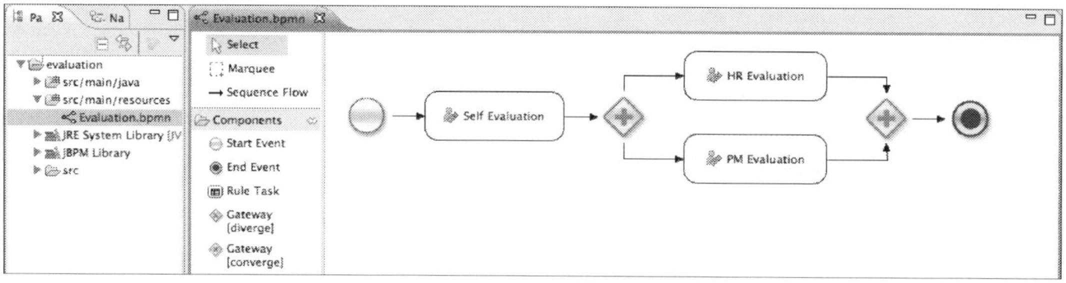

This project also comes with a Java class that tests this process execution, but because this process is composed of human interactions, we need to make sure that the demo environment is up and running in order to interact with this process.

Now we can open the `ProcessTest.java` class and run it as a Java application (right-click in the background of the class file and then go to **Run | Java Application**).

```
public static final void main(String[] args) {
    final KnowledgeRuntimeLogger logger;

    try {
        // load up the knowledge base
        KnowledgeBase kbase = readKnowledgeBase();
        StatefulKnowledgeSession ksession = kbase.newStatefulKnowledgeSession();
        //KnowledgeRuntimeLoggerFactory.newConsoleLogger(ksession);
        logger = KnowledgeRuntimeLoggerFactory.newThreadedFileLogger(ksession, "test", 1000);

        Runtime.getRuntime().addShutdownHook(new Thread() {
               public void run() {
                   if(logger != null){
                       logger.close();
                   }
               }
            });

        ksession.getWorkItemManager().registerWorkItemHandler("Human Task", new WSHumanTaskHandler());
        // start a new process instance
        Map<String, Object> params = new HashMap<String, Object>();
        params.put("employee", "krisv");
        params.put("reason", "Yearly performance evaluation");
        ksession.startProcess("com.sample.evaluation", params);
        System.out.println("Process started ...");

    } catch (Throwable t) {
        t.printStackTrace();
    }
}
```

Notice that the `KnowledgeRuntimeLoggerFactory.newConsoleLogger(ksession);` line is commented out. If you want to see the internal process logs in the console tab, you must uncomment or add this line if it's not there. If you uncomment the console logger, you will see the following output in the console.

```
Properties | Problems | Human Task View | Audit | Guvnor Repositories | Console
ProcessTest [Java Application] /System/Library/Java/JavaVirtualMachines/1.6.0.jdk/Contents/Home/bin/java (Jan 5, 2012 8:33:59 AM)
BEFORE RULEFLOW VARIABLE CHANGED reason=Yearly performance evaluation process:Evaluation[id=com.sample.evaluation]
AFTER RULEFLOW VARIABLE CHANGED reason=Yearly performance evaluation process:Evaluation[id=com.sample.evaluation]
BEFORE RULEFLOW VARIABLE CHANGED employee=krisv process:Evaluation[id=com.sample.evaluation]
AFTER RULEFLOW VARIABLE CHANGED employee=krisv process:Evaluation[id=com.sample.evaluation]
BEFORE RULEFLOW STARTED process:Evaluation[id=com.sample.evaluation]
BEFORE PROCESS NODE TRIGGERED node:Start[id=1] process:Evaluation[id=com.sample.evaluation]
BEFORE PROCESS NODE EXITED node:Start[id=1] process:Evaluation[id=com.sample.evaluation]
BEFORE PROCESS NODE TRIGGERED node:Self Evaluation[id=2] process:Evaluation[id=com.sample.evaluation]
BEFORE RULEFLOW VARIABLE CHANGED content={reason=Yearly performance evaluation} process:Evaluation[id=com.sample.evaluation]
AFTER RULEFLOW VARIABLE CHANGED content={reason=Yearly performance evaluation} process:Evaluation[id=com.sample.evaluation]
AFTER PROCESS NODE TRIGGERED node:Self Evaluation[id=2] process:Evaluation[id=com.sample.evaluation]
AFTER PROCESS NODE TRIGGERED node:Start[id=1] process:Evaluation[id=com.sample.evaluation]
AFTER PROCESS NODE TRIGGERED node:Start[id=1] process:Evaluation[id=com.sample.evaluation]
AFTER RULEFLOW STARTED process:Evaluation[id=com.sample.evaluation]
Process started ...
```

This Java class has started an **evaluation process**; we can see in the console logs that the **Self Evaluation** node has been reached and a human task was created. If we take a look at the **Self Evaluation** activity inside the process diagram, we will see the following values in the **Properties** panel:

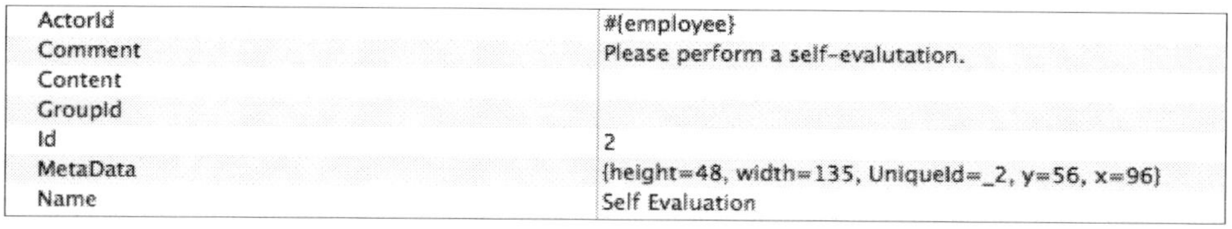

ActorId	#{employee}
Comment	Please perform a self-evalutation.
Content	
GroupId	
Id	2
MetaData	{height=48, width=135, UniqueId=_2, y=56, x=96}
Name	Self Evaluation

As we can see, the **ActorId** attribute contains the expression **#{employee}**. The engine will evaluate this expression; it will look for a process variable called `employee` and it will replace the value of that variable to do the task assignment. If you take a look once again at the `ProcessTest.java` class, you will see that we are starting the process with a parameter called `employee` with the value `krisv`. For this scenario, the **Self Evaluation** task will be assigned to `krisv`.

Now we can go to the **Human Task View** tab, to interact with the created human tasks:

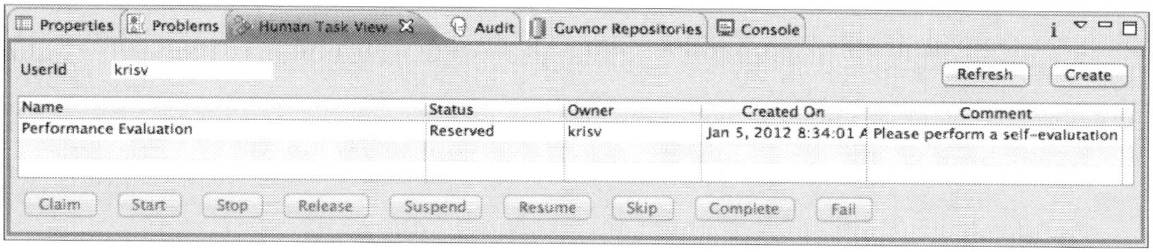

Note that I've typed `krisv` into the **UserId** field and I've hit **Refresh** to see the tasks assigned to **krisv**.

A task was created for the user called **krisv**, and now we can interact with it. In order to enable these action buttons, we need to click on the task row and a different set of buttons will be enabled depending on the task status. Because the **Status** of this task is **Reserved**, we will see that we can now start it. When we click on **Start**, we will see that the task status changes to **InProgress**.

UserId krisv

Name	Status	Owner	Created On
Performance Evaluation	InProgress	krisv	Jan 5, 2012 8:34:01 A

Because the task is now in progress, the **Complete** button will be enabled and we can end the task by clicking on it. Once the task is completed, the Parallel Gateway will be reached and two new tasks will be created. In this case, one task will be created to the user called **john** and the other one to a user called **mary**. You can check these values by clicking on each activity and looking at the **Properties** panel.

Now we can go to the **Human Task View** tab and filter John's tasks:

UserId john

Name	Status	Owner
Performance Evaluation	Reserved	john

Let's start and complete John's task and let's take a look at Mary's tasks:

UserId mary

Name	Status	Owner
Performance Evaluation	Reserved	mary

If we complete Mary's task, the process will reach the Converging Parallel Gateway and the end event will be reached. We will see the following output in the **Console** logs:

```
BEFORE RULEFLOW COMPLETED process:Evaluation[id=com.sample.evaluation]
AFTER RULEFLOW COMPLETED process:Evaluation[id=com.sample.evaluation]
AFTER PROCESS NODE TRIGGERED node:End[id=7] process:Evaluation[id=com.sample.evaluation]
AFTER PROCESS NODE TRIGGERED node:End[id=7] process:Evaluation[id=com.sample.evaluation]
AFTER PROCESS NODE TRIGGERED node:Gateway[id=6] process:Evaluation[id=com.sample.evaluation]
AFTER PROCESS NODE TRIGGERED node:Gateway[id=6] process:Evaluation[id=com.sample.evaluation]
AFTER PROCESS NODE TRIGGERED node:PM Evaluation[id=3] process:Evaluation[id=com.sample.evaluation]
```

Notice that the process was completed successfully. One final thing to know about this example is that we are also using `newThreadedFileLogger`, which creates a logfile in the filesystem that we can open with the **Audit** tab in Eclipse.

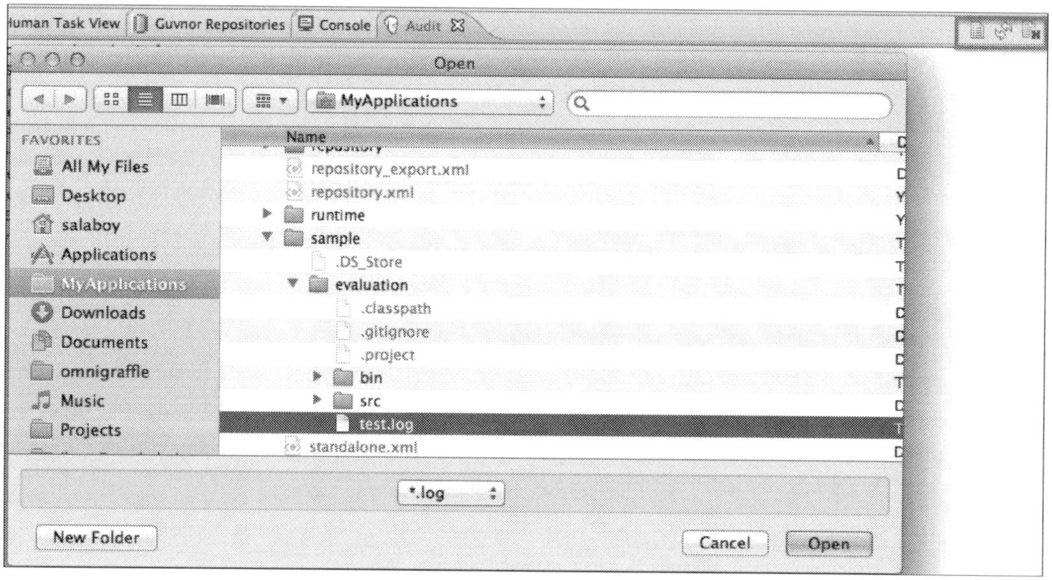

So, if we go to the **Audit** tab and browse (notice the icons in the top-right corner) for the file called `test.log` inside the `Evaluation` project directory, we will be able to see what's going on in a more graphical way:

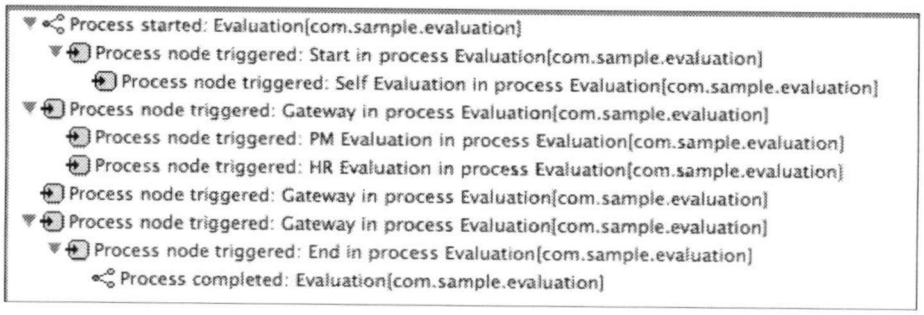

This is a more ordered way of tracking our process execution, as we can easily follow which actions were triggered in each of the execution paths. The different sections of the execution can be collapsed to get a clearer view of a particular execution. Here we have finished the review of the most basic example that comes with the jBPM installer. We will now continue looking at this example, but from the jBPM GWT console perspective. We will usually use the Eclipse IDE for developing and testing our processes, but for real implementations we will need a complete application to handle the human interactions and the processes administration. The next section shows how we can achieve these interactions from the jBPM GWT console.

jBPM GWT console – evaluation sample process

The jBPM console was designed as a generic process administration and task list oriented tool, to handle the interactions between the administrators and users that want to start a process or interact with it in some way. As you may see from the title of this section, the application is built using the **Google Web Toolkit** (**GWT**), and this is a major and important aspect of this application. GWT is growing with a large adoption rate in the market, providing a componentized way of creating a much richer user experience with low barriers of entry from the developer perspective.

Let's take a quick look at the application now. To start the jBPM GWT console we need to start the application server (in this case JBoss AS 7), and to do this, without starting Eclipse, we can run the following command:

```
ant start.demo.noeclipse
```

Running this command, JBoss AS 7 will start deploying all the applications contained inside it. The jBPM server, Drools Guvnor, the web process designer, the human task component, and the jBPM console will be started.

If we go to the JBoss AS 7 administration console (by going to `http://localhost:8080/` and clicking on **Administration Console**), you can check if the applications are up and running:

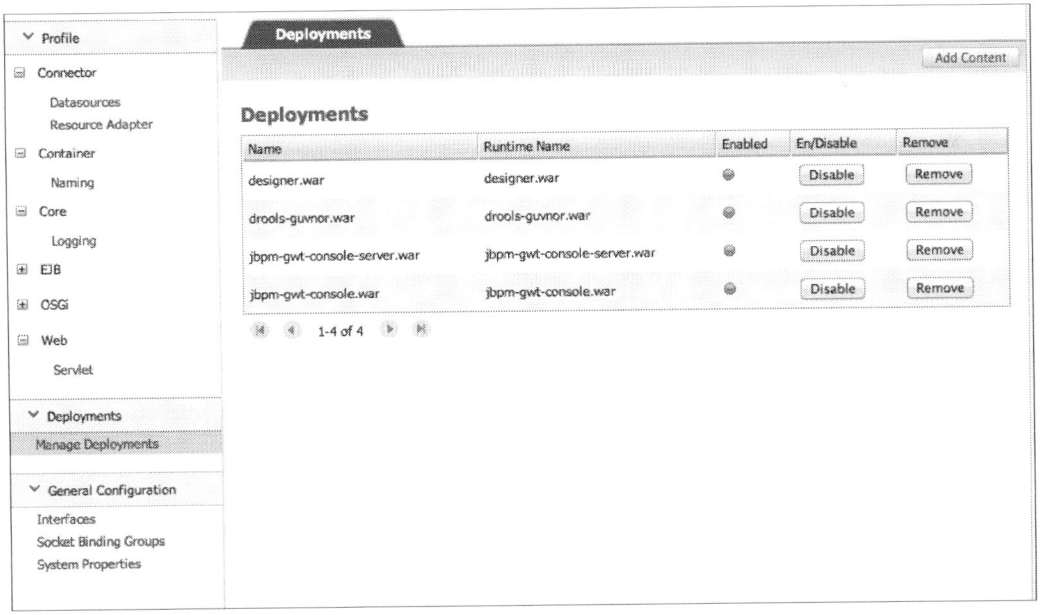

Once the applications are up and running, we can access the jBPM console and start interacting with it (`http://localhost:8080/jbpm-console/`).

Remember to use the username and password `krisv`.

If we go to the **Process** section and click on **Refresh** to update the list of the processes, we should see the **Evaluation** Process. We can select this process and start a new process instance by clicking on the **Start** button.

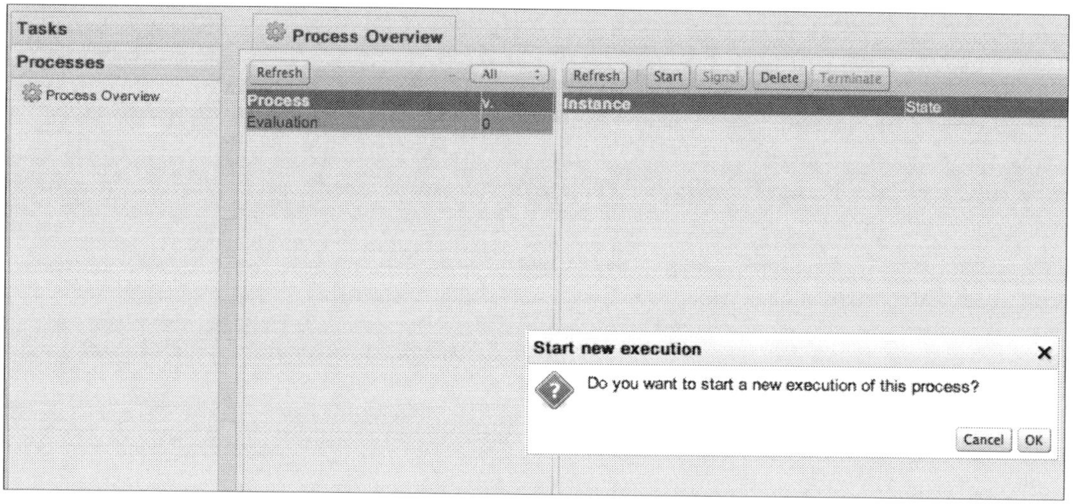

If you remember the previous section, where we programmatically started a new process instance using jBPM5's API, we were sending some information at that point: employee and reason. The process required this information before starting. For this reason, as soon as we click on **OK**, accepting that we want to create a new process instance, a new form will appear letting us enter this initial information.

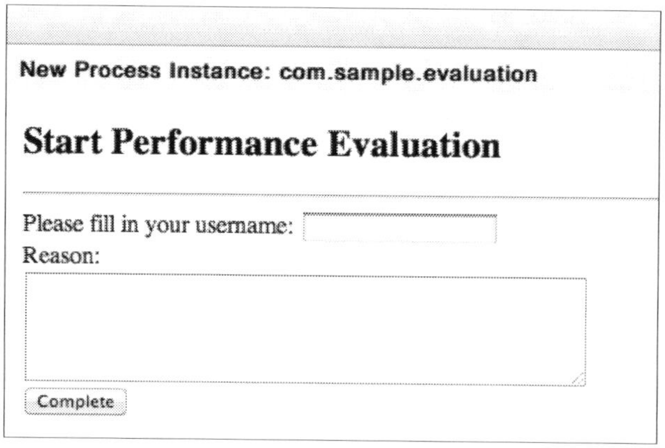

This was a simple example about how to use the current tooling, but you need to know that a huge amount of effort is being done around the tooling for the next version of the project. Feel free to keep an eye on my blog (`http://salaboy.com`) and the project blog (`http://blog.athico.com`) if you are interested in beta testing the new versions.

We can fill these information fields, but we need to be aware that the username that we enter will be the one assigned to the first activity in our business process (the **Self Evaluation** task). Let's enter the username `krisv`, and for the **Reason** field we can put something like `End of the year performance evaluation`; then click on **Complete**. As soon as we close the form window, we will see a new process instance started and running.

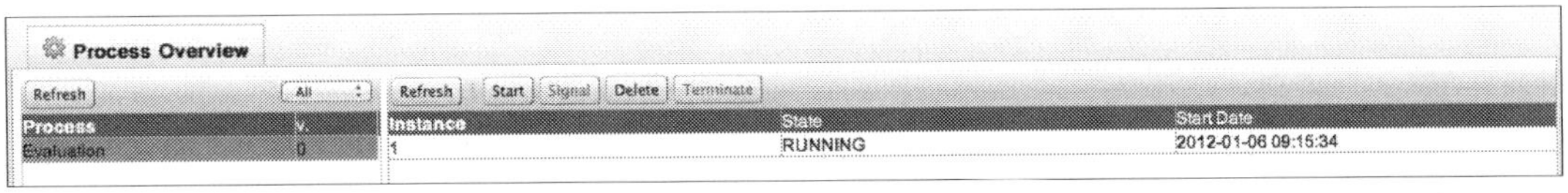

Now we can click on the newly created process instance, and the **Diagram** button and the **Instance Data** button at the bottom of the screen will be enabled. By clicking on the **Diagram** button, we will be able to see the process diagram and where it is stopped, waiting for external interaction.

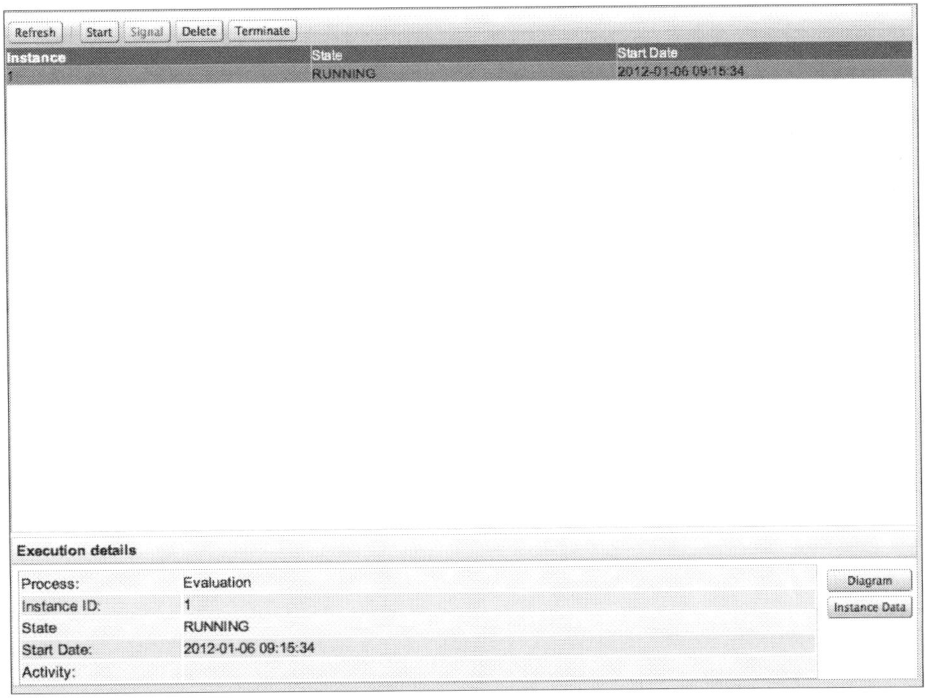

Now we can inspect the instance data and the diagram. For each process instance that we create, we will be able to analyze its internal status. Notice that the Diagram window includes the process instance ID in the window label and the red pointer that lets us know that right now we need to finish the `Self Evaluation` task in order to continue.

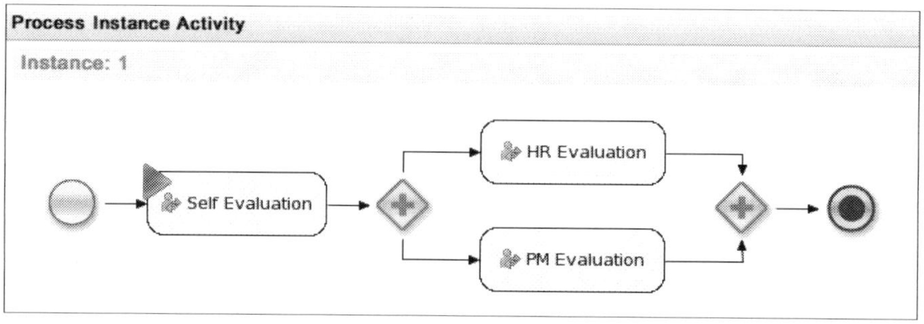

At this point, because we have just started the process instance, the **Process Instance Data** table will look like the following image:

Process Instance Data: 1

Key	XSD Type	Java Type	Value
content	hashMap	java.util.HashMap	n/a
reason	xs:string	java.lang.String	End of the year evaluation
employee	xs:string	java.lang.String	krisv

Notice that this information is organized by key, representing the process variable name, and value. Remember that we will be generating new information inside the process, so feel free to see how the information is being filled out inside the **Process Instance Data** list when we complete the following tasks.

As the process diagram shows, the process has stopped, waiting for external interaction. For that reason, and because we know the process definition, we will go to the **Tasks** section of the console and because we are logged in as **krisv**, we will see inside the **Personal Tasks**, a new task assigned to us:

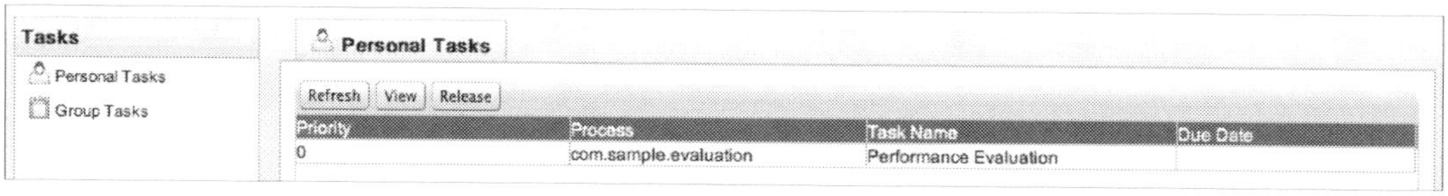

Notice that we can see these tasks because we are logged as **krisv**; other roles and users with different IDs will not be able to see these tasks in their task lists.

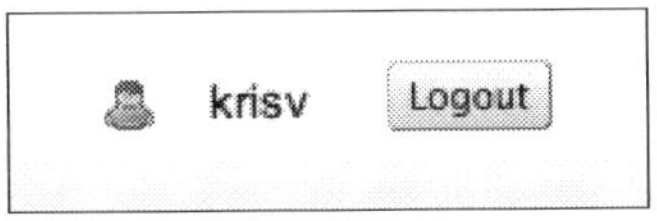

If we want to work and complete the Self Performance Evaluation task, we need to click on the task row and then click on the **View** button at the top of the task list table. This **View** button will open the form associated with that task instance and it will let us interact with it:

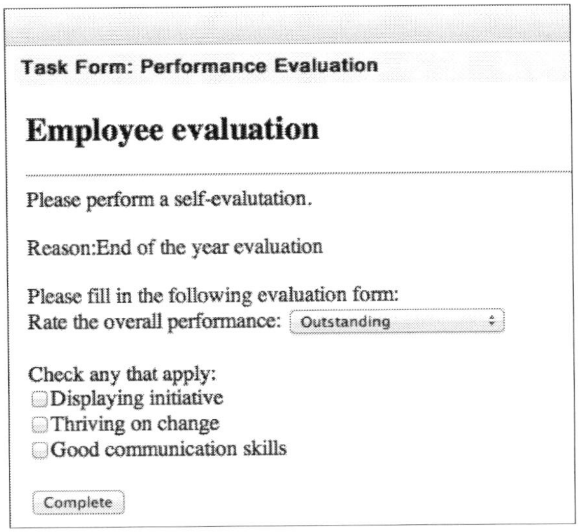

Once again, we will fill the required information; in this case, by selecting a value from the **Rate the overall performance** drop-down box and checking some of the checkboxes at the bottom. Once we are done, we can hit the **Complete** button, close the window, and make sure the user `krisv` doesn't have any other tasks pending in his **Personal Tasks** list.

If we go back to the **Process** section and inspect the process diagram once again, we will see that now there are two pending tasks, one for **john** and another one for **mary**.

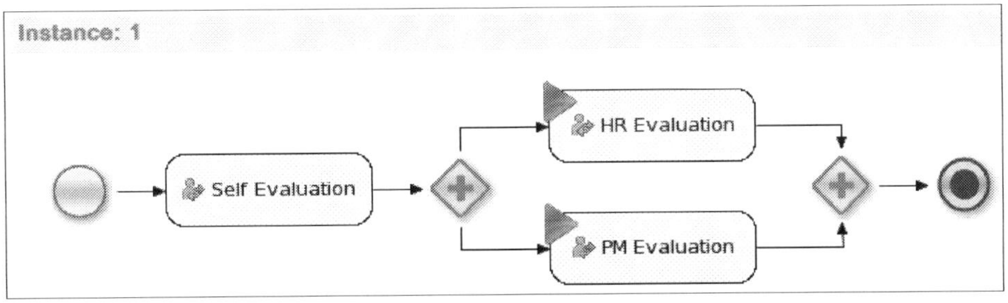

In order to interact with these two pending tasks, we need to switch from the `krisv` user to **john** or **mary**. Because these two tasks can be executed in parallel, no matter which of them is completed first, the Converging Parallel Gateway will always wait until both of the tasks get completed before continuing with the process execution.

Let's log out from the **krisv** session, and using **john** as username and password we can see his pending tasks.

Once we change the user to **john**, go to his pending personal tasks and we will see that **john** has one task assigned. We can go ahead and interact with the task, once again by clicking on the **View** button and completing the task.

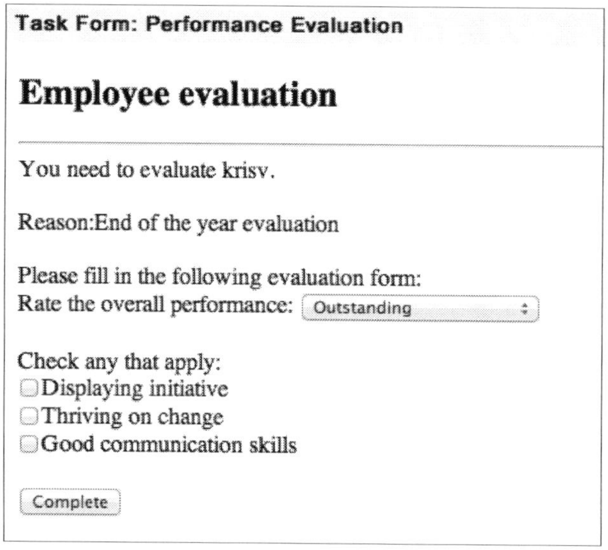

This task form looks very similar to the one that **krisv** has already completed, but in this case it is not a self evaluation for John. In this case John is giving feedback about the performance of **krisv**. The same thing happens with Mary's tasks. If we complete John's task and switch to Mary's user using **mary** as name and password and complete her task, the process instance will be completed and for that reason we will not be able to see it the **Process** section anymore.

Finally, we can go to the **Reporting** Section, where a very simple report can be generated:

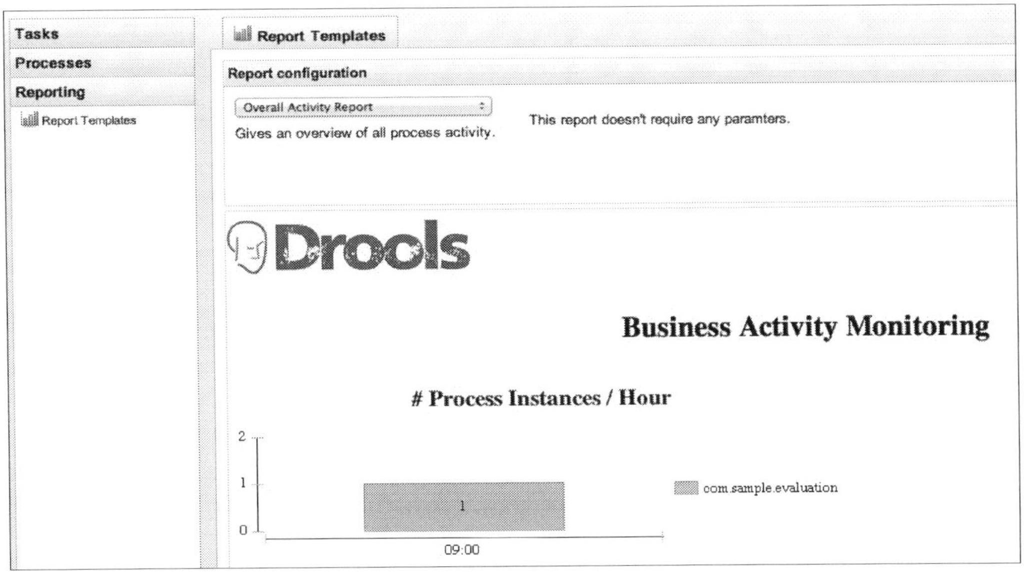

This report shows the overall process activity. As we can see in the graph, we have executed just one single process instance. We have this reporting area, where we can define different report templates and they will be filled with the information that the process engine is gathering from our process executions.

jBPM GWT console summary

The previous section introduced the main areas of the jBPM GWT console. We need to know that this console is interacting with the jBPM server in the back end, as we can see when using this application that we don't need to use or interact directly with any API. Everything is hidden, allowing the user to just interact with the business processes. It's good to mention once again that this is just one generic implementation of a console using GWT as a frontend technology. In other words, you can implement your own BPM console using .NET (a standalone application using `Swing` in Java), another web application using any other technology/ framework that you want, and you can leverage the jBPM process server to do all the backend interactions with jBPM5 process engine for you. Most of the times, companies have specific know-how about certain frameworks/technologies, and if they need to adapt the current GWT console to their needs but don't have trained developers in GWT, they will need to evaluate if the effort required to customize the GWT console is worth it or if start an in-house console for the jBPM5 engine. We will see during the following chapters how we can use the project APIs to create our own embedded consoles inside our applications, no matter the technology that we choose.

The good thing about the jBPM GWT console is that it has a team dedicated to improving it and the whole community reporting bugs and pushing the project forward.

Drools Guvnor and web process designer

As we previously saw, we can use the jBPM GWT console to create and interact with our process instances. But where is the process definition stored? And which tools can we use to create the process definition? One option is the one that we've already seen: using the Eclipse IDE plus the jBPM5 plugins, we can model a business process and then execute it using the jBPM5 project APIs. The Eclipse option is very good when we are developing our business processes, but it is not that good when we want to share those process definitions with our business analysts and/or non-technical people. It's also important to notice that in the Eclipse example we store the process as part of our software project, on the hard drive. Storing our process file in this way will not allow us to version and store meta-information about it as it would if we stored it in a proper content repository.

Drools Guvnor provides us with a knowledge repository where we can store our business processes, business rules, and business assets in a consistent way, making all these assets accessible to non-technical people. Drools Guvnor provides a unified environment to store and manage our business knowledge in a centralized place decoupled from our software project's source code. In this section we will see how the Drools Guvnor knowledge repository can be used in conjunction with the web process designer to create and host the process definitions that will be available inside the jBPM GWT console or our custom implementations. This section is just an introduction for *Chapter 5, The Process Designer*, where we are going to cover the web process designer and some of Guvnor's features in detail.

In order to access Drools Guvnor, you should have the demo running. If you have stopped it because of the previous section, you can start it again:

```
ant start.demo.noeclipse
```

Once the demo is running, we can direct our browser to `http://localhost:8080/drools-guvnor` in order to access the application.

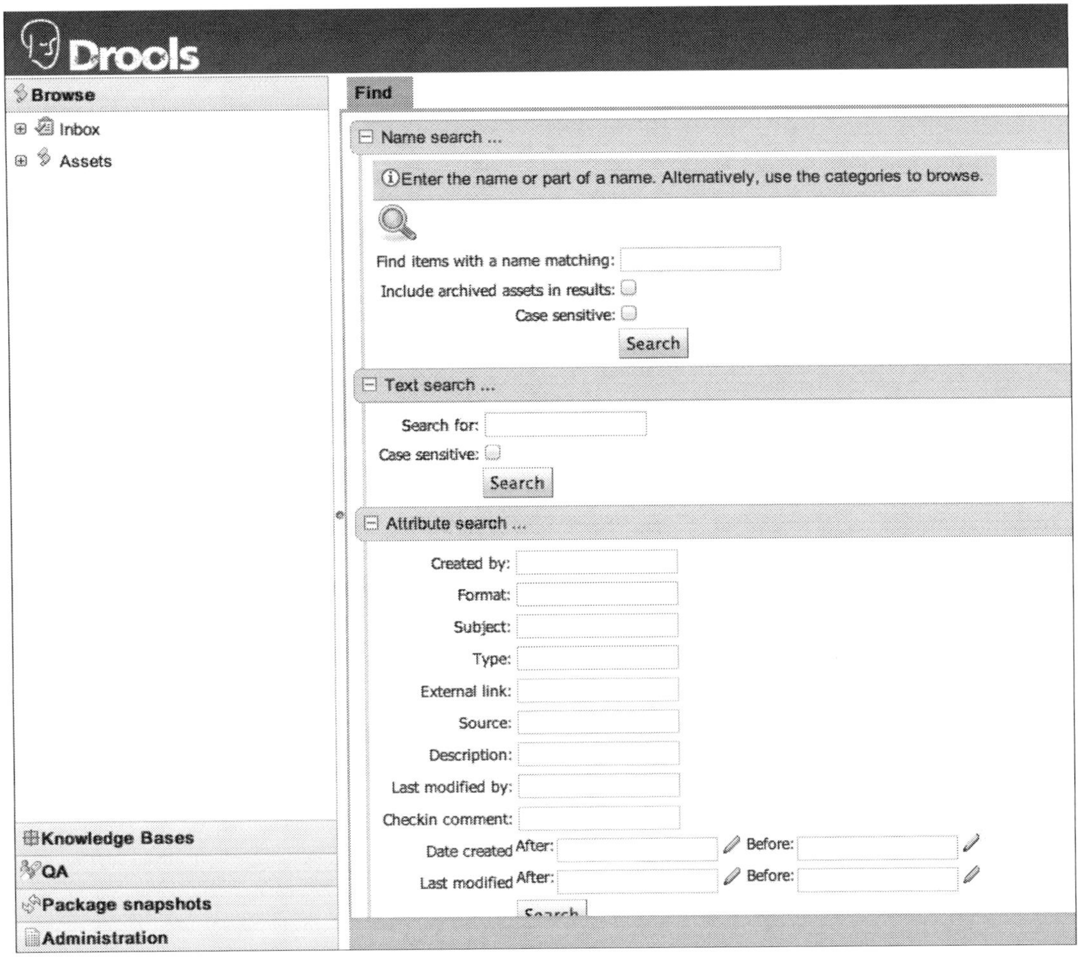

If we go to the **Administration** section, we will find the option **Import Export**, which can be for the repository that contains our assets. Drools Guvnor, by default, doesn't contain any assets when we install it. So, we need to load the content from a previous export provided by the jBPM5 installer.

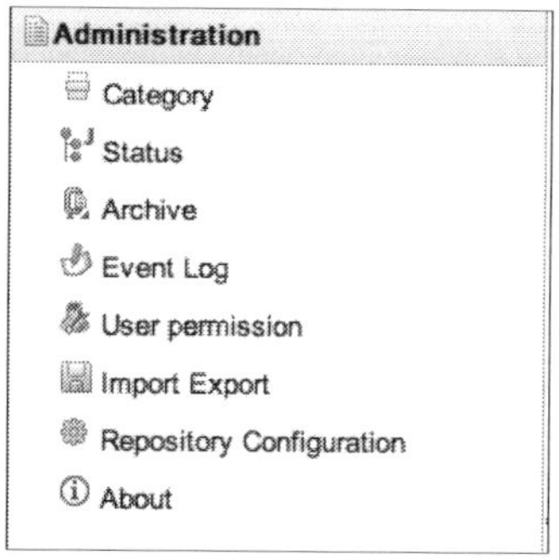

Let's go to the **Import Export** section, click on the **Choose File** browser button, and let's choose the file called `jbpm5_repository_export.xml` that contains the jBPM5 sample assets.

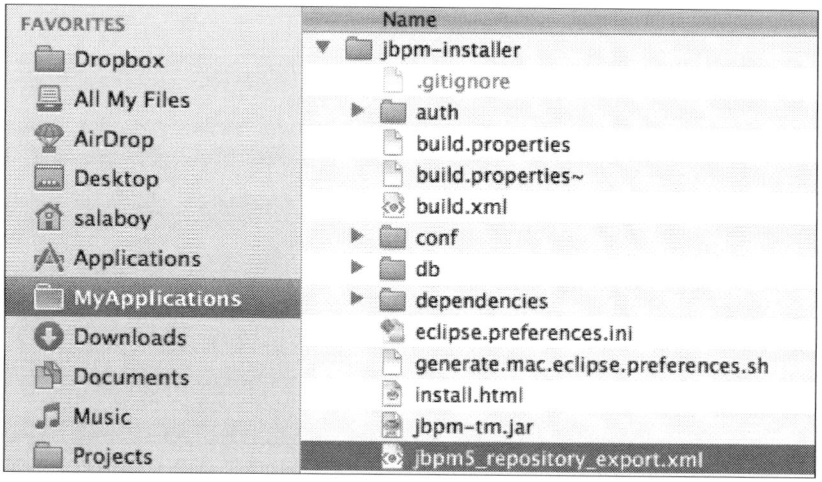

Once we load this repository, we will have all of the assets loaded inside Guvnor and we can go ahead and see what they look like. To do this, we need to go to the **Knowledge Bases** section in the left panel and look at the package called **jbpmExamples**:

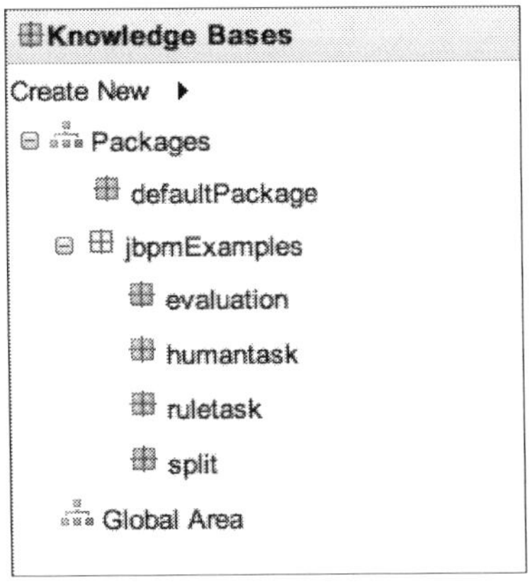

Each of these packages will contain assets related to a specific domain. If we select the package called **evaluation**, the right panel of the screen will show us all the assets stored inside the **evaluation** subpackage.

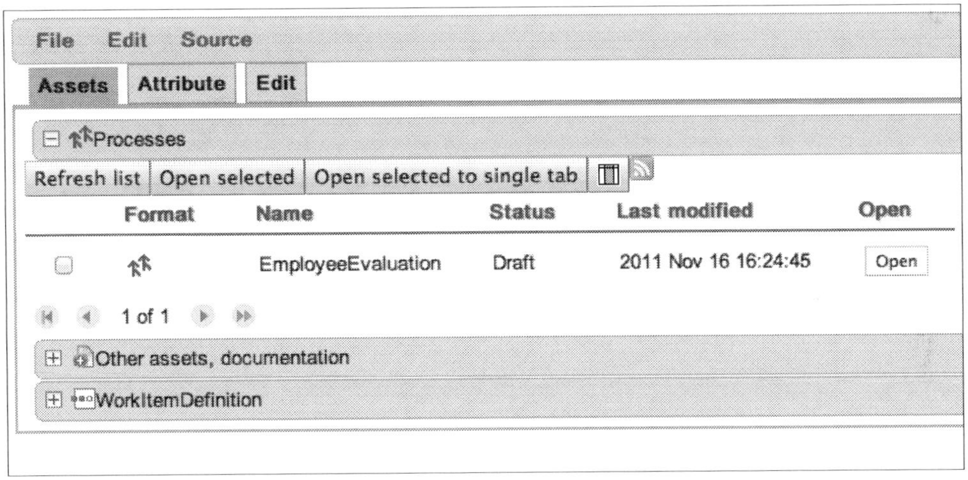

As you can see, the **EmployeeEvaluation** process is stored inside the **Evaluation** package. The repository will be in charge of keeping track of the versioning of these assets and also of keeping track of which users made changes on it. All of the metadata stored inside the repository can be analyzed and used for analyzing how our processes evolve.

If we click on the **Open** button, the process designer will open allowing us to modify the current version of the process.

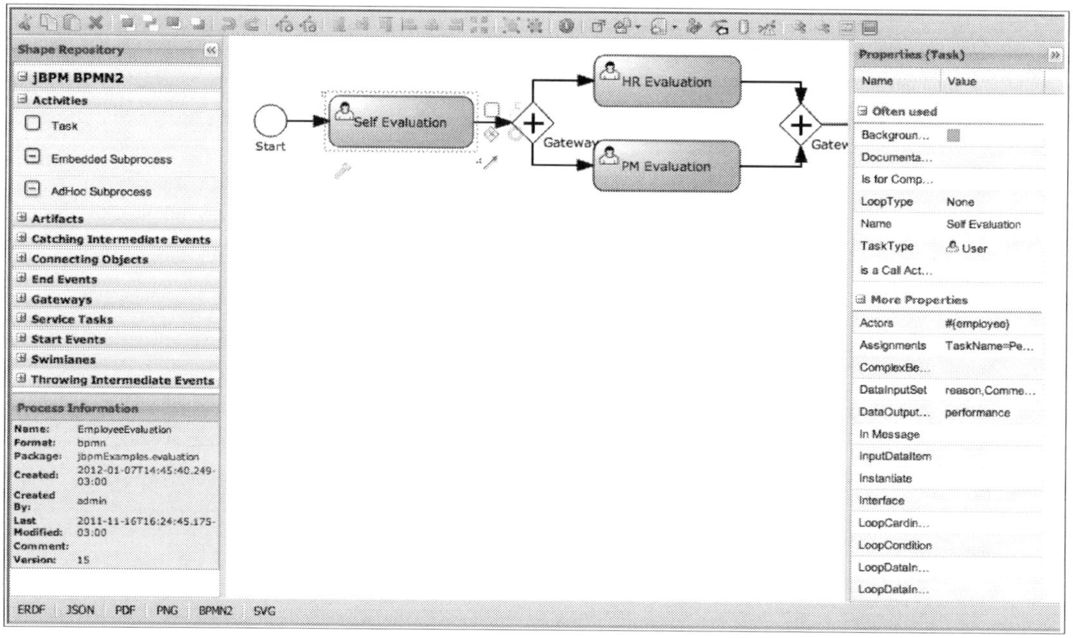

Once the process is opened, we can change it and check a new version into the repository. The next chapter will take a look at the process designer and the properties panel in depth, to help you familiarize yourself with the tooling. The properties of the process can be inspected in the right panel, and if you want to export the process diagram you can look at the footer where there are different buttons for different output formats.

This tool will be extremely helpful for all implementations and we need to know all of the features provided so that we don't reinvent the wheel and implement our own solutions that don't cover all of the things that a real project needs.

The final section of this chapter aims to cover the most frequently asked questions about the tooling and all the projects that were covered in the previous sections.

Frequently asked questions

This section is dedicated to answering some of the common questions I've found in the jBPM5 community forum.

- I don't want to use Eclipse. Is there an alternative environment?

  The answer is yes, of course. You can create your applications using jBPM5 in any IDE. There are no dependencies to Eclipse. I strongly recommend that you use Maven and the `http://search.maven.org` web page to locate the jBPM5 artifacts. Searching for g:`org.jbpm` and v:`5.X.0.Final` you will get all the jBPM5 dependencies that need to be added to your project.

  You also need to know that if you don't use Eclipse, you can still use the web process designer to draw your business processes. There are currently no plugins for Netbeans or IntelliJ to model BPMN 2.0 models or to connect and synchronize the assets that you have inside your project with an external Guvnor repository. You will need to do these steps by hand or you can automate them using scripts.

- How can I change the database being used by the jBPM installer?

  The demo environment requires the configuration of the database for two components:

  1. One for jBPM Runtime (information needed for the process to run) and audit tables.
  2. One for human tasks information.

  Take a look at the following URL, which contains the latest configurations for the different application servers:
  `http://docs.jboss.org/jbpm/v5.4/userguide/ch.installer.html#d0e647`

- All data is erased after I restart JBoss! What happened? How can I change that?

  This is because the Hibernate property `hibernate.hbm2ddl.auto` is set to `create` by default. You will find these properties in both `persistence.xml` files. You can change it to `update` or any other value. You can find more information about this in the Hibernate documentation at `http://docs.jboss.org/hibernate/orm/3.3/reference/en/html/session-configuration.html`

- I've started the demo, but I can't access the tools. What's happening?

  You can check the JBoss startup logs in the jboss/standalone/logs folder. One possible cause is that port 8080 is busy as this is the default port the installer uses.

  So, if you want to start the demo in another port, go to build.xml, and change: <socket server="${jboss.bind.address}" port="8080" />

  You may also need to change gwt-console-server/WEB-INF/classes/jbpm.console.properties to use the port you need.

- How can I add new task forms for the jBPM console?

  You can upload a Freemarker template to the Guvnor default package. The name of this file should be <<task_name>>-taskform.ftl.

  You can find one sample template here:
  https://github.com/droolsjbpm/jbpm/blob/master/jbpm-gwt/jbpm-gwt-form/src/main/resources/DefaultTask.ftl

Summary

In this chapter we have covered all of the tooling provided by jBPM5. This chapter can be used as a reference to choose the required tooling for your specific implementation. You will need to decide yourself if the proposed tools match your needs or if you will need to extend them or provide alternative implementations to suit your needs. For further information about these tools and how to use them, you can look at the jBPM Official documentation where you can find more examples and a detailed description of each of these components. If you are planning to extend or modify any of these tools, it is always recommended that you get in touch with the members of the community and the project leaders to get some advice on which is the right path to implement those extensions. Most of the time, your extensions can be shared with other community members or they can be added to the master source code if they are considered generic enough.

The next chapter will expand one of the most important topics in jBPM5, the web process designer. A step-by-step approach is going to be used to create a new process from scratch.

5
The Process Designer

We need to have a way to easily define our processes; even if jBPM uses BPMN 2.0 syntax as the process definition language, and we can use whatever text editor we want, that's not a good idea.

For technical people, using a text editor to modify an existing process definition might be a viable option, but creating a new process definition from scratch using only a text editor can be a really challenging task.

The BPMN 2.0 specification not only defines the syntax and behavior of each of the elements in our processes, but it also defines the look-and-feel of the processes themselves as well. So the idea of having a graphical representation of the process has been there from the beginning.

This chapter is to serve as an introduction to jBPM5 Web Process Designer. It is going to take a step-by-step approach to cover the minimum set of features we need to know to start designing our own processes. For a reference to all of the features present in the designer you should refer to its documentation: `http://docs.jboss.org/jbpm/v5.4/userguide/ch.designer.html`

An IDE for our processes

One of the main purposes of BPMN 2.0 is to allow users to define business processes that can be understood by people without technical skills. The concepts behind BPMN 2.0 are not technical at all. Having a task that needs to be performed, a decision that has to be taken, the concept of information flowing along a business process—these are all terms that business users are familiar with.

Even if the concepts handled by BPMN 2.0 are not technical, the implementation is! Tasks such as evaluating how a task must be performed, making sure that all of the required information is present before making a decision, the designing and implementation of a model containing the information required by the process, are all technical tasks that must be implemented by people with a deep understanding of IT. Given these two different perspectives, if we want to successfully implement a jBPM solution, we need a tool that's not only flexible enough to be used by technical people to define and model the processes but can also to be used by business users, who validate and verify those process definitions. In order to achieve these two requirements, the BPMN 2.0 specification not only defines the technical part of the language—element types, their attributes and behavior—but it also defines the graphical representation of them—what the process should look like. This technical representation can then be used by technical people to design and implement processes, whereas the graphical representation is for business people who will want to sketch, validate, or review process definitions.

So many jBPM Designers, which one should I use?

When we start using jBPM5, one of the most confusing things is the fact that we have three different process designers to choose from. For those who are new to jBPM or who have used the previous versions of jBPM, it can get very confusing. Let's get a brief introduction to each of the options that we have.

The JBPM5 Eclipse plugin

The jBPM5 Eclipse plugin was the first plugin supplied with the early versions of jBPM5. This plugin was a straightforward migration from the already existing Drools Flow Eclipse plugin. When Drools Flow was re-branded into jBPM5, the decision was to stop supporting the RF proprietary language for process definition and embrace a new standard language called BPMN 2.0 instead.

In the beginning, jBPM5 supported only a small subset of the elements defined in the BPMN 2.0 specification, so what happened was that only the BPMN 2.0 elements that had an existing counterpart in RF were supported. Simply put, the palette of elements existing in the jBPM5 Eclipse plugin was almost identical to the palette of elements present in the Drools Flow Process Editor.

In the early stages of jBPM5, most of its development team was focused on adding new features and improving the already acceptable quality level of the product. Unfortunately, one of the areas that they left behind was the Eclipse plugin.

The result was a powerful business process engine capable of executing most of the BPMN 2.0 specification but with an outdated process editor incapable of letting users make the most of those features.

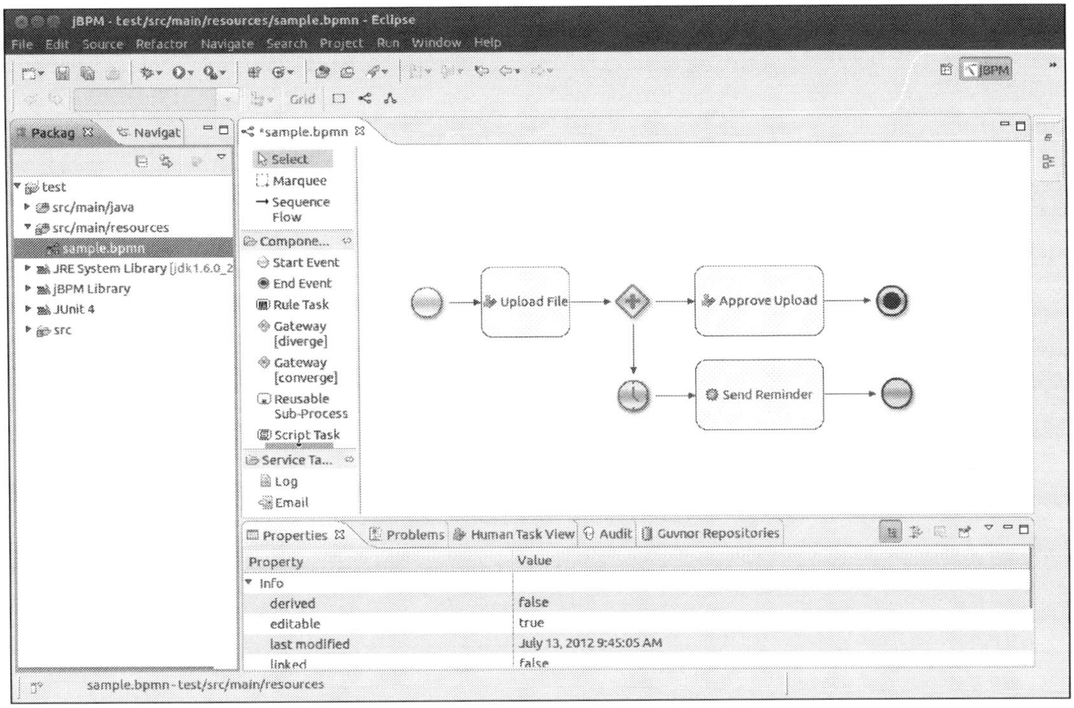

The current status of this editor is, that it is officially discontinued. No new features have been introduced in it for a long time. You can still use this editor to create really simple processes, but its usage is strongly discouraged.

Web Process Designer

At the same time that jBPM5 was being released, a new open source web editor capable of creating full BPMN 2.0 diagrams (among other things) was gaining popularity. The name of this web application was **Oryx**. This web process editor soon caught the attention of the jBPM5 team, as they were looking for a web editor that could be integrated with Red Hat's Guvnor BRMS.

This new editor had only one problem, which was that even though it supported the full BPMN 2.0 palette, the format of the resulting processes was not expressed in BPMN 2.0 XML language but in a proprietary JSON format. The JBPM5 team and some community members had to take charge of translating the proprietary JSON format to BPMN 2.0, as well as taking care of the integration with Guvnor and the implementation of some jBPM5 specific enhancements and features.

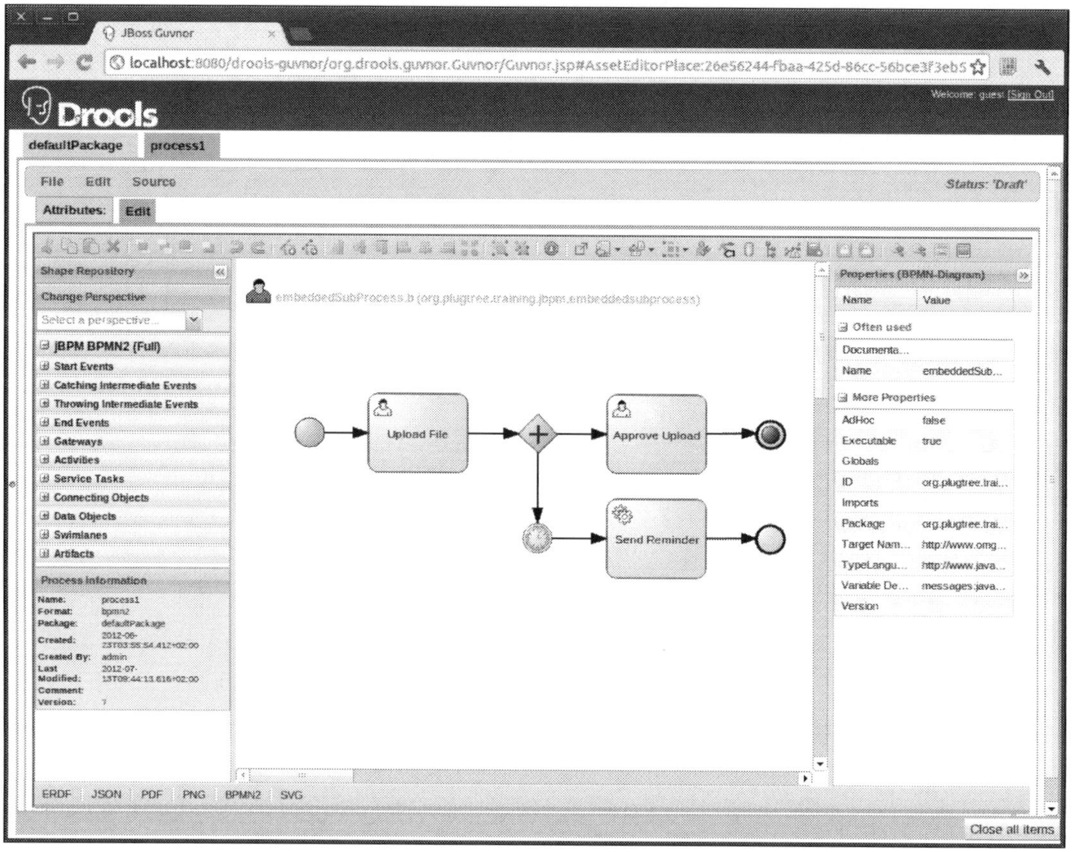

Today the Web Process Designer is the 'official' process editor that comes with jBPM5 installer. It is not configured to be a standalone application but to run embedded within Guvnor instead. This designer is under heavy development, with new features and bug fixes being implemented on a regular basis. For the rest of this chapter we are going to cover the usage of this editor.

The Eclipse BPMN 2.0 plugin

Even if the Web Process Designer does a great job at implementing all of the features present in jBPM5, it lacks one of the characteristics most wanted by almost every programmer—it can't be used inside any of the classic Java IDEs present today. This disadvantage introduces a little inconvenience when developers need to handle both Java code and process definitions seamlessly in just one IDE. This was one of the reasons that a group of Eclipse developers decided to provide a graphical modeling tool for the creation and editing of processes in BPMN 2.0. Now this designer is distributed as a plugin for the Eclipse IDE.

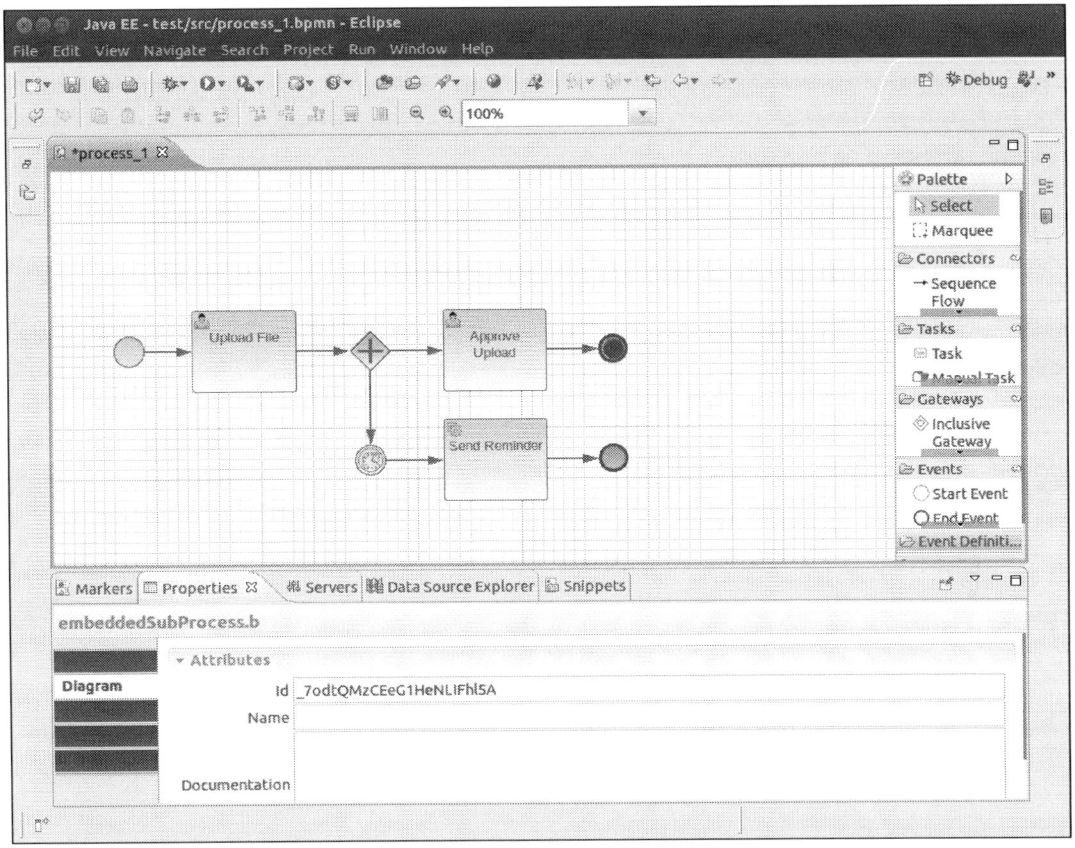

Even if the BPMN 2.0 Plugin is relatively new and still in its incubation period, it has already proved to be a great support for the BPMN 2.0 specification and for some of the jBPM5 specific characteristics.

Interacting with Web Process Editor

The jBPM5 installer comes with the latest stable version of Web Process Editor. After the JBoss instance is launched (see *Chapter 4, Knowing Your Toolbox*), there are two web applications relevant to this chapter—`drools-guvnor.war` and `designer.war`. The first application is Guvnor BRMS and the latter is jBPM5 Web Process Editor.

Guvnor BRMS is part of the Drools **Business Logic Integration Platform (BLIP)** suite, and it has two different purposes: to serve as a business-oriented tool for business assets management and to be used as a repository where those assets can be stored and accessed by external applications. Drools BLIP supports different types of business assets such as (but not limited to) business rules, decision tables, rule templates, and business processes. While Guvnor provides native support for the creation and editing of most of these business assets, it's different in the case of business processes.

For this type of asset, Guvnor relies on another web application—the Web Process Designer. This means that even if the Business Process definitions are going to be stored in Guvnor's repository along with the rest of the Business Assets, the editor used to handle them is not part of Guvnor's implementation.

In this section, we are going to explain how to create, modify, and delete processes in Guvnor. After these three operations are explained we will be ready to cover the different features provided by the Web Process Editor in detail, as well as how we can use them to define some of the processes that have already been covered in previous chapters of this book.

Creating new processes

In *Chapter 4, Knowing Your Toolbox*, we covered how to list the processes residing inside a package in Guvnor. We simply imported an existing Guvnor repository containing a process definition, which is why we didn't have to create a new process from scratch. But of course, before we can list the processes of a package, we have to create them. If what we want is to create a new process, we need to go to the **Knowledge Bases** section in the left panel of Guvnor and click on the **Create new** option at the top of that panel. Guvnor then shows us a list of all the possible business assets that we can define.

The asset type we are interested in is the BPMN2 Process, which is why we have to select the **New BPMN2 Process** option. Before the new process is created, we need to provide some information using the pop-up window that is opened. After this option is selected, Guvnor shows a popup where we can define the initial characteristics of the process we want to create. The first two options in the popup refer to the origin of the process. Do we want to create a completely new process definition? Or do we want to import a process definition that is already defined in Guvnor's global area?

> **Guvnor's global area** is a special package from which you can define the business assets that can be shared among different packages. This area is extremely useful when you have Business Assets that need to be shared among different Guvnor packages. Instead of duplicating the definition of assets, you can store it in a global location and then import it into different packages when you need it.

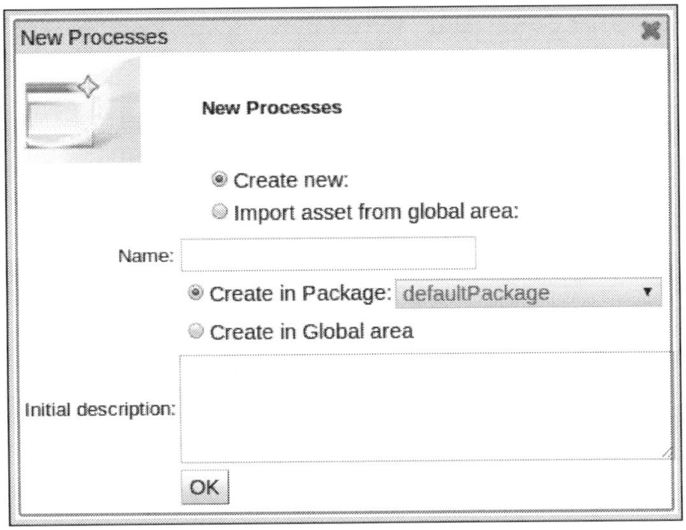

If we decide to create a new process definition, the next piece of information we need to provide is the name of the business process we want to define. The name we choose must be unique among all of the assets in the same package, as it's going to be used by Guvnor to internally identify the process. If we decide to import an existing asset from the global area instead of creating a new one, we select the process we want to import from a drop down list.

Another decision we have to make is whether we want to create the process in a specific package or in the global area. This last choice is only available if we are creating a new process, not importing it from the global area of course. In addition to the package where we want to create the asset, we can also provide a short description of the process that we can use as a sort of initial documentation.

Once we have all of the information in place, we are ready to create a new process (or import it from the global area) by clicking on the **Ok** button. This will create an empty process definition in Guvnor's repository, as well as invoke the Web Process Editor so that we can start working.

Accessing an existing process

Before we can open an existing process in Guvnor, we first need to find it. In Guvnor, there are two different ways to search for an existing process—through the **Knowledge Bases** section in Guvnor's panel on the left-hand side or through the **Browse** section in the same panel.

In *Chapter 4, Knowing Your Toolbox*, we covered how to use the **Knowledge Bases** section to browse through a specific package and list all of the business processes defined inside it. Sometimes this is enough, but there might be other times when we are looking for a process definition but we are not sure which package it's in, or maybe we are interested in processes belonging to different packages. If that is the case, we can make use of the **Assets** option under the **Browse** section in Guvnor's panel on the left-hand side.

Inside this section we have three different ways to find the process(es) we are looking for—we can do a complex search using the **Find** option, filter the processes by their statuses using the **By Status** option, or list the processes according to their categories by using the **By Category** option. No matter which way we choose, the processes listed will always contain an **Open** button that we can use to open the desired process in the Web Process Editor.

Modifying the existing processes

Once we have a process opened in the Web Process Editor, we can start working on it. For the rest of this chapter, we are going to cover the most important options and features in the Web Process Editor for creating your processes. When we want to save the changes we have made in a process, we have to use the **Save changes** option or the **Save and close** option from the **File** menu element present in Guvnor's toolbar.

Before making the changes, Guvnor asks us to add a comment that will be associated with the saving operation. This is pretty much like the comments that developers add every time they commit their changes to a software versioning repository. Actually, that is exactly what Guvnor is: a versioning repository for your business assets.

Every time you save a process, a new version of the process is created in Guvnor's repository. Guvnor keeps a track of all the versions of a particular asset without us needing to do anything special. Later, we can browse the versions of an asset from its **Attributes** tab. From there, we can open any particular version of a process and even bring back a particular version in order to overwrite the current one.

Guvnor's implicit versioning feature is very useful when we want to undo unwanted modifications of a process, or if we want to see the evolution of a particular process over a period of time.

Deleting the existing processes

Deleting an asset in Guvnor is a two-step operation—first we need to archive the asset, rendering it invisible and unusable for most of Guvnor's sections. Once we are sure we want to definitively remove it from the repository, we have to permanently delete it from one of the administrative panels of Guvnor.

In order to archive a process, we need to open it first. In Guvnor's current version, there is no way to archive an asset (using the UI) without opening it up first. Once we do that, we have to select the **Archive** option under **File** menu. When an asset is archived, it will no longer appear in any search or list of assets in Guvnor; furthermore, archived assets are not going to be taken into account during the package's compilation process in Guvnor. For Guvnor, an archived asset is almost like a nonexistent asset. The big benefit of having this extra step is that it gives us the ability to restore an archived asset if required. So if we decide to bring a process back from Guvnor's archive, we only need use one of the administrative panels Guvnor has under its **Administration** section—**Archive**. The **Archive Manager** panel displays a list of all of the assets present in Guvnor's archive. From this panel, we can do two things: restore an archived asset or permanently delete it. Once an asset is permanently deleted, there is no way to undo the operation, so make sure you know what you are doing.

Implementing our first process

Now that we know how to create and access our processes in Guvnor, it's time to create a new process using the Web Process Designer. The process we are going to implement is the Simple Emergency Bed Request introduced in *Chapter 3, Using BPMN 2.0 to Model Business Scenarios*. We are going to use this process to learn not only about its specific implementation but also to cover the different features present in the process editor.

The first thing we need to do is create a new BPMN2 process with the name **Bed Request V1** following the steps mentioned in the previous section.

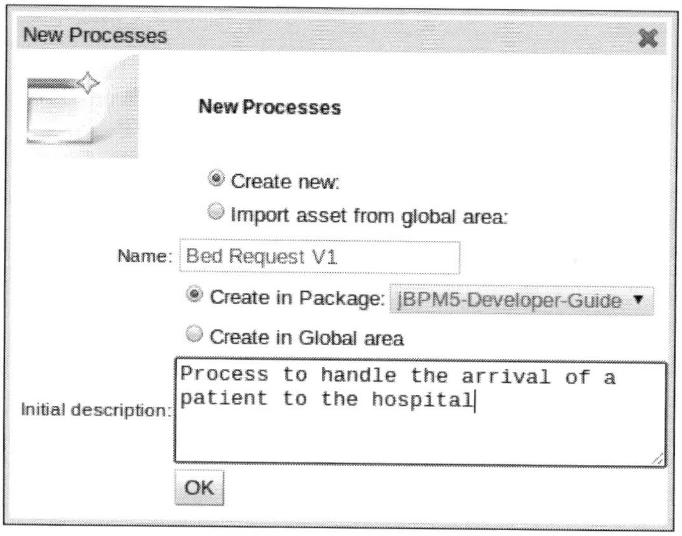

Once that process is created, Guvnor will display the Web Process Designer tool and we can start using it. But before we start implementing the process, let's do a quick review of the different sections we have in the Web Process Designer application as well as its features.

The Web Process Designer sections

The Web Process Designer's UI contains five main sections: **Toolbar**, **Shape Repository**, **Editing Canvas**, **Properties Panel**, and **Footer**. Let's analyze the main purpose of each of these sections.

A clean instance of Web Process Designer looks like the following:

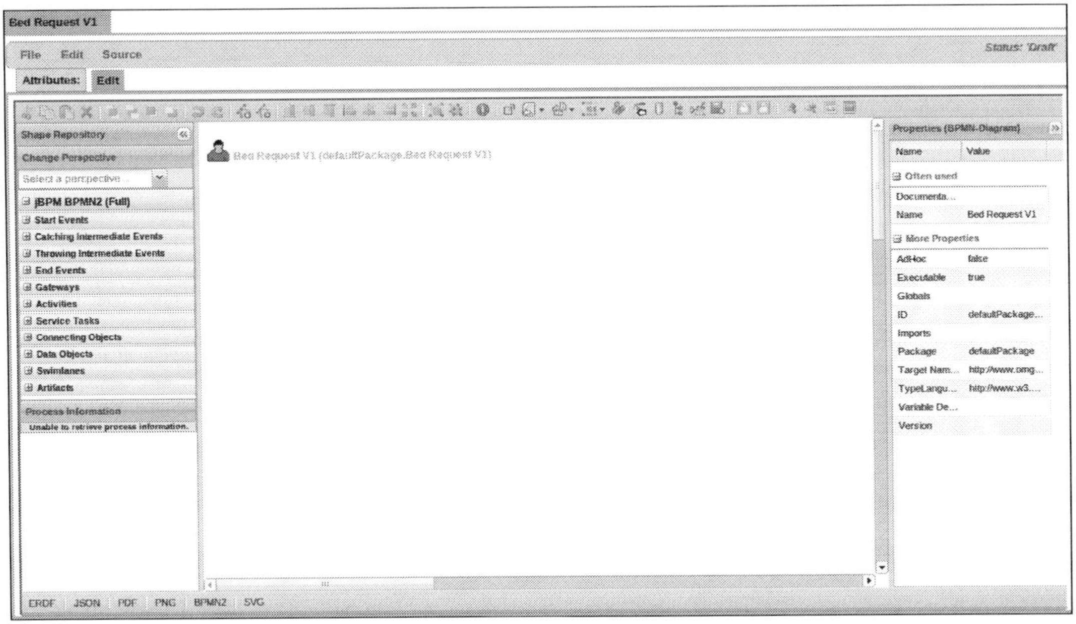

Toolbar

The toolbar contains different buttons that allow us to quickly access most of the features present in the Web Process Designer. Here, we can find shortcut buttons to access the clipboard, as well as other useful buttons regarding the layout of the process and its elements. The toolbar also has some other important features that we are going to cover in this chapter, such as importing process definitions or connecting to the service repository. So feel free to play around with what's in the toolbar until you get used to the options that you have and where they are.

Shape Repository

The shape repository panel contains the palette of BPMN 2.0 elements used to construct business processes. In this palette you will find all of the BPMN 2.0 elements (described in *Chapter 3, Using BPMN 2.0 to Model Business Scenarios*) grouped according to their type. Sometimes having all of the available elements in the palette is not the best thing. After you have designed a couple of processes, you will notice that most of the time you are using only a subset of these elements. That is why in the **Shape Repository** panel, there are two different perspectives: **Full** and **Minimal**. You can switch from one perspective to the other by using the drop-down list present on top of the **Shape Repository** panel.

In the bottom section of the **Shape Repository**, we'll find the **Process Information** panel, where we can see technical information about the current process, such as its name and package (in Guvnor), the creation and last modification times, and so on. All of this information is retrieved from Guvnor's repository.

Editing canvas

The **editing canvas** is perhaps the most important part of the Web Process Editor. It is where we are going to design our processes using the elements present in the shape repository.

When we drag-and-drop an element from the shape repository into the editing canvas, the element is added; we can change its position by simply dragging and dropping it around the canvas. Each element in the canvas has a context menu that we can access by clicking on the element. Using this menu, we can do different things such as creating new linked elements without using the shape repository, changing the type of element, accessing the process dictionary, editing its associated task form (if we are in a user task), or seeing the portion of BPMN 2.0 that is generated by the element.

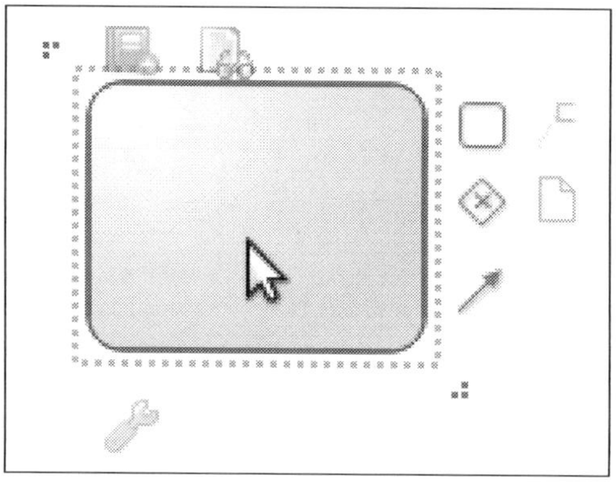

Some elements such as Sequence Flows, have dockers that you can use to bind those elements to some other shape in the editing canvas.

In the upper-left corner of the editing canvas, there's an icon we can use to define the task form that will be displayed by the jBPM5 GWT Console each time an instance of this process is started. In the north, south, east, and west regions of the canvas, we can find little yellow arrows that will only appear when we move the mouse over them. We can use these arrows to increase or decrease the total area of the editing canvas.

The Properties panel

When a BPMN 2.0 element is selected in the editing canvas, its properties are displayed in the right-hand side panel of the Web Process Designer.

Note that not all of the element's properties defined in the BPMN 2.0 specification exist in the Web Process Designer; and not all of the properties present in the properties panel are supported yet by jBPM5. Even though the jBPM5 team is making a big effort to sync up the Web Process Editor and the core process engine with the BPMN 2.0 specification, there are still some rough edges that need to be smoothed out. In this chapter we are going to cover most of the already supported properties of the most frequently used BPMN 2.0 elements.

Obviously, not all of the elements have the same properties set, which is why the **Properties** panel adapts its content to the element currently selected in the editing canvas. If multiple elements are selected in the editing canvas, only the properties that the selected elements have in common will be displayed. In that case, changing the value of a property will modify that property value in all of the selected elements.

Properties can be of different data types: String, Boolean, complex, and so on. Depending on the type of the property being modified, the properties panel can display different editors such as a text area, a checkbox, a popup, and so on.

Footer

In the bottom part of **Process Designer**, we find a toolbar containing options that allow us to export the current process into different formats. The supported formats are: ERDF, JSON, PDF, PNG, BPMN2 and SVG.

Emergency Bed Request Process First Design

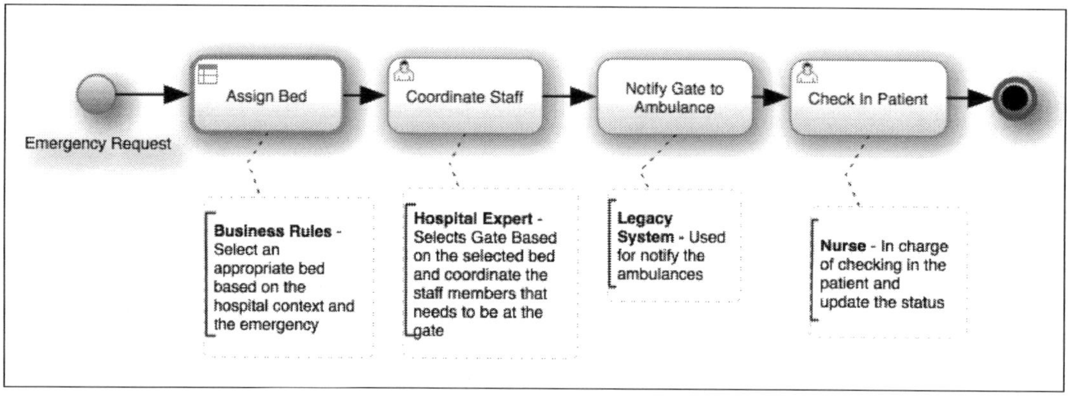

Now that we have a better understanding of the tool, we can create a first definition of the Simple Emergency Bed Request Process introduced in *Chapter 3, Using BPMN 2.0 to Model Business Scenarios*. The idea is to start with a simple definition of the process to explain some of the most used features and options present in the Process Designer. Once we have a simple but running process, we will start adding some advanced nodes in order to create the final version.

To start designing, we will follow the steps previously described in this chapter to create a new BPMN 2.0 process in Guvnor. We'll name it **Bed Request V1**. After the process is created and the Process Editor is opened in Guvnor, we will drag-and-drop a start event (from **Start Events** section) from the **Shape Repository** into the **Editing Canvas**. With the cursor over the new node we just added, we will select the **Task** option from its contextual menu (which should be the small rectangle with rounded corners). This option will add a new **Task** that is connected to the Start Event node, to the **Editing Canvas**. We will repeat these steps in order to add three more task nodes and finally an End Event node. The result should look like the following image:

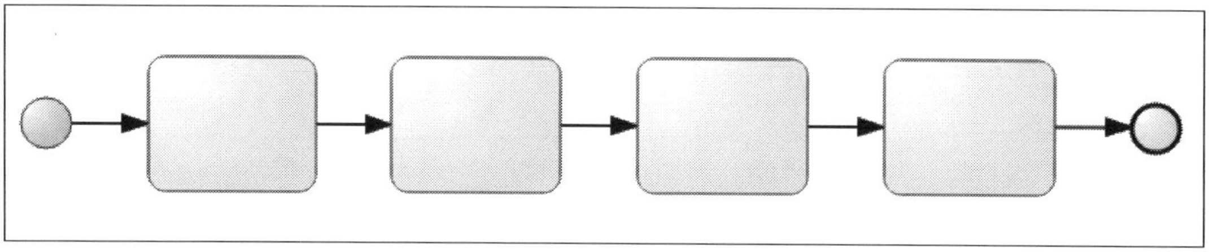

Configuring the process properties

Before talking about each element, we need to populate the mandatory attributes of the process itself. To do this, we have to click on the background of the **Editing Canvas** and go to the **Properties** panel. Each process definition has the following properties:

Property	Description
Documentation	A text document that we can add to the process. This property is not used by jBPM5 at runtime. This value will only be visible inside the Process Editor and in the resulting BPMN 2.0 asset. It is present in all of the nodes available in the palette. When we want to edit the value of this property, a drop-down appears, and when we try to open it, there will be a pop-up containing a text editor.
Name	The name attribute of the generated `<process>` BPMN 2.0 element. In version 5.4 or higher, there is a helper class (`StartProcessHelper`) that allows us to start a process by its name with version filtering, so it gives an option to start the latest version of a process identified by its name.
AdHoc	This Boolean property identifies whether the process is ad hoc or not. Ad hoc processes are special processes where the internal nodes don't have to be connected to each other.
Executable	The BPMN 2.0 specification defines two types of processes-executable and non-executable. Of course because the main idea of Process Designer is to create executable BPMN 2.0 processes, the value of this property is true by default.
Globals	Using this property, we can define Drools globals to share information amongst processes, as well as amongst global services that can be later invoked inside the process. The global editor allows us to define globals by indicating a name and a type. The name must be used to make reference to the global, and the type is the Java full qualified name of the global class.
ID	This property identifies the ID attribute of the generated `<process>` BPMN 2.0 element. The ID of the process must be unique inside a package, and it is used at runtime to identify a process definition.
Imports	Just as in Java, when we're dealing with a process definition, we need to import all of the different classes we want to use in our process. The imports editor is a simple popup that we can use to manage the different imports of the process.

Property	Description
Package	Identifies the Drools package where this process is going to be defined. This property should match the Guvnor's package name. This attribute is not defined by the BPMN 2.0 specification and is one of the few extensions that jBPM5 defines on top of it.
Target Namespace	The target namespace used in the resulting BPMN 2.0 asset. Most of the time there is no need to modify the value of this attribute.
Type Language	This read-only property shows us the language used in the resulting BPMN 2.0 asset.
Variable Definitions	This property defines the variables available in the process. Variables are important for maintaining internal values, sharing information between nodes, and getting some kind of result from the process execution. In the editor available for this property, you can declare a process variable by defining its name and fully qualified type (whether standard or custom).
Version	This attribute can be used to specify the version of a process. This version is then used by the helper class mentioned earlier to instantiate the latest version process given its name.

Now that we have a clear idea of the properties a process has, let's see which ones we need to modify for our example.

The most important property we need to set is the ID of the process. The ID will identify our process in the knowledge base that we need to build, whenever we want to start instances of it. This property must be unique among all of the processes in the knowledge base, no matter which package it's defined in. The process ID is also used to make reference to a process definition when using the Call Activity node (reusable sub-process). In our case, we are going to set the ID of this process to `hospitalEmergencyV1`.

The second property we are going to configure is the package. This property serves as a logical way to group processes together. The value of this property must match the name of the Guvnors' package where the process is defined..

Finally, we need to define all of the process variables required by this definition. In the process that we are designing, we need eleven variables of type String-`bedrequest_id`, `bedrequest_date`, `bedrequest_entity`, `bedrequest_patientage`, `bedrequest_patientname`, `bedrequest_patientgender`, `bedrequest_patientstatus`, `checkinresults_gate`, `checkinresults_checkedin`, `checkinresults_notified`, and `checkinresults_time`. These variables must be defined in the **Variable Definition** property using its corresponding editor. The final result should be as follows:

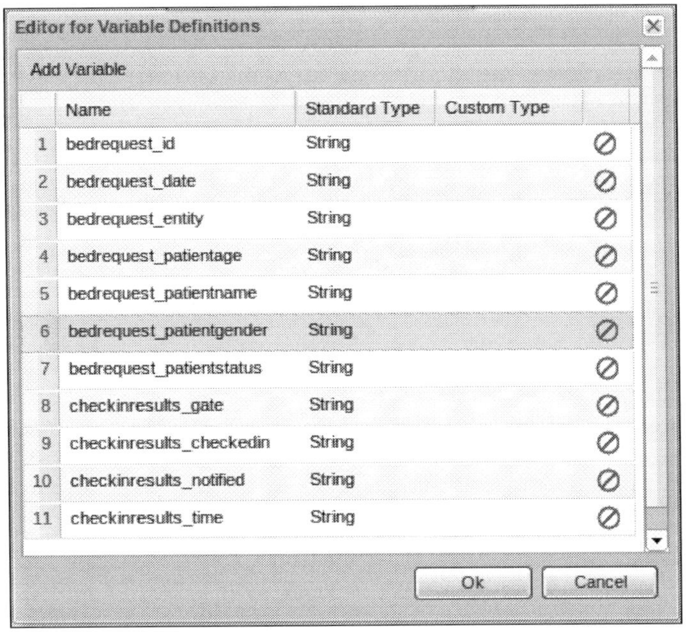

Once we have the process configured, we need to review each of the nodes it has in order to configure their properties.

Configuring the Start Event node

The start event node represents the beginning of the process. From all the different Start Event types that we can use, we have decided to use the None Start Event. In jBPM5, you have to use this type of start event when your process is going to be explicitly started using its ID:

```
ksession.startProcess("id.of.the.process");
```

Besides the common properties that we described earlier, the properties present in this node are as follows:

Property	Description
Background	The background color of the node. This property is present in most of the nodes available in the palette.
Border Color	The border color of the node. This property is present in most of the nodes available in the palette.
Font Color	The font color of the node. This property is present in most of the nodes available in the palette.

Property	Description
Font Size	The font size of the node. This property is present in most of the nodes available in the palette.
DataOutput	This property defines all of the output variables of the node. Each variable has a type (Java class) and a name Specifically, in the case of the None Start Event node, this property has no meaning. The property exists for this node, because it is defined for all of the different Catch Events. In the case of a Signal Start Event, for example, the `DataOutput` can be used to hold a reference to the signal event and the information it contains. The scope of this variable is the node. Once the process runtime leaves the node, the variables are no longer valid.
DataOutputAssociation	This is the way we assign data from the different `DataOutput` variables to process variables. The type of the `DataOutput` and the process variable must be the same (or a subclass). This property is present in each node that has a `DataOutput` property. The editor we have to create the `DataOutput/Input` Associations requires a dedicated section, since it is probably the most complex property editor in the Process Designer. We are going to learn how to use it later in this chapter.

Given that this None Start Event node doesn't have any properties that affect its behavior during execution, we are not going to modify any of them.

Configuring sequence flow elements

Sequence flows are the elements used to connect the Activities, Events and Gateways in our processes. Of all the available properties present in the Process Designer for this type of element, only two of them have an impact on the jBPM5 engine: Condition Expression and Condition Expression Language:

Property	Description
Condition Expression	For sequence flow elements coming from a Diverging Inclusive Gateway or a Diverging Exclusive Gateway, this property defines the condition that needs to be evaluated. Depending on the evaluation result, the execution will either continue through this flow or not. Inside the Condition Expression code, we can access all of the variables defined in our process. The value of this property is a piece of code that is going to be executed each time the gateway is reached. When using the Java language, the last line of the condition must be a sentence of the form: return <expression resolving to boolean>;
Condition expression language	Two different languages are allowed in the Condition Expression property: Java and Drools. We can use this property to specify the language we want to use. When Java is selected, the Condition Expression must be valid Java code. Other than the process variables, a special variable with the name kcontext can be used to get extra information about the process instance. If we use 'drools' as the Conditional Expression Language, the syntax we have to use in the Condition Expression is Drools' DRL. Basically, we have to define a constraint using DRL, which, if true, will propagate the execution of the process through the node connected to this Sequence Flow.

As we are not using any Diverging Inclusive or Exclusive Gateway in the process that we are designing, there is no need to modify either of these properties in any of the Sequence Flows we have. Later in this chapter, when a more complex version of this process is covered, we will see how to use these two properties.

Configuring task nodes

Task nodes in BPMN 2.0 are the place where concrete actions take place. The steps required to achieve our process' goal are going to be defined using task nodes.

Of the eight tasks defined in the BPMN 2.0 specification (abstract task, service task, send task, receive task, user task, manual task, business rule, script task), jBPM5 supports all but the manual task. The predefined implementation jBPM5 provides for these activities is not 100 percent compliant with the BPMN 2.0 specification.

> This chapter will focus on the valid set of properties that you can use for each of the different Tasks supported by jBPM5, but it is not going to cover the detailed behavior of the tasks at runtime.

In the Web Process Designer, all of the different types of tasks are implemented by just one element in the Shape Repository—task. The `TaskType` property of this node is going to specify its concrete type. An empty value for `TaskType` (the default value in Web Process Designer) identifies an abstract task.

Each task type has a different set of attributes that we can use to configure it. Web Process Designer will automatically show only the valid attributes for each specific task type. The following tables explain the valid properties for each type:

Send task	
Property	**Description**
`DataInputSet`	The input variables of the node.
`Assignments`	The assignments between the process variables and the input variables of the node.
`MessageRef`	The name of the message being sent.
`On Entry Action`	A piece of Java code that is invoked before the node gets executed. All of the process variables are available in this piece of code.
`On Exit Action`	A piece of Java code that is invoked after the node gets executed. All of the process variables are available in this piece of code.

The variables you can define in the `DataInputSet` depend on the handler you register for the send task nodes. You can read more about task handlers in *Chapter 6, Domain Specific Processes*.

Receive task	
Property	**Description**
`DataOutputSet`	The output variables of the node.
`Assignments`	The assignments between the output variables and the process variables.
`MessageRef`	The name of the message this node is waiting for.
`On Entry Action`	A piece of Java code that is invoked before the node gets executed. All of the process variables are available in this piece of code.
`On Exit Action`	A piece of Java code that is invoked after the node gets executed. All of the process variables are available in this piece of code.

The variables you can define in the `DataOutputSet` depend on the handler you register for the receive task nodes. You can read more about task handlers in *Chapter 6, Domain Specific Processes*.

Service task	
Property	**Description**
`DataInputSet`	The input variables of the node. If the jBPM5 predefined handler for this task type (`ServiceTaskHandler`) is used, we can define an input variable—its type must be `Object` and its name `Parameter`. This variable is going to be passed as an argument to the method of the object invoked by this node.
`DataOutputSet`	The output variables of the node.
`Assignments`	The assignments between the input/output variables and the process variables.
`Interface`	If the jBPM5 predefined handler for this task type (`ServiceTaskHandler`) is used, this property must be the fully qualified name of the class we want to use as a service. Each time the execution of the process reaches this task, a new instance of this class is going to be created through reflection.
`Operation`	If the jBPM5 predefined handler for this task type (`ServiceTaskHandler`) is used, this property identifies the name of the method we want to invoke in the `Interface` object.
`On Entry Action`	A piece of Java code that is invoked before the node gets executed. All of the process variables are available in this piece of code.
`On Exit Action`	A piece of Java code that is invoked after the node gets executed. All of the process variables are available in this piece of code.

Just like any other task in jBPM5, the runtime behavior of a service task (and the required information such as input and output variables) is going to be determined by the task handler we associate to this node.

User task	
Property	**Description**
`DataInputSet`	The input variables of the node.
`DataOutputSet`	The output variables of the node.
`Assignments`	The assignments between the input/output variables and the process variables.
`Actors`	A comma separated list of actor IDs or an expression of the form `#{<expression>}` that evaluates to a `String`. In the default Human Task implementation of jBPM5, this property defines the possible owners of a task.
`GroupID`	A comma separated list of group IDs or an expression of the form `#{<expression>}` that evaluates to a `String`. In the default human task implementation of jBPM5, this property defines the actor's groups that can own this task.

User task	
Property	**Description**
`Task Name`	The name of the user task. In the default human task implementation of jBPM5, this property defines the task name that should be displayed to the user.
`Comment`	In the default human task implementation of jBPM5, this property defines a comment for the task.
`Priority`	In the default human task implementation of jBPM5, this property defines the priority of the task.
`Skippable`	In the default human task implementation of jBPM5, this property defines whether this task can be skipped or not.
`On Entry Action`	A piece of Java code that is invoked before the node gets executed. All of the process variables are available in this piece of code.
`On Exit Action`	A piece of Java code that is invoked after the node gets executed. All of the process variables are available in this piece of code.

The properties of the user task are tightly related to the default human task implementation of jBPM5. This implementation is going to be introduced and explained in *Chapter 7, Human Interactions*.

Business Rule task	
Property	**Description**
`Ruleflow Group`	This property is used to specify the group of rules that must be executed when the process execution reaches this node.
`On Entry Action`	A piece of Java code that is invoked before the node gets executed. All of the process variables are available in this piece of code.
`On Exit Action`	A piece of Java code that is invoked after the node gets executed. All of the process variables are available in this piece of code.

In jBPM5, the Drools Rule engine performs rule execution. These two frameworks, jBPM5 and Drools, are so well integrated that the switch from one engine to the other is seamless for the user. Actually, the switch has never existed since both engines share the same core.

Script task	
Property	**Description**
`Script`	This property defines the piece of code we want executed when the process execution reaches this node. Inside this piece of code, we have access to all of the process variables and the special variable `kcontext`.
`Script Language`	This defines the language used in the `Script` property. This language could be Java or Mvel, which is a scripting language that runs on top of the JVM.
`On Entry Action`	A piece of Java code that is invoked before the node gets executed. All of the process variables are available in this piece of code.
`On Exit Action`	A piece of Java code that is invoked after the node gets executed. All of the process variables are available in this piece of code.

Business users do not commonly use script tasks, but they are really helpful for technical people. By adding script tasks to a process we can easily modify the behavior of our processes without modifying any Java class. We can use this type of task to add logs, messages, or to perform data transformation tasks in our processes. As a rule of thumb, script tasks shouldn't contain business logic inside them. Abstract tasks, human tasks, and service tasks are a better place to implement this kind of logic.

Abstract Task	
Property	**Description**
`DataInputSet`	The input variables of the node.
`DataOutputSet`	The output variables of the node.
`Assignments`	The assignments between the input/output variables and the process variables.
`Task Name`	This is probably the most important property of this type of Task. It defines the name we have to use to register a handler for this task.
`On Entry Action`	A piece of Java code that is invoked before the node gets executed. All of the process variables are available in this piece of code.
`On Exit Action`	A piece of Java code that is invoked after the node gets executed. All of the process variables are available in this piece of code.

Abstract tasks are used by jBPM5 as an extension point for plugging in our business-related logic. We'll discuss this type of task in detail during the next chapter.

Going back to our process, we have four different tasks to define—one Business Rule (Assign Bed) task, two user tasks (Coordinate Staff and Check In Patient), and one abstract task (Notify Gate to Ambulance). Let's see how we have to configure each node's attributes in order to make this process achieve the goal defined in *Chapter 3, Using BPMN 2.0 to Model Business Scenarios*.

For the first task, the first thing we need to do is to change its `TaskType` property to Business Rule. A little icon similar to a table will appear in the node. The next property we need to change is the `Ruleflow` group. Remember that this property defines the group of rules that are going to be executed when this node is reached. The value we need for this property is `assign-bed`. Finally, and just for representational concerns, we will assign **Assign Bed** as the name for this task.

Regarding the second task, we need to configure it as a user task using its `TaskType` property. A small icon of a person will appear in the node. The `Name` and `Task Name` properties for this task should be set to `Coordinate Staff`. For the `Actors` property, we want to use `hospital`; this represents the possible owner(s) of this task. The `Comment` property of the task, which is a description of the task that will be available to the user at runtime, must hold the value `task for staff coordination`.

Now it's turn to configure the input and output variables for this task. As you may recall from the original definition in *Chapter 3, Using BPMN 2.0 to Model Business Scenarios*, this task has the following input variables—`bedrequest_date`, `bedrequest_patientage`, `bedrequest_entity`, `bedrequest_patientgender`, `bedrequest_patientstatus`. Keep in mind that they are all of type `String`. Using the `DataInputSet` property editor, we have to define all of these input variables. The final result should look like the following:

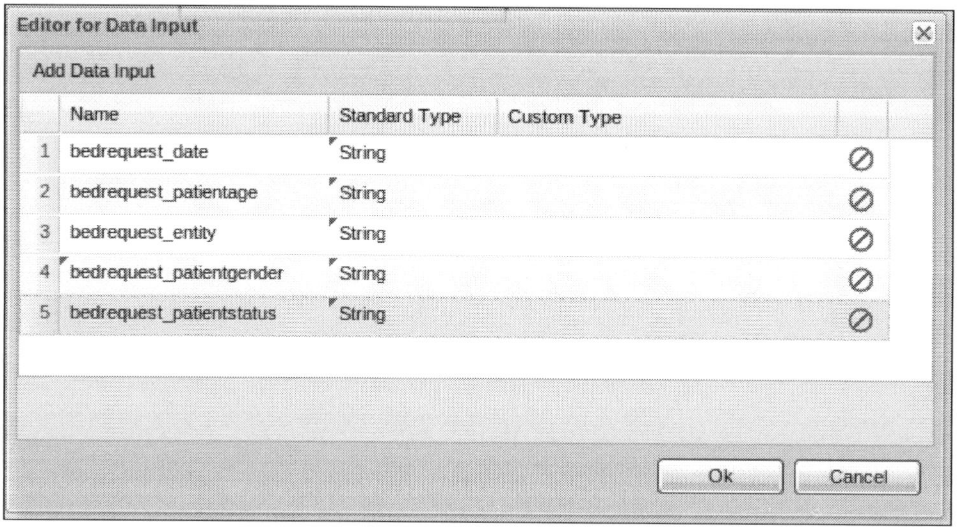

The output variables are defined using the `DataOutputSet` property of the task. In this case, we only have to define one output variable of type `String`, called `checkinresults_gate`. The **Data Output** set editor for this property should look like the following:

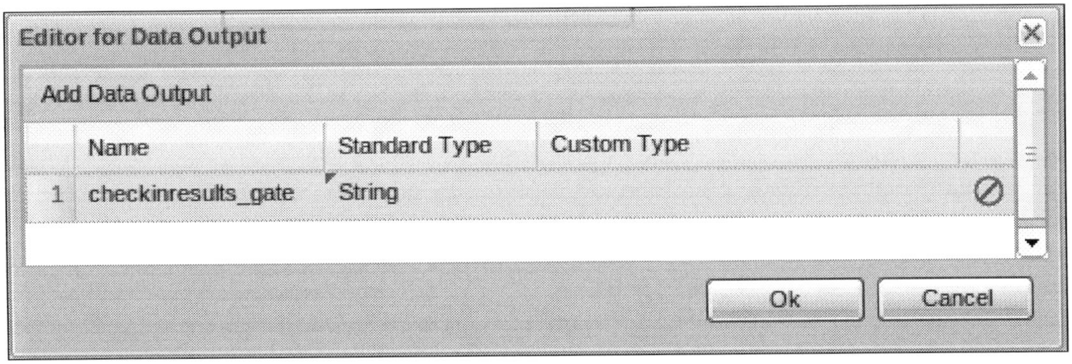

Once we have defined all of our input and output variables, we need to make assignments between the process variables (or fixed values) and the input variables of the task, as well as assignments between the output variables of the task and the process variables. This operation is performed in the editor available for the **Assignments** property of the task. Using this editor, try to create the following configuration:

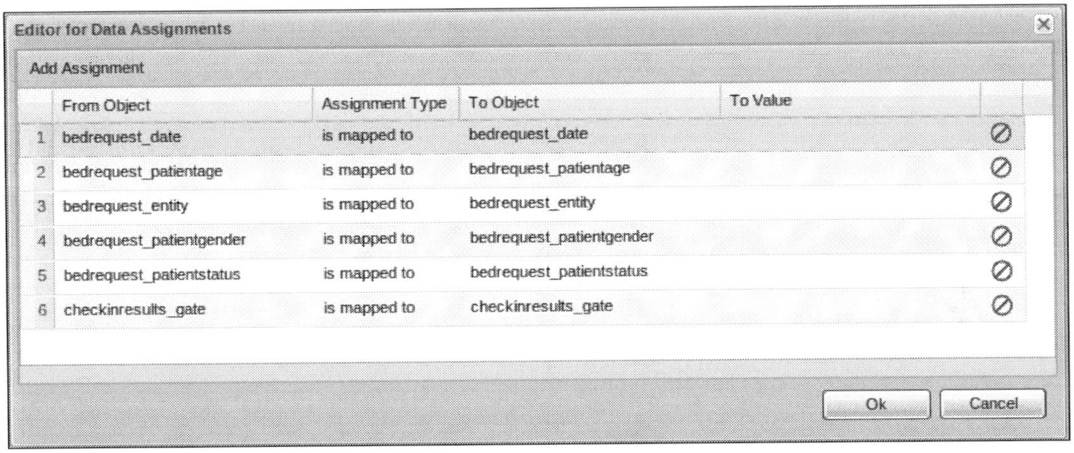

Before we continue, let's explore this editor in more detail. An assignment is composed of three parts—a `From` object, `Assignment` type, and either a `To` object or `To Value` part.

For input assignments—meaning the value we want to assign to one of the input variables of the task—we have to decide whether we want to assign a fixed value to it or if we want to map a process variable to it.

In the case of a fixed value, in the `From` object we have to select the input variable that we want to assign from the drop-down list that contains all of the data input, output variables, and process variables. The `Assignment` type value required to assign a fixed value to a variable is `is equal to`. The third part of the assignment when we are assigning fixed values to an input variable is defined in the **To Value** column, where we have to enter the value we want to assign to the input variable. If what we want to do is map an existing process variable into one of the input variables of the task, we need to select the process variable first in the **From Object** column. Then we have to select `is mapped to` for this column, and finally, we have to select in the **To Object** column the task's input variable that we want to be assigned.

For output assignments, in the **From Object** column, we have to select the output variable we want as the source of the assignation. In the **Assignment Type** column, `is mapped to` is the only valid value, as we can't map an output variable to a fixed value. Because we can't use `is equal to` as the **Assignment Type**, the only column we can use for the third part of the assignment is the **To Object** column, where we have to select the process variable we want to use as the target of the assignment.

In the previous image, the first five entries are input assignments and the last one is an output assignment.

> When processes are saved, some automagic `DataInputSet` variables and assignments may appear in user tasks. These variables correspond to some of the properties that the user task has such as `Comment` or `Skippable`. There is nothing wrong with those variables and assignments, but just ignore them. You can even remove them if you want, but after the process is saved, they'll appear again anyway. If you want to change the value of the assignments, use the property in the **Properties** panel instead of the value in the Assignments Editor.

The third type of task we have in our process is the Abstract task which jBPM5 uses as an extension point for our processes. Using a registration mechanism provided by jBPM5, we can attach custom handlers to this kind of task. In *Chapter 6, Domain Specific Processes*, we will elaborate more on this mechanism and the way we have to extend our processes to make them fit our business needs. For this task, we need to leave the **Task Type** property set to **None**. The **Task Name** property must be set to **Notification System**. At runtime, we will use this name to register the custom handler we want to execute every time the process reaches this node. We'll have to define one String input variable in the node (`checkinresults_gate`) and one String output variable (`checkinresults_gate`).

Then we'll make assignments between the process variable `checkinresults_gate` and the input variable with the same name, as well as assignments between the output variable `checkinresults_gate` and the process variable with the same name.

> In this example, we are using the same name for input/output variables of the Tasks and process variables we are assigning. In jBPM5, this is not mandatory: you can choose the name you want for your process variables and whatever name you like for the input/output variables of your tasks. The relationship between the two is not maintained by the name but by the association table you have in the Assignment property of your tasks.

The input/output variables and the assignment table for the third task should be like this:

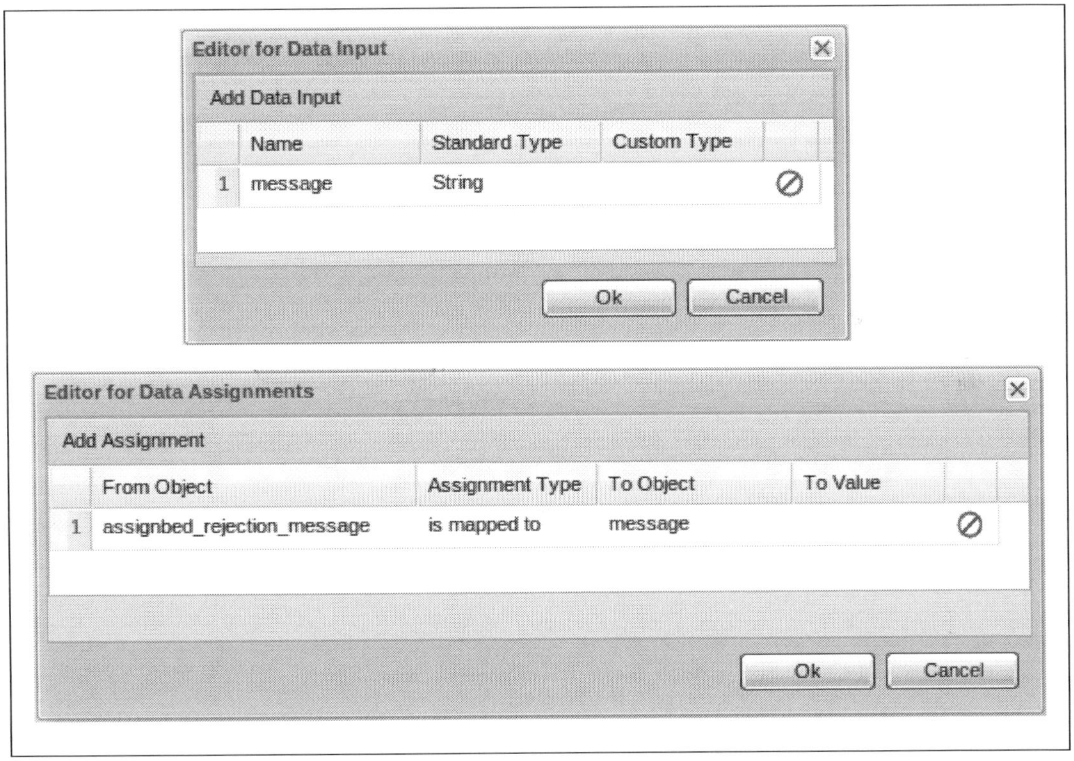

In the process we are modeling, the last task is again a user task. The properties we need to configure are the same properties we have already configured for the second task of the process, described as follows:

- **Name**: **Check In Patient**
- **Task Name**: **Check In Patient**
- **Actors**: **nurse**
- **Comment**: **Task for checking in patient**
- **DataInputSet**: **checkinresults_notified (String)**
- **DataOutputSet**: **checkinresults_checkedin (String), checkinresults_time (String)**
- **Assignments**:
    - **checkinresults_notified ->checkinresults_notified (Input)**
    - **checkinresults_checkedin ->checkinresults_checkedin (Output)**
    - **checkinresults_time ->checkinresults_time (Output)**

Configuring the End Event node

The last node that we have to configure in our process is the End Event node, which represents the end of the execution path of the process. A process can have more than one simultaneous (but, in jBPM5, not concurrent) execution paths. We can use this type of event for two different purposes: to terminate the current execution path (End Event) or to terminate the complete process instance (**Terminating End** event), no matter how many pending execution paths may exist.

Testing the process definition

By now we should have a process definition ready to be executed in the jBPM engine if we've correctly followed all of the steps so far.

If we look for a project called `jBPM5-WebDesignerExamples` inside the `chapter_05` directory, we'll see that it contains all of the tests that we are going to use in this chapter. The test that we are interested in at this point is called `EmergencyBedRequestV1Test.java`. It uses a file called `EmergencyBedRequestV1.bpmn` that contains the definition of the process. So basically the test will execute the process definition to check that everything is working as expected.

What you can do once you have your process definition stored in Guvnor is to get its sources (using the **bpmn2** button in the footer) and replace the content of `EmergencyBedRequestV1.bpmn` to see if your process behaves the same way.

If you want, you can take a look at the source code of the test, but don't worry if you don't understand all of the things that are going on inside it. Some of these things are topics that have not yet been covered, such as Domain-specific processes and user tasks.

Emergency Bed Request Process V2

As you may remember from *Chapter 3, Using BPMN 2.0 to Model Business Scenarios*, the second version of this process introduced a Diverging Exclusive Gateway right after the first task.

Before we start modifying the process we already have, we are going to create a copy of it in Guvnor. This will allow us to have two independent versions of the process. At runtime, we can then choose which version we would like to execute. In Guvnor, we first open the process we want to copy and then select **Edit | Copy** from Guvnor's toolbar. This option will display a pop-up where we have to enter the name we want to give to the copy. The pop-up also allows us to create this copy in a different package. After the copy is created, Guvnor will open the cloned process in Web Process Editor and it will be ready to be worked on. In this case, we are going to name the copy of the process **Bed Request V2**.

In order to add the required modifications to the process, we need to remove the Sequence Flow connecting the first and second tasks. Then we have to drag and drop an Exclusive Gateway from the palette and then connect the first task to it. Now what we need to do is to connect the Exclusive Gateway to the second task and then add a new task connected to the Exclusive Gateway we just added (we can use the gateway's context menu to add this new task node). The last node we have to add is an End Event node connected to the last task that we added. The final result should look like the following:

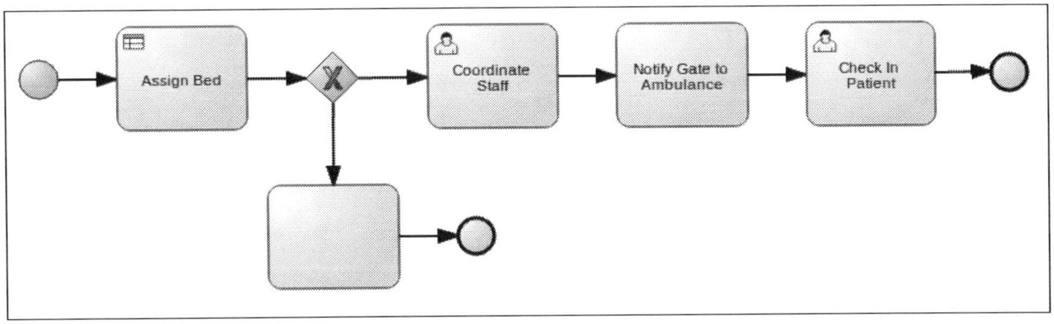

Now that we have the required structure, it is time to configure the new elements we have added to the process.

Configuring process properties

Because we are working on a new version of a process we already have, we must change its ID property. For this version, we are going to use the value `hospitalEmergencyV2`.

> If we don't use different IDs for our processes, we risk one process definition overwriting the other at runtime. We must always use different IDs for different processes and even for different versions of a process.

Configuring the Exclusive Gateway node

In the case of gateways, there are not too many properties we can configure. The behavior of a gateway is determined by its type, which we have implicitly defined by selecting the specific gateway we want to use—exclusive.

Besides the properties we've covered, others present in an Exclusive Gateway are as follows:

Property	Description
X-Marker visible	At the time this book is being written, this property does not work properly. It should display or hide the 'X' marker in the gateway node.
Default gate	Another not-yet-implemented property. It should allow us to select the default Sequence Flow that will be executed if all of the other outgoing Sequence Flows of the gateway evaluate to `false`. There is an open issue in jBPM's bug tracker regarding the lack of support for this property.
Gateway type	This is a Read Only property showing the type of gateway.
XOR type	Another Read Only property displaying the type of Exclusive Gateway a node is.

The only property we are going to modify is the **Name** of the gateway. The name is only used to display a label in the node. We are going to set the value as `Is Bed Assigned?`. As you can see, there's nothing else we can configure in this node, so let's move on to the outgoing Sequence Flows.

Configuring the Sequence Flow elements

According to the BPMN 2.0 specification, the conditions evaluated in an Exclusive or Inclusive Gateway are not defined in the gateway itself but in each of the outgoing Sequence Flows it has. In the process that we are designing, the Gateway needs to check whether a bed was correctly assigned or not. In the case of a correctly assigned bed, we want to continue the execution flow we already had from the previous version of the process. In the case of a rejection in the bed assignment logic, we want to notify the ambulance what to do.

Up to this point, we haven't been interested in the result of the Assign Bed Business Rule task, but things are different now. As we want to make a decision from the rejection or acceptance of a bed request, we need to hold the result of the Assign Bed task inside a process variable. This task will be in charge of modifying the value of this variable, which allows us to use it in the Condition Expression property of our Sequence Flows. The mechanism used by the Business Rule task to change the process variable is out of the scope of this chapter, however we will learn more about this particular task later in *Chapter 9, Smart Processes Using Rules*.

Given that we don't yet have a variable defined to hold the Assign Bed result, we need to create it. Following the directions covered earlier in this chapter, we have to define two new process variables—a Boolean variable called `assignbed_success` and a String variable called `assignbed_rejection_message`.

Now that we have a variable holding the result value of the Assign Bed task, we can configure the outgoing Sequence Flows of the gateway we have added. As we know, the Condition Expression property of a Sequence Flow is a piece of code (by default, in Java) that is executed when the gateway associated with the Sequence Flow is being executed. This code has access to all of the process variables and must return a Boolean value. If that value is `true`, the process execution will continue via the node connected to the Sequence Flow.

In the Condition Expression of the flow that connects the gateway to the Coordinate Staff user task, we are going to write the following piece of code using the ad-hoc editor:

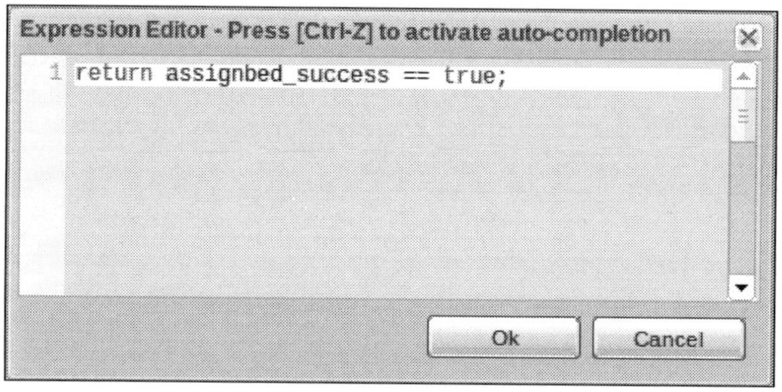

As you can see, the only thing we are doing in the Condition Expression is checking if the value of `assignedbed_success` is `true`.

> The Condition Expression Editor supports basic auto-completion. The *Ctrl+Z* shortcut will give us access to all of the process variables already defined in the process as well as to the automagic `context` object and its attributes.

The **Name** that we are going to set for this flow is **Yes**. In the case of Sequence Flows, the name helps to make sure that users "reading" the process do not need to open the condition editor to see what is being checked internally.

For the second Sequence Flow we added (the one connecting the gateway to the new task), we are going to modify its Condition Expression property as follows:

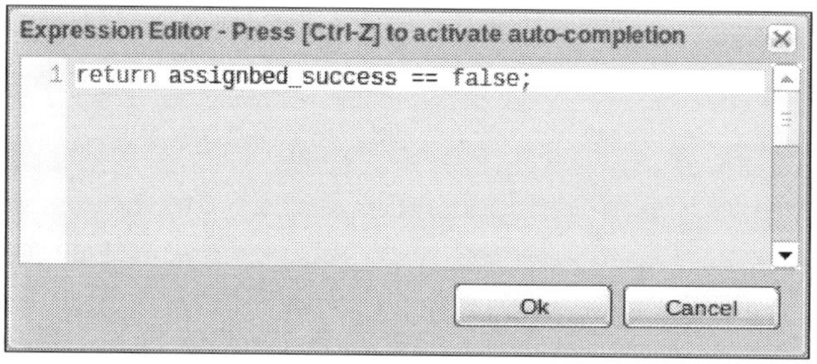

The **Name** attribute of this sequence flow should be set to **No**.

Configuring task nodes

The last task we added should remain as a generic task. The goal of this task is to notify the ambulance of bed request rejections. As already mentioned, we can register Java objects as handlers for generic tasks in jBPM5 in order to achieve our goal at runtime. *Chapter 6, Domain-specific Processes*, is going to cover the use of these handler classes in great detail.

The obvious properties that we need to set first are the **Name** and **Task Name** properties. For these, we are going to use the **Notify Rejection to Ambulance** value.

In the scenario that we are modeling, the input that this task will accept is the message that should be sent to the ambulance. That's why we need to define a new input variable called `message` in the `DataInputSet` property of the task. As we are not expecting any output for this node, we don't need to define any output variables in the task's `DataOutputSet` property.

In the **Assignments** property of the task, we need to map a process variable to the task's input variable. The process variable containing the information we need is `assignbed_rejection_message`. The `DataInputSet` and **Assignments** properties should look like the following:

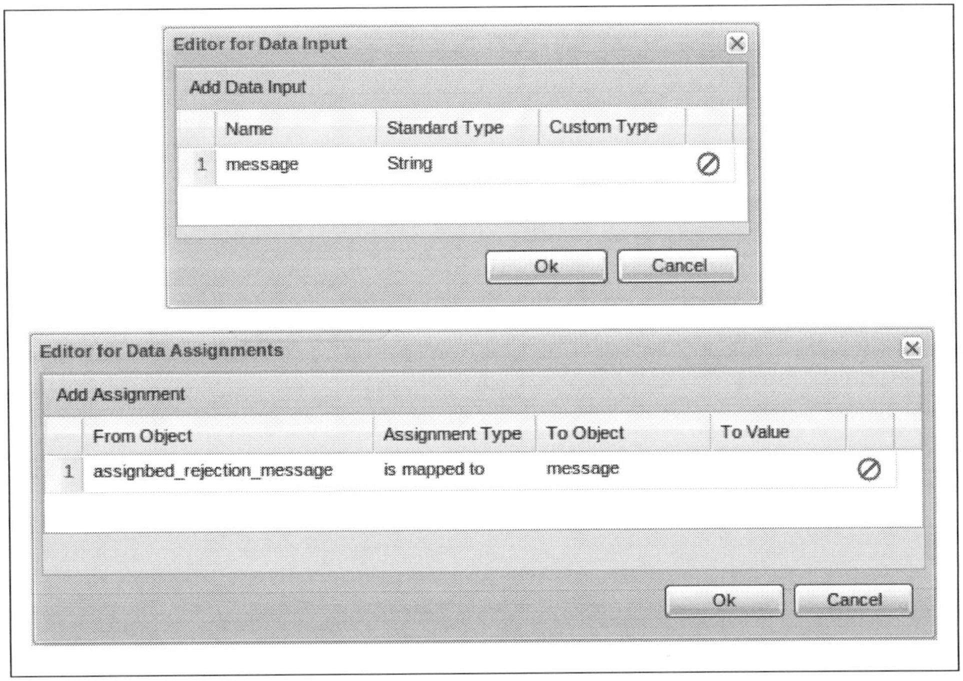

Configuring the End Event nodes

The last node introduced to the process is the None End Event. Just as when we configured the previous None End Event, there is nothing special to do here. Even if we added a new execution path into the process, the new path would be mutually exclusive with the path that already exists (because of the Exclusive Gateway that we are using to split the paths). This is the reason we don't need to convert this None End Event node into a Terminate End Event node. Whenever one of the two End Event nodes that we have in our process is reached, the process execution will finish as there are no further execution paths to be explored. The resulting process after all of the steps we did to upgrade it to Version 2, should be something similar to the following:

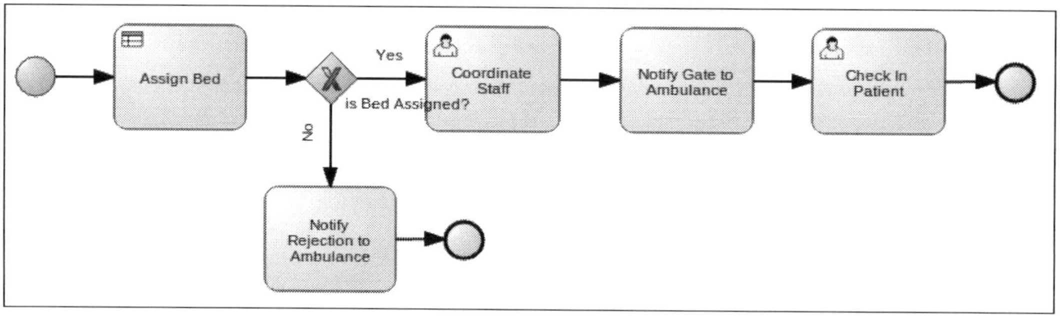

Testing the process definition

This version of the Emergency Bed Request process also has a corresponding test in the `jBPM5-WebDesignerExamples` project—`EmergencyBedRequestV2Test.java`. Just as in the previous version of the process, we can see the final version of the process in the file `EmergencyBedRequestV2.bpmn`. What we can do now is try to recreate the process in Guvnor, replacing the content of that file and checking that the tests still pass.

Emergency Bed Request Process V3

The third version of the process that we are designing includes a brand new and independent execution path that has to wait for an external event to occur in order to be executed. The last user task of the first execution path we had (**Check in Patient**) is now part of the new execution path that we will add.

The steps that we need to follow before we start working on this new version of the process are the same steps we followed for Version 2—create a new copy of the process in Guvnor with the name **Bed Request v3**.

The structural changes we need to make for the new version we are designing are as follows:

1. Delete the incoming and outgoing Sequence Flows of the **Check In Patient** user task.
2. Using a Sequence Flow, link the **Notify Gate to Ambulance** Abstract Task to the orphaned None Event Node we now have.
3. Drag-and-drop an Intermediate Signal Event node from the Shape Repository into the Editing Canvas.
4. Drag-and-drop a Terminate End Event node from the Shape Repository into the Editing Canvas.
5. Using a Sequence Flow, link the new Intermediate Signal Event to the orphaned **Check In Patient** user task.
6. Using a Sequence Flow, link the **Check In Patient** user task to the new Terminate End Event we added in *step 4*.
7. The final structure for version 3 of the Emergency Bed Request process is as follows:

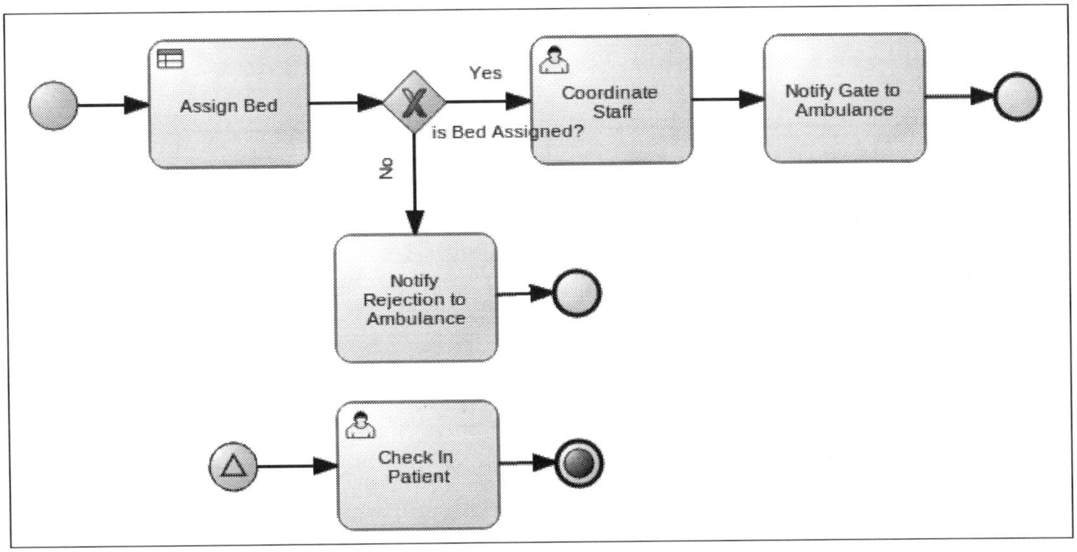

Configuring process properties

Just as we did for the second version, we need to change the ID of the process to avoid naming collisions. The value we are going to set for this property is `hospitalEmergencyV3`.

Configuring Intermediate Signal events

Intermediate Signal Event nodes have to wait for an event to arrive in order to continue their execution. Events can be broadcast from another process or from the Java application.

Using this type of Start node allows us to create more maintainable and robust processes. The properties we can configure in an Intermediate Signal Event are as follows:

Property	Description
`DataOutput`	Just like `DataOutputSet` in task elements, this property is used to specify the output variables of this node. In jBPM5, the only output variable you can define is 'event'. This variable will contain the event object.
`DataOutputAssociation`	In the same way we have Assignments in tasks elements, we have the `DataOutputAssociation` property here, to map the output variable of this event to a process variable.
`SignalRef`	This event type is what the Start node is waiting for. It is just a String that must be used when you want to signal the event.

In our scenario, the event we are going to be waiting for is the Ambulance Arrived event, which is why we need to change the `SignalRef` property to `Ambulance Arrived`. In this case, we don't want to know anything else from the event. All of the information we need to create the Check In Patient user task is already present in our process, so we are not going to define any `DataOutput` or `DataOutputAssociation` in this node. The last change that we are going to make to this node is to add a meaningful name to it, so that users reviewing this process can easily understand what event the node is waiting for. The value we are going to set for the **Name** property is: `Ambulance Arrived`.

Configuring the Terminate End events

The addition of a new execution path in our process has introduced a little problem that requires our attention. The new path expresses the following situation: "When the ambulance arrives at the hospital, the patient has to be checked in". This situation is modeled in the first two nodes of the path—Intermediate Signal Event and user task. Once the user task is completed, the process execution will be completed. We are using a Terminate End Node to explicitly tell the jBPM engine to finish the process instance when this path is completed.

The problem arose when we introduced the failing path in Version 2. In the current state of the process, if the Assign Bed task rejects the assignment, the process will execute Notify Rejection to Ambulance and then the process instance won't be completed. Instead, it will be waiting for the Ambulance Arrived event. This happens, because we are using a None End Event node instead of a Terminate End Node in that path. What we need to do if we want to solve this problem is simply to change the type of End Event we are using from None to Terminate, so that when the failing path is executed, the process instance will be completed.

The final version of the Emergency Bed Request V3 process will be as follows:

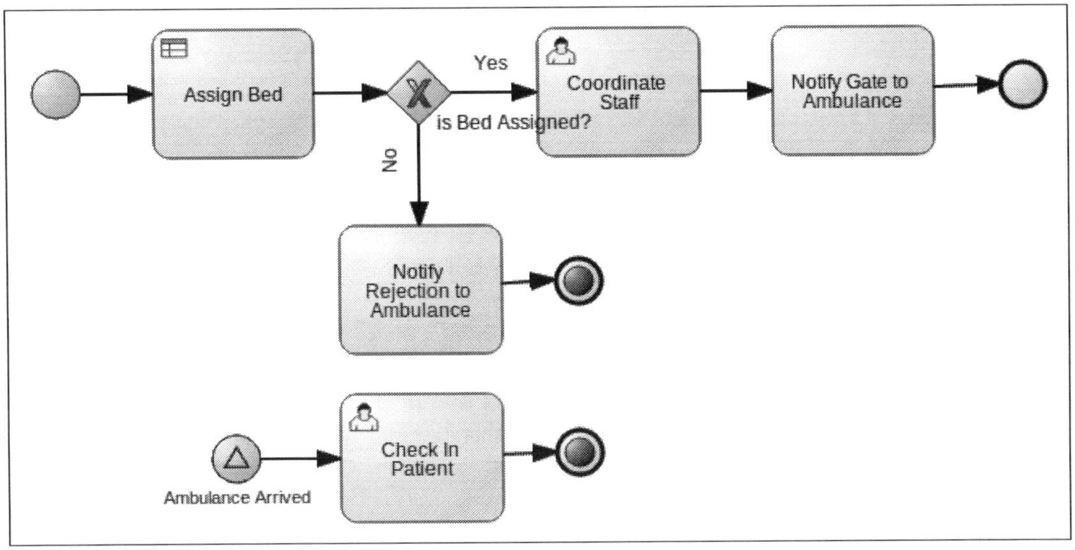

Testing the process definition

At this point, you probably suspect that we also have a test scenario for Emergency Bed Request V3, and you are right! The `jBPM5-WebDesignerExamples` project has a class called `EmergencyBedRequestV3Test.java` that tests this version of the process. You can find the process definition the test is using in the `EmergencyBedRequestV3.bpmn` file. Feel free to replace the content of this file with the definition you've created in Guvnor to see if your process has the same expected behavior.

Process modeling summary

Up to this point, we have learned how we can create and manage process definitions in Guvnor. We have also covered the steps required to design a process from scratch and improve it using some of the elements we have in the Web Process Designer's palette. Even if we have covered some of the most frequently used elements in jBPM5 support, we still need to get a better understanding of the rest of the nodes. For more information, I strongly recommend reading the jBPM5 User Guide, specially the chapter on the Web Process Designer. It can be found at the following URL: `http://www.jboss.org/jbpm/documentation`

The next section will cover some of the advanced topics in the Web Process Designer.

Web Process Designer advanced topics

Even if the functionalities already covered in this chapter are enough to create any kind of process we want, the Web Process Designer has some other features that will make life easier. These features include things like importing existing process definitions into the designer, validating our processes, creating predefined task nodes and more. Let's cover these features now to see how we can improve our productivity in the designer.

Importing process definitions

Sometimes we already have a process definition outside Guvnor that we want to modify. One example is all of the `.bpmn` files that come with the source code of this book; another example would be if someone e-mails us a process definition that he is working on. It would be nice to have a way to import those definitions into Guvnor, so that we can get a visual representation of them, and if required, save or modify them. Fortunately for us, the Web Process Designer has this feature already implemented and ready to be used. In the toolbar, there's the **Import Definition** menu that we can use if we want to import an existing process definition. The supported languages are BPMN 2.0 and JSON. The latter is the internal representation used by the Web Process Designer to maintain the definition of the process while we edit.

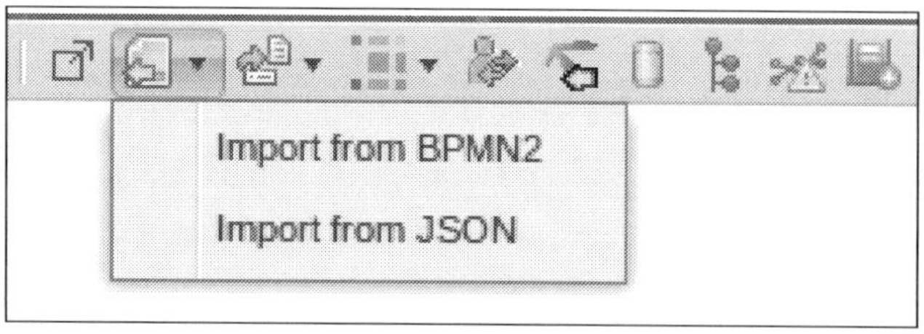

When we select one of the options in this menu, a pop-up window will open that lets us browse for the file containing the definition we want to import. We can also paste the definition of the process directly into the text area of the window.

Regardless of how we choose to import a definition, the process definition will be displayed in the Editing canvas. If an error occurs in the importing process, a generic error message will be displayed in the designer. Unfortunately, for now, the only way to get more information about the error is to check the output of the application server where Guvnor and the Web Process Designer are running.

Visual process validation

Trying to remember all of the mandatory attributes of the different elements that we can use in our processes can be tricky. Each individual element in the palette has unique properties-some that are just optional and others that must be set before a process can be executed.

If we want to make sure that we are not forgetting any of these required properties, we can run the visual validation process option from the Web Process Designer toolbar.

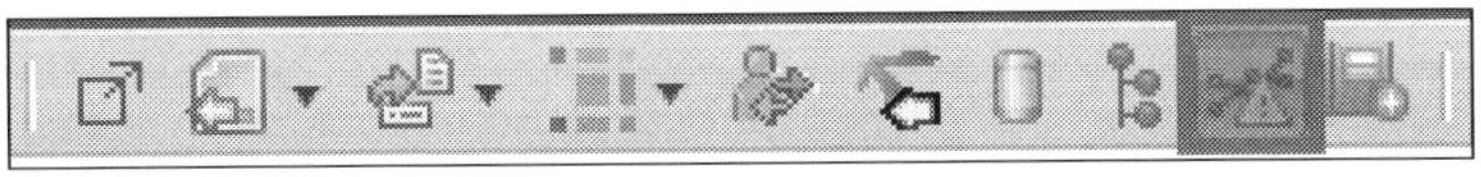

After the validation process ends, a red cross will appear next to any of the business process elements that failed the validation. Moving the mouse over the red cross will display a message for each of the validation errors found in that particular element. This feature is very useful for verifying if the business process meets all of the technical requirements required by jBPM.

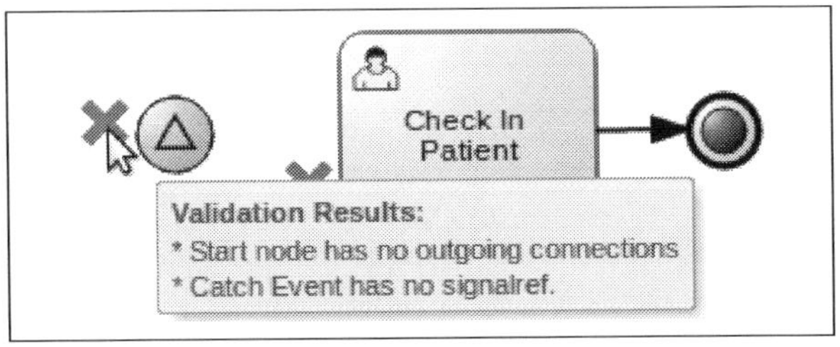

In the previous image you can see part of the Emergency Bed Request V3 process and the errors found by the visual validation process. In the case of the Intermediate Signal Event, two errors have been found — the Start event doesn't have any outgoing connections and the **SignalRef** property has not been set.

Domain-specific tasks

As we now know, the BPMN 2.0 specification defines eight different task types that we can use in our processes. We also know that jBPM5 uses abstract tasks as a way of extending the process definition functionality to fulfill our business needs (even if we are not aware of the specifics yet). But there is one thing that makes this extension mechanism inconvenient—most of the time abstract tasks are too generic. Every time we want to use an abstract task, we have to define its input variables, output variables, the **Name** property, and the **Task Name** property. If we want to reuse that task in another process (or even in the same process), we have to define all of these properties again.

Let's take an example of the Notify Gate to Ambulance task that we are using in Version 2 and 3 of the Emergency Bed Request process. This task has one input variable (`checkinresults_gate`) and one output variable (`checkinresults_notified`). We'll want to notify the ambulance of a specific gate, which means that we'll need to reuse this task in another process definition. To do that, we will need to drag-and-drop an Abstract Task from the palette, create the input variable in its `DataInputSet` property, define the output variable in its `DataOutputSet` property, and then set **Notify Gate to Ambulance** as the task's **Name** and **Task Name** properties. Once the task is configured, we can define the Assignments between the input and output variables of the task, as well as between the process variables. Out of all these steps, only the last one will vary between an instance of this task in one process and another. The assignment between task variables and process variables is the only specific step we have to do, whereas all of the others are the same for each instance we want to use Notify Gate to Ambulance. There must be a better way to reuse task definitions in our processes. And there is—**Domain-specific tasks**.

jBPM5 allows us to create a definition of a task and then reuse it in our processes without having to redefine it every time we want to use it. The definition of this task is created in Guvnor, outside of the Web Process Designer. For example, if we want to create our Notify Gate to Ambulance task, all we have to do is go to the left-hand side panel of Guvnor, and under the **Knowledge Bases** section, select **Create New | Work Item Definition**. **Work Item** is the technical name for Domain-specific tasks.

> You will find a lot of references to the concept of Work Items in jBPM5 documentation, examples, and code. Work Items are the main concept behind *Chapter 6, Domain-specific Processes*, as we use them to create Domain-specific processes. Using Work Item definitions, we can create reusable tasks that will be independent elements in the Web Process Designer's palette.

Work Item definition editor

A complete description of this editor is outside the scope of this book. We are only going to give a brief overview of this feature. For further information, you can refer to the jBPM5 documentation.

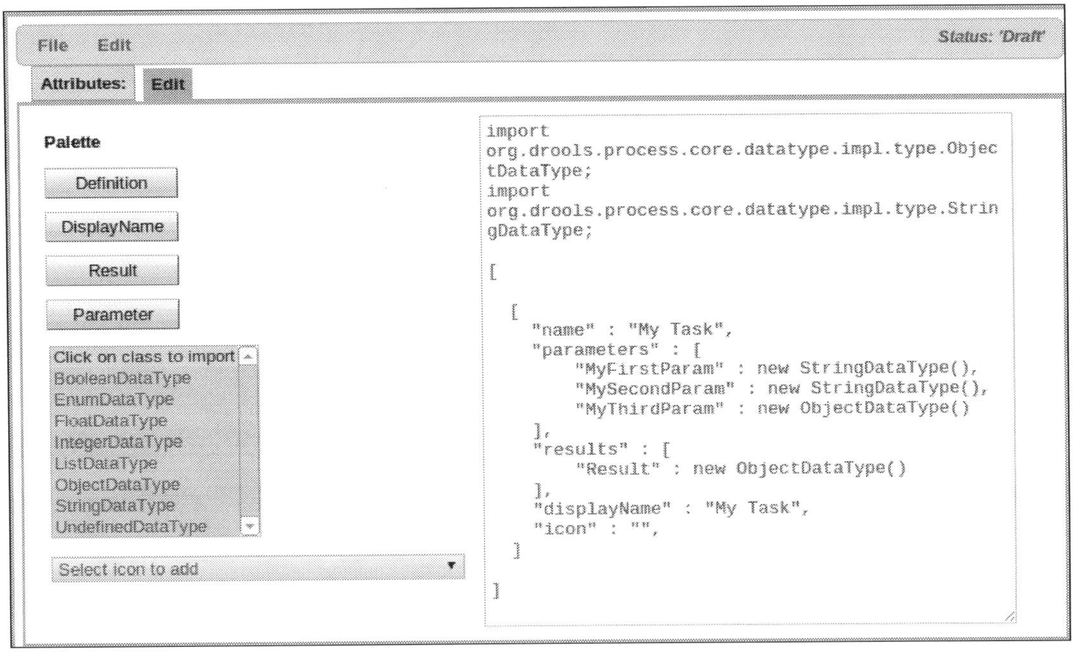

The **editor** is basically a text area where we can write the structure of a Work Item definition that we are creating. The format of this structure is similar to JSON syntax, but in reality it is Mvel syntax.

A Work Item definition is composed of the following five sections:

- **Name**: This is the value of the **Task Name** property of the resulting Task element.
- **Parameters**: These are the input variables of the resulting task. Each of the elements in this array is going to be a variable definition in the `DataInputSet` property of the task.
- **Results**: This is the same as parameters but for output variables. Each of the elements in this array is going to be a variable declaration in the `DataOutputSet` property of the resulting task.
- **Display name**: This is the name that the resulting task is going to have in the Web Process Designer palette.

- **Icon**: This property defines the icon that the Web Process Designer is going to use for the resulting task. The icon must be specified as a URL and is going to be used both in the Web Process Designer's palette and in the task representation inside the Editing Canvas.

> The Web Process Designer still doesn't support Work Item definitions without input or output parameters. If we don't have any input or output parameters for a Domain-specific task, the whole parameters or results section must be removed from the definition.

Using Work Item Definitions in the Web Process Designer

For each Work Item definition, the Web Process Designer is going to add a new element to the Shape Repository. Only the Work Item definitions belonging to the same package (where the process we are editing is defined) are going to be used by the Process Designer.

All of the Work Item definitions are placed in a special section of the Shape Repository, which you'll find in the **Full** perspective under **Service Tasks**.

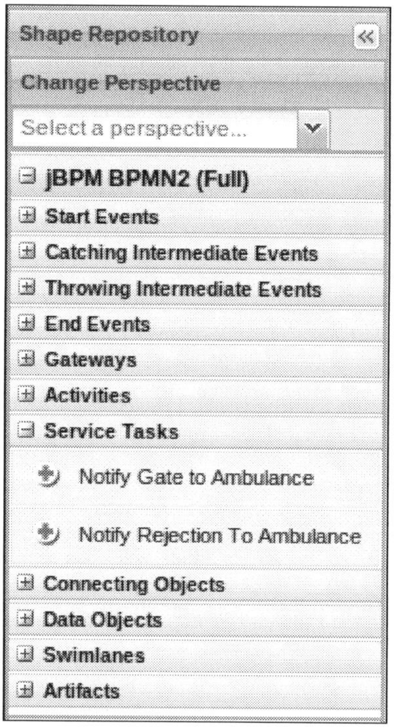

In this image we can see two domain specific tasks—Notify Gate to Ambulance and Notify Rejection To Ambulance.

> In order to see the domain-specific tasks we have created, we have two options: close the process we are designing and re-open it or simply save it. The same applies for modifications in the Work Item definitions.

In the properties of these new tasks, we can check that the `DataInputSet` and `DataOutputSet` are pre-populated with the values we have defined in the Work Item definition.

Service Repository

Instead of defining and storing our Work Item definitions in Guvnor, we can keep them in a separate place—a repository—that is shared among multiple Guvnor instances.

Simply put, a Service Repository is a web server exposing Work Item definitions through HTTP.

For common tasks such as interacting with an FTP server, sending an e-mail, invoking a REST web service, and so on, jBPM5 already provides a public Service Repository we can use. You can refer to jBPM5 documentation in order to configure the jBPM5 public Service Repository and get a detailed explanation on how to use it, as well as how to implement your own.

Web Process Designer integration with Service Repository

In the Web Process Designer, we can connect to an instance of the Service Repository in order to get the domain-specific tasks that are exposed. If we want to connect to a Service Repository, we just have to use the **Connect to a Service Repository** option, available in the Process Designer's toolbar.

When this option is selected, a pop-up window will open and ask us to connect to a Service Repository instance. After we insert a valid URL and click on the **Connect** button, the Web Process Designer will retrieve all of the definitions present in that service and display them in a table, as shown next:

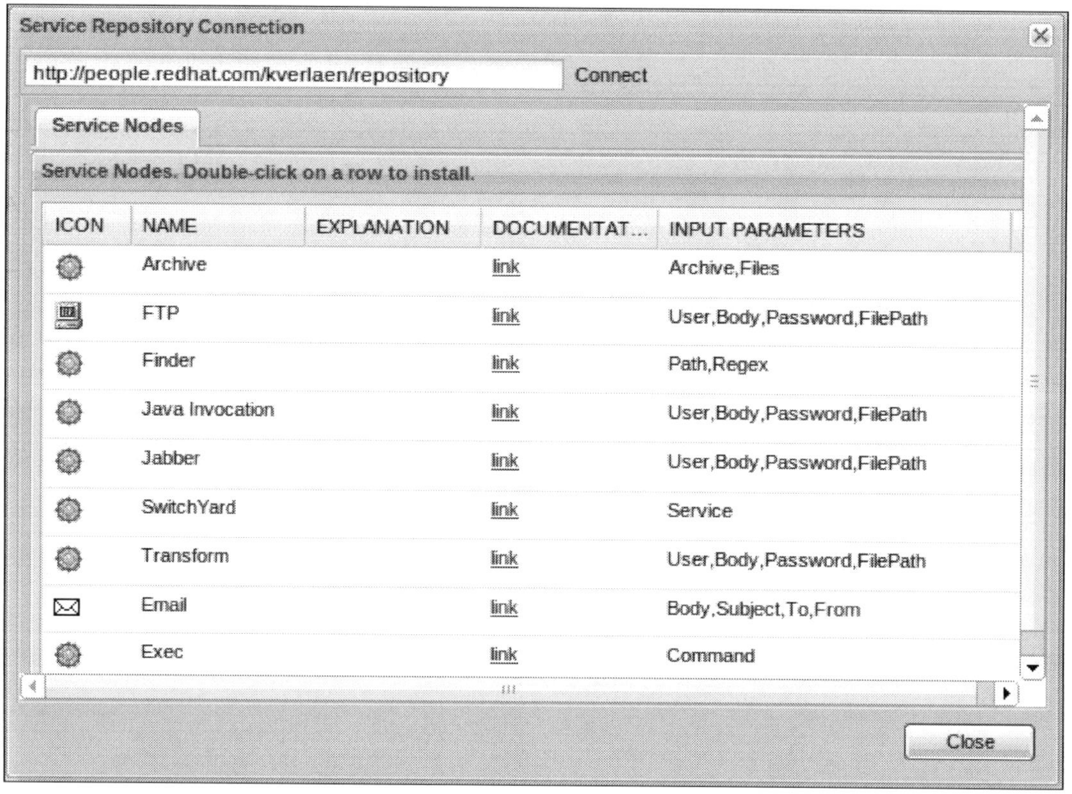

Domain-specific tasks can be installed into the Web Process Designer by double-clicking on them. After we have installed all of the necessary definitions, we have to close and re-open the Process Designer (or just save the current process) so that we can see the new elements in the Shape Repository.

Summary

In this chapter, we covered the main characteristics and features of the Web Process Designer. We learned how to create and manipulate process definitions in Guvnor and how to design our business processes using the Web Process Designer.

Using one of the processes introduced in *Chapter 3, Using BPMN 2.0 to Model Business Scenarios*, as a guideline, we have reviewed the different BPMN 2.0 elements and properties that we might use if we want to create an executable version of that process in jBPM5. While designing the process, we learned about some of the most frequently used BPMN 2.0 elements, as well as the properties required by the jBPM5 engine for execution.

This chapter introduced some executable examples that we can use to test not only the processes introduced by this chapter but also any other process we might create using the Process Editor.

Now we should be familiar not only with the Web Process Designer's UI but also with the underlying BPMN 2.0 code it generates. Let's move to some of the most advanced topics of jBPM5, such as domain-specific processes, human tasks, and transaction management.

6
Domain-specific Processes

Having a generic specification such as BPMN 2.0 and a generic engine such as jBPM5 is great. The amount of flexibility that this mix provides lets us express tons of different business situations. This flexibility is awesome, but we need to know how to handle it for our own benefit.

Most of the time we need to design business processes that reflect how a company solves different tasks to achieve a business goal. There is no generic way to describe specific business situations and the specific behavior of each of the activities within the context of that situation.

The BPMN 2.0 specification not only describes each word of the language used to model processes, it also describes how the processes will behave at runtime. But the description that we find in the specification is broad and generic. Unless we have very simple scenarios to model, we will need to define our own domain-specific behavior for each activity that cannot be considered generic.

Like every BPM system that implements the BPMN 2.0 specification, jBPM5 provides a mechanism for plugin extensions and custom behavior.

In this chapter we will cover:

- How to define domain-specific connectors?
- How to use these connectors in our applications?
- How to deal with synchronous and asynchronous interactions?

We will also see how we can centralize and re-use these extensions across different business processes to speed up the development and modeling phase. In order to understand how jBPM5 allows us to plugin our domain-specific connectors, we need to understand how the BPMN 2.0 specification and our BPMN models will expose this custom behavior.

BPMN 2.0 task

In *Chapter 3, Using BPMN 2.0 to Model Business Scenarios*, we covered the two most frequently used task subtypes: User Tasks and Service Tasks. Both represent interactions that happen outside the context of the process, one for human interactions and the other for system interactions. *Chapter 7, Human Interactions*, will deal with human interactions, and here we will analyze systems and services interactions.

The Service Task activity defined in the BPMN 2.0 specification represents any interaction with external services. We interpret external service as anything external to the process' scope.

Some things that can be considered external services are:

- Web service: An external or internal service to the company that exposes a piece of functionality in a remote procedure call fashion
- Third party system interaction: If we want to interact with any system that is hosted on a different machine, we will need to have a way to send and receive information between the process and the external system
- A machine that you want to control
- A sensor that receives information that the process wants to use

Again, note that all these interactions will happen outside of the scope of the process. The process engine will be in charge of the coordination of these different interactions. We will see that the process is in charge of defining which pieces of information are required by each interaction; it does this by scoping and gathering the information before the interaction takes place. After the interaction happens, the engine is in charge of taking the results and making them available to the process' scope. The information that is being copied into the process' scope can be used later by different activities.

In order to achieve a successful system interaction, we need to understand the behavior of the external system as well as the technical requirements. Evaluating the information that is required by the interaction is very important in defining the input and output mappings. Understanding the external system behavior will also allow us to choose the most appropriate mechanisms to achieve the interactions. From the modeling perspective, having domain-specific activities will help us improve communication between different teams that don't need to know the underlying technical mechanisms required for the interactions.

In the following section, we will see the mechanisms provided by jBPM5 to plugin domain-specific behavior.

Domain-specific behavior in jBPM5

We already know all the advantages that come with defining our domain-specific activities, from both the process-modeling and the technical perspectives. Now we need to understand how these concepts and advantages are mapped to the jBPM5 internals. Inside jBPM5, an internal concept is defined to handle external interactions. The work item concept is used as the extension point to provide the engine a custom block that represents custom behavior to execute an external interaction. A work item inside jBPM5 can be defined as "any piece of work that needs to be done by an external entity".

Notice that this definition uses the external-entity concept, in contrast to the external service that the BPMN 2.0 specification defines. The work item concept covers external interactions with systems as well as with humans. Both interactions are considered external interactions from the process' perspective. We will discuss in depth how jBPM5 implements the mechanism to handle human/user interactions using the work item concept in *Chapter 7, Human Interactions*.

In jBPM5, we can say that each task we define in our processes will reference a work item (except Rule Tasks). Each of our different service interactions will be classified into different types of services. For each type of service that we have, we will need to have at least one implementation of a work item handler that will represent the service connector in charge of the external interaction.

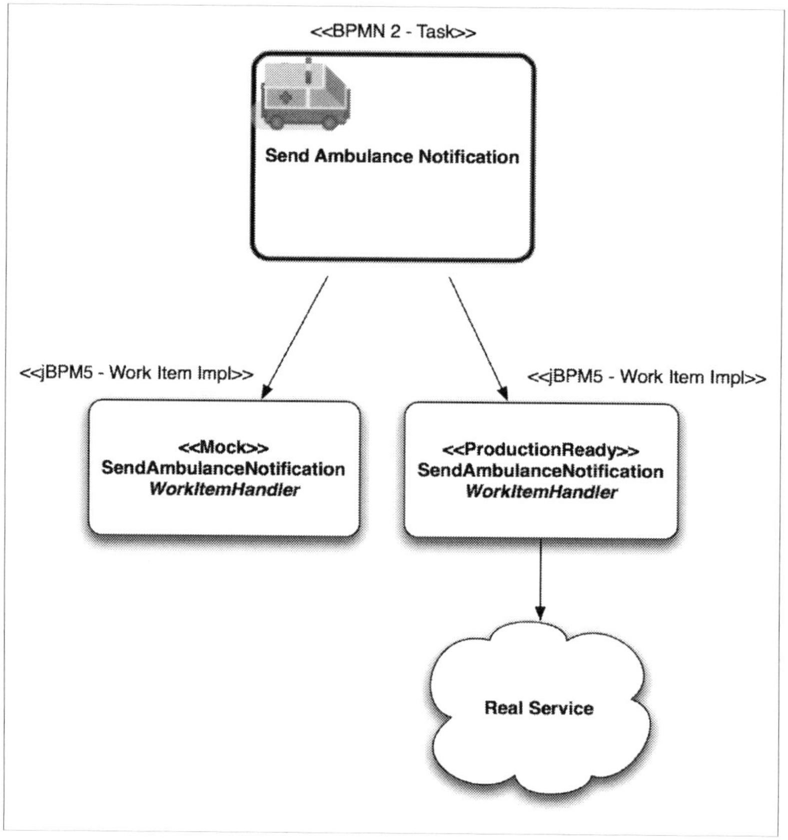

The previous figure shows the relationship between the concepts defined by the BPMN 2.0 standard specification and the internal concepts defined inside the jBPM5 implementation. At runtime we will need to bind our process definitions to a set of work item handler implementations that could be chosen based on the environment where our process will run.

Notice the use of <<BPMN 2.0 Task>> instead of <<BPMN 2.0 Service Task>> in the previous figure. A distinction needs to be made in order to differentiate a generic Service Task, which can be handled as a simple method call, or a domain-specific activity, which can be much more specific to the domain. In jBPM5, if we need to call a Java method or a web-service method, we will use the Service Task (`<serviceTask/>`) tag defined by the specification. But if we want to use our custom domain-specific behavior, the task (`<task/>`) tag will be used instead.

No matter which tag we decide to use, we need to make sure that we have the set of work item handlers that will be needed for the process to run. The process engine will fail at runtime if an unbounded work item handler is found. This allows us to dynamically plugin different implementations if we want to, but at the same time we need to be careful to make at least one implementation available.

Before jumping to the examples, we need to know a little bit more about the APIs that jBPM5 exposes for defining and binding our custom work item definitions.

The work item handler interface

Each time we want to define an interaction with an external entity, we need to implement the work item handler interface. Then we can re-use the implementation in multiple tasks and multiple processes, if we require the same behavior in a different situation. If we create parameterizable implementations, we can improve the reutilization of our code.

The work item handler interface located inside the package `org.drools.runtime.process` defines the following method's signatures:

```
public void executeWorkItem(WorkItem workItem,
                            WorkItemManager manager);
public void abortWorkItem(WorkItem workItem,
                            WorkItemManager manager);
```

In order to create our service connector, we will need to implement this work item handler interface. The `executeWorkItem()` method will be in charge of containing the logic needed to contact the external service. The `abortWorkItem()` method will be in charge of cancelling the external interaction.

Once we have a custom implementation of our work item handler, we need to bind it to our session runtime. For this binding, we will access the work item manager from the session and then we will register our implementation associated with a task name:

```
ksession.getWorkItemManager()
                 .registerWorkItemHandler(
                               "Notification System",
                               myHandlerInstance);
```

This will make the notification system handler available to all our processes in the current session.

```
<task id="_1" tns:taskName="Notification System"
               name="Notify Gate to Ambulance">
```

Notice that the `tns:taskName` attribute set inside the `task` tag (where `tns` is the namespace `xmlns:tns=http://www.jboss.org/drools`) is the one that defines the custom domain-specific behavior name that needs to be registered into the session.

When we use a `serviceTask` tag, there is no need to specify the `taskName` attribute inside the BPMN 2.0 XML definition:

```
<serviceTask id="_1" name="Notify Gate to Ambulance">
```

In such cases, in order to register a work item handler to the session, we will use the reserved string: `Service Task`.

```
ksession.getWorkItemManager()
                 .registerWorkItemHandler(
                               "Service Task",
                               new ServiceTaskHandler());
```

For Service Tasks, there is a predefined work item handler that we can use, called `ServiceTaskHandler`. You can find an example on how to use this handler to call web services or simple POJO beans inside this chapter's source code, in a test called `ServiceTaskTest`, which can be found inside the project `jBPM5-Executor-AsyncWorkItems`.

> Registering work item handlers in the knowledge session is a step that is needed before running those of our processes that use them. If we use persistence mechanisms or if we recreate our session, we need to re-register them. In other words, work item handler bindings are volatile and the binding information is not persisted anywhere.

Another important aspect of work item handlers is the fact that each implementation decides if it will interact with an external entity in a synchronous or asynchronous fashion. The following section covers the mechanisms that we have to define the nature of each interaction.

Synchronous interactions

Different systems have different methods and requirements for interaction. That's why we need to know all the mechanisms provided by the engine to achieve each type of interaction. We will need to evaluate each interaction and decide if we can do it in a synchronous way or in an asynchronous way. Usually, synchronous interactions are considered to be the simplest and most intuitive way to interact; but we need to understand how and when asynchronous interactions become handy.

In order to define the nature of the interaction, we will use the work item manager to decide if an interaction ends when the `executeWorkItem()` method finishes or if we need to wait for an external stimulus to consider the interaction complete.

The work item manager, the same one that we use to register work item handlers to our knowledge session, is used to notify the engine of the completion of one particular instance of the work item. The work item manager interface located in the same package (`org.drools.runtime.process`) exposes the following methods:

```
public interface WorkItemManager {
    public void completeWorkItem(long l,
                                 Map<String, Object> map);
    public void abortWorkItem(long l);
    public void registerWorkItemHandler(String string,
                                        WorkItemHandler wih);
}
```

We can access the work item manager from the knowledge session or from inside the work item handler implementation, where we receive the work item manager reference as an argument of the `executeWorkItem()` and `abortWorkItem()` methods.

Synchronous interactions simply call the `completeWorkItem (long workItemId, Map results)` method at the end of the `executeWorkItem()` method. When we are done executing the external interaction, a notification will be sent to the engine to continue the process execution. The following code snippet shows what a synchronous work item handler implementation looks like:

```
public void executeWorkItem(WorkItem workItem,
                            WorkItemManager manager) {
  System.out.println(">>>> Executing External Interaction …");
```

```
        <<Your Logic Goes Here>>
    System.out.println(">>>> Completing External Interaction");
    manager.completeWorkItem(workItem.getId(), null);
  }
```

As soon as our logic ends, we use the `manager` reference to notify the engine that the interaction has been completed and that we are ready to continue. The logic that we add here can be anything. We are able to write Java code to interact with a web service, to query information from a database using JDBC or JPA, to send an SMS message, to send a Twitter message, and so on. The only consideration that we must understand is the fact that as soon as the code gets executed, the engine will continue with the next task in the chain. In other words, if we call the `completeWorkItem()` method, the engine will consider this logic ended and it will not wait for any other external stimulus to continue.

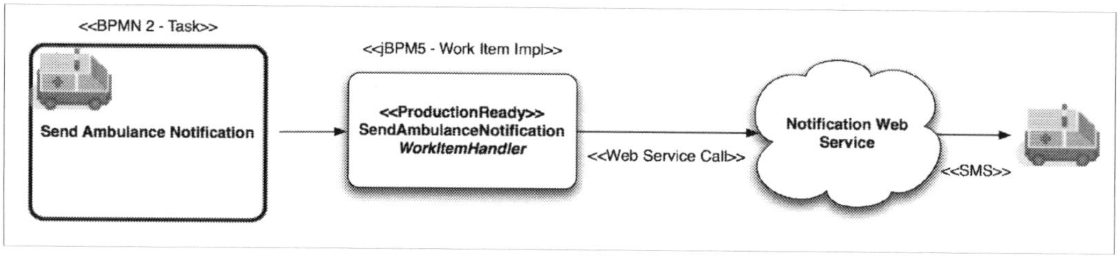

In this example, the `SendAmbulanceNotificationWorkItemHandler` implementation will make a web service call to contact the Notification Web Service item. Because this web service provides a synchronous behavior, the call inside our work item handler implementation will be blocked until the web service invocation has finished. When the invocation is finished, we will be able to retrieve the results and complete our work item by calling the `completeWorkItem()` method.

If we analyze this behavior from the process engine's perspective, we can see that we will be blocking the execution thread until the automatic and synchronous activities end.

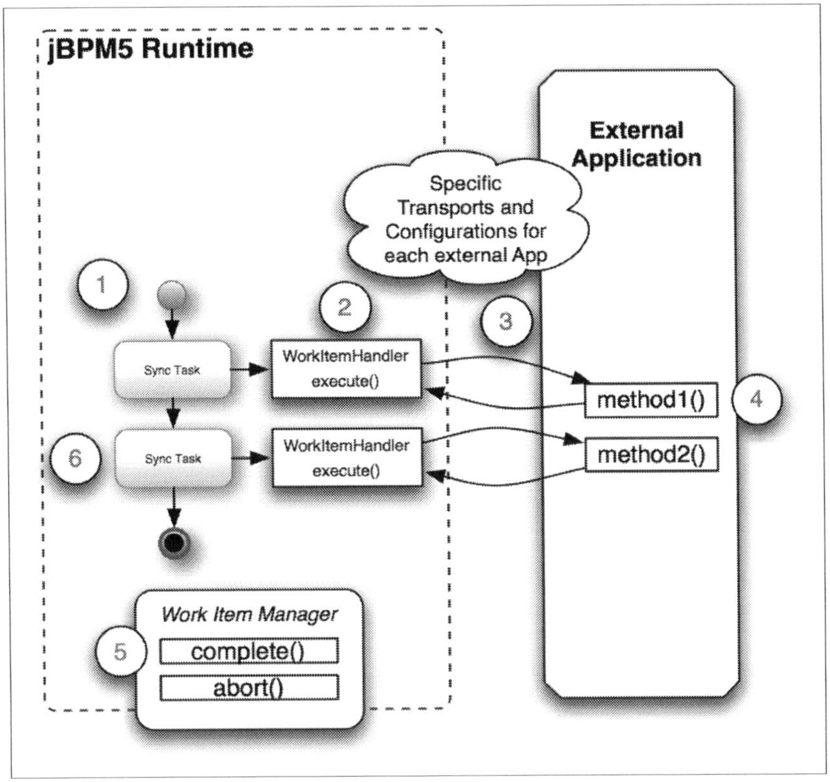

The previous figure shows the complete path of interactions and how they happen inside the engine. The first step from the engine's perspective (1) is when we start a new process instance. In order to start a new process instance, we use the process-engine APIs—more specifically, the `startProcess()` method or one of its variants. As soon as we start the process, the start event will be executed, leading us to the first Sync Task that needs to be executed. This task will contact a previously bonded work item handler (by using the `registerWorkItemHandler()` method from the work item manager) and call the `executeWorkItem()` method (2). The logic inside the work item handler will be in charge of calling `method1()` inside the external application (3).

To do that, we usually need to provide specific configurations and make sure that the external application is available. Executing the `method1()` logic is the responsibility of the external application. This application will work as if other clients are interacting with that method; that's why it will take its time to answer the request. How the application handles the request is up to the application, and there is nothing that we can do about it. If we know how the application reacts in some situations (for example, timeouts), we can take the appropriate precautions inside our work item handler logic. After the execution of `method1()` is over (4) and we get a result inside our work item handler code, we first process those results, decide exactly which part of them we are going to use, and then we call the method `completeWorkItem()` from the work item manager (5) to continue the execution to the next Sync Task (6). The same steps will be executed for the new sync Service Task. We will see that steps (3), (4), and (5) will be executed to invoke `method2()` and the end-event node will be reached, terminating the process instance. We need to understand that until this point (where the process ends in this example), our application—the one that calls the `startProcess()` method—will be blocked. We need to understand this fact in order to analyze if we will be able to afford this kind of interaction. There are some scenarios where we cannot be blocking the application thread until all the synchronous interactions end. Imagine a process that contains more than 10 of these sync interactions; our application would be blocked until all the work is done. Imagine if just one of those sync interactions was a batch process that took 10 hours to be completed. For these kinds of scenarios, we need to understand how asynchronous interactions work from the process' perspective.

Asynchronous interactions

As introduced in the previous section, we need to understand how asynchronous interactions work in order to not block our application when the external interactions require long periods of time. Asynchronous interactions provide a more realistic way of interacting with external systems when we are looking for robustness. In the real world, most of the time we cannot trust in plain synchronous interactions. If we called a web service and for some reason the web service was not available, we would need to implement retry mechanisms, acknowledge mechanisms, persistence mechanisms to deal with faults, and so on. Most of these mechanisms are already implemented in asynchronous messaging frameworks that we can leverage. Before going into more technical details, let's analyze how the interactions will work for these kinds of scenarios.

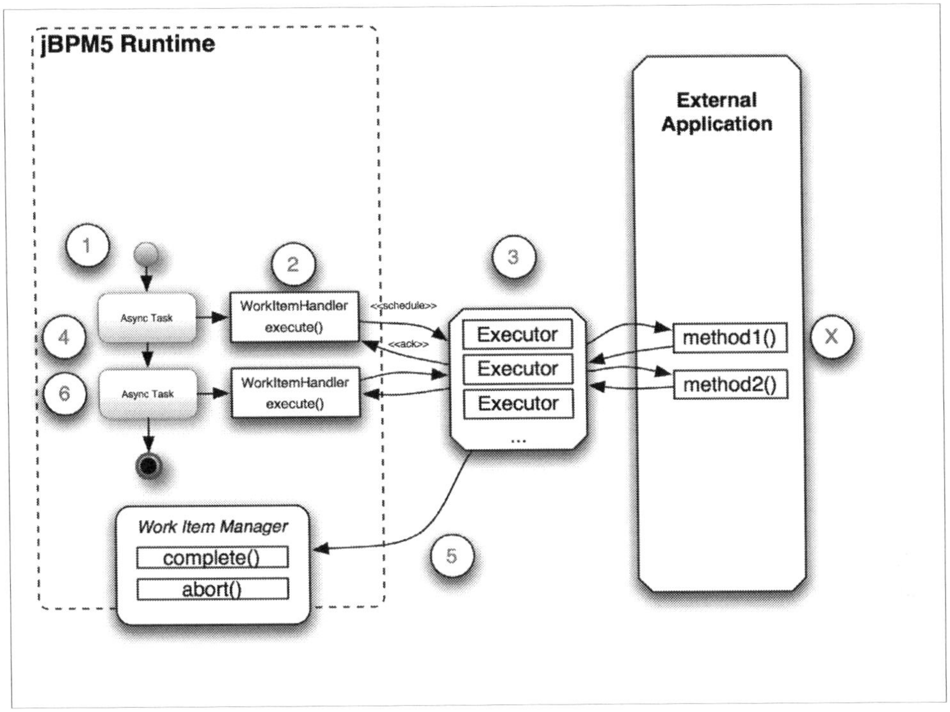

As we can see, a new external component appears in the middle of the process engine and the External Application. This new component is in charge of receiving requests to interact with the external application. It has a set of available executors that will pickup the requests sent by the process engine (or any other app that wants to schedule an asynchronous execution) and executes the real interactions with our external applications. Once the execution is done, this component will be in charge of notifying the requester that the execution was successfully completed.

Let's see how this component works in contrast to the sync interactions introduced previously.

Once again, our application calls the `startProcess()` method (1) in order to start a new process instance. The start event propagates the execution to the first task. The asynchronous work item handler associated with this task is located and the `executeWorkItem()` method (2) is invoked. Now, instead of calling the external service inside our `executeWorkItem()` method, we will schedule a new execution in our intermediary component.

Now, as you can see in (3), the work item handler will contact this component to schedule a remote execution, and then the component will return with an acknowledgement that the request was received. With the acknowledgement received, we are now in step (4) and the control returns to the application that has called the `startProcess()` method. At some point (X), the executor component will execute our request and the interaction with the remote service will happen. Once the interaction is over, the executor component will need to notify the requester (in this case, the jBPM5 process engine) of the request completion (5). This notification will include contacting the work item manager and executing the `completeWorkItem()` method for the corresponding work item identifier (`workItemId`). As soon as the `completeWorkItem()` method is executed, the process instance is notified and the process can continue to the next asynchronous activity. For the next Sync Task, we will see the same behavior, meaning that the application will gain control once again when the work item handler schedules the request.

From the application's perspective, we call the `startProcess()` method and get control to continue working on other tasks. Now the execution will be the responsibility of the executor component. Let's analyze this component in more detail.

Executor component

There are several ways of implementing and designing a component like this. In this book I've decided to include a simple implementation that is not included in the jBPM code base yet. This simple implementation, based on CDI/WELD (`http://jcp.org/en/jsr/detail?id=299` and `http://seamframework.org/Weld`), provides most of the features described in the following sections without tying the whole application to a specific environment. The provided implementation can be adapted to work in EE environments as well, but that's not the focus of this section. This section describes some of the common requirements for this component.

Generally speaking, this component needs to be able to receive requests to schedule asynchronous tasks' executions. In some way, this component will be exposed as a service. It will need to be available to the requester; it could be a client or a direct (in JVM) reference. Once this component receives and acknowledges the request, it needs to have a way to pickup a request (from a request inbox or list) and execute it. Usually, this mechanism contains retry mechanisms as well as an exception-handling mechanism that allows us to recover the execution if something fails with the external application (for example, if it's not available at a particular point in time). This component must have a way of contacting the requester to notify it when the execution is complete. To do this, the component usually stores a business key that allows us to make the notification successfully.

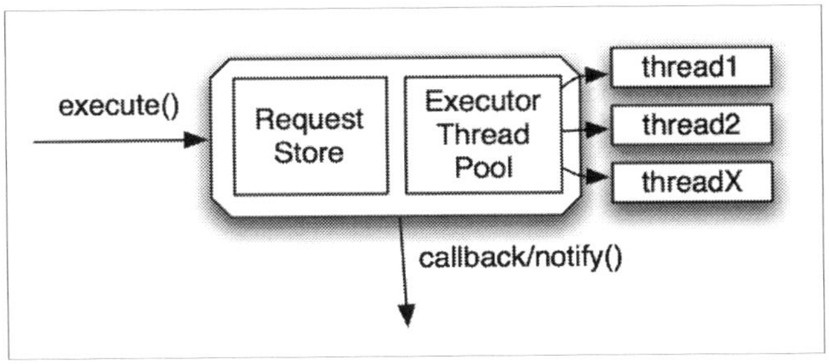

This executor service will use the command pattern (`http://en.wikipedia.org/wiki/Command_pattern`) in order to schedule remote executions. These commands will contain the logic that needs to be executed, allowing us to create new commands if we have special requirements.

The `Executor` service interface exposes two methods:

```
public interface Executor extends Service{
    public String scheduleRequest(String commandName,
                                  CommandContext ctx);
    public void cancelRequest(String requestId);
}
```

The schedule method will receive the name of the command that we want to schedule and a `CommandContext` parameter containing among other things the business key that we can use to make reference to this particular execution, which will be used to gather all the information required to execute the request.

In order to use this service we will need to configure it accordingly, based on our business requirements. For some scenarios we need a very reactive `Executor` service, which executes the requests as soon as they are scheduled. Other situations that require large-batch executions can be scheduled to be executed twice a day.

The `Executor` service will be running as a separate component of our application and it will need to be initialized before any other component tries to schedule new requests to be executed.

The project called `jBPM5-Executor-Service` inside the `chapter_06` directory contains a very simple implementation of this service. The following section covers this implementation to show the features that must be provided by the component. Depending on your business requirements, you will need to validate if this component is sufficient for your use case or if you will need a more robust solution.

Executor service implementation

Inside the project called `jBPM5-Executor-Service`, you will find the internal implementation of the Executor component. This particular implementation uses a database to store and query the pending requests. Once a request is found in the database, a thread from a thread pool is requested to execute the scheduled command.

In order to use this component, we will need to either include this project as a dependency to our application or start it up in a separate JVM as a standalone component.

This implementation requires you to set up only three parameters:

- The `interval` parameter defines the total idle time between each cycle of this component. In other words, we will tolerate a maximum of 5 seconds delay between one execution and another. By default, this parameter is `3` seconds.
- The `threadPoolSize` parameter defines how many threads we will use to monitor the pending requests. By default, this parameter is `1`.
- The `retries` parameter allows you to define how many times a request needs to be retried in case of failure. By default, this parameter is `3`.

Besides configuring these parameters for each `Executor` instance, we need to make sure to have a `persistence.xml` file with the database configuration. An example is provided inside the `jBPM5-Executor-Service` project (`src/test/resources/META-INF/persistence.xml`).

If we are inside a CDI application, in order to get a reference to the Executor component, we can execute the following code:

```
@Inject
private ExecutorServiceEntryPoint executor;
```

The `ExecutorServiceEntryPoint` interface gives us unified access to all of the `Executor` internal services. You can find a CDI example using Arquillian (`http://www.jboss.org/arquillian.html`) in the test classes called `ArquillianCDISimpleExecutorTest` and `BasicExecutorBaseTest`.

If we are not in a CDI environment, we can use the `ExecutorServiceModule` helper to get hold of the reference.

```
ExecutorServiceEntryPoint executor =
                            ExecutorModule.getInstance()
                               .getExecutorServiceEntryPoint();
```

You can find an example for non-CDI environments in a test class called `NoCDIExecutorTest`.

When we get the component reference, we will be able to change the default configuration by setting the previously mentioned parameters. If we don't want to change the default configuration, we can just start the component using the `init()` method.

```
executor.setThreadPoolSize(1);
executor.setInterval(3);
executor.setRetries(3)
executor.init();
```

Once the component is initialized, for this example, we will see in the logs that a query to the database will be executed every three seconds. This query is looking for pending requests to be executed. As soon as this query finds one pending request, it will pick up that request and execute it using a thread pool. Obviously, nothing will happen until we schedule a request to execute something.

In order to do so, we will use the `scheduleRequest()` method:

```
CommandContext commandContext = new CommandContext();
commandContext.setData("businessKey",
                       UUID.randomUUID().toString());
executor.scheduleRequest("PrintOutCmd", commandContext);
```

Notice that we are using the `PrintOutCmd` value to reference a command name. If you take a look at the class called `PrintOutCommand`, you will see that a CDI annotation is being used to specify the bean name.

```
@Named(value="PrintOutCmd")
public class PrintOutCommand implements Command{

  public ExecutionResults execute(CommandContext ctx) {
    System.out.println(">>> Hi This is the first command!");
    ExecutionResults executionResults = new ExecutionResults();
    return executionResults;
  }
}
```

The `Executor` component will scan the application classpath looking for each command that we send, trying to find a CDI bean annotated with `@Named` corresponding with the command that we want to execute.

The test `simpleExcecutionTest()` inside the `BasicExecutorBaseTest` class shows the usage of this method. As you can see, the `scheduleRequest()` method receives two parameters that describe the request and its context. The first parameter is the command that we want to execute, in this case `PrintOutCmd`. This command will just print out a hello message to the console.

The second parameter represents the command context that enriches the environment where the command will run. Inside this context, which is basically a map of parameters, we need to provide a business key value that will be used by the command and by the callback handlers to gain access to the context required during and after the command execution.

Because we are now delegating the execution of our interaction to a different component, the business key value will allow the Executor component to have a reference to the requester. Using this reference, we will be able to build a context to execute the command or contact the requester as soon as the command execution finishes.

For the command execution, we can add inside the `CommandContext` object the parameters that are required for the interaction. For example, if the command will execute an interaction against a web service, the arguments for the web service call can be included inside the context. The command will then need to contain the logic to get the parameters from the `CommandContext` map and make the web service call.

But now what happens if you want to do something with the web service execution's results? For that kind of situation, when we need to obtain some results, we can attach a set of callbacks to the command execution. These callbacks will be in charge of contacting the application notifying it that the execution finished correctly or directly execute some extra steps required after the command execution.

These callbacks can work in several ways, but here I will show you two of the most common techniques:

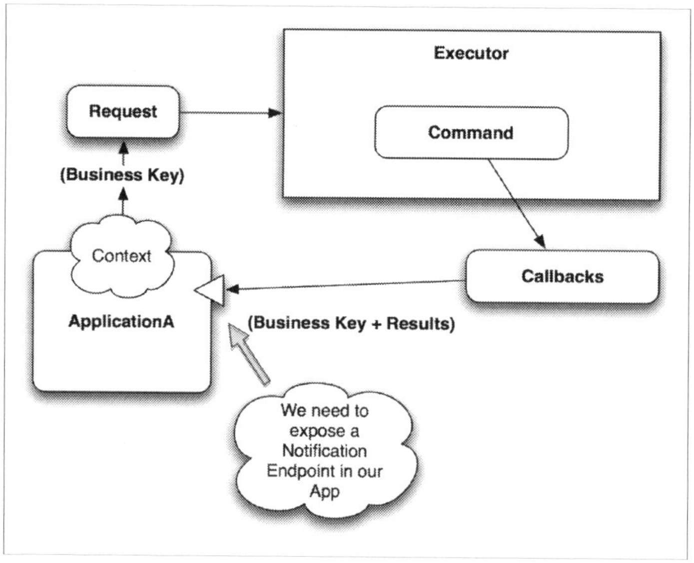

The first option is to expose in our application an endpoint that is in charge of receiving the notifications of the task completions. Usually, these endpoints will take the Business Key that identifies the request and the information that results from the execution. This option assumes that you can add that endpoint and that the application will know how to handle these notifications in an appropriate way. Sometimes, when you don't have these kind of endpoints exposed you will not be able to change the application. In such cases you can consider the following option:

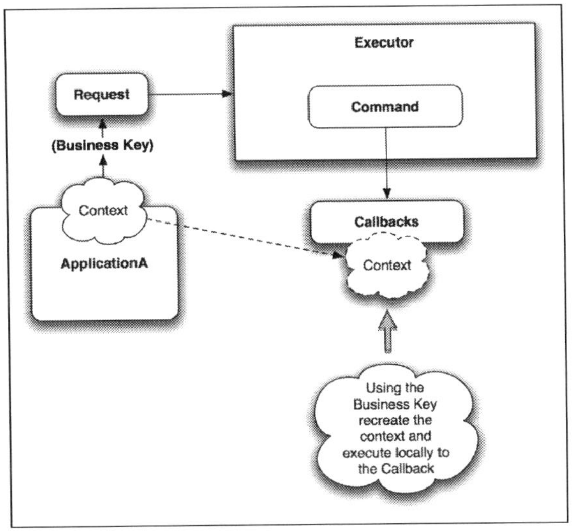

In this second option, we use the Business Key to recreate the execution context needed to continue the execution that was started by the application. This option is based on the assumption that our original application is not only delegating the execution of the request to the Executor component, it is also delegating the execution of the next steps. This option really makes sense if the application that is delegating the execution of the requested job can be continued by the executor thread and there is no real requirement to go back to the requester in order to continue. We will see how this option is applied to delegate the execution of different bits of our business processes.

In order to set up callbacks to our requests, we need to create a list with all the callbacks that will be called after the command execution ends. Take a look at the test called `executorSimpleTestWithCallback()` inside the `BasicExecutorBaseTest` class, which defines a callback to increment a global value:

```
CommandContext commandContext = new CommandContext();
commandContext.setData("businessKey",
                       UUID.randomUUID().toString());
```

```
cachedEntities.put((String)commandContext
        .getData("businessKey"), new AtomicLong(1));

List<String> callbacks = new ArrayList<String>();
             callbacks.add("SimpleIncrementCallback");

commandContext.setData("callbacks", callbacks);

executor.scheduleRequest(
      PrintOutCommand.class.getCanonicalName(),
      commandContext);
```

Notice that we are setting, inside `commandContext`, a special value called `callbacks` with a list containing all the names of the callbacks that need to be invoked after completing the command execution. For this simple implementation, these callbacks will be executed one after the other in the same thread that executes the command in the first place.

Notice also that we are using a static final map called `cachedEntities`, which allows sharing data between the Executor component and our application. This is just for demonstration purposes and is obviously not recommended for real-life implementations.

The callback class, in this case `SimpleIncrementCallback`, looks like this:

```
@Named(value = "SimpleIncrementCallback")
public class SimpleIncrementCallback implements
                                            CommandCallback{

 public void onCommandDone(CommandContext ctx,
                           ExecutionResults results) {
  BasicExecutorBaseTest.cachedEntities
                          .get(businessKey))
                           .incrementAndGet();
 }
}
```

All the callback handlers will need to implement the `CommandCallback` interface, which forces us to implement the `onCommandDone()` method, which propagates the command-execution results, and `CommandContext`, which was originally used to execute the command. The previous example shows how, by using the business key that was propagated to the command execution and to the callback execution, we can locate an object that was stored initially by the application, changing it inside the callback calls. For resolving the name of `CommandCallbacks`, we use the same technique as in the commands with the `@Named` annotation.

Executor service internals

This simple implementation provides you the following out-of-the-box mechanisms:

- Asynchronous processing
- Execution delegation via commands
- Callbacks
- Error handling
- Retry mechanism
- Failover recovery

The following figure shows how the component is using the database to monitor the pending requests and retry them in case of failures:

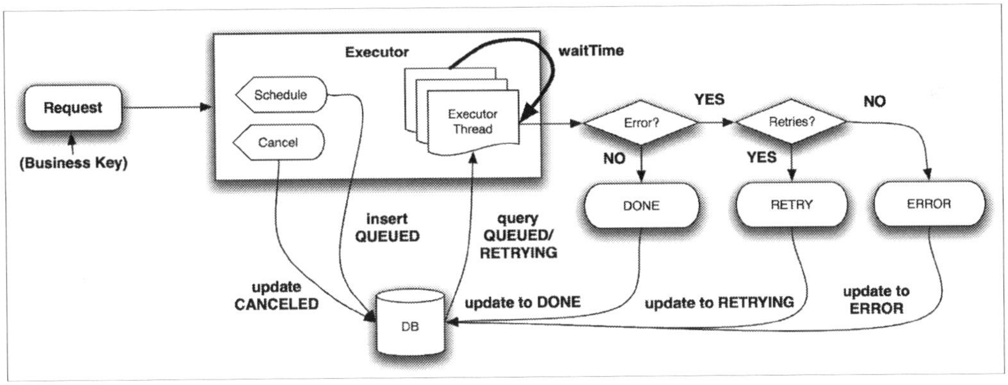

As you can see, the Executor component heavily relies on the database to keep the status of each request. All the requests will be stored in a table called `RequestInfo`, which is defined as a JPA entity. Based on the configurations, the Executor component will have a pool of threads that will be in charge of querying the database to pickup the queued and retry requests. When an executor thread picks up a Request record, it will try to execute the specified command and mark the request as running. If everything goes well, it will mark that request as DONE. If for some reason the Executor component catches an exception from the command or callback executions, the retry mechanism will kick in. For the retry options, there are two main points of configuration. The Retries property, at the Executor-component level, will be used if no other configuration is present. For each request that the execution component receives, it will tag each request with the number of retries available. There are some cases where this solution is not sufficient, and for that reason you can also specify the number of retries per request.

In order to do that you will need to add an extra property to `CommandContext`, called retries:

```
commandContext.setData("retries", 0);
```

This property will override the global configuration for this request only. In this case, the command executed using this context will not retry its execution in the case of failure.

If a command gets executed and it fails until the retry limit is reached, our request will be marked as an ERROR, and the intervention of an administrator will be required to fix the issue. A separate table is provided to log the errors, called `ErrorInfo`, which can be analyzed to understand why the requests and all the retry executions failed. Each `ErrorInfo` object has a timestamp, a stack trace for the error, and a reference to the original `RequestInfo` object that was scheduled. You can take a look at the implementation details inside the `jBPM5-Executor-Service` project provided with this chapter.

There are several improvements that can be made to that project, for example:

- A JMS-based implementation of the service
- A dead letter queue approach
- Administrator notifications when a request cannot be executed after multiple retries
- A nice administration UI to be able to solve any problems and retrigger failing executions

The following section analyzes an example where a business process uses the executor command to delegate an external interaction.

External service interactions

Now that we understand how the Executor component works, we will analyze how it could help us in the context of business processes. This section introduces a new example scenario in order to see an end-to-end process using the Executor component for its external interactions and how this can be compared with simple synchronous interactions.

The following business process represents the insurance validations that are executed for every patient that is checked-in to the hospital:

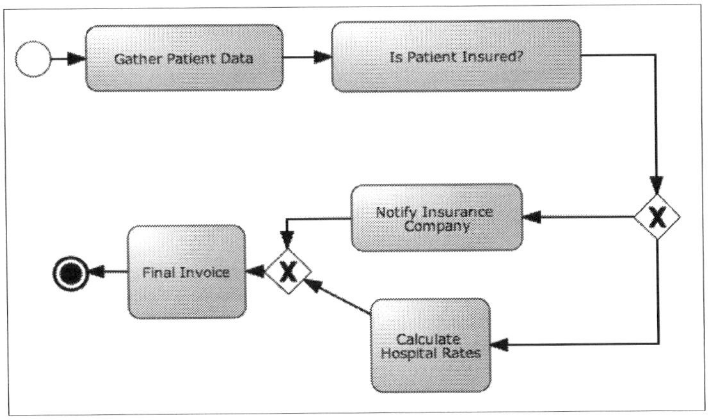

As described in the process image, the first activity is to gather all the available data for that patient. The hospital uses an external service that allows the hospital to query, using the patient's social security number, all of the relevant data. Once they get this information, the hospital uses a different service to validate if the patient is covered under health-care insurance. Depending on the output of this interaction, and based on the patient status, it will calculate the rates for the patient's hospitalization. For this example, if company X insures the patient, the hospital will charge a flat rate already defined. For this case, the insurance company will be notified about this patient's hospitalization through a service call. If the patient doesn't have insurance, the rates will be calculated based on the accommodations and services that the patient will require. In such cases, the process will use the hospital's internal service to calculate the final rates. Finally, when all the rates are calculated, the invoice system is in charge of creating the initial patient invoice, which can be modified in the future if the patient requires more services than the ones initially calculated.

Technically speaking, this is an automatic process that doesn't requires human interaction. This means that the process will be started and will coordinate all the service interactions moving all the necessary data between the different service calls.

In order to simplify the examples, all the services will be exposed by the same web service that exposes all the business logic required by this business process.

The project `jBPM5-Patient-Insurance` defines different tests and configurations showing synchronous and asynchronous interactions. If you open the test class called `HospitalInsuranceServiceTest`, you will find a set of tests that check the service's logic implemented in the `InsuranceServiceImpl` class. Look at the `InsuranceService` interface inside the package called `com.salaboy.jbpm5.dev.guide.webservice`, which describes the methods that will be exposed and used by the business-process activities.

Each method inside this interface will represent a different service that can be called by our processes. We will now see how we can plug these service calls in inside our activities. There are several ways of doing this, but here we will only analyze the most common ones.

The simplest approach in jBPM5 is to create, for each interaction, a work item handler that will be in charge of contacting the service, sending the required data, and processing the results. Our work item handlers will be in charge of gathering the information provided by the processes and will contain the logic to call the external service. Take a look at the `PatientDataServiceWorkItemHandler` implementation, which is in charge of contacting the `getPatientData()` method of `InsuranceService` and handing the results back.

This is a very straightforward work item handler implementation, where we get some information from the process context (`wi.getParameter("gatherdata_patientName")`), which was mapped inside the business process definition. Using this information, the work item handler contacts the service:

```
InsuranceService client = getClient();
patientData = client.getPatientData(patientId);
```

Finally, the work item handler has the responsibility of mapping the results back to the process context. Notice that this mapping can select, based on the results, which bits of information are required by the process and which are not.

```
Map<String, Object> result = new HashMap<String, Object>();
result.put("gatherdata_patient", patientData);

wim.completeWorkItem(wi.getId(), result);
```

As you may notice, as soon as we gather all the results we can complete the work item (with the `completeWorkItem(id, results)` method), notifying the process engine to continue with the next activity in the sequence.

This work item handler implementation doesn't use the Executor component, and for that reason the thread that starts the process will block until the web service call finishes. In the case that an exception is thrown by one of our service interactions, the work item handler code will be in charge of dealing with it. If we don't deal with the exceptions inside it, they will be propagated to the caller—in this case, our application. To put it in a different way, if we don't deal with these low-level exceptions inside our work item handler implementations, the caller application will need to do it. If the error happens in the last activity, we need to start all over again because no previous state of the process is known. Most of the time, we need to deal with these exceptions in the same way; for that reason, the following section explains how we can deal with these situations by using the Executor service.

The Executor service and our work items

The Executor service will be in charge of dealing with exceptions and retrying the execution in case of failure. In order to be able to use the exception handling and retry mechanisms from the Executor service, we will need to delegate the logic for the service interaction to a command that will be executed remotely by the Executor service.

If we want to do that with our `PatientDataServiceWorkItemHandler` `executeWorkItem()` method logic, it will look like the following code snippet:

```
public void executeWorkItem(WorkItem workItem,
                            WorkItemManager manager) {
  long workItemId = workItem.getId();
  String command = (String) workItem
                           .getParameter("command");
  String callbacks = (String) workItem
                             .getParameter("callbacks");
  this.execKey = workItem.getName() + "_" +
                 workItem.getProcessInstanceId() + "_" +
                 workItemId + "@sessionId="+this.sessionId;
  CommandContext ctx = new CommandContext();
  for (Map.Entry<String, Object> entry :
               workItem.getParameters().entrySet()) {
                      ctx.setData(entry.getKey(), entry.getValue());
  }
  ctx.setData("_workItemId", String.valueOf(workItemId));
  ctx.setData("callbacks", callbacks);
  ctx.setData("businessKey", this.execKey);
  Long requestId = executor.scheduleRequest(command, ctx);
  workItem.getParameters().put("requestId", requestId);
  String sWaitTillComplete = (String) workItem
                            .getParameter("waitTillComplete");
  Boolean waitTillComplete =
                   sWaitTillComplete == null ? null :
                     Boolean.valueOf(sWaitTillComplete);
  if (waitTillComplete == null ||
                 !waitTillComplete.booleanValue()) {
    manager.completeWorkItem(workItemId,
                             workItem.getResults());
  }

}
```

The previous code snippet is, in a generic way, picking up a command passed as a work item parameter and using the Executor service component to schedule a remote interaction. The command that this work item receives is the command that will be remotely scheduled for execution. This generic implementation can be found inside the project `jBPM5-Patient-Insurance` in a class called `AsyncGenericWorkItemHandler`. In order to have the same logic that we had inside the `PatientDataServiceWorkItemHandler` implementation, we just need to create a command implementation that contains the service call.

```
public class GetPatientDataCommand implements Command {

  public ExecutionResults execute(CommandContext ctx)
                      throws MalformedURLException {
    String patientId = (String)
                     ctx.getData("gatherdata_patientName");
    InsuranceService client = getClient();
    Patient patientData = client.getPatientData(patientId);
    ExecutionResults executionResults =
                                  new ExecutionResults();
    executionResults.setData("gatherdata_patient",
                            patientData);
    return executionResults;
  }

  private InsuranceService getClient()
                          throws MalformedURLException {
    URL wsdlURL = new URL(
                     "http://127.0.0.1:19999/
                     InsuranceServiceImpl/insurance?WSDL");
    QName SERVICE_QNAME = new QName(
               "http://webservice.guide.dev.
                jbpm5.salaboy.com/",
               "InsuranceServiceImplService");
    Service service = Service.create(wsdlURL, SERVICE_QNAME);
    InsuranceService client =
                   service.getPort(InsuranceService.class);
    return client;
  }
}
```

Notice that the logic inside this command, called `GetPatientDataCommand`, is exactly the same as the one proposed by our original work item handler implementation. It just creates the web service client and then calls the `getPatientData(patientId)` method, getting back a patient instance as a result.

The only missing piece is to map the name of the `GetPatientDataCommand` and `CompleteWorkItemCallback` classes to the task-input parameter. Inside the BPMN file called `InsuranceProcessV2.bpmn`, look for the following tag:

```
<bpmn2:task id="…" name="Gather Patient Data">
```

Within the `dataInput` associations defined inside tasks, we will find three properties related to the `Executor` service configuration:

- Command (`commandInput`): This `dataInput` mapping contains the name of the command class that will be scheduled to be executed by the Executor component
- Callback (`callbacksInput`): If we want to add callbacks at the end of the execution, we need to use the callback's variable to specify the chain of callbacks that we want to execute. We can specify multiple callbacks, using a comma (,) to separate each class name. You need to know that these callbacks will be synchronously executed after the command.
- WaitTillComplete (`waitTillCompleteInput`): This parameter will be picked up by `AsyncGenericWorkItemHandler`, and based on its value it will decide if we need to wait for a callback to complete the work item or if we will continue with the next task in the process as soon as we schedule the message to be executed.

Note that `GetPatientDataCommand` returns `executionResults`:

```
ExecutionResults executionResults = new ExecutionResults();
executionResults.setData("gatherdata_patient",
                                    patientData);
return executionResults;
```

`executionResults` needs to be filled with the information that we want to inject back into the process. The command class itself doesn't have access to the context of the process and for that reason we need to add a callback that will know how to get `executionResults`, map them to the process variables, and complete the pending work item.

Notice that we are using a generic callback called `CompleteWorkItemCallback`. This generic `CompleteWorkItemCallback` callback looks like this:

```
public class CompleteWorkItemCallback
                            implements CommandCallback {

  public void onCommandDone(CommandContext ctx,
                             ExecutionResults results) {
   Map<String, Object> output = new HashMap<String, Object>();
```

```
        if (results != null) {
         for (Map.Entry<String, Object> entry :
                                    results.getData().entrySet()) {
          output.put(entry.getKey(), entry.getValue());
         }
        }
        String sWorkItemId = (String) ctx.getData("_workItemId");
        String businessKey = (String) ctx.getData("businessKey");
        String[] key = businessKey.split("@");
        StatefulKnowledgeSession session =
                        SessionStoreUtil.sessionCache.get(key[1]);
        session.getWorkItemManager().completeWorkItem(
                               Long.valueOf(sWorkItemId), output);
      }
    }
```

This generic callback has three main responsibilities:

- First, it maps the `executionResults` to an output map to be able to complete the work item with it.
- Second, it has a business key that is used to locate the session where that work item was running and the ID of the work item that needs to be completed. This version of `CompleteWorkItemCallback` is using `SessionStoreUtil` to locate the session, but several options can be used to locate it. We will see a more advanced version of this callback that can be applied when we are storing the session into a database.
- Third, when it locates the session, it completes the work item on that session and causes the continuation of the process to the next activity.

If an error occurs in the execution of the command or in the chain of callbacks, the Executor component will automatically retry the execution. How many times and how often the retries happens will be up to the configuration. If we want to configure per command the number of retries that the Executor component will retry that specific operation, we can extend `AsyncGenericWorkItemHandler` to receive the retries parameter and add that to `CommandContext`. Doing this, we would be overriding the global configuration.

You can open all the command and callback classes implemented for the hospital insurance check example to see how each of them is implemented following the same patterns. You can find all the implementations inside `jBPM5-Patient-Insurance/src/main/java/com/salaboy/jbpm5/dev/guide/commands/`. The `CompleteWorkItemCallback` implementation can be found inside the test sources because it's tied to the way we are storing the sessions for this particular test: `jBPM5-Patient-Insurance/src/test/java/com/salaboy/jbpm5/dev/guide/callbacks/CompleteWorkItemCallback.java`

The following section briefly explains how the execution of our process is affected by this approach.

Execution flow

Because we have introduced the Executor service, we will see a different behavior in our processes' executions. All the external interactions that use the Executor service will have asynchronous behavior now, and this will definitely affect how our process gets executed.

The following diagram shows what a sync execution looks like:

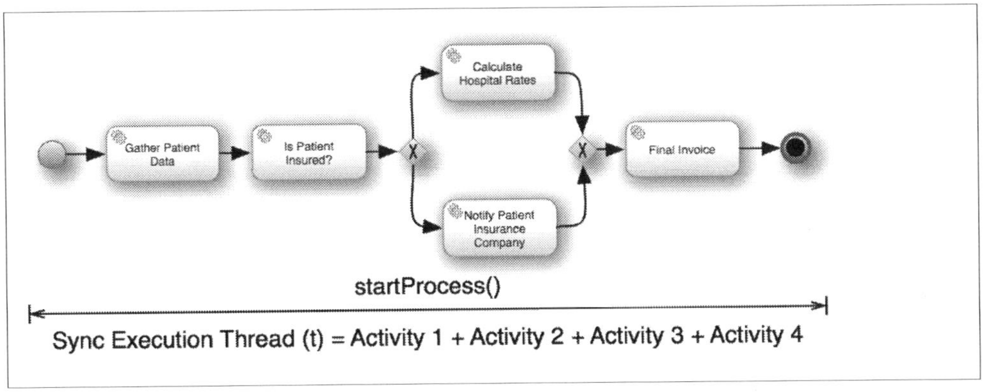

This figure describes how the `startProcess()` method will behave if all our activities have synchronous behavior, which is usually the most common behavior for web-service calls. The amount of time (*t*) required to complete the `startProcess()` method can be calculated as the sum of the times taken to execute all the external interactions. If one of these external interactions is a lengthy operation, the application that calls the `startProcess()` method will be blocked for a long time. This is usually not desired behavior from an architectural and design perspective. If we use the Executor service, we will see that our application will delegate the execution to the Executor service threads without blocking for long periods of time.

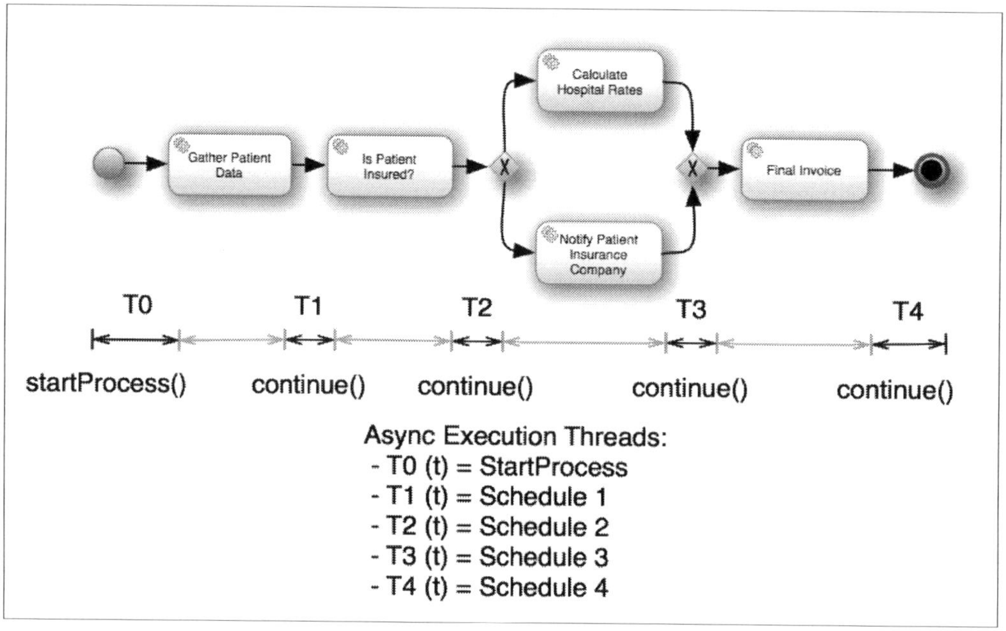

The previous diagram shows how our application thread (*T0*) starts the process by calling the `startProcess()` method, which will run until it finds the first external interaction that needs to be delegated to the Executor component. The segments (between the Txs) represent the time that will be used by the Executor component to execute a scheduled task, but it also means that during those periods our application will be free to do something else and it will not be blocked while waiting for an external interaction. *T1*, *T2*, *T3*, and *T4* represent the time used by the Executor component to schedule new external interactions. Once the scheduling is done, the threads from inside the thread pool of the Executor component will be in charge of doing the real work. Obviously, all the executions that happen in threads that belong to the Executor component will be monitored and retried in the case of any error.

The test called `SlowWebServicesInteractionsTest` shows an example where some lengthy operations are scheduled to be executed by the Executor service. Here the main thread of execution (the test class) is just waiting for the executor thread to finish its job; but in real situations it could be executing any other application logic.

Data flow

This section briefly explains the data flows between all these different components. Now that we have a more complex architecture, we need to understand exactly how our information is being propagated to the different components and threads that are participating in our external executions.

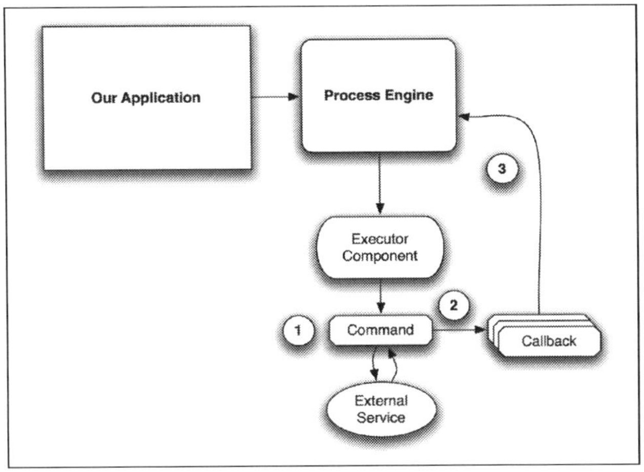

When we start using the Executor Component to delegate external executions, we decouple where the real calls to our external services will happen. For this reason, each command implementation will need to be able to gather or carry the information that will be required to finally execute the internal interaction. As we saw in `GetPatientDataCommand`, we use `CommandContext` to transport the information that will be required by the interaction. This `CommandContext` object will be populated by our `AsyncGenericWorkItemHandler` instance, which will take the information from our business process data mappings and will inject those variables into `CommandContext`. Because the command will be scheduled to be executed by a different thread, the information that we are moving inside `CommandContext` will be serialized and persisted into the database (for this executor implementation). We can provide different ways to locate this information, but usually persisting a copy that can be restored by any other thread is a good option. If this option doesn't fit into your scenario, you will need to store only a reference to that piece of information and then write the mechanism to be able to retrieve that information from a different thread that could be running in a different JVM/machine.

Once the command gets executed successfully (1), `ExecutionResults` and `CommandContext` will be propagated to Callback (2). Because this implementation of the Executor component uses the same thread to execute the Command and all of the Callback instances, this information will be moved only in memory; but more advanced implementations can use different threads to process the callbacks. A similar approach of serializing `ExecutionResults` can be used in such cases.

Once the callbacks are done, usually they will need to contact the Process Engine again to be able to complete the pending activity. The following section will explain how this lookup happens, based on the information that is being kept inside `CommandContext`. At this point (3), the callback will need to copy back to the work item scope the information gathered by the command and callbacks execution. As soon as the callback completes the work item, the resultant information will be copied back to the process scope based on the data output associations defined in the process.

Keeping track of the context

In order to be able to continue the process execution from a different thread, in this case one of the threads from the Executor service, we need a way to get a reference back to the context that was used initially to start the process. In some way we need to recreate, in a different thread, the execution context in order to be able to continue the process execution from that thread.

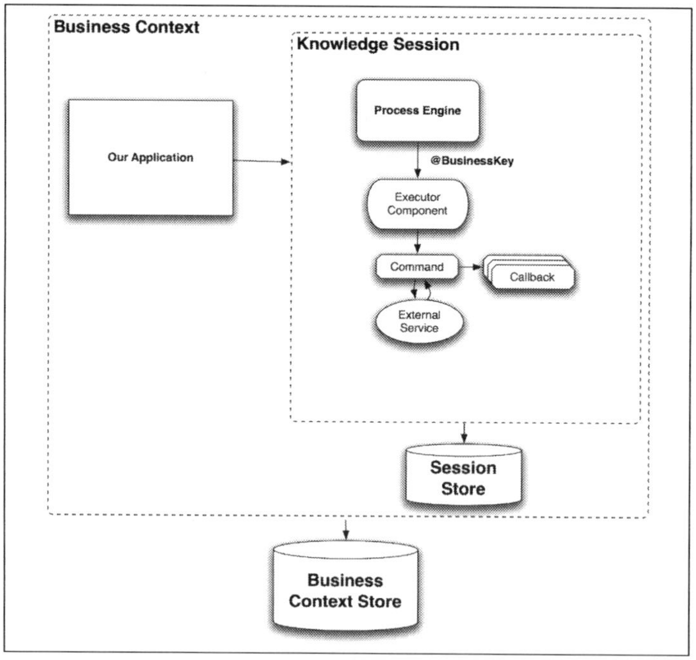

In order to interact with the Process Engine, our application will need to have a reference to a Knowledge Session that was created containing our process definition; if the application has a direct reference to the Knowledge Session object, them there is not much business context required to perform the execution. In cases where we need to locate the session where our process is being hosted, we will need to have some mechanism that gathers all the information that will be used to interact with the Process Engine. This kind of mechanism uses a business key, which will allow us to load all the necessary data to be able to interact with our business processes. The previous diagram shows two types of contexts, the bigger one is called business context, which will contain all the business information required to interact with our process engine or even the rule engine. Usually, this store allows us to store all the references that we need using just a simple key. This means that if our application knows which key is required to load the entire context, we can re-create the execution environment regardless of the thread we are in.

The same approach can be used to locate and restore the Knowledge Session where our process instance was initially executed. The Session Store allows us to locate by ID the sessions that we are using. The only requirement that we have is to have the Session Store in a global scope so different threads can locate the sessions. The examples provided use a class called `SessionStoreUtil`. This class contains a static map that is in charge of storing our sessions. This approach will work well for applications that run on the same JVM, but if we have a more distributed environment we will need a more advanced approach. As we will see in *Chapter 8, Persistence and Transactions*, we can leverage the Drools & jBPM5 persistence layer to store and locate our sessions. But no matter where we store the sessions, we will need to have a business key which stores the `sessionId` and the relationship with the process instance.

As you can see in our examples, the one in charge of generating this business key is the class called `AsyncGenericWorkItemHandler`:

```
this.execKey = workItem.getName() + "_" +
               workItem.getProcessInstanceId() + "_" +
               workItemId + "@sessionId="+this.sessionId;
```

If we want to add more information to the business key, we can do it; usually we will want to add all the information that is being propagated by the application. This business key will usually be required by the callbacks to contact the application or to locate the knowledge session that contains the process that needs to be continued after the command execution. You can see how `CompleteWorkItemCallback` gets the `sessionId` value from the business key to be able to complete the pending work item and notify the process that it can continue to the next activity.

```
String businessKey = (String) ctx.getData("businessKey");
String[] key = businessKey.split("@");
StatefulKnowledgeSession session =
                  SessionStoreUtil.sessionCache.get(key[1]);
session.getWorkItemManager().completeWorkItem(
                         Long.valueOf(sWorkItemId), output);
```

Summary

In this chapter we have covered how external interactions can be achieved from inside our business processes. We discussed the different approaches that are available to execute external interactions with synchronous or asynchronous behavior. This chapter also covered, with examples, how an external component such as the Executor service helps us achieve more robust interactions, delegating the executions to an external component from our application's point of view. This technique allows us to implement different error-handling mechanisms that are usually required by our business process executions. The following chapter will discuss how, using the same mechanism inside jBPM5, we achieve human interactions. We will also examine the main differences between an automated activity and a human interaction, which usually requires a user interface to be created.

7
Human Interactions

Business processes are about how a company works towards a well-defined goal. Human actors play the most important role inside the work that needs to be done. We need to understand how people will interact with the company's business processes and how each of them will be responsible for their different tasks.

This chapter will be about understanding the mindset proposed by the BPM discipline about human interactions. This chapter will also introduce the **Web Services Human Task (WS-HT)** standard specification which has been created to standardize the information, life cycle, and interaction with software components that are specialized in achieving human interactions.

By the end of this chapter, we will learn how to work with and handle human tasks inside jBPM5. Our emergency service example will be extended to use new user interfaces based on the task list concepts described in the first section of this chapter.

Human interactions

There are a lot of studies aimed at improving and finding better ways to deal with human-to-system interactions. Here we will analyze a common approach derived from the BPM discipline that is widely used by most of the BPM systems. Some changes will be introduced to the way that we think about and design our end user interfaces. Developers that are used for building standalone or web applications in general will notice a huge paradigm shift derived from the system integration field.

Let's take a quick look at the context in which human activities will take place inside our business processes.

Human interactions inside our processes

Remember that we are modeling our business processes using the BPMN 2.0 standard notation that includes different types of activities. Two of the most frequently used activities are User Tasks and Service Tasks. Our processes will be in charge of coordinating these system-to-system and human-to-system interactions that guide the company's day-to-day activities.

When a User Task is reached in our process, a new task will be created and assigned to the corresponding business actor. At that point, we will need a way to notify the user that a new task was created and assigned to him/her. When the user is notified, he/she will then need a way to interact with the newly created task.

This task, like every User Task in our process, contains information that is contextually relevant to a specific process execution that will allow the user to perform the task.

Usually, a business actor will handle multiple tasks at the same time, and the contextual information, in addition to the task type/name, will differentiate one task from another. Depending on how many business processes the actor is involved in, there are a number of different types of tasks that the user must be prepared to complete. Comparing the task type with the user role, we can easily check that the person assigned is prepared for the job.

At this point we need to have a set of generic mechanisms to deal with the notification, presentation, interaction, and completion of each of the human tasks that our process' instances will create at runtime.

The Web Services Human Task (WS-HT) standard specification formalizes these mechanisms as well as defines the task life cycle. The task life cycle will define the stages that a task can be in at a certain point in time. The following section is a quick review of the important topics covered inside the WS-HT specification. For further details, you can check out the following link which contains the full WS-HT specification definition as a PDF format: `http://docs.oasis-open.org/bpel4people/ws-humantask-1.1.pdf`

Web Services Human Task specification

The OASIS group, composed of international companies, has defined the WS-HT specification to standardize the structure and the information that a human interaction must contain to be interoperable between different vendors. Like every standard specification, the WS-HT specification serves as a guideline and as a generic description of the features that a component in charge of the human interactions must have. All the features described inside the specification are based on industry best practices, as well as on the most implemented and used features. Standards always describe a way to solve a problem based on how different companies have solved that problem in the past, merging different experiences, and defining best practices. Being compliant with this kind of specification means that our component implements the most required features using a previously tested solution. It also means that if we want to replace our component with a different one provided by another vendor, we can do so without affecting other components that rely on them.

Traditionally, BPMS has provided a built-in component in charge of handling human interactions. Nowadays, not only business processes require human interactions but other components can use this functionality. That's why a new component has been introduced by the specification.

The following diagram shows an architectural overview of what BPMS traditionally provides, compared against the new Task Component proposed by the WS-HT specification and implemented inside jBPM5:

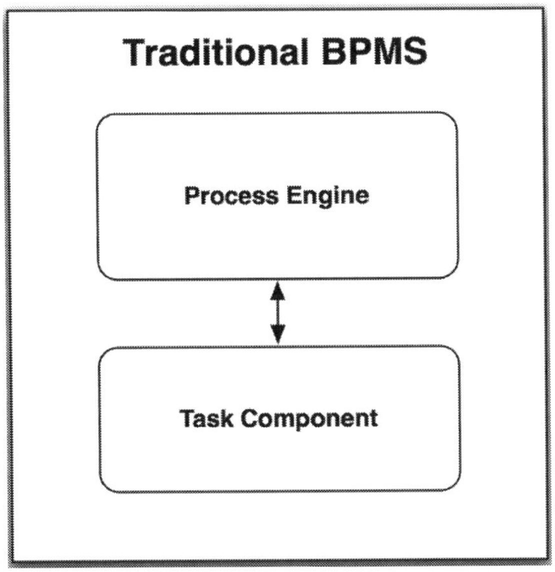

As we can see, the previous designs include the responsibility of handling the human interactions tightly coupled with the process engine. This fact causes complications for other applications and components that may also want to create human interactions. The more tightly coupled the Task Component is to the BPM system, the more difficult it becomes to enable third-party applications to interact with it.

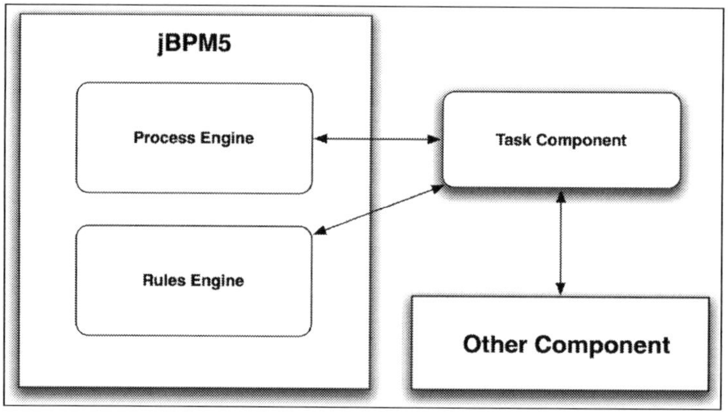

In jBPM5, because of the strong need to share the ability to create and interact with human tasks from different components, the human task component was externalized. Now, a wide range of applications can influence the status of, and create and monitor human interactions.

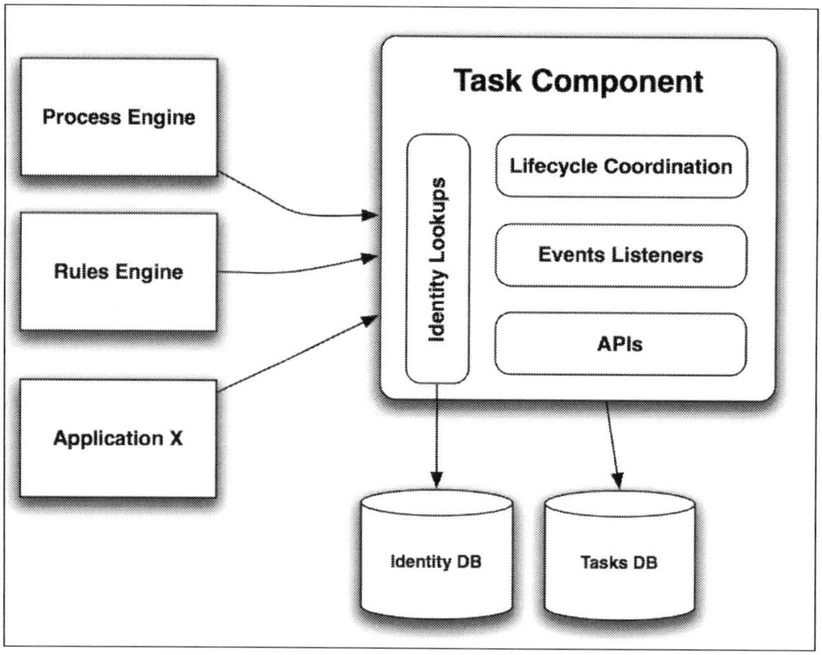

Here we will cover the four most important aspects of this component:

- Human tasks service API
- Human tasks life cycle
- External identity component integration
- Human tasks and business processes' interactions

Human tasks service APIs

Like every **Application Programming Interface** (**API**), the WS-HT API exposes the services provided by the human task component. The human task component can be used in any other system that requires creating and managing human interactions. One of those systems will obviously be the process engine, but it's not limited to it.

Two types of systems will usually consume the human task service APIs:

- The one that creates the tasks, and usually wants to get notifications about those tasks
- The one that consumes the tasks, exposing them to the end users and letting them work until each task is completed

A common scenario is described in the following figure:

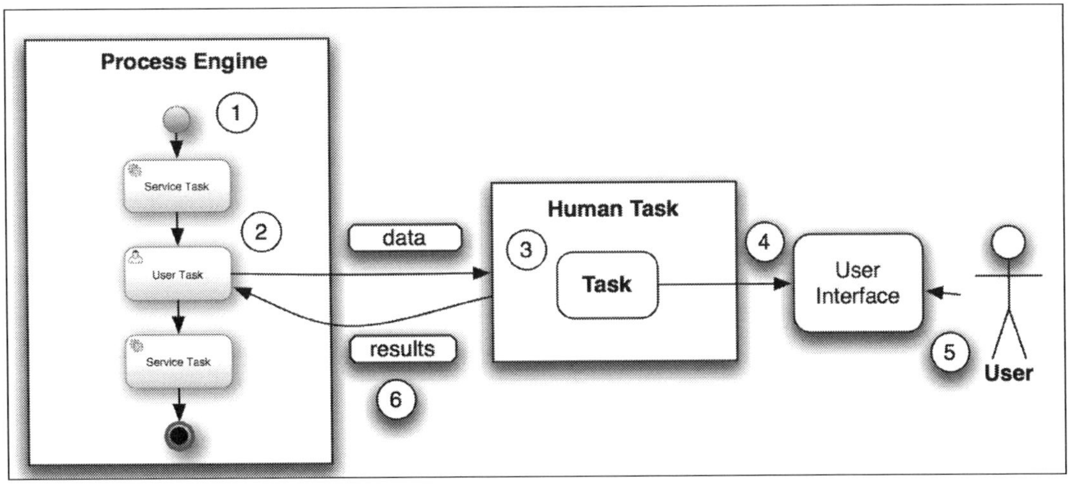

As you can see in (1), a business process is started. When the execution reaches a User Task, the process engine will contact the Human Task service to create a new human task (2). The process in this case will need to wait until the human interaction ends in order to continue. Once the task is created in the Human Task service (3), all of the information and the status of each task will be managed by this component.

Usually, a User Interface component will query the Human Task service to find all of the tasks related to a specific user or group. The result of the query should allow the User Interface component to render the information required by the interaction (4).

Finally, in (5) the end user will do the work, (usually loading or reviewing information provided by the User Interface) and when the task is finished, the UI will notify the Human Task service of the task completion. At that point, the Human Task service will notify the Process Engine (6) that the task is complete and the process can move forward to the next activity.

In order to render a UI, the Human Task component exposes a well-defined API that allows the UI to query and interact with the created Human Tasks.

The following code snippet is an extract from the interface defined inside jBPM5 that provides a subset of the functionality described in the WS-HT specification:

```
package org.jbpm.task;

public interface TaskService {
  // Deploy a Task Definition
  void addTask(Task task, ContentData content);

  // Query Tasks
  Task getTask(long taskId);
  Task getTaskByWorkItemId(long workItemId);
  List<TaskSummary> getTasksAssignedAsBusinessAdministrator(
                           String userId, String language);
  List<TaskSummary> getTasksAssignedAsExcludedOwner(
                           String userId, String language);
  List<TaskSummary> getTasksAssignedAsPotentialOwner(
  String userId, String language);
  List<TaskSummary> getTasksAssignedAsPotentialOwner(
  String userId, List<String> groupIds, String language);
  List<?> query(String qlString, Integer size,
                                         Integer offset);
  // Tasks Operations
  void start(long taskId, String userId);
  void stop(long taskId, String userId);
  void skip(long taskId, String userId);
  void suspend(long taskId, String userId);
```

```
    void resume(long taskId, String userId);
    void claim(long taskId, String userId);
    void release(long taskId, String userId);
    void complete(long taskId, String userId,
                       ContentData outputData);
    void fail(long taskId, String userId, FaultData faultData);
    void forward(long taskId, String userId,
                                     String targetEntityId);
    // Event Listeners
    void registerForEvent(EventKey key, boolean remove,
                        EventResponseHandler responseHandler);
    void unregisterForEvent(EventKey key);
    //Omitted Methods
}
```

As you can see, the `TaskService` interface defines the following:

1. The signature for the task's operation methods.
2. The method to deploy a new task definition.
3. The methods to query already existing tasks.
4. Methods to register listeners to receive notifications of task status changes.

Our task clients will be in charge of using these methods from the human task service to provide the user with a way to interact with their tasks. In the following section, we will see how we can use these methods to interact with our human tasks and how we can build user interfaces using them.

In order to understand why these methods have been defined, we need to understand the life cycle of each of these human tasks.

Human tasks life cycle

The WS-HT specification defines a detailed and complete set of states that every task can be in, ranging from its creation to its end.

This set of states is designed to cover a wide range of scenarios related to human interactions. These states also cover what we call Group Tasks, which are not assigned to any particular person. Business processes can create these tasks, but any of a pool of qualified people can complete them. When these tasks are created, every person who has the ability to complete them will need to claim each task in order to work on it. Once the task is claimed, it's assigned to the user who claimed it, and no one else can claim that task. If the person who claimed the task cannot work on it, he/she has the option to release it.

The specification introduced in the following graph represents the possible states and transition of a task:

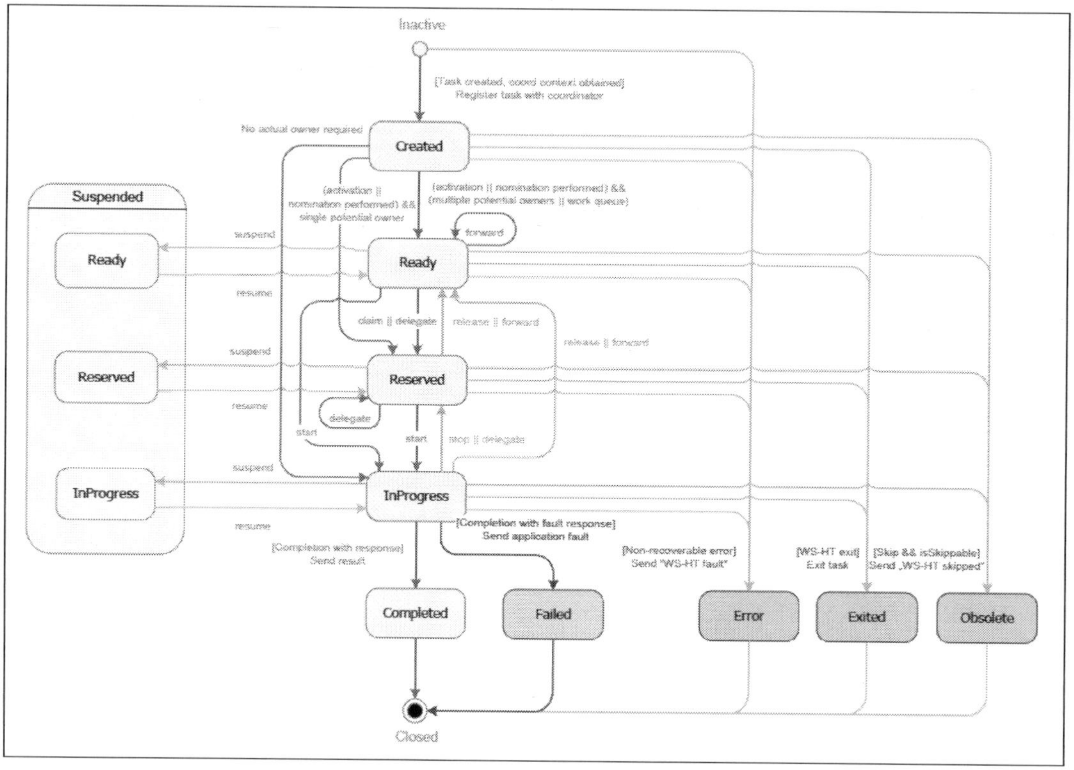

As you can see, there is clear definition of how our tasks flow from one state to another. These task states have a direct relationship with the task operations defined in the `TaskService` interface. By using the task operations against a particular task instance, we change the internal state of that task. If we call an operation that is not valid for the current state of the task, the human task service will notify us of the error.

Usually, our business process will create a task and initially it will be set up at the Created state. If the task has no direct assignment (that is, the process or the task definition doesn't contain information about who is in charge of it), the task will be moved to the Ready state. At this point the task will be ready and waiting for a user assignment in order to be moved to the Reserved state. When we find a task in the Reserved state, we know that the task is ready to be started by the person who is assigned to it. When the person is ready to work on the task, he/she will start the task—moving it to the InProgress state. The task will usually remain in the InProgress state until the user in charge of that task completes it, thereby moving the task to the Completed state. Alternatively, we can suspend or stop a task, which means that we need to resume it or start it again.

It's important to notice that a task in the Ready state is unassigned—it needs to be claimed by one of the potential owners. If the person who claims the task for some reason cannot continue working on it, he/she can release it so that any other person in the group can claim it.

For exceptional situations such as when a task cannot be completed successfully, there are four other options to close that task execution. If for some logical issue, the task cannot be successfully completed, the user can finish the task by adding a Fault and moving the task to the Failed state. This usually happens when the user in charge of the task doesn't have all of the information or the means required to finish the task. Error, Exited, and Obsolete are used when there is a non-recoverable technical error happening inside the task, when we want to abort the task, or when the task is not needed any more.

Now that we understand the states that a task can be in, we can go back to the API side to understand the concepts that are used to define each method. The following section introduces the human task service provided in jBPM5 by showing us an example of how we can create human tasks.

External identity component integration

Human interactions will be directly related to the people inside our company. This forces the human task service design to be flexible enough to integrate with the existing user/group directories. Different companies use different storages/mechanisms to store and organize the users' hierarchy and information. Most of the time, an LDAP tree or a set of database tables are used to keep this information centralized. For this reason, we need to learn how jBPM5 provides a set of classes to plugin the already existing identity storage that will be consumed every time that a task is assigned, re-assigned, delegated, or escalated. Look at the *The user/group callbacks* section, which introduces a mechanism to plugin an existing LDAP repository to obtain the user's information and assign the human tasks related to a process.

Human tasks and business processes' interactions

Before going into the technical details related to the jBPM5 implementation, we need to understand that the human task service will provide a way for the process to create tasks and also a set of event listeners to be able to receive notifications when a task changes its internal state. The same mechanisms can also be used by third-party applications that want to create tasks and want to receive notifications about them. The *The Human task work item handler* section covers a process execution, which contains a set of human tasks in addition to the configuration of an external identity provider.

jBPM5 human task component overview

Based on the WS-HT specification, the current version of the Human Task component inside jBPM5 can be found inside the master GIT repository:

`https://github.com/droolsjbpm/jbpm/tree/master/jbpm-human-task`

This repository contains all the source code for this component, but you don't need to worry about the source code, because a compiled version of the component is provided with the jBPM5 installer. In this section, we will cover some important aspects from the architectural side and we will see an example that shows how we can use this component from outside and inside our business processes.

From the architectural perspective, this component can be configured in different ways depending on our application needs. Because the Human Task service is a very simple and lightweight component, the simplest way of starting to use it is to embed it in your application.

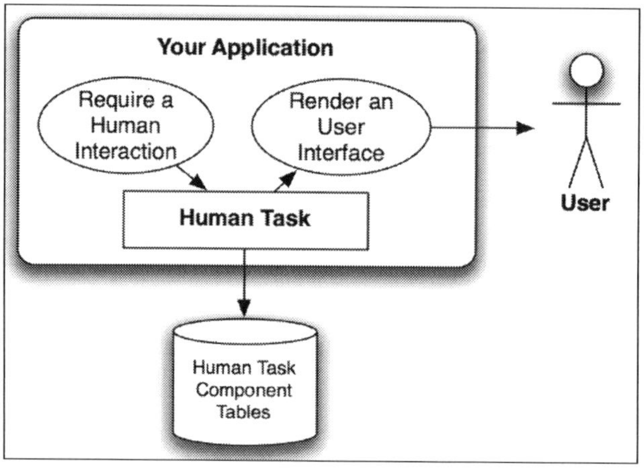

Notice that this option adds the Human Task component to your application like any other library. The Human Task service will use **Java Persistence API (JPA)** to store the information about the task's status into a database. As you may know, JPA needs a persistence provider to be configured, which by default is Hibernate in jBPM5. In these kinds of scenarios, our application will have direct access to the Human Task service APIs to create new human tasks and queries for their status. The application will be the one responsible for rendering a user interface.

Because all the information about the tasks is being stored in a database, we can have multiple applications embedding the human task library and querying the same database. By using the Human Task service as a library inside our application, we are not adding a new separate component to our architecture—we keep it simple. As a con, we will need to configure all the component parameters from inside our application, and now our application will be the one responsible for containing all the configurations required for this component to work. If we have several applications embedding the human task component's features, we will need to keep track of all the configurations in each application, which can be a pain to maintain. Obviously, by using this approach we will be running all the human task operations in the same JVM as our application.

The second option is to use this component as an external component. Our application will need to contact—via a transport protocol—a component that can be located in a different JVM or machine.

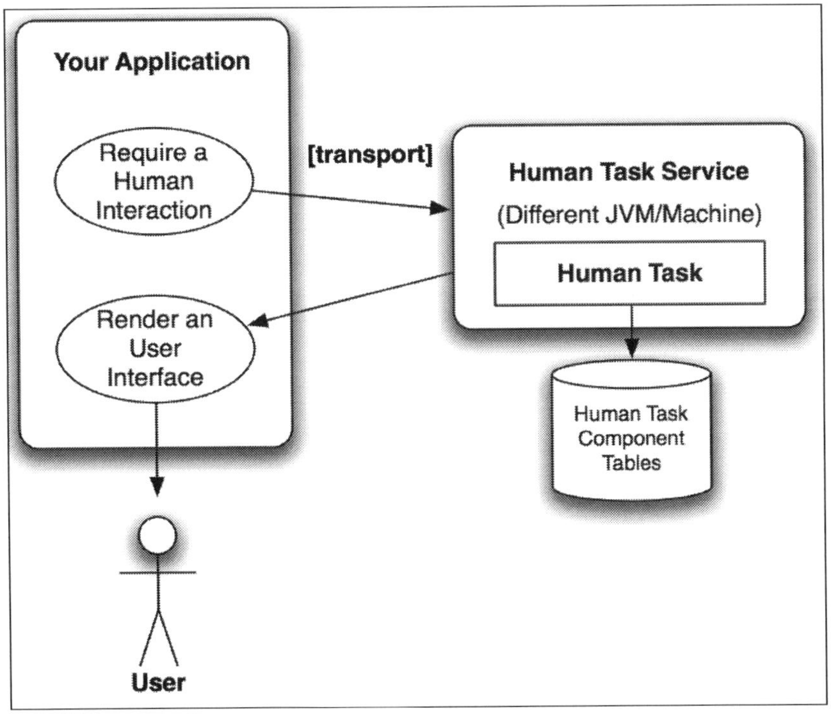

As you can see, between the application and the Human Task service, we will need to choose a communication protocol, which will allow our application to communicate with the Human Task Service. Usually we base our decision on the business requirements that we have for that component. There are two transports available in the latest version: Apache Mina (`http://mina.apache.org/`) and JMS via HornetQ (`http://www.jboss.org/hornetq`), and ActiveMQ (`http://activemq.apache.org/`). Apache Mina provides us a fast transport layer and both JMS implementations give us a highly reliable and configurable messaging service. JMS is usually the best choice if we will have a large infrastructure where we need to guarantee message delivery and where a cluster of Human Task Services may be required.

When using the Human Task Service decoupled from our application, we will be centralizing all the configurations and responsibilities of maintaining the Human Task Service in a single place. We will be using a different JVM from our applications, which means that we will not be adding extra load to our applications, which can be a very good advantage if we are planning to tune them to improve their performance. The obvious con with this approach is that we are now adding a network and transport overhead if the component runs in a different JVM.

If you are planning to expose the Human Task Service via web services, your architecture will be similar because you will only be changing the transport to HTTP/SOAP.

Human task service APIs example

We will start with a simple example of how we can embed the human task service in our application. We will also cover the main APIs that we can use to create, query, and interact with our human tasks.

If you open the project called `jBPM5-HumanTasksSimple` located inside the `chapter_07` directory, you will find a test called `HumanTasksLifecycleAPITest` that shows how to create a task definition, deploy it to the human task service, and then how to interact with it.

This example allows us to get a quick overview of the most common methods that we will be using from the `TaskService` interface, the data structures that we will need to handle, and all the configurations required for getting you started.

Let's analyze the `HumanTasksLifecycleAPITest` test class. From the configuration point of view, we need to set up a couple of things first.

- The human task service dependencies
- The persistence configuration

You can find a quick explanation about how these example projects are configured inside the `README` file of *Chapter 7, Human Interactions* (`https://github.com/Salaboy/jBPM5-Developer-Guide/blob/master/chapter_07/README`).

Once our project is correctly configured, we can start using the human task service APIs.

We will look at three different places inside the `HumanTasksLifecycleAPITest` class. The first method that needs our attention is the `setUp()` method annotated with the `@Before` annotation. This method will be executed before each test (method annotated with `@Test`):

```
@Before
public void setUp() {
  // Create an EntityManagerFactory based on the
  // PU configuration
  emf = Persistence
   .createEntityManagerFactory("org.jbpm.task");
  // The Task Service will use the EMF to store our
  // Task Status
  taskService = new TaskService(emf,
  SystemEventListenerFactory.getSystemEventListener());
  // We can use the Task Service to get an instance
  // of the Task Session which
  // allows us to introduce to our database the users
  // and groups information before running our tests
  taskSession = taskService.createSession();

  // Adds 1 Administrator, 2 users and 1 Group
  addUsersAndGroups(taskSession);

  //We need to set up a user to represent the user
  //that is making the requests
  MockUserInfo userInfo = new MockUserInfo();
  taskService.setUserinfo(userInfo);
}
```

Trying to sum up the comments inside the code, we can say that before running a test, we will need to:

1. Create a new `EntityManagerFactory` entity using the PU configuration provided by the `persistence.xml` file.
2. Create the `TaskService` instance.
3. Add our users and groups using `TaskServiceSession`.
4. Set up the current user that is requesting the interactions.

Once the environment is set up, we can start running our tests. Looking at the `regularFlowTest()` method, annotated with `@Test`, we can see what our task interactions will look like. Before looking at the code, let's define what this test is doing:

1. We need to instantiate a local and synchronous implementation of our human task component to use inside the test. For that, we use the `TaskService` instance to create a `LocalTaskService` instance.
2. We need to create a task definition and a new instance of that task in order to enable a user to work on it.
3. Once the task is ready, the user can query for his/her pending tasks.
4. Once the user has a task in a reserved status, he/she can start working on it.

The next code snippet shows the test interactions without the comments that have been included in the test class. Feel free to open the test class and run it and debug it to see the output as well as to get comfortable with the behavior:

```
LocalTaskService localTaskService =
                          new LocalTaskService(taskService);
List<User> potentialOwners = new ArrayList<User>();

potentialOwners.add(users.get("salaboy"));

Task task = createSimpleTask(potentialOwners,
                              users.get("administrator"));

localTaskService.addTask(task, new ContentData());

List<TaskSummary> tasksAssignedAsPotentialOwner =
     localTaskService
       .getTasksAssignedAsPotentialOwner("salaboy", "en-UK");

// Get the first task
Long taskId = tasksAssignedAsPotentialOwner.get(0).getId();

localTaskService.start(simpleTask.getId(), "salaboy");

// PERFORM THE TASK ACTIVITY HERE

localTaskService.complete(simpleTask.getId(), "salaboy",
                                                    null);
```

A couple of things to note here! First of all, there's a method called `createSimpleTask()`, which creates a very simple and basic task of assigning the users (that are sent as the method arguments) as potential owners and the administrator. If we send just one user, the task will have only one potential owner who will be automatically assigned as the owner of the task. Once we have the task structure, we use the `addTask()` method on the `LocalTaskService` instance to notify the human task service of this new definition. This `addTask()` method will also create automatically an instance of the task and set up everything to expose that task to the users. Using the `getTasksAssignedAsPotentialOwner()` method, we can query for all the tasks which have, the user that we sent in the method arguments as a potential owner. Notice that all the query methods return to `List<TaskSummary>`, which means that not all the task information is available. We will see in the next sections why it is very useful to get a summary first, and then if we need it, we can get the complete task data. Notice that the task status cannot be obtained from `TaskSummary`, so we can use the `getTask()` method to retrieve all the available data from that particular task.

When the human task service instantiates this task definition, because it only has one potential owner, the task is automatically forwarded to the Reserved state.

After ensuring that we are in the expected task state, we can start interacting with the task. Notice that we are only using the `start()` and `complete()` methods, which are the most commonly used ones. We will usually complete a task by sending results back; in this case we are not doing that, because we are only testing the life cycle.

Finally, the `@After` annotated method will be executed to clean up our environment. We are disposing off `EntityManagerFactory` and releasing the task session that we used to insert users and groups.

Ok, that was a quick introduction to the APIs and how we can interact with them. Feel free to review the `LocalTaskService` methods so that you'll have a complete overview of what you can do with them. The following section describes the main classes that we need to know in order to achieve the interaction between our human tasks and our business processes.

The human task work item handler

In the same way that we learnt about work item handlers in the previous chapter, this chapter covers a specific work item handler implementation for interacting with the human task service. As with every work item handler, it will need to be registered to the current knowledge session in order to be called when a user task is reached inside our processes. Because human interactions are considered always asynchronous interactions, the human task work item handler will use the event listeners provided by the human task service to receive notifications of when a task has been completed, skipped, or failed.

The class called `GenericHTWorkItemHandler` implements the specific logic to interact with the human task service. If we are using the human task service embedded in our application, we will use a subclass of `GenericHTWorkItemHandler` called `LocalHTWorkItemHandler`. If you choose to use the human task service as a remote service, a different work item handler that knows how to use the selected transport will need to be selected. For example, you will find `MinaHTWorkItemHandler` for the Apache Mina implementation, and `HornetQHTWorkItemHandler` for the HornetQ implementation. If you want to implement your own transport you can use these implementations as guidelines.

If you take a look at the `GenericHTWorkItemHandler` implementation and its superclass called `AbstractHTWorkItemHandler`, we will find the following important points:

- The task will be created based on the data inputs and outputs defined inside the business process. Based on the data mappings, the human task created will provide information to the user to work on it, and it will expect some information to be filled in. Based on the data output mappings, this information filled in by the user will be copied back to the process scope when the human task gets completed.
- A set of listeners will be registered to receive notifications about the task's completion.
- A mechanism is defined to notify the knowledge session about the completion of a human task. This mechanism will decide if the work item associated with the task needs to be completed to allow the process to move forward to the next activity. It's important to note that the session must be active/running in order to notify it about the human task completion, or an exception will be thrown.

You can take a look at these classes inside the GitHub repository here:

https://github.com/droolsjbpm/jbpm/blob/5.4.x/jbpm-human-task/jbpm-human-task-core/src/main/java/org/jbpm/process/workitem/wsht/GenericHTWorkItemHandler.java

After the next section, an example showing `GenericHTWorkItemHandler` in action, in conjunction with the user/group callbacks will be introduced.

The user/group callbacks

As mentioned in the *External identity component integration* section, a strong ability to integrate with existing user/group repositories is required for real-life implementations. For that reason, jBPM5 provides the concept of `UserGroupCallback`. jBPM5 will allow us to provide different implementations of an interface called `UserGroupCallback` to integrate our existing user repositories with the human task service. Out-of-the-box jBPM5 provides implementations for LDAP, DB, JAAS, and `Properties` file (used by default).

```
public interface UserGroupCallback {
  boolean existsUser(String userId);
  boolean existsGroup(String groupId);
  List<String> getGroupsForUser(String userId,
                              List<String> groupIds,
                        List<String> allExistingGroupIds);
}
```

The implementations for this interface will provide the necessary mechanisms to contact the identity repository to look up existing users and groups. The `getGroupsForUsers()` method will be used to retrieve information about the groups where a specific user belongs. The following section shows an example that uses `GenericHTWorkItemHandler` and an implementation of the `UserGroupCallback` interface for an LDAP repository.

HT work item handler and UserGroupCallback example

The project called `jBPM5-HumanTaskAndProcesses` contains an example test that shows how to execute a process containing three user tasks.

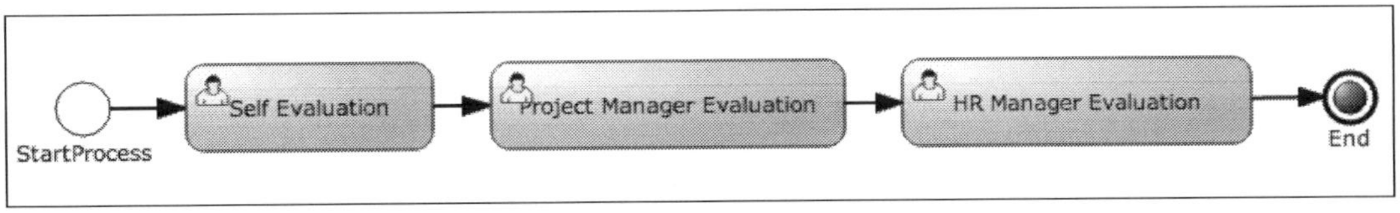

The process consists of three user tasks. The first task will be assigned based on a process variable called `user_self_evaluation` that will be assigned at the beginning of the process. The following two tasks are group tasks that will be automatically assigned to the groups **HR (Human Resources)** and **PM (Project Managers)**. This means that the users inside these groups will need to claim the tasks in order to work on them.

In order to correctly execute this process, we will need to register an instance of `LocalHTWorkItemHandler` to the session. This handler will use a local instance of the human task service to create the required human tasks.

```
TaskService ts = new TaskService(
                Persistence.
                  createEntityManagerFactory("org.jbpm.task"),
                  SystemEventListenerFactory
                                 .getSystemEventListener());
LocalTaskService taskService = new LocalTaskService(ts);
LocalHTWorkItemHandler taskHandler =
                    new LocalHTWorkItemHandler(taskService,
                                                    ksession);
```

Note that the `LocalHTWorkItemHandler` subclass as well as other subclasses of the `GenericHTWorkItemHandler` class require the reference to the `ksession` that needs to be notified when a task is completed.

This example also uses an implementation of the `UserGroupCallback` interface called `LdapUserGroupCallback`. In order to register our own implementation of the `UserGroupCallback` interface, we need to register a system variable, as shown here:

```
System.setProperty("jbpm.usergroup.callback",

     "org.jbpm.task.identity.LDAPUserGroupCallbackImpl");
```

Note that we can access the instance of the registered implementation by executing the following line:

```
UserGroupCallbackManager.getInstance().getCallback();
```

The test class called `ProcessAndHumanTasksTest` shows these configurations and an execution of the previously introduced process.

For testing purposes, the JUnit test sets up an embedded LDAP repository using the Spring Security and Apache DS LDAP integration, which allows us to have an instance of an LDAP server based on a configuration file called `identity-repository.ldif`. This file contains the users and groups in our company. Using the LDAP APIs provided by Apache DS LDAP, we will be able to query the user and group structures.

I strongly recommend that you open up the project and run the test class called `ProcessAndHumanTasksTest` to familiarize yourself with the behavior of the previously introduced mechanisms. In order to fully understand how all of the pieces fit together you can debug the test and place break points inside the `LdapUserGroupCallback` and `GenericHTWorkItemHandler` classes. This will give you a deep understanding about the execution flow.

The following section deals, in my opinion, with the most important aspect of human interactions, that is, how to build our user interfaces.

Task list oriented user interfaces

A good way to understand the APIs functionality is to clearly define what we are trying to achieve with it. That's why the following section will introduce something that we call task list oriented user interfaces.

Based on the standardization of a generic structure for a human task, we can build generic user interfaces. This will facilitate user interactions by unifying the method of accessing the information.

The screens that will contain and handle human tasks can be split into two different blocks:

- Task lists
- Task forms

Task lists

When a user needs to know what tasks are outstanding, he/she needs a screen that quickly shows a list of pending tasks. This list will just contain a brief description (or an abstract) of the real task. It's the minimum information required by the user to understand the task that is pending, without interacting or retrieving the full structure of the task.

A task list, which is only a summarized view of the pending tasks, allows the user to choose which tasks in the list to start working on first. We can say that a task list is an entry point for users to understand what they need to do. The users should use their task list screen to get a quick and complete understanding of the priorities of the job.

Some of the common pieces of information that are displayed in a task list are:

- **Task name**: Short, descriptive name for the task.
- **Due date**: The date and time when the task is due.
- **Creation date**: The date when the task was created.
- **Description**: A textual description of the task. It can contain contextual information which clarifies the task purpose.
- **Last update**: The last date of modification.
- **Priority**: Priority information can help sort tasks depending on their required time of completion.

The human task service clients use this information to build a data grid / table UI component, which the users will load when they want to know about their pending tasks.

It's important to notice that no matter the technology or the communication protocol used to build the clients, the structure of the information will be the same. In one way or another, our clients will allow the end user to check the status of their pending tasks. Someone somewhere will retrieve the information from the human task service and render it to the end users.

A task list screen should look like the following figure:

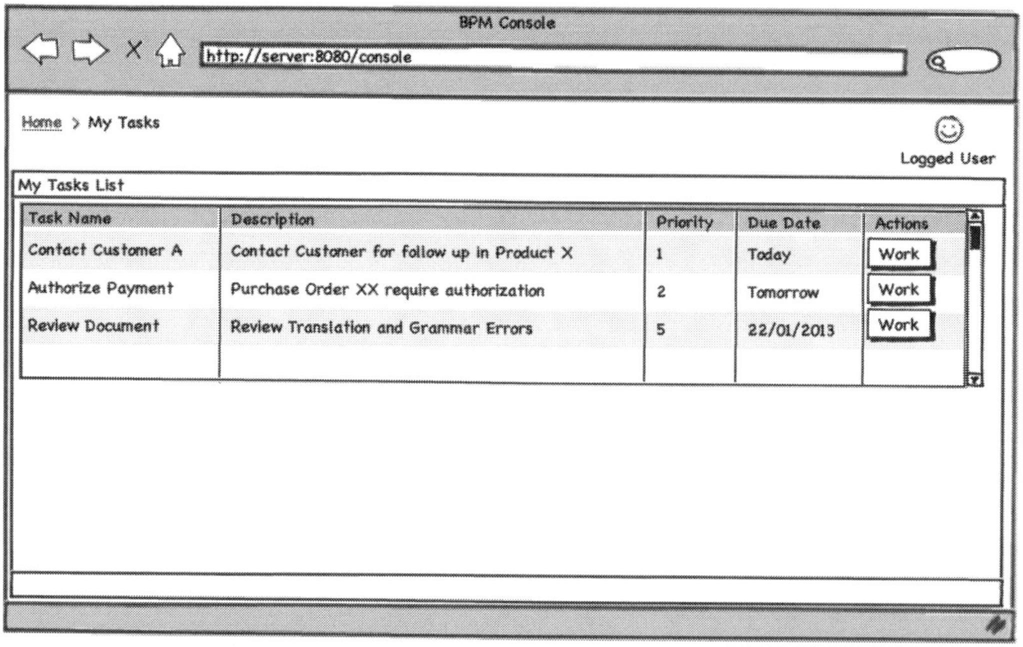

Group task lists

Usually used in conjunction with the user tasks list, the group tasks list will display all of the tasks that a business user can do but is not yet assigned to.

The big difference with a pending task list is that users need to have a way to claim each task displayed in the list.

So the user ends up with a screen containing both, a personal task list and another list of tasks that are not assigned but that he/she can claim. When the user claims a task, it's automatically moved to his/her current pending tasks. At this point, no one else can see this task anymore; none of the other potential owners can claim it now, because it has an owner and its state is Reserved.

But because these tasks have more than one potential owner in the first place a new action can be executed on those tasks. Users who have claimed a task have the option to release the task if they are not able to work on it anymore. If a user chooses to release a task, it will be automatically moved to the group task list again and every potential owner has the chance to claim it.

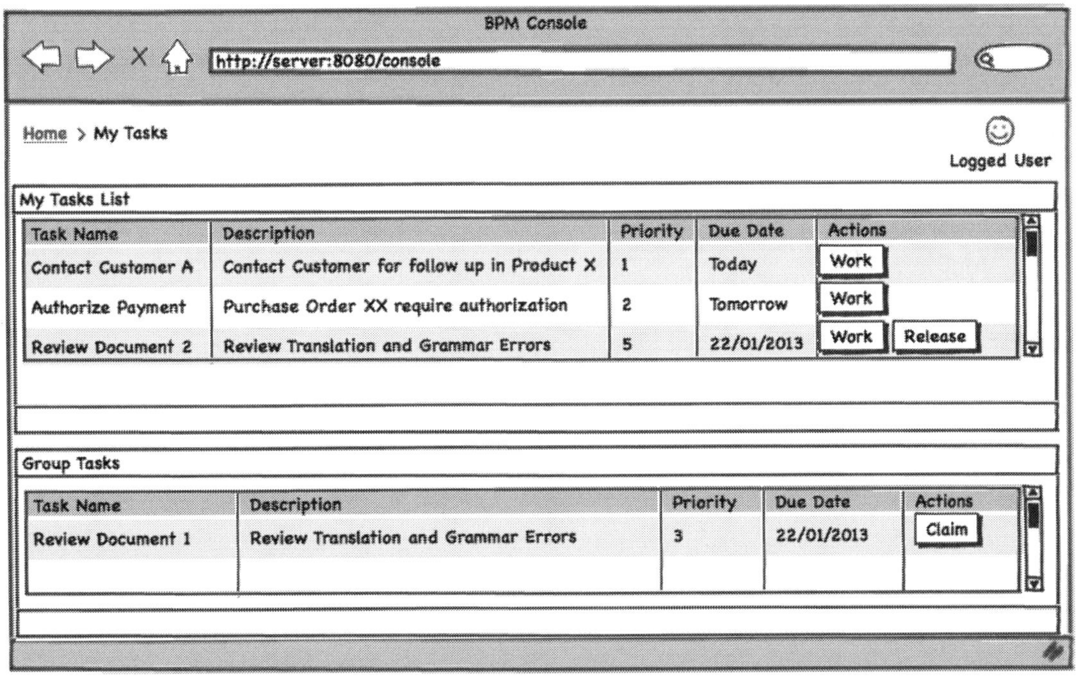

With just these task lists, our end users can have a quick overview about their status and current workload. Notice that in some implementations these task lists (Group and Personal) can be merged into just one. I've decide to show both in separated tables to explain the different concepts. We can customize this screen with different mechanisms, such as different color palettes, to highlight prioritized tasks or tasks that are nearly due. Most of the time, these task lists are enriched with domain-specific information and domain-specific search capabilities. Looking at all of the tasks associated with a specific customer could also be something extremely useful and vital for a company.

The next section covers the other side of the story, when the user wants to work on a specific task.

Task forms

Now that we understand the concept of task lists and how they help us to order and prioritize the work that needs to be done, we can jump directly to the representation of each task.

Each type of task needs to have a different task form that enables user interaction.

Task forms usually have the following requirements:

- Reviewing and approving information
- Gathering information required by the task
- Doing manual work and reporting the outcome

We usually try to digitalize the paper work that needs to be done in the processes, but sometimes it is not possible, at least in the first stages of the project. In such cases, we can just add a reference—a unique reference—to the filled paper form or resultant artifact generated by the manual work. If you are dealing with invoices, for example, the invoice number could be recorded as part of the task to keep a reference to the real invoice.

Depending on the nature of each task, we can create a task form to handle the information managed by that task. These task forms can be reused each time a task with similar requirements is needed.

Some examples of task forms are as follows:

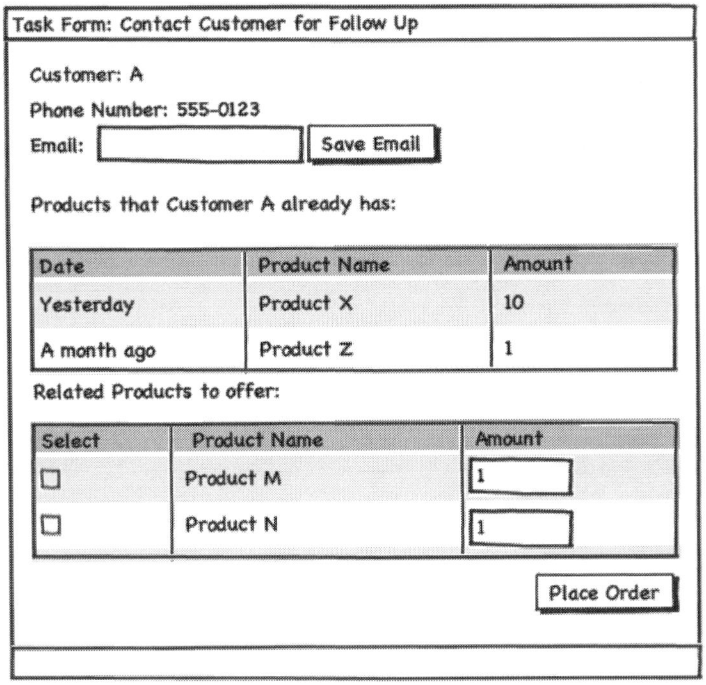

The **Contact Customer for Follow Up** task form provides the user with all the information required to contact customers as well as offer them products related to the ones that they've already bought. Like almost all the task forms, this one contains a huge amount of domain-specific information. The ultimate idea of providing generic task lists and domain-specific task forms is to organize the work that needs to be done in a generic way, but when the user needs to do the real work, we provide very specific tools. The other cool thing about task forms is that multiple processes that require this functionality can use them.

As you can see in the previous task form example, the task also has some intermediate steps that can assist the user to gather all the necessary information.

The following screenshot shows the **Authorize Payment for Purchase Order** task form. Once again, each task form will provide very specific functionality to achieve that specific task. We can notice that in this case, the person in charge of authorizing the payment is also in charge of selecting the shipping option and can add some notes for the provider delivering that order. How you will organize your task form and the data contained in them depends on the business context. There is no best practice other than trying to be as concise as possible with the scope of the tasks. The more concise you are, the more reusable the task forms are.

The following example shows a more advanced task form that requires us to integrate an external plugin in order to read and review documents. Because this is a common requirement, we need to be ready to integrate with different external tools that the user may need in solving a task. The **Review Translated Document** task form shows a task that requires a more advanced internal workflow. Reviewing a document is not a matter of just finishing the review; the user needs to read the document multiple times, adding notes, highlighting different sections, and finally scoring the document translation. Before completing the task, the reviewer can decide to accept the translation or reject it. Depending on how the business process is modeled, the output of this task can affect the process execution. Based on this output, different activities can be chosen. Notice that this task form consists of two different tabs; one uses a specialized tool, such as an embedded PDF reader, to review a document. The second tab gathers information pertinent to the process, which will be kept as process information.

In cases like these, keeping the document reference inside the process is enough. There is no need to keep all the content of the document as a process variable. You will find it a common practice to keep the document in a content repository and have a process variable that points to the actual document. If for some reason the business process requires some bits of information from inside the document to make some decisions, you can usually store metadata about the document inside the repository and use that information inside the process context.

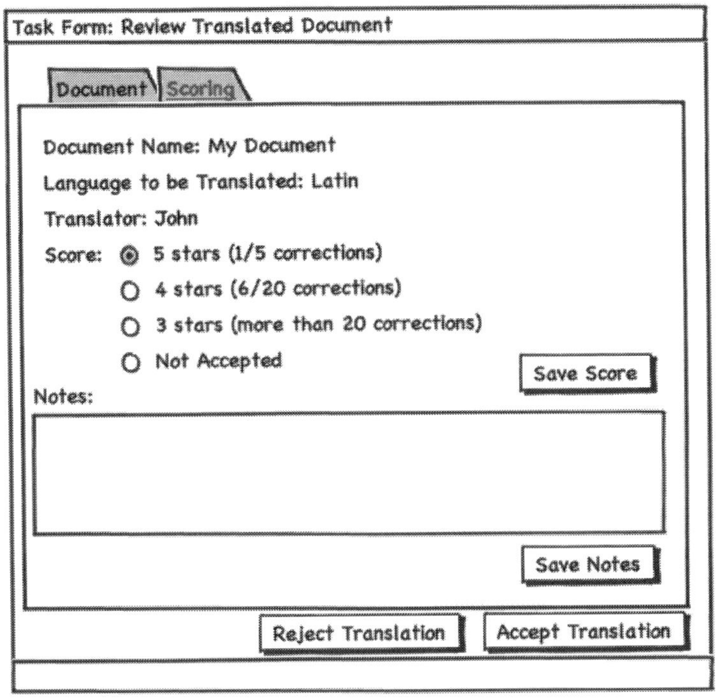

As you can see in the previous examples, the main responsibility of generic implementations of tasks forms is to get task input and output information. Based on this mapping and the type of each parameter, a dynamic form can be generated to display and collect the required information. These kinds of mechanisms will have defined generic components to do the work such as:

- Simple text fields
- Password / hidden text fields
- Calendar component for handling dates
- Select lists (list of values)
- Multi-selection lists
- Checkboxes / radio buttons

The previously mentioned visual components are available in most of the UI-related frameworks. But sometimes it´s not enough—we need to go one step further. It is common to find tools that allow business users to create the task forms. In jBPM5, we have a component called form builder that allows business users to design the task forms and hook them with their corresponding task. The form builder is not covered in this book but keep an eye on the jBPM5 website for more information on it.

It is important to remember that each human task represents a real world task that needs to be done. We need to find the best way to represent and allow the user to do the task. Depending on the nature of the task, we may need to create custom components to deal with domain-specific users' interactions.

As we saw in the **Review Translated Document** task form, external components can be used so we need to search for and choose which component is best for our needs. For this particular example, the following list can be helpful in making our decision since it itemizes what we really need when we're handling a document inside our process and task form (this list is not exhaustive):

- Plain text file
- **Rich Text File (RTF)**
- Microsoft Word (`.doc`) / Open Office Document (`.odp`)
- Cloud / Google Drive link
- PDF / EPub

In cases like our example, a simple task form with text fields will not work. We need more advanced components and also need to add plugins to enable users to do their work.

Each of these task forms can be handled as a knowledge asset, which will be used as a bridge between the process and the users. Tasks forms are displayed to the end user applying a rendering strategy and a templating mechanism.

We need to understand that it's just one possible solution to enable the user interaction. We need to be open minded about how we can expose the task lists and task forms, so that users can easily access the information required to complete their tasks.

Here are some of the things that we can do to improve how the end users access the information related to human tasks:

- Provide mobile implementations for task lists and task forms
- Email-based services
- SMS-based services

- Social network client interfaces: Twitter, Facebook, and other such implementations
- Excel-based task forms

The more ways we provide users to work, the faster (and less painful!) the adoption phase is. The following section discusses how we can build these task forms and task lists, no matter what technology we choose to render them in.

Building our own user interfaces

Nowadays developers can choose from more than 20 frameworks in the Java world that allow them to build applications using different approaches. This section describes generic features that our user interfaces will need to implement in order to enable the end users to perform their tasks. No matter what technology you choose, the underlying concepts as well as how we use the jBPM5 human task service APIs will be the same.

In order to get started, we need to first build our task's lists screens. Remember that a task list is a generic way to organize tasks that are assigned to a particular user, and so we need to render inside our task list all the tasks for the currently logged user.

In order to build a task list, we first need to get the ID for the currently logged user. If we are in a web application, we can usually get this information from the HTTP session. If you are not in a web application, you will need to find out how you can get the currently logged user. Once we get the ID of the currently logged user, we can query the human task service directly. We don't need to interact with the process engine for rendering our task lists. This is a very good way of removing load from the process engine. Imagine if we had a large number of users querying for their tasks concurrently—we could suffer a performance impact! But because jBPM5 provides a separate component to deal with human interactions, this is not a problem at all. If we need to optimize our infrastructure to deal with more user interactions, we know that the only component that will be affected is the human task component so we can focus on optimizing only this component.

Tasks lists are usually rendered when the user accesses his/her account. In most of the BPM systems and implementations, task lists are the entry point for the users to start working, which is why they are usually rendered as part of the home screen of each user console.

In order to get all the tasks associated with a user, we will need to have a task client that in some way connects to the human task service.

From the jBPM5 API's perspective, we will usually use one of the task client's query methods that accepts the user as a parameter:

```
List<TaskSummary> userTasks =
        client
          .getTasksAssignedAsPotentialOwner(loggedUser,
                                            "en-UK");
```

There are several query methods, depending on the role that the user has against different tasks. Most of the time we want to know the tasks to which the user is already assigned as a potential owner. Notice that the query method returns a list of `TaskSummary`. Because we don't need all the information about the task for rendering the task lists, the jBPM5 human task service API returns just a summary that allows us to quickly render each row inside our task lists with the minimum information required to give the user a context to understand the nature of the task.

Once we get the `TaskSummary` list, we need to iterate it and render a row per element of our task list. Usually each row ends up inside a data grid, where we can define which bits of the `TaskSummary` object will be displayed. We can also provide different perspectives with more detailed information if it's required.

The following screenshot shows a very simple task list that I've created in a couple of hours (using Swing: `http://docs.oracle.com/javase/tutorial/ui/overview/intro.html`) to demonstrate how easy it is to create your own, using the technology that you feel comfortable with:

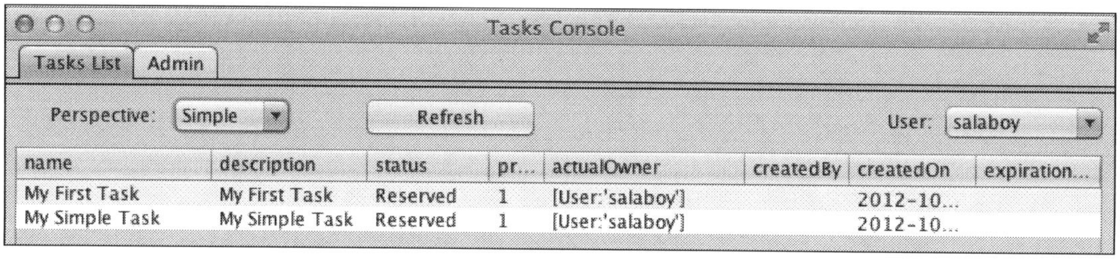

As you can see, the most basic components are in place. We have a data grid that is in charge of listing the task for the selected user. In this case, we have a way to select the current user, which enables us to test more quickly. We also have a perspective list that allows us to get more information about each task. Finally, the **Refresh** button is in charge of executing the query, which will retrieve all the current pending tasks for the selected user. In real scenarios, we can implement a pooling mechanism that executes the query every *x* minutes to keep the task list updated for each user.

Depending on the technology that we are using, we can create a link that allows the user to move from one selected task summary to the task form.

For this Swing example, if we double-click in a row of our task list, a task form will be opened in a different tab.

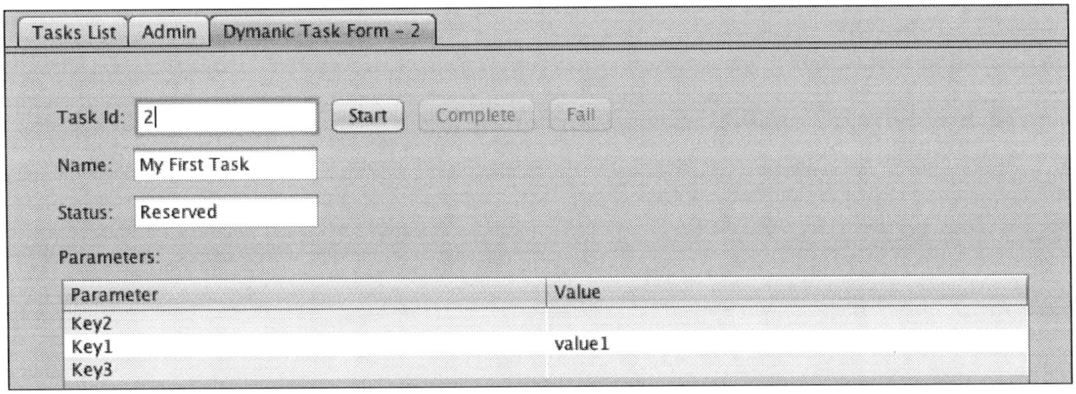

The generic functionality of this task form allows us to interact with the task via actions. In this case, the most basic ones are **Start/Complete**. The space between the buttons and the task status and the action buttons will be filled by domain-specific tools to gather data or achieve different business tasks.

Take a look at the **Admin** tab, which allows you to create new tasks and the task content **Parameters**, which are the required data to work on each specific task instance.

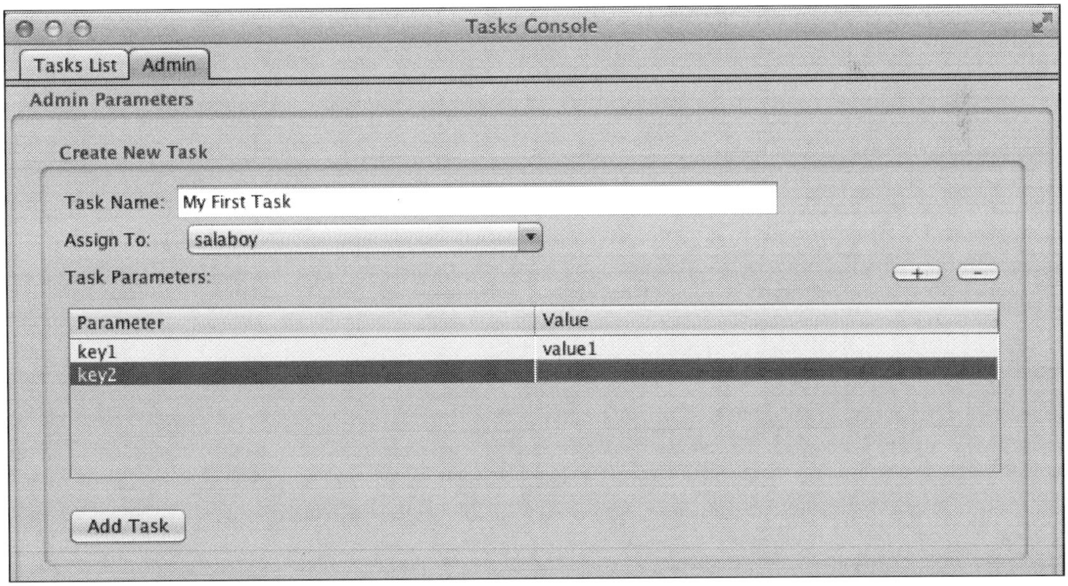

I strongly suggest that you open this project and take a look at the source code to understand which methods from the jBPM5 human task API are being used, where, and when. You can find the source code for this example inside the `chapter_07` directory. The project is called: `jBPM5-HumanTaskUI-Swing`. Take a look at the project dependencies.

To run the example from the console or from your IDE, you need to run the following Maven goal:

```
mvn exec:java
```

Summary

In this chapter we have discussed the main points of providing human interactions. As you may know by now, human interactions are not necessarily tied to a business process execution and can be independently created by any other application. We have learned how we can expose and organize the task that needs to be executed by a specific role, using task lists and task forms. The following chapters will show how this component can be used in conjunction with the rule engine, the complex event-processing features and how extracting information from this component can allow us to provide valuable information for decision-making.

8

Persistence and Transactions

In this chapter we will cover the most important aspects of persistence and transactions in order to understand and configure these mechanisms inside the Drools and jBPM5 platform.

Both persistence and transaction services are topics that usually confuse newcomers. This is because, depending on the environment in which we are trying to run our application, different polices can be applied and the runtime behavior can be affected, causing unexpected failures. If we don't understand exactly why we need to configure them, the application behavior can frustrate us. We need to understand the problems that we are trying to tackle in order to apply the most appropriate configuration when needed.

Real-life scenarios require handling processes that can last for days, months, or even years, involving multiple component interactions. These requirements force BPMSs to provide specific mechanisms, which we developers need to understand in terms of how they are designed and how they affect our process' execution.

This chapter will cover the following points:

- Why we need the persistence mechanism?
- Why we need to handle transactions?
- Frequently asked questions on these topics

Why we need persistence mechanisms

When we talk about processes, we know that we can run them in memory if they are quick and can be completed in a couple of minutes. Up to now, all the examples presented in this book have been in-memory processes, with a focus on showing how the jBPM5 process engine works. When we have processes that take more than a couple of minutes (which is usually the case), we will be forced to analyze and choose a persistence mechanism.

For every process that we want to run in our production environment (not just in a test), we need to define a set of functional requirements in order to guarantee their correct performance and execution. Remember that a business process is supposed to be guiding a company in its daily activities. These activities can be very different, so the requirements to fulfill them can vary. It's up to you to understand the nature and requirements of each process that you want to run, so that you recognize and decide which configuration is best in a given situation. For processes, there are two high-level categories:

- In-memory processes
- Long-running processes (also known as persistent processes)

As mentioned before, **in-memory processes** are usually short-lived processes that execute quick (synchronous and asynchronous), automatic interactions. These processes are usually very low-level technical operations, such as service orchestrations. We cannot predict exactly how much time a short-lived process will take, but we know that it will be over in matter of seconds or minutes.

On the other hand, for **long-running processes** we know for sure that a long period of time will be required to complete an instance. A typical example is when human tasks are involved. When a process depends on asynchronous external interactions, the process engine won't know if the external entity will take 1 second, 1 minute, or 1 month to complete an activity.

The following set of questions have been designed to help you decide which category a given process falls under:

1. Does your process run from beginning to end without waiting for an external interaction?

   If your answer is yes, you are potentially facing an in-memory process. If your answer is no, you will need to evaluate the external interaction's average completion time in order to decide if you can afford to wait out the overall process time.

2. Can your process instances be started again from the beginning if something goes wrong in the middle of the execution?

   If your answer is yes, you are safe to run it as an in-memory process. If you can restart your process instance when something goes wrong, it means that your process instance doesn't require you to store any previous state to be recovered from an anomalous situation. This fact makes our life simple; if something goes wrong, we can just create a fresh instance to do the work.

If your answer is no, you will need to analyze if there is a simple mechanism that allows you to recover from an error without persisting the process status. If this is not possible, your process is most likely a long-running process.

3. Does your process interact with other transactional services?

   If your answer is yes, you will probably need to use persistent processes to make the process status consistent with all the other transactional resources that are being used. If your answer is no, a simple in-memory configuration will do the work for you.

If we identify that we have long-running/persistent processes, we will need to find a way to store the process status in a persistent storage.

Generally, whenever we have to store the state of our running processes, we need a mechanism that gets the current state from the main memory (RAM / volatile memory) to a secondary (non-volatile) storage such as a database or a filesystem. Depending on the information that we are handling inside our processes, the performance requirements, and the data structures that we want to persist, we will configure the persistence mechanism differently.

Here are the most common approaches used to persist states:

- Filesystem: Since we are using Java, we will need a way to transform the process engine internal objects to a byte[], which will represent the process status
- Relational database: Since we are using Java, using JPA is the standard way of interacting with relational databases by using well-known object relational mapping frameworks (such as Hibernate)
- Not Only SQL (NoSQL) / key value storage / graph-oriented DBs

These approaches allow us to get the current status of a process in the main memory and store it in a safe place. The fastest approach is usually to create a binary representation of the objects that hold the state (a byte[] representation), in contrast to the database approach, which can take too much time if the structures that we are handling are really complex. If we look at the file-based approach versus the database approach though, the first one lacks some serious features, such as concurrent access, transaction ability, and integrity checking. The enterprise software that is being built today usually requires all these features. We will see how jBPM5 mixes these approaches to provide a fast storage of runtime data.

The next section covers how the persistence mechanism is used in most BPM systems available. We will see how these standard mechanisms are then applied in jBPM5 and Drools.

Persisting long-running processes

Let's analyze the behavior of a **long-running process** for a second. When we refer to "a running process instance", we are saying that it is active. It means that the business goal is still not fulfilled and that there are pending activities to be executed. From the business-process perspective, the process instance is running. From the technical perspective, we can say that the process is probably waiting for some external activity to be finished before it can continue to the next step. Let's take a look at the following example:

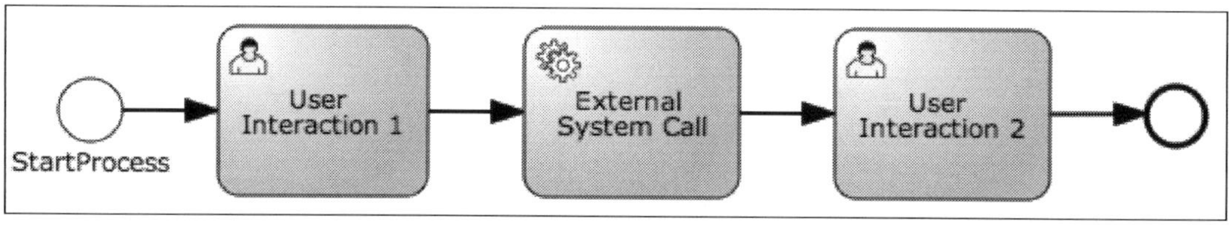

This very simple business process contains two human interactions and an automated interaction with an external system. When we start a new instance of the business process, the start event will be executed, the user task will create a new task for the user, and the process will need to wait for the task to be completed. The process state will remain the same until the user completes the task, thereby triggering the process continuation. Technically speaking, if the user never finishes the task, the process will be waiting forever.

There are some common terms to define this situation of waiting, such as **wait state**, **safe point**, and **safe state.** The term wait state makes reference to the fact that the activity needs to be executed by an external entity (in this case, a human actor). Safe point or safe state, in contrast, makes reference to the fact that we can safely persist the state of the process instance. We can do this as well as remove the process from the server's/machine's main memory, because there are no actions being executed internally by the engine at that point. It is safe to store the state, because we are waiting for an external entity that can take a day, a month, or a year to execute the activity. The following figure shows the concept of the safe point explicitly:

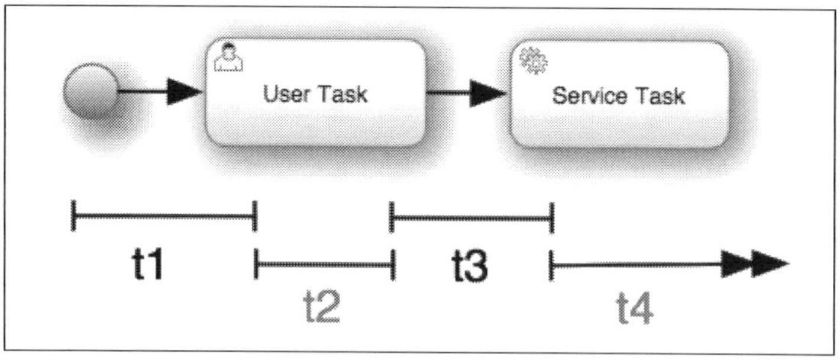

Notice that t1 represents the initial creation time and t2 represents the idle time until the external entity finishes the task. Most of the time, t2 is extremely large compared to t1, which is why we can state that most of our process technically runs for small amounts of time and waits for an external operation for long periods. In order to not depend on the server's/machine's main memory, our process state can be stored in a persistent storage during t2 and t4. In this example, t2 and t4 are external to the process engine, which means that we can support server crashes. It is much safer to store the process status than to trust that the server will not crash. Based on some private benchmarking of the engine, t1 and t3 are of a maximum magnitude of 50 ms in contrast to a human task, like for example t2, which could be unattended for long periods if the person in charge of it is not in front of his/her computer.

Persistence in jBPM5

Drools and jBPM5 share the declarative power that allows us to formalize and execute domain-specific knowledge (Rules & Processes). The persistence component itself was created and designed with the idea in mind that persistence is a common mechanism between Drools and jBPM5. From now on, you need to be aware that the persistence component is not only in charge of dealing with the process engine but also with the rule engine in a unified way.

The concept of a safe point remains the same from the process perspective, but now we also need to understand how it works from the rule engine's perspective.

The previous section shows what a safe point looks like. It's important to understand that there is a one-to-one relationship between a safe point and a method of the API. For example:

```
ksession.startProcess(<id>, <params>);
```

This method execution starts the process, executing all the activities until the process reaches a safe point, such as the first user task defined in the previous example. This method will return as soon as there is nothing more to do than wait for an external interaction (system or human). If we define a process without safe states, this method will execute the process until the end without persisting the state.

As we already saw in the API introduction section, `StatefulKnowledgeSession` serves as the main access point for us to interact with the rule and process engines. Some common methods that we can use to interact with the rule engine are:

- `ksession.insert(<fact>);`
- `ksession.update(<facthandle>, <fact>);`
- `ksession.retract(<facthandle>);`
- `ksession.fireAllRules();`

These methods behave the same way as the processes do. When we interact with the rule engine, each method can execute different bits/chunks of logic, depending on the present rules, processes, and the facts in that particular session.

For example, the `insert()`, `update()`, and `retract()` methods will do all the evaluations for the fact that you are inserting / updating / retracting in the knowledge session. The `fireAllRules()` method will execute all the activated rules for a specific fact set. Because of the recursive nature of the Rule Engine's internal algorithm, and depending on the knowledge that is being evaluated, the time required to complete the execution will vary. The good thing is that we know when one of these methods returns the control to the application, we are at a safe point.

The current implementation of the persistence component can be found in these two projects: `drools-persistence-jpa`, `jbpm-persistence-jpa`.

Here you can see that the jBPM5 project has extended Drools' capabilities by adding the specific entities related to the processes. These two projects define the mechanisms to take snapshots of the knowledge session state at safe points. These snapshots contain a serialized version of the current internal status of the knowledge session. Since Drools 5.3 and jBPM5 5.2 releases, we use a framework called Protobuf (`http://code.google.com/p/protobuf/`) to perform the serialization process. Compared to the standard serialization methods used in the Java environment, Protobuf offers some very interesting extra features. It provides a language-neutral, platform-neutral, extensible way of serializing structured data.

So once we get a snapshot containing the current session state, we use JPA to store it in a very simple table inside a database. These tables contain the byte array that represents the session state plus additional metadata, which will allow us to restore the session whenever we need to. The examples in this book use JPA1 with Hibernate 3 as a persistence provider, but JPA2 with Hibernate 4 can also be configured.

The entities and tables used by JPA are:

- `SessionInfo`
- `ProcessInstanceInfo`
- `EventTypes`
- `WorkItemInfo`

For more information on the tables that are being used to store the binary snapshot, you can take a look at the official documentation:

`http://docs.jboss.org/jbpm/v5.4/userguide/ch.core-persistence.html#d0e3334`

Remember that the persistence mechanism needs to be configured at the session level, which is why a helper class is introduced, `JPAKnowledgeService`. This helper class contains two static methods that allow us to create and restore a previously persisted knowledge session.

If we take a look at the methods implemented by the `JPAKnowledgeService` class, we will notice that in order to create a persistence session, we will need the following:

```
StatefulKnowledgeSession newStatefulKnowledgeSession(
KnowledgeBase kbase,
KnowledgeSessionConfiguration configuration,
Environment environment);

StatefulKnowledgeSession loadStatefulKnowledgeSession(int id,
KnowledgeBase kbase,
KnowledgeSessionConfiguration configuration,
Environment environment);
```

Essentially, the `newStatefulKnowledgeSession()` method allows us to create a new persistent `StatefulKnowledgeSession` instance.

The environment variable will be used to configure—in both engines—the persistence and transaction providers. In other words, this variable will contain a reference to `EntityManagerFactory` and Transactional Manager. If we choose not to use a JPA implementation, we can set up an equivalent of `EntityManagerFactory` inside the environment variable. Drools and jBPM5 allow us to extend and provide our own implementation, so we can define how we want to handle the persistence and transactional mechanisms.

If we create a persistent knowledge session, the `id` field will be initialized by the persistence layer (or the backend database, if we are using the JPA implementation). We can obtain the actual ID by using the `ksession.getId()` method. This ID can be used later to restore the session using the `loadStatefulKnowledgeSession(...)` method provided by the `JPAKnowledgeService` helper class.

But how does it work internally?

Internally, the `JPAKnowledgeService` helper class creates a `CommandBasedStatefulKnowledgeSession` instance that implements the `StatefulKnowledgeSession` interface. The term `CommandBased` is used to make a reference to the command design pattern (`http://www.oodesign.com/command-pattern.html`) that is being used to execute the session's internal logic.

Drools defines a set of commands that implements the `GenericCommand` interface:

```
public interface GenericCommand<T extends Object> extends Command<T> {
    public T execute(Context cntxt);
}
```

The commands that implement this interface represent a piece of logic that can be executed by a command executor. If you take a look at the current implementations of this interface, you will find that there is one command per method exposed in the `StatefulKnowledgeSession` interface. You will see that we have implemented commands such as `StartProcessInstanceCommand`, `InsertObjectCommand`, `RetractCommand`, and `FireAllRulesCommand`.

You will also see that this command pattern is widely used inside the Drools/jBPM platform. Now that we know the commands' responsibility, we can analyze how the `CommandBasedStatefulKnowledgeSession` instance works internally. This gives us a hook point to take a snapshot and persist the status of the session after each command execution.

From a high-level perspective, we have the following interaction:

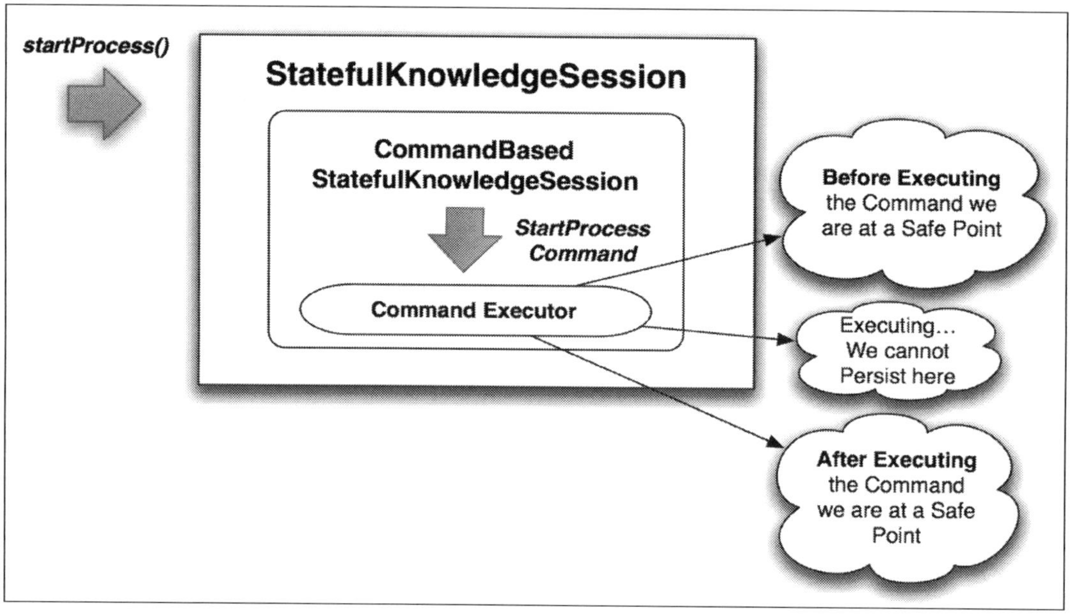

When we create a new `StatefulKnowledgeSession` interface using the `JPAKnowledgeService` helper class, we obtain a `CommandBasedKnowledgeSession` instance instead of a `StatefulKnowledgeSessionImpl` instance. The user interacts with the session normally, but in the back, a `CommandBasedKnowledgeSession` instance will be dealing with the user requests. As you saw in the previous figure, the command-based implementation is in charge of creating the corresponding command and its execution. From the API's perspective, we are able to use a `StatefulKnowledgeSession` interface without worrying about the persistence mechanisms. Now we have clear hook points, before and after executing the command, where the persistence mechanism kicks in. If everything is configured correctly, a binary snapshot will be created after each interaction and then stored in the database.

The following section describes how transactions come into the picture and why they are extremely important.

Why we need a transaction mechanism

I assume you are already familiar with the concept of **transaction**. The basic idea of transactions is to keep our data coherent. When we talk about database transactions, we make reference to a unit of work that needs to be executed completely or rolled back if something fails. The same principle applies to other transactional resources such as messaging queues, and transactional services.

This section gives us an introduction to why we need to deal with transactional resources and how we need to configure our runtime to support them.

As introduced in the previous section, Drools and jBPM5 share the same persistence and transaction mechanisms. This ensures that the snapshots that we take from our sessions (which contain processes and all the information that is being stored inside the knowledge session, such as facts and process variables) are stored consistently in the database. The `CommandBasedKnowledgeSession` instance creates a transaction before executing each command and then commits the transaction if the command was successfully executed. If something goes wrong, the transaction is rolled back and the previous status of the session is recovered.

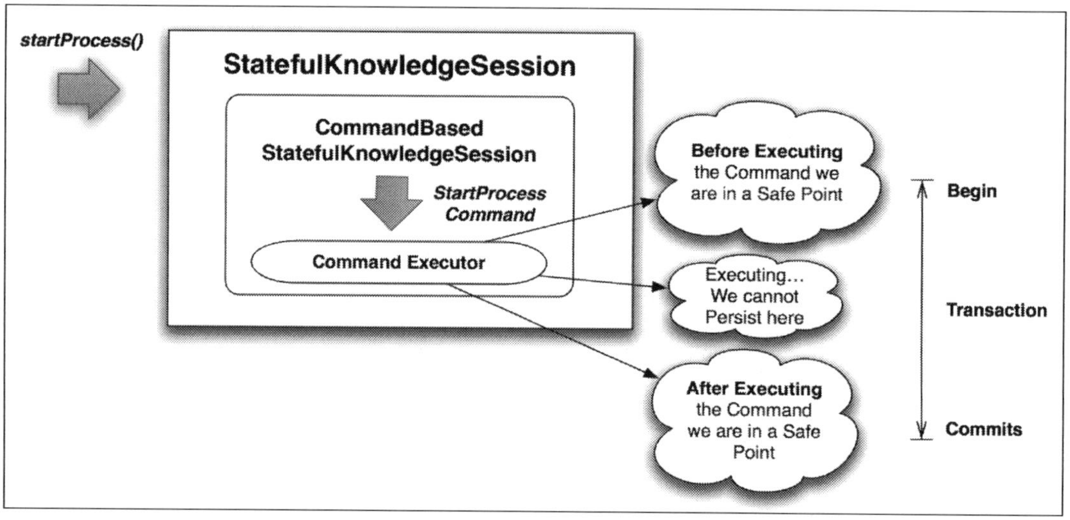

In simple cases, we will deal with just one transaction created by each command execution. During the transaction's lifespan, the command will be executed, the snapshot of the current status of the session will be taken, and all this information will be persisted in the database as soon as the transaction ends and gets committed. If at any time the command execution fails, the transaction is rolled back and the changes in the session are discarded.

In real-life scenarios, the execution of a command (for example, `StartProcessCommand`) involves more than just the database. This fact forces us to understand the nature of each one of these components and make decisions on how we want to configure our system.

Let's go back to our previous example:

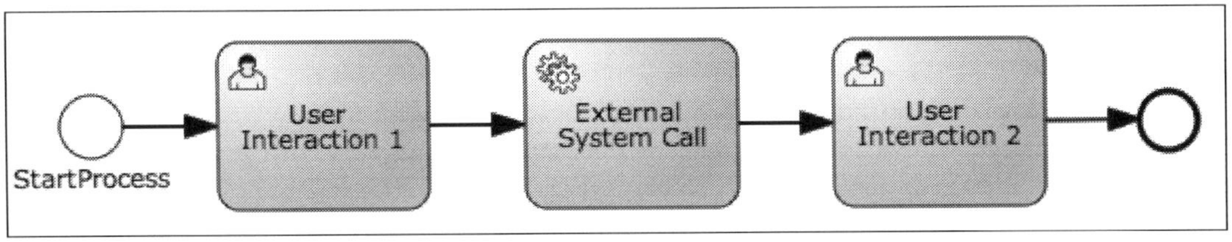

Imagine we want to run this process using a persistent knowledge session. Using the `JPAKnowledgeService` helper class, we obtain a `CommandBasedStatefulKnowledgeSession` instance that will be in charge of creating `StartProcessCommand` when we call the `startProcess()` method. Before starting the execution of `StartProcessCommand`, a new transaction is created. For this example, because we have a human interaction, the transaction will be committed as soon as the engine creates the corresponding human task inside the human task service. Now, because we have two different components, we need to make sure that if we persist our process instance status as waiting for an external interaction, this external interaction has been correctly created; if it has not, we will end up with an incoherent situation.

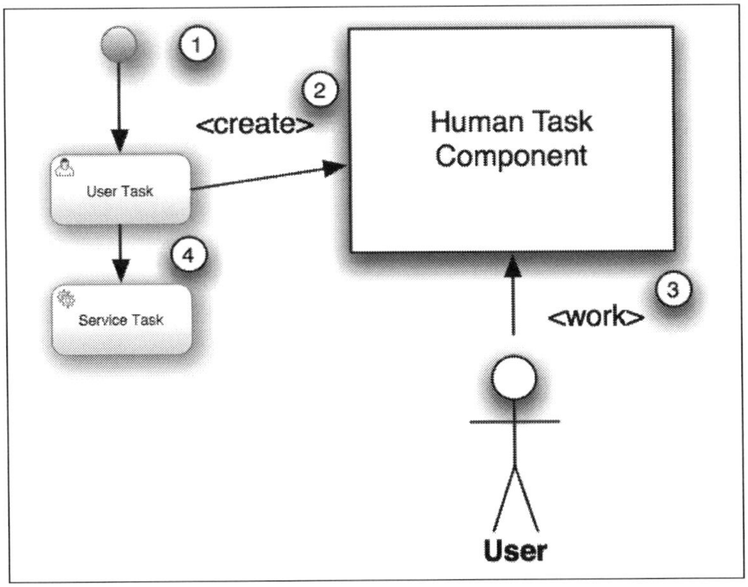

We can see how 1 and 2 need to be inside the same transaction boundaries to guarantee that we are waiting for a human interaction to be completed. If for some reason the `StartProcessCommand` execution fails or the task creation at the Human Task Component fails, the process state and the task creation need to be undone. The same happens when the user works on the human task that was created for him/her. As the completion of the human task will begin a transaction, this transaction will encapsulate the steps 3 and 4 until the process reaches the next wait state. For this example the service task is an asynchronous activity, which means that the transaction will be committed right after the service task schedules the activity in the external system.

The previous example assumes that we can include the human task service in the same transaction that is being used by the `JPAKnowledgeService` helper class to store the session. This assumption is correct if we use the human task service as a local service instead of having it as a separate component, like the remote transport (Mina, HornetQ, or JMS) implementations for the human task service.

The following section introduces an example project, which shows these mechanisms in action.

Simple jBPM5 persistence and transactions configuration

This section covers the basic persistence and transaction configurations for jBPM5. It also covers some additional things that you need to know in order to start working with persistent knowledge sessions. We will see the technical and practical aspects of how to configure transactions, since there are some basic configurations that need to be done before we can work with the persistence mechanisms.

The project called `jBPM5-PersistentProcess` inside the `chapter_08` directory contains a simple test class that shows how to set up all the configurations when working with the `JPAKnowledgeService` helper class. Take a look at the `README` file provided in this chapter's source code directory for a full description of the provided tests.

If you open the test class called `PersistentProcessTest`, you will find a test that creates a persistent session using the `JPAKnowledgeService` helper class:

```
Environment env = EnvironmentFactory.newEnvironment();
EntityManagerFactory emf = Persistence.
createEntityManagerFactory("org.jbpm.runtime");

env.set(EnvironmentName.ENTITY_MANAGER_FACTORY, emf);
```

```
env.set(EnvironmentName.TRANSACTION_MANAGER,
          TransactionManagerServices.getTransactionManager());
final StatefulKnowledgeSession ksession =
        JPAKnowledgeService.newStatefulKnowledgeSession(kbase,
                                                    null, env);
```

As you can see, now we need to create an `Environment` object, which will contain all of the configurations required to create a persistent session. Two properties are required for the basic settings: `EnvironmentName.ENTITY_MANAGER_FACTORY` and `EnvironmentName.TRANSACTION_MANAGER`.

As you may notice, we are creating `EntityManagerFactory` based on a persistence unit called `org.jbpm.runtime`. The `persistence.xml` file that you can find inside the `META-INF` directory located at `src/test/resources` defines this persistence unit.

```
<persistence-unit name="org.jbpm.runtime"
transaction-type="JTA">
<provider>org.hibernate.ejb.HibernatePersistence</provider>
<jta-data-source>jdbc/testDS1</jta-data-source>
<mapping-file>META-INF/JBPMorm.xml</mapping-file>
<mapping-file>META-INF/ProcessInstanceInfo.hbm.xml</mapping-file>
<class>org.drools.persistence.info.SessionInfo</class>
<class>
org.jbpm.persistence.processinstance.ProcessInstanceInfo
</class>
<class>org.drools.persistence.info.WorkItemInfo</class>
<properties>
<!—Other Hibernate Properties Ommited à
<property
name="hibernate.transaction.manager_lookup_class"
value=
"org.hibernate.transaction.BTMTransactionManagerLookup"
/>
</properties>
</persistence-unit>
```

To do unit testing, we usually use Bitronix (`http://docs.codehaus.org/display/BTM/Home`), which is an easily embeddable transaction manager. Basically, Bitronix allows us to create a data source, which can be linked to multiple transactional resources. The `transaction.manager_lookup_class` property set up will be in charge of looking at `TransactionManager` associated to the data source defined inside the `jta-data-source` tag. If you are planning to use jBPM5 inside JBoss AS for example, instead of using Bitronix you will probably use JBoss transactions (`http://www.jboss.org/jbosstm`) that are provided by the container.

In order to start a data source using Bitronix, we do the following:

```
@Before
public void setUp() {
  ds.setUniqueName("jdbc/testDS1");
  ds.setClassName("org.h2.jdbcx.JdbcDataSource");
  ds.setMaxPoolSize(3);
  ds.setAllowLocalTransactions(true);
  ds.getDriverProperties().put("user", "sa");
  ds.getDriverProperties().put("password", "sasa");
  ds.getDriverProperties().put("URL", "jdbc:h2:mem:mydb");
  ds.init();
}
```

The previous snippet creates a data source against an embedded instance of H2, the database that we have already used for the human task, and executor components.

Once again, if we are inside an application server we will need to find out how to create and manage data sources, all of which should be in the documentation for that specific server. For JBoss Application Server 7, the one installed by the jBPM installer, you can find a quick how-to on data sources at `https://community.jboss.org/wiki/DataSourceConfigurationInAS7`

Finally, because Bitronix also creates a JNDI tree to enable JNDI lookups, we need to add the following property inside a file called `jndi.properties` in our resources directory:

```
java.naming.factory.initial=
bitronix.tm.jndi.BitronixInitialContextFactory
```

Or you can set this property as a system property by using the following code snippet:

```
System.setProperty("java.naming.factory.initial",
 "bitronix.tm.jndi.BitronixInitialContextFactory");
```

If you try to run a project without specifying the Naming Initial Factory, you'll get the following exception:

```
Caused by: javax.naming.NoInitialContextException: Need to specify class
name in environment or system property, or as an applet parameter, or in
an application resource file:  java.naming.factory.initial
        at javax.naming.spi.NamingManager.getInitialContext(NamingManager.
java:645)
        ...
```

Once we have all the configurations in place, we can start using our knowledge session. I have created two mock work-item handlers for this test, which will simulate human interactions and the external service interaction. Because the business process that we are trying to run will need to have the work-item handlers' definitions, we need to register them:

```
MockHTWorkItemHandler mockHTWorkItemHandler =
new MockHTWorkItemHandler();
MockExternalServiceWorkItemHandler
mockExternalServiceWorkItemHandler
= new MockExternalServiceWorkItemHandler();
ksession.getWorkItemManager().registerWorkItemHandler(
"Human Task", mockHTWorkItemHandler);
ksession.getWorkItemManager().registerWorkItemHandler(
"External Service Call",
mockExternalServiceWorkItemHandler);
```

> If we are using persistent-knowledge sessions, it is a requirement for all our entities to be serializable/externalizable in order to be stored correctly.

In the previously introduced test class, you will see that we are using a process variable, which is a `Person` instance. If you open this `Person` class, you will notice that this class needs to be serializable.

If all our domain data can be serialized, the persistence layer will be able to work correctly. Running the test called `processInstancePersistentTest()` inside the `PersistentProcessTest` class should show the following console output:

```
>>> Let's create a Persistent Knowledge Session
Hibernate: insert into SessionInfo ...
>>> Let's Create Process Instance
Hibernate: insert into ProcessInstanceInfo ...
Hibernate: update SessionInfo ...
Hibernate: update ProcessInstanceInfo ...
>>> Let's Start the Process Instance
Hibernate: select pI from ProcessInstanceInfo
Hibernate: insert into WorkItemInfo
>>> Completing a Human Interaction
Hibernate: insert into WorkItemInfo
>>> Completing an External Interaction
Hibernate: insert into WorkItemInfo
>>> Completing a Human Interaction
```

```
Hibernate: select pI from ProcessInstanceInfo
Hibernate: update SessionInfo
Hibernate: delete from EventTypes where InstanceId=?
Hibernate: delete from ProcessInstanceInfo where InstanceId=?
Hibernate: delete from WorkItemInfo where workItemId=?
Hibernate: delete from WorkItemInfo where workItemId=?
Hibernate: delete from WorkItemInfo where workItemId=?
>>> Disposing Session
```

> The queries' details were omitted to present the output in less than one page.

As you can see, as soon as we create the persistent-knowledge session using the `JPAKnowledgeService` helper class, a new row is inserted inside the `SessionInfo` table. This table will contain all the persistent sessions. When we create a new process instance inside our session, a new row inside the table called `ProcessInstanceInfo` is also inserted, containing the information about our just-created process. The two following updates are being triggered to set the references between the process and the session (and vice versa).

> This persistence mechanism should be considered internal to the process engine. The users should not influence how the engine handles the information internally. You, as a developer, need to know how it works and how to externalize the data that is being stored if you are interested in querying it. You should discard any attempt at consuming the serialized information contained in the tables created by the persistence mechanism.

When we start the created process instance, we can see that the first `select` gets the corresponding process instance and then the three activities get executed. As soon as the process finishes its execution, we can see how all the runtime information about the process is being cleaned up after completing the second human interaction. This example shows how, for this process, we are using a persistent session, but because the process runs from beginning to end, the process instance is quickly removed.

The next example test called `processInstancePersistentAsyncTest()` shows the same scenario, but here there are two safe points introduced to simulate a real asynchronous human interaction. If you run this test alone, you should see the following output:

```
...
>>> Let's Start the Process Instance
```

```
Hibernate: select pI from ProcessInstanceInfo
Hibernate: insert into WorkItemInfo
>>> Working on a Human Interaction
Hibernate: update SessionInfo
Hibernate: select eT EventTypes
Hibernate: update ProcessInstanceInfo
Hibernate: update WorkItemInfo
>>> Completing the first Human Interaction
Hibernate: insert into WorkItemInfo
>>> Completing an External Interaction
Hibernate: insert into WorkItemInfo
>>> Working on a Human Interaction
Hibernate: update ProcessInstanceInfo
Hibernate: update WorkItemInfo
...
```

As we can see, when a human interaction takes place, a safe point is reached where the process will wait until the external task is completed. That's why `SessionInfo`, `ProcessInstanceInfo`, and `WorkItemInfo` are updated.

Now we need to complete the human interaction manually in order for the process to move forward:

```
ksession.getWorkItemManager()
.completeWorkItem(mockAsyncHTWorkItemHandler.getId(), null);
```

As soon as we complete the work item, the process continues to the next activity, which is completing the external interaction and automatically moving forward to the next human interaction. At this point, we are once again at a safe point, so we can see that `ProcessInstance` and `WorkItemInfo` are being updated.

Feel free to check the next test called `processInstancesPersistenceFaultTest()` to examine what happens if one of the work-item handlers fails and throws an exception. If you take a look at the output, you will see that the process state is rolled back to the previous safe point (in this example, the initial status).

Finally, before moving on to the next section, check out the test called `processInstancesAndLocalHTTest()`, which shows how we configure the process to use a persistent session along with a local implementation for the human task functionality. Now let's take a look at the important points to be noted in this example.

The first important thing is the persistence unit that is used in this test, `org.jbpm.runtime.ht`. It has been included in the same `persistence.xml` file shown before.

```
<persistence-unit name="org.jbpm.runtime.ht"
transaction-type="JTA">
<provider>org.hibernate.ejb.HibernatePersistence</provider>
<jta-data-source>jdbc/testDS1</jta-data-source>
<mapping-file>META-INF/JBPMorm.xml</mapping-file>
<mapping-file>META-INF/ProcessInstanceInfo.hbm.xml</mapping-file>
<mapping-file>META-INF/Taskorm.xml</mapping-file>
<!-- Tasks -->
<class>org.jbpm.task.Status</class>
<class>org.jbpm.task.Task</class>
<class>org.jbpm.task.TaskData</class>
<!– other entities mappings ommited à
<class>org.jbpm.task.User</class>
<!-- Session -->
<class>org.drools.persistence.info.SessionInfo</class>
<class>
org.jbpm.persistence.processinstance.ProcessInstanceInfo
</class>
<class>
org.drools.persistence.info.WorkItemInfo
</class>
<properties>
<!–other hibernate properties omitted à
<property
name="hibernate.transaction.manager_lookup_class"
value="org.hibernate.transaction.BTMTransactionManagerLookup"
/>
</properties>
</persistence-unit>
```

The persistence configurations are the same; we've just added the entities required by the human task classes and the human task specific queries inside the `Taskorm.xml` file.

Inside the `pom.xml` file we've added the `jbpm-human-task-core` dependency, because we are only using the local implementation contained in the core module.

Then, instead of registering a mock work item handler, we will register the `LocalHTWorkItemHandler` instance provided by the `jbpm-human-task-core` module.

```
TaskService client = createTaskService(emf);
LocalHTWorkItemHandler localHTWorkItemHandler =
                new LocalHTWorkItemHandler(client, ksession);
```

Now we can use the client variable to interact with our human tasks. As soon as we start a process instance, a user task will be created; in order to complete it, we will need to use the human task APIs. The behavior from the persistence point of view will be the same as the one simulated in the previous test. The only difference is that in the output we will see how a real human task is created and persisted inside the human task service tables.

Take a look at the code inside the `createTaskService()` method used to initialize the task service.

Notice that when we are interacting with our tasks, the work item handler associated with the human task component will be in charge of notifying the session of any task completion.

```
  ksession.startProcessInstance(processInstance.getId());

System.out.println(" >>> Looking for Salaboy's Tasks");
  List<TaskSummary> salaboysTasks =
client.getTasksAssignedAsPotentialOwner("salaboy", "en-UK");

TaskSummary salaboyTask = salaboysTasks.get(0);

client.start(salaboyTask.getId(), "salaboy");

client.complete(salaboyTask.getId(), "salaboy", null);
```

This means that as soon as we call `client.complete()` to finish a task, the knowledge session will be notified and the corresponding work item will be completed so that the process can move forward. Instead of completing the work item manually, the `LocalHTWorkItemHandler` instance contains the logic that automatically notifies the session of the task's completion using the mechanisms described in the previous chapter.

This configuration—which uses `LocalTaskService` plus `LocalHTWorkItemHandler` and just one persistence unit (containing the session's and the tasks' tables)—is referred to as Persistent Session with Local HT Configuration. Using this configuration, the transactions will be shared by the mechanisms that persist the knowledge session and the mechanisms that persist the human task interactions.

The next section discusses more advanced scenarios, where the persistent-knowledge session needs to interact with external components that are transactional.

Advanced jBPM5 persistence and transactions configuration

When we are running all of our components in the same JVM, the configurations are easy and straightforward. You just need to copy and adapt the configurations to our specific database. When we want to coordinate multiple components, the configuration can become more complex, depending on our requirements as well as the robustness needed.

We will analyze a scenario similar to the one introduced in the previous section, but now the human task service will be a decoupled component that runs in a separate JVM. The same concepts used for the human task service can be applied to any other component or third-party service that we want our knowledge session and the processes hosted inside it to interact with.

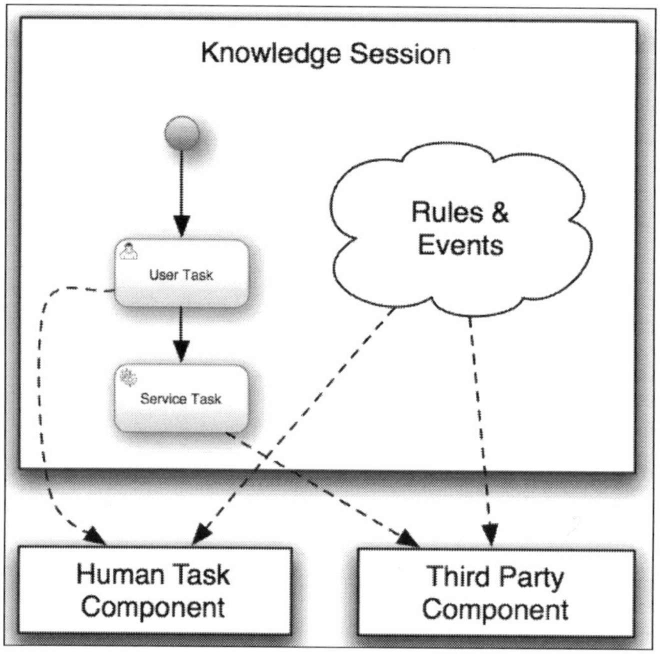

Having an external component changes our architecture and our requirements for configuration. Because jBPM5 is inside the system-integration field, we will need to deal with these situations in one way or another, so let's see how we can interact with external components.

Because the human task service can be configured to run as a service, our application and the process and rule engine will need to contact it using a transport (JMS, Mina, HTTP, and so on). These interactions with the human task service will all be asynchronous because of the nature of human interactions, and from the process engine's perspective, they will all create safe points. These safe points will be intercepted by the persistence mechanism, and the status of the process will be saved right after the creation of the human task.

Now we have two different components, so we will have the transaction split into two different components, as if they were two completely different applications. You need to be aware of what this means in terms of robustness and configurations.

If we want to interact with external components, such as the human task component, we will need to define three important technical aspects:

- Where the component will run?
- Which transport(s) will be used to interact with the component?
- The robustness of our interactions with this particular component

These factors influence how our scenario will behave under different circumstances. Defining and understanding these different scenarios will help us to quickly identify issues when they appear. They will also serve us as guidelines to decide which is the best path, architecturally speaking.

The first point is easy to answer; the new component can run in another instance of the JVM if it's a Java-based application, or on another machine. Once we define the location(s) of the component, we will need to figure out the available transport that we can use to interact with it. For the human task component, as of now you can choose between three different transports: Mina, HornetQ, and JMS. Usually the JMS and HornetQ options are the most appropriate for enterprise environments, where we can rely on reliable messaging mechanisms that are easy to cluster.

Once we choose the transport that we want to use, we need to start analyzing the functional requirements of these interactions and the robustness required by our business.

How much robustness do we need?

The amount of robustness needed is a serious matter to consider! We need to define how much we are willing to pay for robustness. There are several levels of solution that give us greater guarantees that our systems will always work coherently and that the interactions between our components will be secure and reliable. Most of the time, there is no need to use complicated methods and mechanisms to have the highest degree of robustness, because we can create a simple mechanism to recover our runtime from a faulty operation (that is, if it doesn't happen too often).

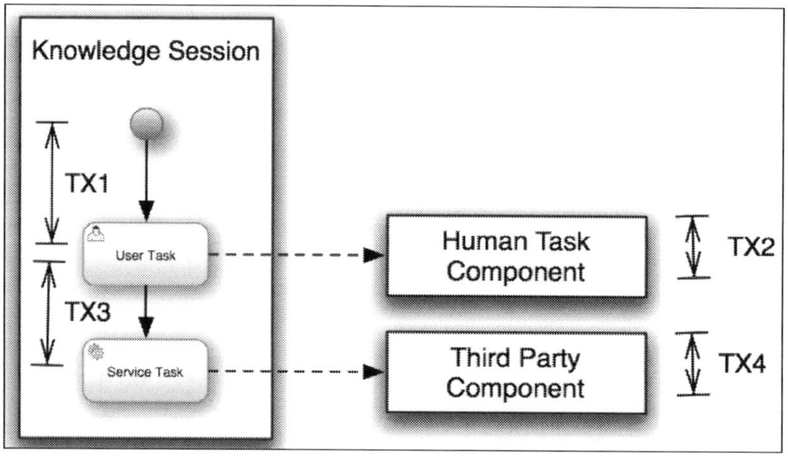

As you can see in the previous figure, we can have multiple components that our process will be contacting. The difference now is that each component will handle their transactions internally. TX1 and TX3 are transactions created inside our knowledge session, but TX2 and TX4 are created outside the process context, so they cannot be monitored or controlled unless each component exposes this functionality.

What does this mean exactly? What kinds of problems might we find when we have these split transactions?

Looking at the previous figure, imagine that TX1 is committed in the process engine (meaning that our process will be waiting for a human interaction). Because the user task will interact with the human task service to create the human task remotely, we can expect an acknowledgement (ACK) from the external service before committing TX1. We can use this approach if the service that we are contacting behaves in an asynchronous way and gives us an ACK confirming that the operation was queued correctly. So, for example, if we are interacting with the human task service via Mina or HTTP, we expect to receive the response as soon as the task is created. But if we are interacting with an asynchronous component and transport, we will expect an ACK. In other words, this means that TX1 will be committed without knowing for sure that the task was created.

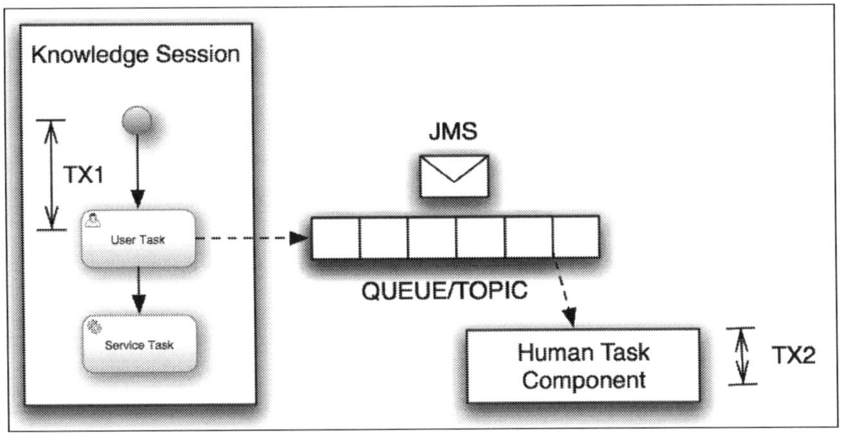

As an example, let's take a component like the human task component working with JMS. From the user task perspective, we will receive an ACK that the JMS message has been placed inside the message queue correctly. Because JMS works asynchronously, we don't know for sure if the message reaches the queue. We just get a confirmation that the JMS sent the message asynchronously to the queue. If we trust in our environment, and 99 percent of the times the JMS provider places the message in the queue, we might be fairly sure—but not 100 percent sure—that the human task component will pick up the message and TX2 will be created and committed successfully. At this point, we need to decide which component we trust (and which one we don't).

Depending on how we configure our JMS provider, we can say that when our process sends a message to the queue, it will arrive 99 percent of the time. Most of the JMS providers out there allow us to configure our queues in clusters, which increases their reliability. If we have a cluster of JMS queues, the chances of failure drastically decrease, but there is still a chance of not being able to contact any of the clustered queues. We can avoid these situations by adding the JMS message creation inside the same transaction of the knowledge session using XA drivers. If we use XA drivers and XA-enabled resources (JMS, Databases, and so on), we can use two-phase commits, allowing the engine to roll back multiple operations if one of them goes wrong. Using this approach, we will be safe because all the possible scenarios are covered. For example, let's analyze the opposite scenario, where the JMS message is correctly placed inside the queue but the process state is being committed to the database; here, the transaction fails and needs to be rolled back. If we don't use two transactional resources for that scenario, we might find an inconsistent state: a situation where the human task that was created by the process state was rolled back before the human task creation.

Another important thing to note is that if we want to avoid these kinds of situations, we are going to be forced to use XA drivers, which is not always possible and usually requires a more sophisticated setup.

As an alternative, we can always build recovering mechanisms, depending on how often these kind of errors occur. These mechanisms are usually simpler to implement and configure than dealing with XA drivers, which add overhead and complications to our setups. With an in-house mechanism, we will not cover 100 percent of the problems; but depending on our requirements and our recovering mechanisms, we can end up with cleaner solutions.

Frequently asked questions

Based on the user forums and our experience consulting with customers around the world, this section covers the frequently asked questions that newcomers have when they start working with persistent sessions and transactional resources. Notice that neither these sections nor this chapter are intended to explain the basic concepts behind transactional mechanisms (local/global transactions, distributed transactions, and two-phase commits) and persistence mechanisms such as JPA/hibernate. Drools & jBPM5 rely on these concepts to work; so if you don't want to get caught in a situation where you don't understand what is happening, I strongly recommend you to read about them to gain confidence.

- Can I control when my process instances are persisted?

  As this chapter described, jBPM5 already comes with an out of the box persistence mechanism that we must configure if we want to use it. Persisting a process instance (and all its variables) at an arbitrary point in time is not possible. Process instances are automatically persisted whenever they reach a safe state. Whenever your application gets the execution control back after interacting with a `StatefulKnowledgeSession` or a `WorkItemManager` interface, you know for sure that the content of the session (including all the process instances) were persisted.

- Why do we need to register the work item handlers every time a session is restored from the database?

All instances of `WorkItemHandler` implement the logic to interact with external systems. The reference to `WorkItemHandler` registered in a session is not persisted as part of the `StatefulKnowledgeSession` state. They must be registered again each time we reload the session from the database. The reason behind this is that most of the times `WorkItemHandler`s depend on the environment where they are being executed. For example, consider a `WorkItemHandler` object containing a reference to a file in the filesystem or a database connection. In this case, the `WorkItemHandler` object cannot be simply serialized, persisted, and then deserialized into another environment. You will find a common pattern of the following steps:

1. Create the persistent knowledge session.
2. Register `WorkItemHandler` and event listeners.
3. Interact.
4. Dispose.
5. Load session.
6. Register `WorkItemHandler` and event listeners.
7. Interact.
8. Dispose (and then repeat from step 5).

- How can we continue a process instance after a session is restored from the database?

  A common thought is that after `StatefulKnowledgeSession` is restored from the database, we need to do something special in order to continue with the execution of the process instances that it contains. In order to understand what needs to be done, we first need to understand why and when `StatefulKnowledgeSession` was persisted. As we already know, `StatefulKnowledgeSession` is persisted after one of the process instances that it contains reaches a safe state. There are basically three different ways to reach a safe state.

  1. The process instance is waiting for the completion of an asynchronous `WorkItemHandler` object and there is no other execution path in the process instance to be executed. This means that it is waiting for something (probably an external system) to complete its execution.

2. The process instance is waiting for a human task to be completed and there is no other execution path in the process instance to be executed. This is a specific case of the previous scenario where the `WorkItemHandler` object is a subclass of `AbstractHTWorkItemHandler` and the external system is the human task service.
3. The process instance is waiting for an external event to continue with its execution and there is no other execution path in the process instance to be executed.

So, under normal circumstances, we don't need to do anything special after `StatefulKnowledgeSession` is restored from the database. If the process instance was waiting for a `WorkItemHandler` instance to be completed, it will be completed as soon as the external system execution ends and `WorkItemManager` is notified. If the process instance was waiting for an event coming from our own application or even from outside the scope of the application, it will eventually be notified by the application or external system when necessary. Simply put, there is nothing we must do after we restore `StatefulKnowledgeSession` in order to continue with the execution of the process instances it contains.

- After a system crash, do we have to reload all the `StatefulKnowledgeSessions` instances from the database?

  The table `SessionInfo` contains all the persisted sessions of our application. We need to be aware though that this table contains not only the sessions having active process instances but *all* the sessions we have created over time (unless we have explicitly deleted them). It is the responsibility of an application using jBPM5 to keep the list of active sessions or to keep `SessionInfo` table in sync with the application's active sessions. When the application is restarted (after a crash or a regular shutdown), we have two different approaches to deal with persisted sessions:

  1. Reload all the active sessions from the database using the `JPAKnowledgeService` helper class.
  2. Reload sessions on-demand, by using `JPAKnowledgeService`, when we need to interact with them.

  The first approach is easier to implement and maintain. The main disadvantages it has are the time and memory footprint required to reload and keep in memory all the sessions we have persisted and the fact that load balancing a cluster of applications following this approach could be very hard, if not impossible. The second approach requires our application to have a mechanism to load a session only when needed. For this approach, it is better to have all the interactions with a session in a centralized piece of code.

It is important to note that if we are using human tasks, the second approach could be a little bit trickier to implement. We not only need to make sure we have a living session before we can interact with it, but we also need to make sure we have a living session before we interact with the human tasks service as well. Since the relation between the human task service and the session is weak (meaning that they only communicate through events), if we complete a human task before restoring the proper session from the database, the process instance will never be notified of this event. This means that the process instance will not continue with its execution.

- Why is the session not removed from the `SessionInfo` table after all the process instances that it contains are completed?

  jBPM5 runtime tables contain the minimum amount of information required to continue with the execution of process instances. The `ProcessInstanceInfo` and `WorkItemInfo` tables only contain the active processes and work item instances. After a work item is completed, its reference is removed from `WorkItemInfo`. The same thing happens for process instances, they are removed from `ProcessInstanceInfo` after they are completed. On the other hand, `StatefulKnowledgeSessions` doesn't follow the same behavior. jBPM5 is flexible enough to let us decide the session-handling strategy we want to use:

  1. 1 session per process instance.
  2. 1 session for all the process instances in our application.
  3. 1 session per business unit / domain / context.

  Since jBPM5 doesn't know which strategy we are using, it would be erroneous on its part to automatically remove a session from the `SessionInfo` table after all the process instances it contains are completed. It may be the case that we want to re-use the session for further process instance executions. It is also important to understand that a session can contain business rules. Business rules follow a very different life cycle than business processes and a per use-case analysis needs to be done in order to understand when the state of the session is not needed any more. For that reason, and based on the selected strategy, it is our responsibility to decide when a session is no longer needed and to remove its reference from the `SessionInfo` table.

- Why do we need to dispose `StatefulKnowledgeSessions`?

  When we are using persistent sessions, we can only trust in the state that has been stored inside the database. If multiple applications load the same session from the database, and they all interact by changing the state, only one of them will be able to persist those changes. The rest will obviously get an exception when they try to apply changes to an inconsistent state. All these other applications will need to retry their actions. In order to avoid such cases, we need to reduce the time between when we load and interact with the session. Every time that we use the `loadStatefulKnowledgeSession()` method from the `JPAKnowledgeService` helper class, we get the latest consistent state from our session. When we call the `dispose()` method, we are saying "The session instance that I have in my application could no longer be the latest consistent state". When we call the `dispose()` method, we force ourselves to reload the latest consistent state from the database.

Summary

In this chapter we have learned how the persistence and transaction mechanisms are shared by Drools and jBPM5 to provide a unified and reliable layer that is in charge of keeping our runtime information coherent. We also have learned how to classify our different business processes in defining which configuration fits best. The next two chapters will give you a quick overview of the rule engine and the complex event processing features also provided by the Drools and jBPM5 platform.

9
Smart Processes Using Rules

This chapter covers some of the common uses of business rules and business processes together. In order to understand how these two worlds are merged inside the Drools & jBPM5 platform, we need to appreciate how a rule engine works. This chapter covers:

- Good old integration patterns between processes and rules
- A quick introduction to the Drools Rule Engine
- How to leverage the power of the rule engine in our business processes
- Common usage patterns

Most of the examples covered in the rest of the chapter are generic enough to be adapted to your business scenarios. The main goal of all the examples is to give you an overview of the wide range of scenarios that can be covered and improved with the introduced patterns. The flexibility provided by the rule engine and the process engine allows us to build very complex scenarios, but we need to learn how to use that flexibility to meet our own needs without being overwhelmed by the number of different patterns that can be implemented.

Good old integration patterns

What we've learnt from experience about jBPM3 is that a rule engine can become very handy when evaluating different situations and making automatic decisions based on the information available. Based on my experience in consulting, I've noticed that people who understand how a process engine works and feel comfortable with it, start looking at rule engines such as Drools. The most intuitive first step is to delegate the business decisions in your processes and the data validations to a rule engine. In the past, adopting one of these two different technologies at the same time was difficult, mostly because of the learning curve as well as the maturity and investment required by a company to learn and use both technologies at once. At the end of the day, companies spend time and money to create in-house integrations and solutions so that they can merge these two worlds.

The following example shows what people have done with jBPM3 and the Drools Rule Engine:

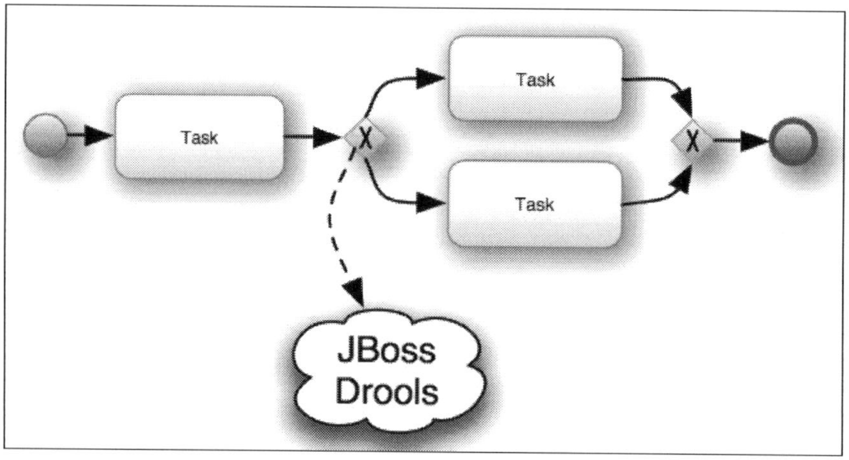

The first and most typical use case is to use a rule engine to choose between different paths in a process. Usually, the information that is sent to the rule engine is the same information that is flowing through the process tasks or just some pieces of it; we expect a return value from the rule engine that will be used to select which path to take. Most of the time, we send small pieces of information (for example, the age or salary of a person, and so on) and we expect to get a Boolean (true/false) value, in the case that we want to decide between just two paths, or a value (integers such as 1, 2, 3, and so on) that will be used to match each outgoing sequence flow. In this kind of integration, the rule engine is considered just an external component. We expect a very stateless behavior and an immediate response from the rule engine.

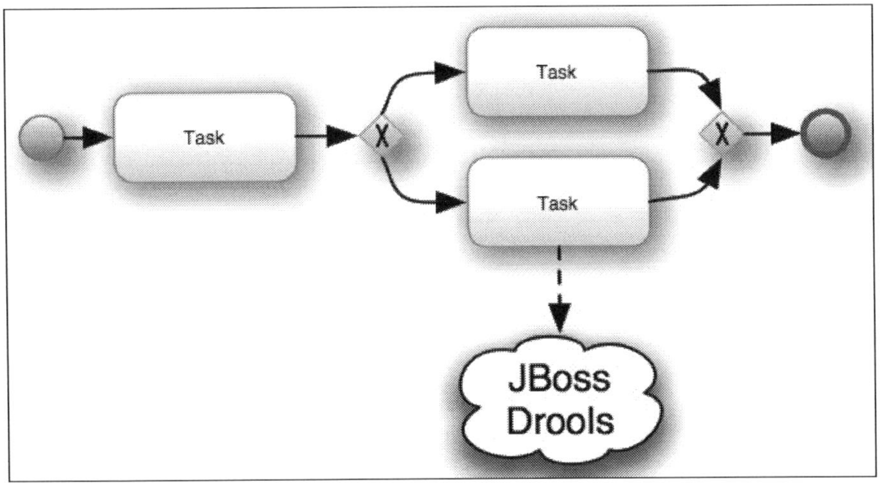

The previous figure shows a similar situation, when we want to validate some data and then define a task inside our process to achieve this information's validation or decoration. Usually we send a set of objects that we want to validate or decorate, and we expect an immediate answer from the rule engine. The type of answer that we receive depends on the type of validation or the decoration rules that we write. Usually, these interactions interchange complex data structures, such as a full graph of objects.

And that's it! Those two examples show the classic interaction from a process engine to a rule engine. You may have noticed the stateless nature of both the examples, where the most interesting features of the rule engine are not being used at all. In order to understand a little bit better why a rule engine is an important tool and the advantages of using it (in contrast to any other service), we need to understand some of the basic concepts behind it.

The following section briefly introduces the Drools Rule Engine and its features, as well as an explanation of the basic topics that we need to know in order to use it.

The Drools Rule Engine

The reason why rule engines are extremely useful is that they allow us to express declaratively what to do in specific scenarios. In contrast to imperative languages such as Java, the Rule Engine provides a declarative language that is used to evaluate the available information.

In this chapter we will analyze some Drools rules, but this chapter will not explain in detail the Drools Rule syntax. For more information on this take a look at the official documentation at `http://docs.jboss.org/drools/release/5.5.0.Final/drools-expert-docs/html_single/`.

Let's analyze the following simple example to understand the differences between the declarative approaches and the imperative approaches:

```
rule "over 18 enabled to drive"
  when
    $p: Person( age > 18, enabledToDrive == false)
  then
    $p.setEnabledToDrive(true);
    update($p);
end
rule "over 21 enabled to vote"
  when
    $p: Person( age > 21, enabledToVote == false)
  Then
    $p.setEnabledToVote(true);
    update($p);
end
```

Before explaining what these two rules are doing (which is kind of obvious as they are self-descriptive!), let's analyze the following java code snippet:

```
if(person.getAge() > 18 && person.isEnabledToDrive() == false){
  person.setEnabledToDrive(true);
}
if(person.getAge() > 21 && person.isEnabledToVote() == false){
  person.setEnabledToVote(true);
}
```

Usually most people, who are not familiar with rule engines but have heard of them, think that rule engines are used to extract `if/else` statements from the application's code. This definition is far from reality, and doesn't explain the power of rule engines.

First of all, rule engines provide us a declarative language to express our rules, in contrast to the imperative nature of languages such as Java.

In Java code, we know that the first line is evaluated first, so if the expression inside the `if` statement evaluates to true, the next line will be executed; if not, the execution will jump to the next `if` statement. There are no doubts about how Java will analyze and execute these statements: one after the other until there are no more instructions. We commonly say that Java is an imperative language in which we specify the actions that need to be executed and the sequence of these actions.

> Java, C, PHP, Python, and Cobol are imperative languages, meaning that they follow the instructions that we give them, one after the other.

Now if we analyze the DRL snippet (DRL means Drools Rule Language), we are not specifying a sequence of imperative actions. We are specifying situations that are evaluated by the rule engine, so when those situations are detected, the rule consequence (the `then` section of the rule) is eligible to be executed.

Each rule defines a situation that the engine will evaluate. Rules are defined using two sections: the conditional section, which starts with the `when` keyword that defines the filter that will be applied to the information available inside the rule engine. This example rule contains the following condition:

```
when
  $p: Person( age > 18 )
```

This DRL conditional statement filters all the objects inside the rule engine instance that match this condition. This conditional statement means "match for each person whose age is over 18". If we have at least one `Person` instance that matches this condition, this rule will be activated for that `Person` instance. A rule that is activated is said to be eligible to be fired. When a rule is fired, the consequence side of the rule is executed. For this example rule, the consequence section looks like this:

```
then
     $p.setEnabledToDrive(true);
     update($p);
```

In the rule consequence, you can write any Java code you want. This code will be executed as regular Java code. In this case, we are getting the object that matches the filter—`Person ( age > 18 )`—that is bonded to the variable called `$p` and changing one of its attributes. The second line inside the consequence notifies the rule engine of this change so it can be used by other rules.

> A rule is composed of a conditional side, also called Left-Hand Side (LHS for short) and a consequence side, also called Right-Hand Side (RHS for short).

```
rule "Person over 60 - apply discount"
  when //  LHS
    $p: Person(age > 60)
  then //  RHS
     $p.setDiscount(40);
end
```

We will be in charge of writing these rules and making them available to a rule engine that is prepared to host a large number of rules.

To understand the differences and advantages between the following lines, we need to understand how a rule engine works. The first big difference is behavior: we cannot force the rule engine to execute a given rule. The rule engine will pick up only the rules that match with the expressed conditions.

```
if(person.getAge() > 18)
```

And

```
$p: Person(  age > 18 )
```

If we try to compare rules with imperative code, we usually analyze how the declarative nature of rule languages can help us to create more maintainable code. The following example shows how application codes usually get so complicated, that maintaining them is not a simple task:

```
If(…){
  If(){
    If(){
    }
  }else(){
    if(…){
    }
   }
}
```

All of the evaluations must be done in a sequence. When the application grows, maintaining this spaghetti code becomes complex—even more so when the logic that it represents needs to be changed frequently to reflect business changes. In our simple example, if the person that we are analyzing is 19 years old, the only rule that will be evaluated and activated is the rule called `"over 18 enabled to drive"`. Imagine that we had mixed and nested `if` statements evaluating different domain entities in our application. There would be no simple way to do the evaluations in the right order for every possible combination. Business rules offer us a simple and atomic way to describe the situations that we are interested in, which will be analyzed based on the data available. When the number of these situations grows and we need to frequently apply changes to reflect the business reality, a rule engine is a very good alternative to improve readability and maintenance.

> Rules represent what to do for a specific situation. That's why business rules must be atomic. When we read a business rule, we need to clearly identify what's the condition and exactly what will happen when the condition is true.

To finish this quick introduction to the Drools Rule Engine, let's look at the following example:

```
rule "enabled to drive must have a car"
  When
    $p: Person( enabledToDrive == true )
    not(Car(person == $p))
  then
    insert(new Car($p));
end
rule "person with new car must be happy"
  when
    $p: Person()
    $c: Car(person == $p)
  then
    $p.setHappy(true);
end
rule "over 18 enabled to drive"
  when
    $p: Person( age > 18, enabledToDrive == false)
  then
    $p.setEnabledToDrive(true);
    update($p);
end
```

When you get used to the Drools Rule Language, you can easily see how the rules will work for a given situation. The rule called `"over 18 enabled to drive"` checks the person's age in order to see if he/she is enabled to drive or not. By default, persons are not enabled to drive. When this rule finds one instance of the `Person` object that matches with this filter, it will activate the rule; and when the rule's consequence gets executed, the `enabledToDrive` attribute will be set to `true` and we will notify the engine of this change. Because the `Person` instance has been updated, the rule called `"enabled to drive must have a car"` is now eligible to be fired. Because there is no other active rule, the rule's consequence will be executed, causing the insertion of a new car instance. As soon as we insert a new car instance, the last rule's conditions will be true. Notice that the last rule is evaluating two different types of objects as well as joining them. The rule called `"person with new car must be happy"` is checking that the car belongs to the person with `$c: Car(person == $p)`. As you may imagine, the `$p:` creates a binding to the object instances that match the conditions for that pattern. In all the examples in this book, I've used the `$` sign to denote variables that are being bound inside rules. This is not a requirement, but it is a good practice that allows you to quickly identify variables versus object field filters.

Please notice that the rule engine doesn't care about the order of the rules that we provide; it will analyze them by their conditional sections, not by the order in which we provide the rules.

This chapter provides a very simple project implementing this scenario, so feel free to open it from inside the `chapter_09` directory and experiment with it. It's called `drools5-SimpleExample`. This project contains a test class called `MyFirstDrools5RulesTest`, which tests the previously introduced rules. Feel free to change the order of the rules provided in the `/src/test/resources/simpleRules.drl` file. Please take a look at the official documentation at `www.drools.org` to find more about the advantages of using a rule engine.

What Drools needs to work

If you remember the jBPM5 API introduction section, you will recall the `StatefulKnowledgeSession` interface that hosts our business processes. This stateful knowledge session is all that we need in order to host and interact with our rules as well. We can run our processes and business rules in the same instance of a knowledge session without any trouble. In order to make our rules available in our knowledge session, we will need to use the knowledge builder to parse and compile our business rules and to create the proper knowledge packages. Now we will use the `ResourceType.DRL` file instead of the `ResourceType.BPMN2` file that we were using for our business processes.

So the knowledge session will represent our world. The business rules that we put in it will evaluate all the information available in the context. From our application side, we will need to notify the rule engine which pieces of information will be available to be analyzed by it. In order to inform and interact with the engine, there are four basic methods provided by the `StatefulKnowledgeSession` object that we need to know.

We will be sharing a `StatefulKnowledgeSession` instance between our processes and our rules. From the rule engine perspective, we will need to insert information to be analyzed. These pieces of information (which are Java objects) are called facts according to the rule engine's terminology. Our rules are in charge of evaluating these facts against our defined conditions.

The following four methods become a fundamental piece of our toolbox:

```
FactHandle insert(Object object)
void update(FactHandle handle, Object object)

void retract(FactHandle handle)
int fireAllRules()
```

The `insert()` method notifies the engine of an object instance that we want to analyze using our rules. When we use the `insert()` method, our object instance becomes a fact. A fact is just a piece of information that is considered to be true inside the rule engine. Based on this assumption, a wrapper to the object instance will be created and returned from the `insert()` method. This wrapper is called `FactHandle` and it will allow us to make references to an inserted fact. Notice that the `update()` and `retract()` methods use this `FactHandle` wrapper to modify or remove an object that we have previously inserted.

Another important thing to understand at this point is that only top-level objects will be handled as facts, which implies the following:

```
FactHandle personHandle = ksession.insert(new Person());
```

This sentence will notify the engine about the presence of a new fact, the `Person` instance. Having the instances of `Person` as facts will enable us to write rules using the pattern `Person()` to filter the available objects. What if we have a more complex structure? Here, for example, the `Person` class defines a list of addresses as:

```
class Person{
  private String name;
  private List<Address> addresses;
}
```

In such cases we will need to define if we are interested in making inferences about `addresses`. If we just insert the `Person` object instance, none of the `addresses` instances will be treated as facts by the engine. Only the `Person` object will be filtered. In other words, a condition such as the following would never be true:

```
when
  $p: Person()
  $a: Address()
```

This rule condition would never match, because we don't have any `Address` facts. In order to make the `Address` instances available to the engine, we can iterate the person's addresses and insert them as facts.

```
ksession.insert(person);
for(Address addr : person.getAddresses()){
  ksession.insert(addr);
}
```

If our object changes, we need to notify the engine about the changes. For that purpose, the `update()` method allows us to modify a fact using its fact handler. Using the `update()` method will ensure that only the rules that were filtering this fact type gets re-evaluated. When a fact is no longer true or when we don't need it anymore, we can use the `retract()` method to remove that piece of information from the rule engine.

Up until now, the rule engine has generated activations for all the rules and facts that match with those rules. No rule's consequence will be executed if we don't call the `fireAllRules()` method. The `fireAllRules()` method will first look for activations inside our `ksession` object and select one. Then it will execute that activation, which can cause new activations to be created or current ones canceled. At this point, the loop begins again; the method picks one activation from the Agenda (where all the activations go) and executes it. This loop goes on until there are no more activations to execute. At that point the `fireAllRules()` method returns control to our application.

The following figure shows this execution cycle:

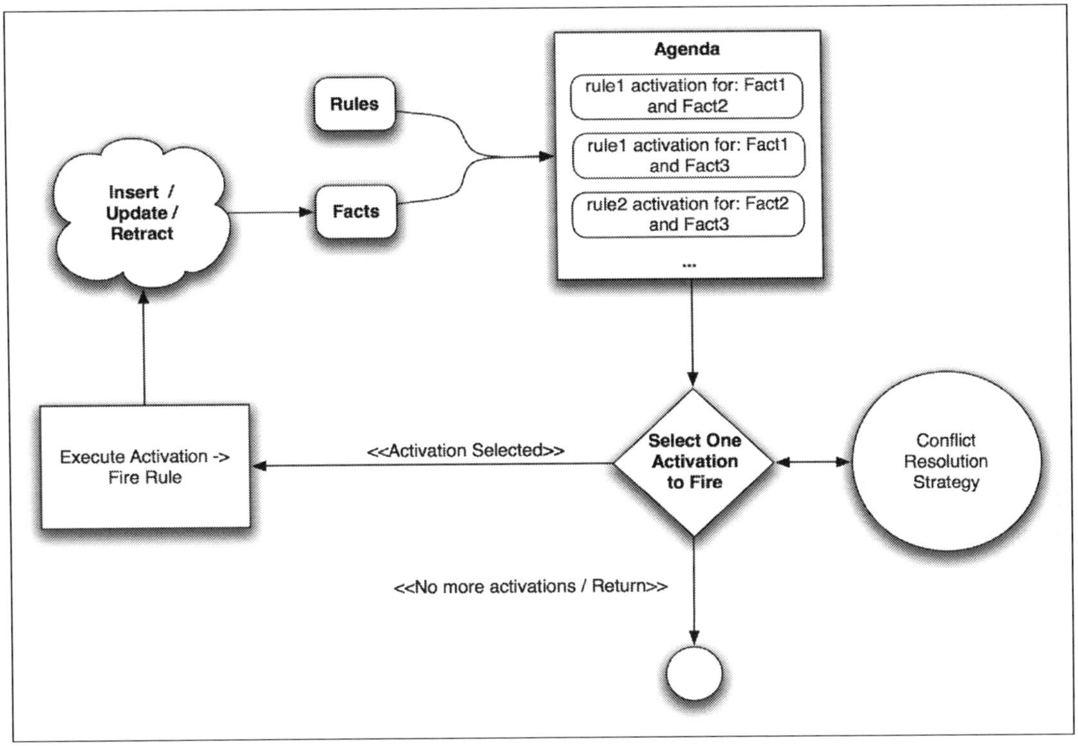

This cycle represents the inference process, since our rules can generate new information (based on the information that is available), and new conclusions can be derived by the end of this cycle.

> Understanding this cycle is vital in working with the rule engine. As soon as we understand the power of making data inferences as opposed to just plain data validation, the power of the rule engine is unleashed. It usually takes some time to digest the full range of possibilities that can be modeled using rules, but it's definitely worth it.

Another characteristic of rule engines that you need to understand is the difference between stateless and stateful sessions. In this book, all the examples use the `StatefulKnowledgeSession` instance to interact with processes and rules. A stateless session is considered a very simple `StatefulKnowledgeSession` that can execute a previously described execution cycle just once. Stateless sessions can be used when we only need to evaluate our data once and then dispose of that session, because we are not planning to use it anymore. Most of the time, because the processes are long running and multiple interactions will be required, we need to use a `StatefulKnowledgeSession` instance. In a `StatefulKnowledgeSession`, we will be able to go throughout the previous cycle multiple times, which allows us to introduce more information over time instead of all at the beginning. Just so you know, the `StatelessKnowledgeSession` instance in Drools exposes an `execute()` method that internally inserts all the facts provided as parameters, calls the `fireAllRules()` method, and finally disposes of the session. There have been several discussions about the performance of these two approaches, but inside the Drools Engine, both stateful and stateless sessions perform the same, because `StatelessKnowledgeSession` uses `StatefulKnowledgeSession` under the hood.

> There is no performance difference between stateless and stateful sessions in Drools.

The last function that we need to know is the `dispose()` method provided by the `StatefulKnowledgeSession` interface. Disposing of the session will release all the references to our domain objects that are kept, allowing those objects to be collected by the JVM's garbage collector. As soon as we know that we are not going to use a session anymore, we should dispose of it by using `dispose()`.

The power of the rules applied to our processes

Going back to our very simple integration patterns, you may notice that back in the old days, the process engines interacted with the rule engines in a very stateless fashion, leaving out more than 90 percent of the rule engine features.

In jBPM5, the rule engine and the process engine have been designed to work together in a stateful context, which gives us a rich environment to work in. This new design encourages us to build smarter and simpler process diagrams, as well as to leverage the power of the rule engine to identify business situations that require attention.

If we re-examine the first process rule integration pattern (the one that analyzes an order to choose the right path), we will notice that in jBPM5 we are defining the XOR gateway using expressions or rules. This is the most basic usage of rules in our processes; if we choose to write the gateway's conditions using the rule language, a rule will be generated.

This section is intended to show you some of the available alternatives to model and design different behaviors, depending on your business situation. You will notice that there are several ways to do similar things; this is because the engine is extremely flexible, but sometimes this fact confuses people.

Gateway conditions

As we said before, the most basic way of using rules is applying them inside process gateways. Because it is the simplest way, we need to master it and know all the possibilities.

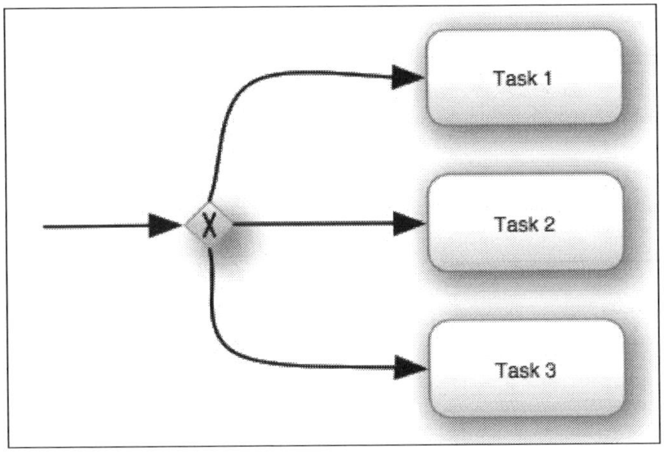

Each outgoing sequence flow can define a condition that must be fulfilled by the available data in the context. An evaluation will be done to select the path for each process instance. As mentioned before, these conditions can be expressed in Java code (using the imperative nature of the language) or in DRL, in which we can leverage its declarative nature in order to analyze more complex conditions.

Java-based conditions

This is the simplest scenario and the most intuitive for non-rules users. Most people who feel comfortable with process engines will probably decide to use Java to express the conditions.

If we now open the test class called `GoodOldIntegrationPatterns` provided inside the project called `jBPM5-Process-Rules-Patterns`, the method called `javaBasedDecisionTest()` shows you an example using Java conditions. Notice that these tests load the process file `process-java-decision.bpmn`. Feel free to open and debug these tests in order to follow the process execution.

If we open this process in the Process Designer, it looks like the following figure:

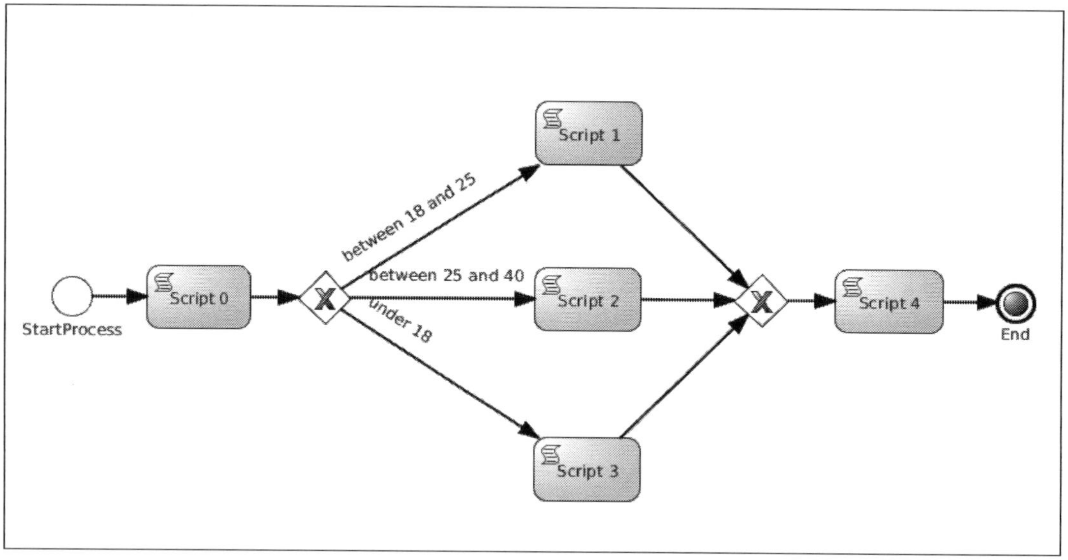

It is important for us to notice the following points:

- The conditions are not inside the gateway, they are placed inside the sequence flows.
- Each condition expression needs to be evaluated and it must return a Boolean value using the `return` keyword.
- We can use the context variable to access the process variables. The knowledge runtime also allows us to access the rule engine context.
- Each sequence flow's condition is evaluated in a sequence; in an exclusive gateway (the one used in the example), the process will continue through the first condition that returns `true`, without evaluating any remaining conditions.
- Any Java expression can be included in these conditions.
- The engine evaluates these conditions at runtime for each process instance, but at compile time, these expressions are checked.

- 99 percent of the time that we choose to use Java expressions inside the gateway's conditions it is because we need to evaluate the process information. For wider analysis, the following section explains how we can use the power of rules.

Rule-based conditions

Let's take a look at the same situation but with a rule-based approach using the DRL language. If we choose to go with this option, at compilation time the engine will create the appropriate rules to perform the evaluations. If you want to, take a look at the example provided in the test class called `NewCommonIntegrationPatternsTest` — the method called `testSimpleRulesDecision()` shows how these conditions can be written in the DRL language.

Consider the following DRL snippet:

```
Person( age < 18 )
```

This will only propagate the execution for that sequence flow when there is a person that matches that age restriction.

One interesting thing to note here is the fact that the previous example does not look at the process variables; instead, it is matching the objects/facts inside the current knowledge session. In this case, we need to have at least one `Person` object that matches these conditions in order for the process to continue.

If we want to check for conditions in the process variables using the DRL approach, we need to do something like this:

```
WorkflowProcessInstanceImpl( $person: variables["person"])
Person( age< 18 ) from $person
```

In order to make this evaluation, we need to have inserted the process instance as a fact inside the knowledge session. We usually insert the process instance after creating it, in order to be able to make inferences. For example:

```
ProcessInstance processInstance =
                ksession.createProcessInstance("myprocess");
ksession.insert(processInstance);
ksession.startProcessInstance(processInstance.getId());
```

You can check the test called `testSimpleDecisionWithReactiveRules()`, which shows this example in action.

If we don't want to insert the process instance manually into the session, there is a special `ProcessEventListener`, which comes out-of-the-box to automatically insert the `ProcessInstance` object before the process is started and also to keep it updated when the process variables change. Look at the `README` file provided with this chapter's source code to find more information and tests showing the behavior of the `RuleAwareProcessEventListener` object.

Notice that when we start using rules and processes together, we usually want to put the engine in what we call reactive mode. This basically means that as soon as a rule gets activated, it will be fired. The engine will not wait for the `fireAllRules()` invocation.

There are two ways of achieving this mode:

- Fire until halt
- Agenda & process event listeners

The fire until halt alternative requires another thread to be created, which will be in charge of monitoring the activations and firing them as soon as they are created. In order to put the engine in a reactive mode by using the `fireUntilHalt()` method, we use the following code snippet:

```
new Thread(new Runnable() {
  public void run() {
    ksession.fireUntilHalt();
  }
} ).start();
```

The test called `testSimpleDecisionWithReactiveRules()` inside `NewCommonIntegrationPatternsTest` shows the fire until halt approach in action. Notice that the `Thread.sleep(...)` method is also used to wait for the other thread to react.

The only downside of using the fire until halt approach is that we need to create another thread—this is not always possible. We will also see that when we use the persistence layer for our business process using this alternative is not recommended. For testing purposes, relying on another thread to fire our rules can add extra complexity and possibly race conditions. That's why the following method, which uses listeners, is usually recommended.

Using the agenda and process event listeners mode allows us to get the internal engine events and execute a set of actions as soon as the events are triggered. In order to set up these listeners, we need to add the following code snippet right after the session creation, so that we don't miss any event:

```
ksession.addEventListener(
   newDefaultAgendaEventListener() {
     @Override
     public void activationCreated(ActivationCreatedEvent event) {
       ((StatefulKnowledgeSession) event.getKnowledgeRuntime())
                                              .fireAllRules();
     }
});

ksession.addEventListener(new DefaultProcessEventListener(){
   @Override
   public void afterProcessStarted(ProcessStartedEvent event) {
       ((StatefulKnowledgeSession) event.getKnowledgeRuntime())
               .fireAllRules();
   }
});
```

The test `testSimpleDecisionWithReactiveRulesUsingListener()` inside the `NewCommonIntegrationPatternsTest` class shows how these listeners can be used.

Notice that we are attaching `DefaultAgendaEventListener` and `DefaultProcessEventListener`; both define several methods that will be called when internal events in the engine are generated. The implementations of these listeners will allow us to intercept these events and inject our custom and domain-specific code. In this example, we are overriding the behavior of the `activationCreated(...)` and `afterProcessStarted(...)` methods, because we need to fire all the rules as soon as an activation is created or a process has started. If you have the source code of the projects (jBPM5 and Drools), look at the other methods inside `DefaultAgendaEventListener` and `DefaultProcessEventListener` to see the other events that can be used as hook points. This approach, using listeners, gives us a more precise and single-threaded approach to work with.

It is important to know that both approaches—fire until halt and agenda and process event listeners—give the same results in the previous tests, but they work in different ways. We need to understand these differences in order to choose wisely.

Do you remember when we used the DRL filter with the following restriction in our gateway?

```
Person( age< 18 )
```

We will be filtering all the objects inside the current session. This is an extremely flexible mechanism to write conditions not only based in the process information but also in the available context. We need to understand what exactly happens under the hood in order to leverage this power.

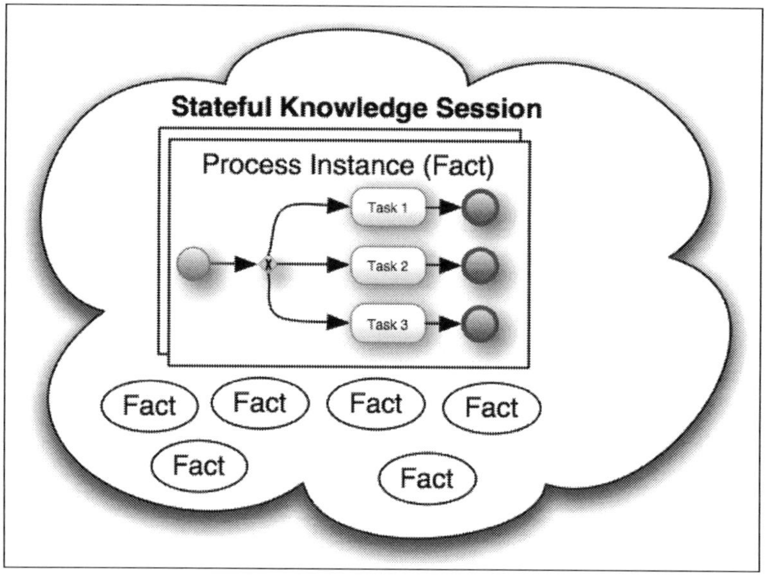

We need to know how and when to use it. If we learn how to write effective rules in the Drools Rule Language, we will be able to express quite complex conditions inside our business processes.

To show you what kind of things can be done using this mechanism, let's analyze the following example called multi process instance evaluations.

Multi-process instance evaluations

In jBPM5, if we start multiple processes in the same knowledge session, all of them will run in the same context. One of the big advantages of running multiple processes under the same knowledge session umbrella is that we can analyze those instances and make global decisions about them. This feature allows us to go one level up in the organization level, so we avoid being focused on just one process execution at a time. Most of the old process engines were focused on offering mechanisms to work with a single process instance.

This fact pushes process composition (embedding a process inside another to have different layers and process hierarchy) as the only way to take control of multiple process instances that are related to each other. Compared to the new paradigm, of having our process instances as facts inside the rule engine, we can now start writing rules that will evaluate multiple processes instances to find more complex and specific situations.

Take a look at the following process definition, which chooses between two different paths based on the available resources at execution time.

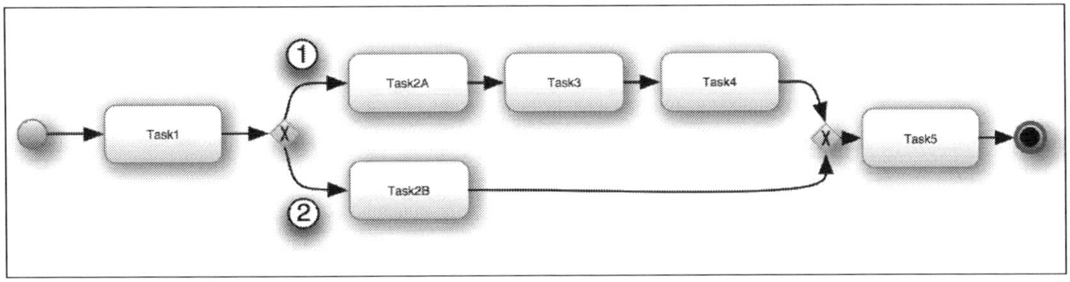

When we start the first process instance, the XOR diverging gateway will evaluate the following conditions:

- For path 1: `Resources ( available > 5 )`
- For path 2: `Resources ( available <= 5 )`

Each task requires and consumes one unit of the available resources. Here we have defined `Resources()` for the example, but it can be anything that you need to have in order to perform the task. For instance, if these tasks were automated activities and we were interacting with an external system that charged our company per transaction, these resources would represent the amount of money that the company was spending consuming that service. If these tasks were human activities performed by external contractors, these resources could represent once again the budget that the company can spend in order to perform the work. For both cases, when we are out of resources, we need to stop working.

Let's imagine that we start with 50 resources available. Technically, these resources will be represented by a new instance of the `Resources` class with the `available` attribute set to `50`. We can easily predict what will happen and how much a complete process execution will cost us. We know that if our process instance chooses path number 1, five tasks will be executed, consuming five units of our resources. Path number 2 will cost us only three units.

For simplicity's sake, in our example we will consider that only one instance of our `Resources` class can exist inside the session. This instance will contain the number of available resources at all times.

If we start creating instances of this process definition with the restrictions mentioned previously, the first nine instances will choose path number 1, whereas instance number 10 will choose path number 2. After executing instance number 10, we will have only two remaining resources available. When instance number 11 starts, it will choose path number 2 but will fail while executing the second task because of the lack of resources.

You can check this scenario in the test class called `MultiProcessEvaluationTest`. The test method called `testMultiProcessEvaluation()` shows this execution behavior. The process file that is being used is called `multi-process-decision.bpmn`—it looks like the following figure:

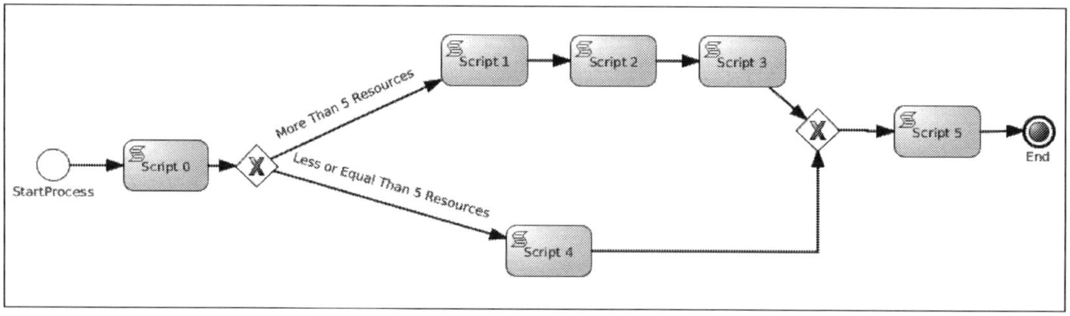

Some important points that will help you to understand what is happening are as follows:

- The example process uses Script Tasks; you will not use these Script Tasks in real situations.
- Each Script Task executes the code to reduce the available resources by one unit. The example implements a very simple approach; in a real implementation, you will probably have a service to do this.
  The following code is executed inside each Script Task:

```
QueryResultsqueryResults = kcontext.getKnowledgeRuntime()
        .getQueryResults("getResources", new Object[]{});
QueryResultsRow row = queryResults.iterator().next();
Resources resources = (Resources)row.get("$r");
resources.setAvailable(resources.getAvailable() - 1);
FactHandle handle = kcontext.getKnowledgeRuntime()
                            .getFactHandle(resources);
kcontext.getKnowledgeRuntime().update(handle, resources);
```

This code basically executes a query against the knowledge session. You can consider a query to be exactly the same as a rule without the consequence, which allows us to retrieve information from within the session. This snippet is calling the `getResources` query that can be found inside the `resources.drl` file. It looks like this:

```
query getResources()
  $r: Resources()
end
```

Because we know that there is one and only one `Resources()` fact, we just get the first result using the `iterator().next()` method. Once we get the reference to the `resource` object, we just decrement the available resources. In order for the engine to know about this change, we need to update the fact so we need to get the fact handle that was created at insertion time. We have two options: one is to keep a registry where all the fact handles for our application are kept, or we can just use the `getFactHandle()` method, which accepts the object and returns the fact handle.

- Notice that inside the `resources.drl` file, a rule was included to check when there are no more resources available:

```
rule "Out of resources"
  when
   $r: Resources( available == 0 )
  then
   throw new IllegalStateException(
             "No More Resources Available = "+$r);
end
```

  This rule is a little bit harsh, but it clearly states that we cannot execute a task if we are out of resources. `IllegalStateException` will break the execution, stopping the current process instance.

- In this simple example, we are starting one process instance after the previous one is already finished.

The next section will build on this example, adding more complexity and showing more advanced decisions.

Rule-based process selection and creation

Our previous example showed us how we can share information between different process instances and make decisions inside each particular instance based on global information.

Now we will see an enhanced version of this process that uses more of the available domain information in choosing between different paths, as well as saving resources, which improves the process' business performance. First of all, we will add a restriction to the condition declared in the diverging XOR gateway. We will analyze the process variable called `Person` for each process instance. If the person associated with the process has a Platinum Plan and there are enough resources available, Path number 1 will be chosen. For all of the other persons, path number 2 will be selected. This business decision allows us to execute more process instances while taking special care of our platinum customers and saving resources for the rest of the plans.

Now, in order to really take advantage of the rule engine, we will write some rules to verify that we will not be able to start a new process if we don't have enough resources to finish it. We have several ways of implementing this, but here I will describe only two options:

- Delegate the creation of the process instance to the rule engine
- Warn—based on rules—when a process will not be able to finish its execution

Starting with the first option, we can say that an extremely useful feature inside the Drools Rule Engine is that we are able to start processes and influence the process executions from inside the business rules. If our process requires some input data, our rules can be in charge of gathering that data, and as soon as the data is ready, we can trigger the process creation.

In order to start a process from within a business rule, we only need to know the process ID (the name of the process definition) and the input parameters required by the process. Using a very simple rule, we can start a process instance for each `Customer()` that we have in our session:

```
rule "Customer Basic Process"
  when
    $c: Customer()
  then
    Map params = new HashMap();
    params.put("customer", $c);
    ProcessInstance pi =
                    kcontext.getKnowledgeRuntime()
                            .createProcessInstance(
                       "com.salaboy.process.CustomerBasicProcess",
                            params);
    insert(pi);
    kcontext.getKnowledgeRuntime()
            .startProcessInstance(pi.getId());
end
```

This rule will be activated for each customer that we insert into our knowledge session and it will create an instance of `CustomerBasicProcess`, setting the customer as a process variable.

There is a test called `testProcessCreationDelegation()` inside the `MultiProcessEvaluationTest` class that demonstrates the previous rule (`simple-process-trigger.drl`) in action.

> Take note that because we are trying to start a process from a rule consequence, this rule needs to be fired in order to create the process. Because we are creating the process instance inside the inference cycle and our process will run from start to end in a single shot, all the activations created by the process execution will be queued up and executed as soon as the process ends. This is usually not a problem, because most of the time we will have long running processes—but you need to be aware of this behavior.

To show this feature in more advanced use cases, let's twist our example. Instead of having a gateway, to choose between two paths in our process, we can just split our process into two well-focused and simpler processes:

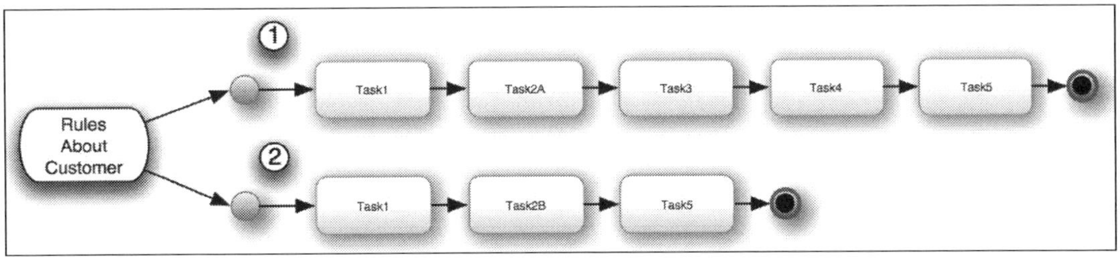

As you can see, we don't need an XOR gateway anymore; instead, a set of rules defines which process to start. Each process definition contains only the tasks required for each specific scenario. If we start having complicated conditions inside our gateways, we can consider this approach of creating a decoupled set of rules and start different process instances. In order to make these kind of changes, you will need to understand the business scenario and evaluate if you can split it into more than one process definition. Now you have two different process definitions to maintain, so it is a trade-off between simplicity in your models and maintainability. Using these mechanisms, we can build custom processes and use the rule engine to choose exactly when we need to use our business processes based on the contextual information that we have available.

The test class called `RuleBasedProcessSelectionTest` contains four tests showing these concepts in action. These tests show a simple scenario where various features of the rule engine are being used to check the resource availability and choose between two different processes.

Another possibility, instead of splitting the process, is to use subprocesses to only define a fragment of the process that can be selected at runtime. Using a subprocess also creates a new process definition, but this definition can be reused. Most of the time, using sub-processes is recommended to define several layers of abstraction, where subprocesses represent more specific tasks that need to be done.

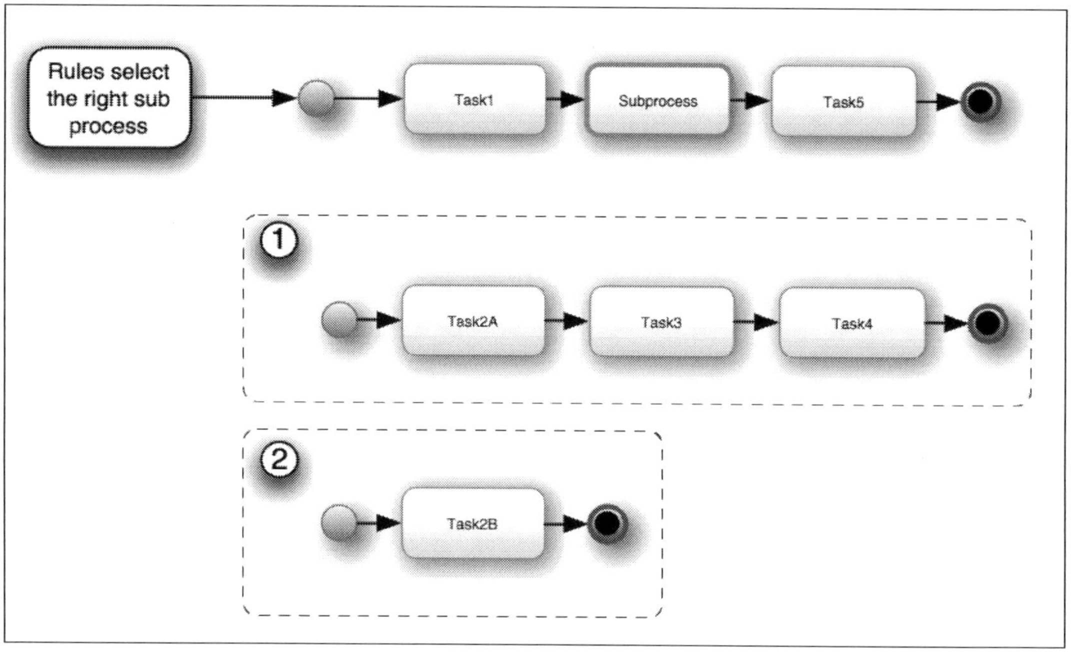

In this case, the rules (which start the process instance) need to define the subprocess that will be used by that instance. The rules, in this case, will need to decide which subprocess ID will be used and sent as a parameter. At runtime this parameter will be evaluated and the correct subprocess will be instantiated.

Note that in both cases (when we split the process versus when we use subprocesses), the resource allocation can be done more effectively, because we know how much each set of tasks will cost.

Summary

In this chapter, we have covered important patterns that we need to know in order to leverage the power of the rule engine in improving our business processes. It is important for you to remember that there are usually several ways to model a problem and you will be responsible for the flexibility of the solution. You can use the patterns mentioned in this chapter in order to decide which is the best option. One chapter is not enough to cover all the possible scenarios; if you are interested in getting a deeper understanding of these topics look at the `README` file provided with the chapter's source code for further details and more advanced patterns.

In the next chapter, we will cover how our business process can leverage the power of Drools Fusion, which enables us to do complex event processing with the events generated by our business processes. Using the power of complex event processing, we will add another layer of flexibility and we will also have an extra tool to model our business situations.

10

Reactive Processes Using Drools Fusion

The previous chapter introduced the concept of business rules that enable us to model a smarter process depending on contextual information; different evaluations can be executed to influence how our business as a whole will behave in different scenarios. The combination of processes and rules is a very powerful mix that we need to master. This will not happen in just one day or by just reading the previous chapter. What we need to do is to put all the previous concepts into practice and start developing solutions with them. When we mix rules and processes, we can discover new patterns and take advantage of all the rule engine features; we are merging how the activities that we define need to be executed in sequence and how our application needs to react to very specific situations. Up to this point, we haven't included any strong temporal information in the mix that our system can receive, such as notifications, streams of data, or live data. As you may have noticed in the previous chapter, we weren't using any temporal reference, so whenever we insert our facts into the rule engine—if we have a rule that matches the current facts—a rule or a set of rules may be fired.

This chapter will cover the following topics:

- An introduction to Drools Fusion, which enables temporal reasoning within the rules engine
- A quick review of the **Event Driven Architectures** (**EDA**) and **Complex Event Processing** (**CEP**) fields that will put us in context, so that we understand how we can now model and react to different scenarios
- We will also analyze how our business processes can react in real time to situations that are heavily based on temporal constraints using Drools Fusion

In order to understand these fields, we need to know what an event is.

What is an event?

A core concept behind EDA and CEP is the idea of an event. If you start reading books on this subject, you will find multiple definitions of what an event is, but for this book's context and for Drools Fusion, an **event** can be defined as *a significant change of state in our application Domain*.

Depending on the scenario that we are modeling, we will need to choose which events are significant for us. Some real-life examples of events are:

- A person finishing an activity
- Real-time data about the stock market
- Real-time data about a patient's vital signs
- Real-time data about an aircraft route
- GPS coordinates of a vehicle
- An incoming text message
- Someone opening the door
- Someone sending a tweet using a specific hash tag
- Someone checking into a restaurant using Four Square
- A vehicle running out of gas

As you can see, there is a lot of activity around us, at every second, and any of this information can be modeled as events. Depending on our business, we will decide which events are relevant and can be used to improve the working of our company. For example, in some contexts, recording when someone opens a door could be important; if we were running a monitoring/security company that keeps track of who is accessing a specific room or house, this type of event could be extremely important, but if we were running a stock brokering company, recording this information would not be necessary at all.

At the modeling stage, the **Subject Matter Experts** (**SMEs**) define which events are relevant so that we can use them to enrich our context. Usually when we are interested in capturing events that happen in real time, it is because we have situations where we need to react as soon as an event or a set of events occurs. For example, in the case that we are capturing events from a patient's vital signs monitor, we will be interested in notifying the nurse in charge of that patient if the temperature rises over a certain threshold as soon as it happens. If we are in the security field monitoring unauthorized access and we capture an event about a security breach, we need to quickly inform the administrators of the situation.

Once we define which events are relevant to our scenario, we need to define what information the events will contain. In order to define the information that will be captured about the change of state, we need to understand the domain context and the specific reasons we need to capture that data. We also need to know some common characteristics of events so that we can capture and model them correctly.

Event characteristics

To define whether a piece of information is an event or just information, we need to know the set of common characteristics events generally share. We shouldn't confuse our entity models and structures with events. Both store information, but what varies is how the information will change over time as well as how we capture the information. Here are the common characteristics we find in events:

- Events are immutable
- Events contain strong temporal information
- Events store information related to the change of state

Events are usually immutable, so if something happens, we cannot change it. This means that we can analyze what has happened, decorate the event information, and use it to reach a conclusion—but we cannot change the past.

In some way, the event has to contain a temporal reference to the moment where the change of state has happened. We will see that Drools Fusion is flexible enough to allow us to define which attribute of the event object contains this information. If the event doesn't contain any temporal information, we can tag it with the current timestamp as soon as we receive it. The temporal information related to our events is extremely important because it lets us know the interval of time for which an event is relevant to our domain. If we want to react in real time, we will not be interested in a patient's vital signs that are two years old unless we are trying to find something that happened in that period.

At modeling time, we need to define which attributes will be relevant to our domain, and based on that, we will need to consider what kind of analysis we want to do. As with an entity model, there are performance implications regarding the amount of information that we store for each instance of our events. So we will need to think carefully about the information that we handle inside an event definition, considering the fact that we can be receiving many event instances in short periods of time.

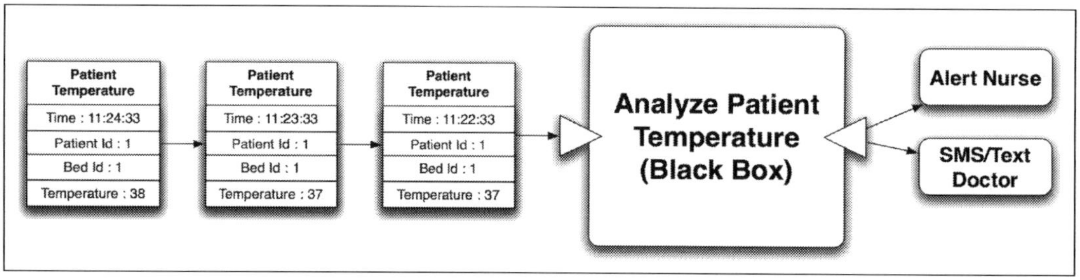

The preceding figure shows an example of the Patient Temperature event. As you can see, the event is being generated every minute and contains information on a given patient's location (which bed he/she is in as well as his/her temperature). In this case, the event contains the time when the temperature was taken. Note that, in the last event, the temperature has risen. If we are monitoring this situation, the black box will detect that spike in temperature and will notify the nurse and the doctor in charge of that patient as soon as the events is processed.

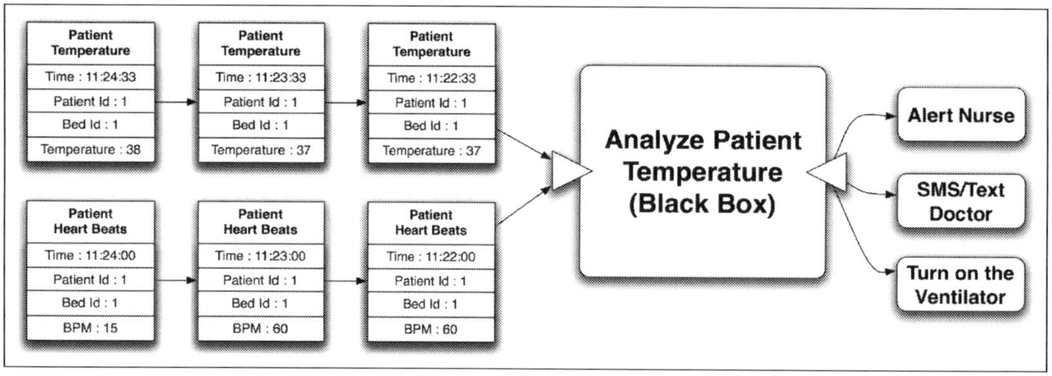

Note that we are not limited to capturing or analyzing just one single type of event; we can mix and match different types to detect more complex scenarios. In this case, the event structures are similar, but they can be completely different. It just depends on the type of data we are capturing.

As you can see in this example, the events are generated every minute, and depending on the source of events we have, we may receive a large number of events simultaneously. Events of the same type arriving together are usually referred to as a stream of events because they are flowing with time. These streams of events can be considered quiet or aggressive, depending on the number of event instances that they are delivering. For performance reasons, we need to define the number of event sources and how aggressive they are, to define system requirements such as memory, network latency, and so on.

Event-driven architectures

When we start working with events, we will see that what is being proposed by event-driven architectures becomes very useful. EDA proposes a much decoupled way of building infrastructure based on events. As we have learned from **Service Oriented Architectures (SOA)**, having well-defined components to create our systems helps us to break our application into different components with well-defined responsibilities. This allows us to upgrade each of them, if necessary, without the need to change the entire system. SOA is based on the concept of services, while EDA relies on the concept of events.

Because all the components in EDA will need to work using events, the following main components are proposed:

- Event producers
- Event consumers
- Event channels
- Event processing agents

The following figure shows the relationship between these components:

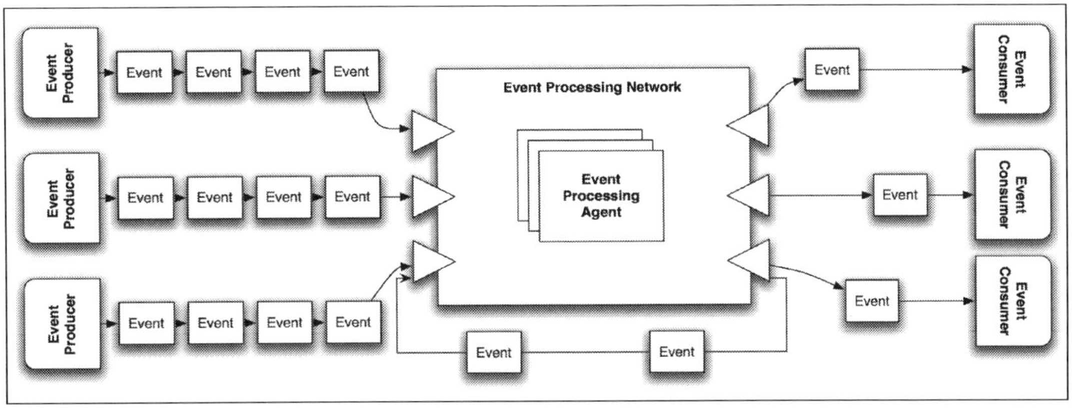

As you can see, the main responsibility of an event producer is to generate streams of events. These event producers can be anything that emits information which we capture as events. Here are some common sources of events that can be considered as event producers:

- User interfaces
- Monitors of any type
- An alert system
- A sensor of any type
- A person pushing a button or interacting with a machine

Each of these event producers can generate different types of events that are propagated to the event processing network via event channels. The event processing network contains a set of event processing agents that are in charge of analyzing the incoming event streams. Each processing agent can analyze events from multiple channels and notify an event consumer of a specific event if a situation of interest is found. As you can see, the event processing network or one of its processing agents can generate events that will be consumed by another processing agent.

An event consumer can be anything interested in receiving a notification of a change of state. Some examples of event consumers are:

- An application
- A business process
- A business dashboard
- A person waiting for a notification
- A machine waiting for instructions

One big advantage to these types of architectures is that event producers don't need to know the event consumers nor the event processing network. These concepts can easily be applied to any existing infrastructure in a non-intrusive way, so we don't need to consider EDA as a completely different approach to SOA. Rather, we can use them in conjunction to enrich our overall system capabilities.

A true EDA environment is not just this set of concepts. It should provide a set of tools to define, manage, and maintain the events required for a business scenario. Usually, an EDA environment should also provide all the infrastructure requirements that guarantee we will be able to operate with the number of events and the time responses (service-level agreements) that our business scenario requires.

The following section covers the complex event processing field that is considered the core of **EDA**.

Complex event processing

If we take the core concepts of EDA and analyze what happens inside the event processing network, we're going to be dealing with **complex event processing (CEP)**. CEP can be considered a small and core subset of the components that we find in an EDA environment. But what's the main goal of CEP?

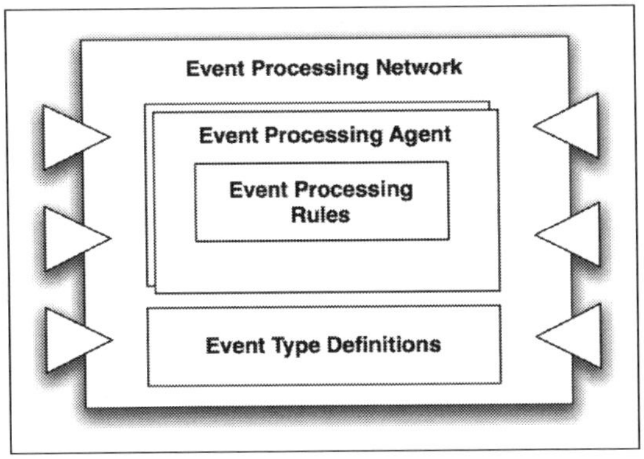

CEP is all about analyzing events and reacting as soon as a situation of interest is found. Each event processing agent defines a set of rules to describe these situations. The rules specified inside a processing agent will be in charge of aggregating, composing, and correlating events from different sources, in order to identify different situations. To analyze these events, we need to clearly define the event type structures as well as the processing agents that need to know these structures in order to operate. Once the structures are defined, we can start writing rules that will define the behavior of our agents.

> Note that, within these components, we don't know our event producers or the event consumers, and we have a limited vision of the event channels. We will only know the entry points from which we are going to receive the event streams.

In order to examine CEP with some examples, let's jump directly to Drools Fusion, which is the component inside Drools and the jBPM5 platform that deals with CEP.

Drools Fusion

Drools Fusion can be considered an extension to the Drools Rule Engine that understands and deals with events. Usually, rule engines don't deal with temporal data; in general, they work with facts that are considered pieces of information that are true for a given context. Facts can contain temporal information, but the engine itself has no idea of the current time, so it can't do temporal reasoning.

Drools Fusion tackles this problem by adding the following list of capabilities:

- Event definition capabilities
- System clocks
- Temporal operators and DRL extensions
- Sliding windows
- Event life cycle management

Let's quickly cover these features to see them in action.

Event definitions

With Drools Fusion, we have a way of defining our events. Since we are in a Java environment, our event definitions will be Java objects, the same as our facts, which means that we'll need a way to differentiate them. At this point, you may be wondering if all our facts will be events from now on or if the events are facts, so remember:

> All events are facts but not all facts are events.

In order to define a fact as an event, we decorate our fact type inside a DRL file with the following syntax:

```
define MyEvent
 @role(event)
end
```

By using this decoration, we are informing the engine that, now, instances of `MyEvent` need to be treated as events instead of facts. In this case, because we just want to decorate an existing class, we are only specifying the `@role` annotation, but we can define the entire structure in the DRL file just as we define our facts in it. This example requires a Java class called `MyEvent` to be imported into the DRL file to work.

As we already discussed, events are relevant only for a period of time. That's why we can also inform the engine of the validity of each event. In other words, we can express the expiration time for each type of event that we have by using the `@expires` annotation:

```
define MyEvent
 @role(event)
 @expires(2h)
end
```

Using the `@expires` annotation says that after two hours we will no longer be interested in that event instance. For this example, we will analyze events that are relevant only for the first two hours. This will enable the engine to perform automatic life cycle management, which includes removing events from the rule engine session when they are no longer relevant to our business scenario; this drastically reduces the amount of memory required to operate.

For example, if we needed to store all the credit card transactions that happened in a city for 30 days, we would require a lot of memory to host the objects that represent those transactions. If we were doing analysis that identified fraud patterns in real time, we would be more interested in shorter periods (for example, days). Automatic life cycle management allows the engine to dispose of the events that are no longer relevant for our analysis.

Finally, because our events need to contain a temporal reference, we can use the annotation `@timestamp` to define which property inside our class represents the time of the event.

```
define MyEvent
 @role(event)
 @expires(2h)
 @timestamp(time)
end
```

In this case, the class `MyEvent` contains a property called `time` that contains the long representation of when the event has happened. There are some cases when our class doesn't contain the temporal reference as a property; for those cases, if we don't specify the `@timestamp` annotation, the engine will automatically tag and decorate our class with the timestamp attribute using the current JVM clock.

Before moving forward, it is important for us to understand that there are two types of events:

- Point-in-time events
- Interval events

Point-in-time events are instantaneous. In other words, point-in-time events don't have duration. In contrast, **interval events** have duration, meaning that we can clearly see when an interval event starts and when it ends. Depending on the nature of the event that we are trying to model, we will need to choose between these different types.

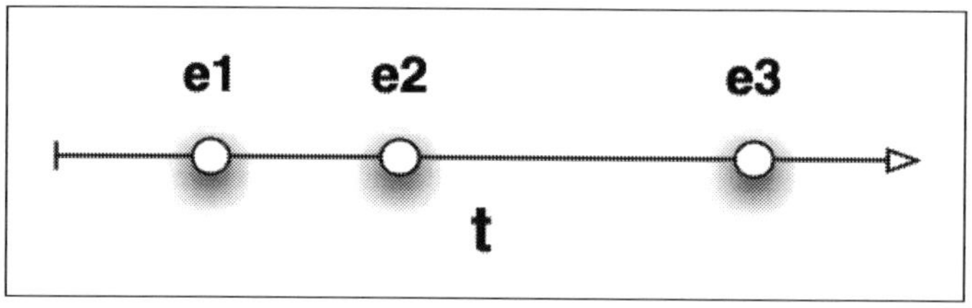

As we can see, point-in-time events happen at a single point. The preceding figure shows three point-in-time events that happen at three different moments. Because the time is continuously flowing—using the temporal operators (which will be introduced in the next section)—we will be able to create rules, which detect patterns in the occurences of these events. An example for a point-in-time event could be when a phone starts ringing.

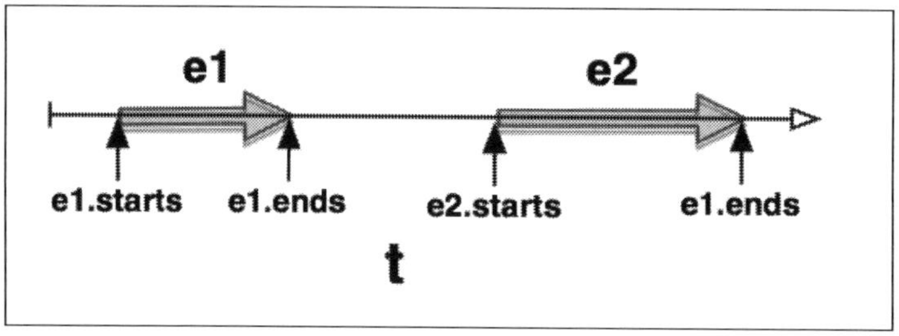

When we define interval events, each event instance contains a specified duration. As we can see in the previous figure, each event instance has a segment of time associated with it. Instead of just capturing when the phone rings as an event, we may also want to capture the phone call as an event. In that case, using an interval event definition is appropriate. If we have an entity to represent the information about that phone call, we will need to extract the duration of each phone call from that entity. By default, events are defined as point-in-time events. If we want to define an interval event, we need to use the `@duration` annotation, which will allow us to define a fixed duration for that event or specify the property that will contain that information inside the event type.

```
define MyEvent
 @role(event)
 @expires(2h)
```

```
    @timestamp(time)
    @duration(connectedTime)
end
```

Because we now have duration associated with the event, the engine will have references to two different timestamps: the event start time and the event end time. In the temporal operator sections, we will see how the engine uses these timestamps to evaluate the relationship between the events.

System clocks

In order to provide temporal reasoning capabilities, Drools Fusion introduces the concept of a clock to measure time. Because the engine needs to understand the concept of "now", Drools Fusion allows us to plugin different clock implementations. There are two very useful implementations provided with the engine. The most common one is Real Time Clock, which uses the JVM clock implementation. This is extremely practical for building real-time analysis tools and reactive systems that require a fine-grained perception of time. Because the real-time clock will be using the JVM internal clock, we will not be able to stop or manipulate this one, and the time will continuously flow.

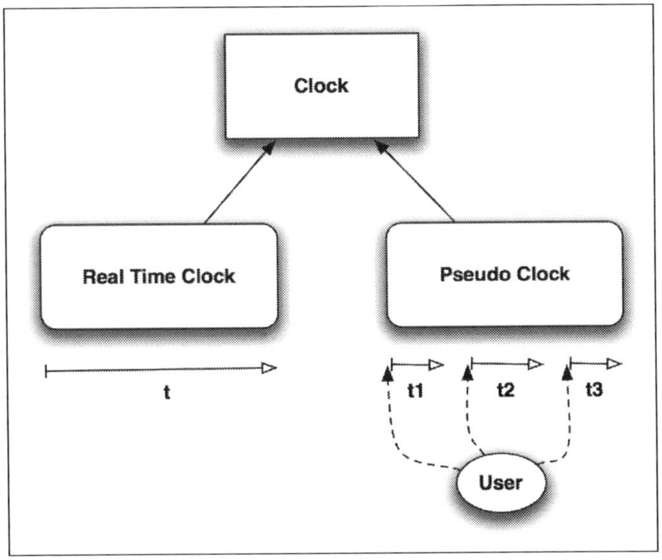

We can also use a different implementation, called Pseudo Clock, that enables us to have control of time; we can influence the clock when we want to. We will see some examples in the following sections, but it's important for you to know that this implementation becomes very handy when testing or simulating scenarios where we need to have control of how the time flows.

Now that we have the concept of time inside the engine via the clock implementations, we can perform temporal reasoning using the temporal operators defined by Drools Fusion.

Temporal operators

Temporal operators are extensions of the DRL language that enable us to operate and compare different instances of events. Using these operators, we will be able to write rules that identify situations where time is an important factor.

13 temporal operators have been outlined by James F. Allen to specify all the possible relationships between two events. Note that they are defined to operate with interval events, so some of them don't make sense for point-in-time events.

These are the 13 temporal operators available in Drools Fusion:

- After
- Before
- Coincides
- During
- Finishes
- Finished By
- Includes
- Meets
- Met By
- Overlaps
- Overlapped By
- Starts
- Started By

The following section briefly explains these temporal operators so we can quickly review them in action.

Before and After temporal operators

In order to compare two interval or point-in-time events using the temporal operators Before or After, we need to understand how the engine decides whether one event is before or after another.

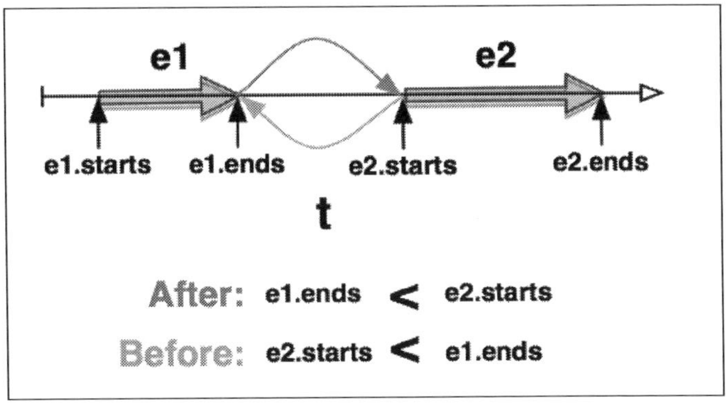

The previous figure also applies to point-in-time events, where the events' start and end timestamps are considered to be the same. Now in the DRL language, we can use these operators as in the following example:

```
$t1: TemperatureEvent( temperature <= 37)
$t2: TemperatureEvent( temperature > 38, this after $t1 )
```

As you can see, we can now use the After/Before temporal operator to correlate two events. The previous rule will evaluate to `true` only when we have two temperature events, where the first has to be less than `37` degrees Celsius and the second needs to be more than `38` degrees Celsius and is after `$t1`. As you may notice, this rule is not very restrictive when it comes to saying the relevant period of time. If we have two events on different days that match the previous restriction, the rule will be activated. We can define more restrictive periods if or when we are expecting events to happen. The following example shows how we can constrain the time interval that the engine will wait for, until `$t2` happens. The previous DRL snippet shows how we define *t'*, which only specifies that `$t2` needs to happen after `$t1`.

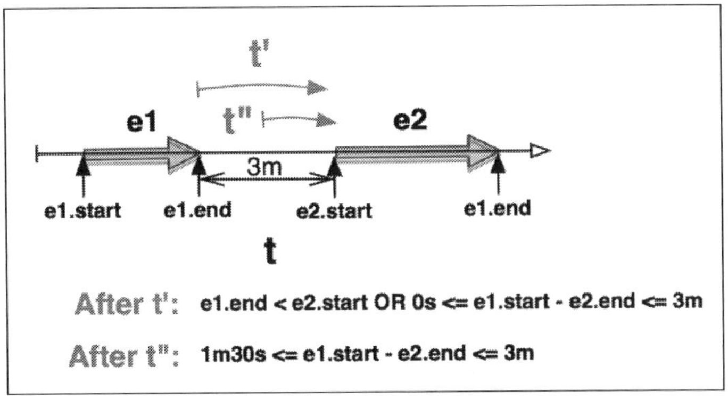

The DRL equivalent to the preceding figure will look like the following lines:

```
$t1: TemperatureEvent( temperature <= 37)
$t2: TemperatureEvent( temperature > 38, this after[1m30s, 3m] $t1 )
```

We are looking for events that happen between 1 minute, 30 seconds and 3 minutes after `$t1`. Events that don't match these temporal restrictions will not activate the rule. The previous example shows how *t*" can be specified using the DRL syntax.

One important thing to note at this point is that if we are using the real time clock, each timestamp will be precise to the millisecond. When we are dealing with business scenarios, business users usually don't need that kind of precision, so that's why using intervals with the operators allows us to map higher-level business requirements.

Another interesting example using the After temporal operator is when we want to monitor a situation where we didn't receive something that we were expecting, for example:

```
$order: OrderReceived($orderId: id)
Not( OrderConfirmation(orderId = $orderId,
                         this after [0s, 4m] $order))
```

In this case, after receiving the `OrderReceived` event, we delay the activation of this rule to wait for 4 minutes to see if we receive an `OrderConfirmation`. If we remove the `"this after [0s, 4m] $order"` constrain, the rule will be activated as soon as we receive the `OrderReceived` Event, without waiting the `OrderConfirmation` event. When we add this temporal restriction, the engine knows that it needs to wait for 4 minutes before activating this rule. This behavior is called **delayed activation**.

The Coincides temporal operator

Sometimes we need to know if two events are happening at the same time. When we talk about interval events, the Coincides temporal operator will check start and end timestamps for both events .

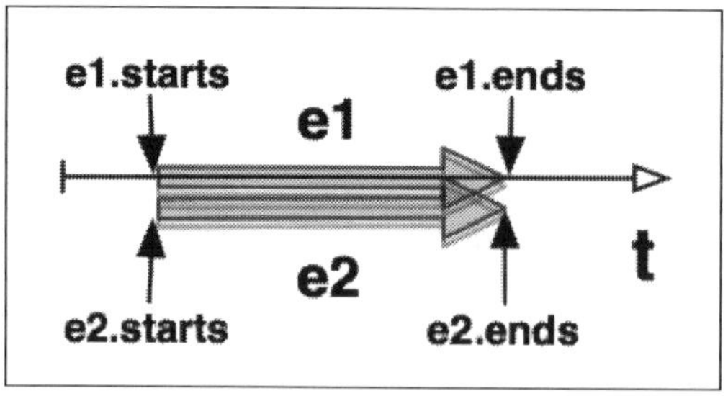

The following DRL shows the Coincides temporal operator in action:

```
$e1 : MyEvent( )
$e2 : MyEvent( this coincides $e1 )
```

As mentioned before, if we use the real time clock and the engine tags the events with the current timestamp, it will be extremely difficult for those two events to happen at the exact same millisecond. So, that's why we can also use time intervals to define how the Coincides operator needs to be evaluated.

```
$e1 : MyEvent( )
$e2 : MyEvent( this coincides[3m] $e1 )
```

These DRL conditional elements enable a 3-minute threshold, meaning that if the two events happen within a period of 3 minutes, they will match, and the rule will be activated.

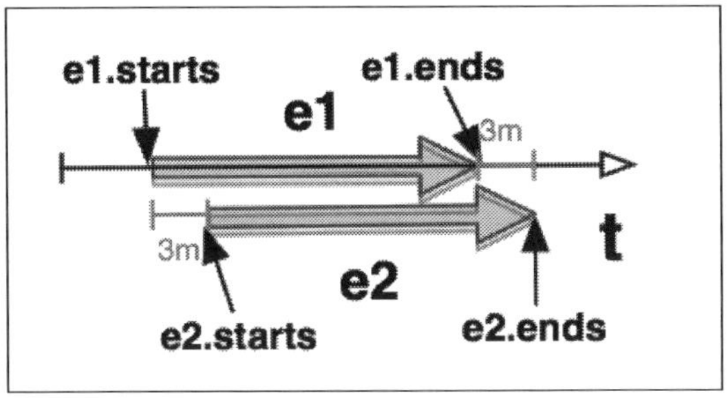

The engine does the following calculations in order to decide whether two events coincide or not:

```
abs( e1.start - e2.start ) <= 3m &&
abs( e1.end - e2.end ) <= 3m
```

Having these configurable thresholds makes sense at the business level, where it doesn't matter, for example, if two bank transactions were to occur in the exact same millisecond, so the scope of the analysis can be seconds, minutes, or hours.

Temporal operators summary

If you want to see a full description of all the temporal operators, you can look at the Drools Fusion official documentation at `http://docs.jboss.org/drools/release/5.5.0.Final/drools-fusion-docs/ html_single/index.html#d0e548`. Here, we'll explain just three of them because we will see how they can be used in conjunction with business processes in the following sections.

Sliding window support

Another cool feature that Drools Fusion provides is support for sliding windows. Sliding windows allow us to define an interval of interest. There are two types:

- Time sliding windows
- Length sliding windows

Drools Fusion provides two keywords for defining sliding windows: time and length.

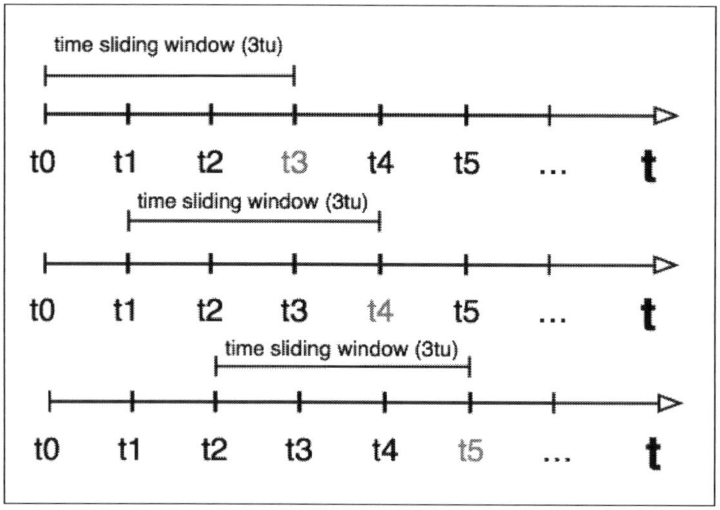

Using the DRL rule language, we can define a time sliding window as follows:

```
TemperatureEvent() over window:time( 2m )
```

This reads: all the `TemperatureEvent` instances that have happened in the last 2 minutes. Another example that uses a length sliding window would be:

```
FailureEvent() over window:length( 10 )
```

This reads: the last 10 instances of `FailureEvent` that have happened.

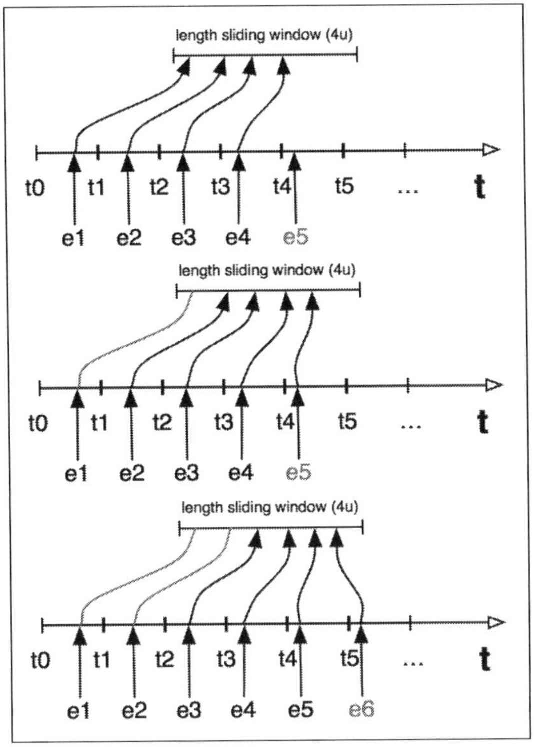

Events life cycle management

Because the engine now knows the relevance of each of our events, it can automatically manage the events life cycle for us. In other words, the engine will drop all the events that are no longer relevant to our system. As soon as the engine notices that an event is not being used any more, it will automatically retract the event from the knowledge session, freeing up space and memory for more events. Drools Fusion uses the `@expires` annotation as an explicit way to define when an event needs to be retracted, but it also infers from the rules (that we have in our rules base) when an event is not needed anymore.

For example, let's look at this previously introduced rule:

```
$order: OrderReceived($orderId: id)
not( OrderConfirmation(orderId = $orderId,
                       this after [0s, 4m] $order))
```

We can say that the `OrderReceived` event has an implicit expiration time of 4 minutes because we need to wait for up to 4 minutes to receive the `OrderConfirmation` event. In the case that we have set an explicit expiration time, the longer of the two will be used. Note that the implicit expiration time is calculated based on all the rules that are using the event type. The previous examples only analyze one rule, but in real-life scenarios, a more complex algorithm is used to calculate the implicit expiration times.

Drools Fusion in action

Let's get our hands dirty with code to see Drools Fusion in action, applying all of the concepts covered so far. First, we will analyze a very simple example that allows us to generate events and see how the rules react. Once we understand the basics, we will see how we can mix processes and events to build real-time reactive environments.

This section will analyze the example provided in the `chapter_10` directory that contains a project called `drools5-fusionSimpleExample`. Because this project is only using Drools, there is no reference to jBPM5 inside the `pom.xml` descriptor file.

This simple example is divided into two sections. The first one is the tests section, which contains the test showing the Drools Fusion core functionality. All these tests use the pseudo clock to execute the rules in a controlled way, where the application is in charge of moving the clock forward as needed.

The second part of the example is a GUI that lets us interact using the real time clock.

Both the tests and the GUI use the same rules to evaluate events generated by pressing keys on our keyboard. Definitions for the following rules and events are included in the `simpleEventAnalysis.drl` file:

```
rule "more than 3 key A in the last 10s"
    when
        Number($value: doubleValue > 3) from accumulate( $a: KeyA()
over window:time(10s), count($a))
    then
        System.out.println(" >>> KeyA Pressed - count: "+$value);
end
rule "key A + key S + key D pattern"
    when
```

```
        $a: KeyA()
        $s: KeyS( this after[1ms, 100ms] $a)
        $d: KeyD( this after[1ms, 100ms] $s)
    then
        System.out.println(" >>> KeyA +Key S + KeyD pattern
detected");
end
```

Take a look at the `README` file provided in this chapter's source code directory for a detailed description of the tests and configurations, including the pseudo clock. Inside this `README` file, you will find valuable information on how to configure the engine to work with events and how to set up the desired clock implementation.

The same project provides Swing client, which captures the keyboard events and automatically creates and inserts the appropriate event type in real time, using the real time clock to analyze the events. In order to run this Swing client, you can right-click on the class and select **Run as | Java Application**. You can also run it from the console, using Maven, by executing the following command:

```
mvn exec:java
```

So, each time you press a key, an event will be generated and inserted into the knowledge session. Both rules—the one that uses the sliding window and the one that checks for the *A+S+D* pattern—will wait to be activated.

These examples use the real time clock, so if you want to test how the rules work, you will need to move very fast to get the second rule (*A+S+D*) activated and fired. You will see the output in the console.

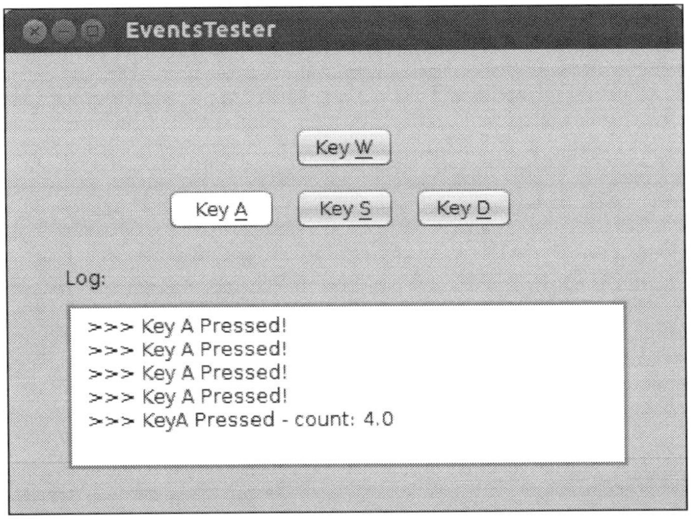

To fully understand event processing and how these rules get activated and fired, you need to play around with it. The following section describes how we can leverage the power of events to monitor and influence our process's execution.

Mixing processes and events

As we have seen in the previous section, Drools Fusion allows us to detect patterns in different streams of events arriving at our knowledge session. This section covers a simple example (built using Drools Fusion and jBPM5) where we can monitor the execution of multiple business processes and influence them as a group.

If you take a look at the example project called `jBPM5-Process-Events-Patterns`, you will see a very simple process definition that will be executed multiple times. Each activity/node triggers an event that will be analyzed by two rules.

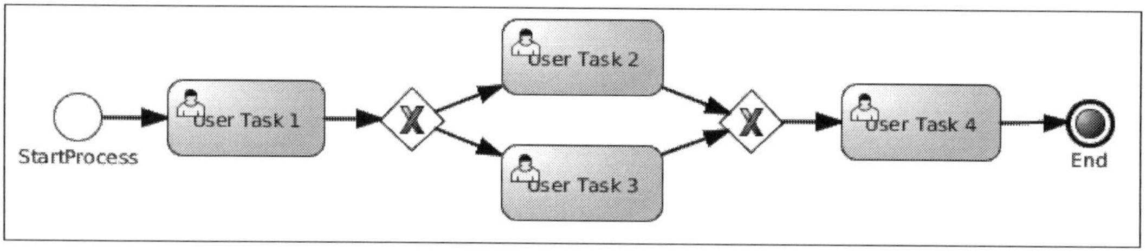

Each User task on this process will have an associated time of completion. A set of rules designed to monitor the events generated by the process instances will be in charge of speeding up or slowing down this task's completion time, in essence trying to find a balance to meet business requirements.

To omit events from the process' execution, we don't need to modify the process definition; rather, we can just attach a `ProcessEventListener` instance to the session that is running the process instances. This `ProcessEventListener` method will be in charge of catching all the events generated by the process and then forwarding them to a different session that is in charge of analyzing them.

```
processKsession.addEventListener(new DefaultProcessEventListener() {

            @Override
            public void beforeProcessStarted(ProcessStartedEvent
event) {

                System.out.println(" >>> Before Process Started: " +
event.getProcessInstance().getProcessName());
                eventsKsession.insert(event);
            }
```

```
            @Override
            public void afterProcessCompleted(ProcessCompletedEvent
event) {
                System.out.println(" >>> After Process Completed: " +
event.getProcessInstance().getProcessName());
                eventsKsession.insert(event);
            }

            @Override
            public void beforeNodeLeft(org.drools.event.process.
ProcessNodeLeftEvent event) {
                System.out.println(" >>> Before Node Left: " + event.
getNodeInstance().getNodeName());
                eventsKsession.insert(event);
            }
        });
```

Note that we are overriding the methods that are relevant to us, and those methods just propagate the events to a different session. As you can see, we are interested in three different events `ProcessNodeLeftEvent`, `ProcessCompletedEvent`, and `ProcessStartedEvent`. You can find these configuration options inside the `ProcessAndEventIntegrationTest` class. You will also find a couple of methods that initialize both sessions: the one that runs all the processes instances and the one that is in charge of analyzing the events generated by these processes. There is no real rule of thumb to decouple the process execution from the event analysis, but sometimes you will not want to do everything in the same session; this example highlights that situation. Based on the scenario/problem that you are trying to model, you'll have to decide if multiple sessions are required for it to work.

As mentioned earlier, each User Task will have an associated time of completion. In this case, we simulate a person working on the task, and for this we register a custom work item handler, which in this case will put the current thread to sleep. This simulates a person working for a designated amount of time.

```
processKsession.getWorkItemManager()
  .registerWorkItemHandler("Human Task",
    new WorkItemHandler() {

   public void executeWorkItem(WorkItem wi,
                               WorkItemManager wim) {
    try {
      System.out.println(" >>> Working on Task! it will take: "
                 + taskSpeed.getAmount() / 1000 + " seconds.");
      Thread.sleep(taskSpeed.getAmount());
```

```
    } catch (InterruptedException ex) {
      //Log error
    }
    System.out.println(" >>> Completing Task! -> " +
                      wi.getName() + " - id: " + wi.getId());
      wim.completeWorkItem(wi.getId(), null);
    }

    public void abortWorkItem(WorkItem wi,
                              WorkItemManager wim) {
               // do nothing
    }});
```

The `taskSpeed.getAmount()` method will affect how much time the task takes to be completed. We will influence this value from within the rules that measure the process execution performance.

Note that we are setting the initial value of `taskSpeed.amount` to 1000 milliseconds (equal to one second).

```
final TaskSpeed taskSpeed = new TaskSpeed(1000L);
eventsKsession.setGlobal("taskSpeed", taskSpeed);
```

Now, if we analyze the rules in the `analyze-process-events.drl` file, we will see that these two rules are trying to monitor the two following SLAs:

- If more than 10 User Tasks are executed in the last 10 seconds, we need to slow the pace down, so we don't stress our workers out
- If a process execution, from the beginning to end, takes more than 10 seconds, we need to hurry up and increase the task completion speed (`taskSpeed.amount`)

The two following rules define the previously described behavior:

```
rule "too much work - slow down"
    when

        Number( doubleValue > 10 ) from accumulate($e: Process
NodeLeftEvent(nodeInstance.nodeName contains "User Task") over
window:time(10s), count($e))
        not( TaskSpeedCorrected())
    then
        taskSpeed.setAmount(taskSpeed.getAmount()*2);
        System.out.println(" XXX Slowing down! Current task speed:
"+taskSpeed.getAmount());
```

```
        insert(new TaskSpeedCorrected());
end

rule "A Process Completion cannot take more than 10 secs - more power
needed"
    when

        $e: ProcessStartedEvent($id: processInstance.id )
        not ( ProcessCompletedEvent( processInstance.id == $id, this
after [1s, 10s] $e))
        not( TaskSpeedCorrected())

    then
        taskSpeed.setAmount(taskSpeed.getAmount()/2);
        System.out.println(" XXX Hurry Up! Current task speed:
"+taskSpeed.getAmount());
        insert(new TaskSpeedCorrected());
end
```

As you can see in the previous DRL snippet, in order to slow down the pace, we increase the value of `taskSpeed.amount` by multiplying the current value by `2`. The opposite happens when we want to complete our process executions faster; we decrease the value of `taskSpeed.amount` dividing the current value by `2`.

If you take a look at the first bits of the DRL file, where we define our events, you will find that we are once again defining a new event type called `TaskSpeedCorrected`. This is used to apply speed corrections once every 10 seconds.

```
declare ProcessNodeLeftEvent
    @role( event )
end
declare ProcessCompletedEvent
    @role( event )
end
declare ProcessStartedEvent
    @role( event )
end
declare TaskSpeedCorrected
    @role ( event )
    @expires (10s)
end
```

Defining the `TaskSpeedCorrected` event's expiration time and checking in the rules will stop the engine from applying speed corrections until the `TaskSpeedCorrected` event is retracted automatically after 10 seconds.

```
not( TaskSpeedCorrected())
```

If you run the test called `processEventsWithListenerTest()` inside the `ProcessAndEventIntegrationTest` class, you will see that, because of the business restrictions, the task completion time will vary between 2 and 4 seconds. You should see, in the console, output similar to this:

```
User Task 3 - On-exit
 >>> Before Node Left: User Task 3
 >>> Before Node Left: Gateway
User Task 4 - On-entry
 >>> Working on Task! it will take: 4 seconds.
 XXX Hurry Up! Current task speed: 2000
 >>> Completing Task! -> Human Task - id: 36
User Task 4 - On-exit
 >>> Before Node Left: User Task 4
 >>> Before Node Left: End
 >>> After Process Completed: Simple Process
Starting Process Instance: 13
 >>> Before Process Started: Simple Process
 >>> Before Node Left: StartProcess
User Task 1 - On-entry
 >>> Working on Task! it will take: 2 seconds.
 >>> Completing Task! -> Human Task - id: 37
User Task 1 - On-exit
 >>> Before Node Left: User Task 1
```

This variation is because there is no way to accomplish both rules at the same time using these values. If we set the time to `4` seconds, a process that needs to execute three User Tasks will take 12 seconds (causing the second rule to kick in). Once this rule gets fired, the time will be reduced to half (two seconds, now) allowing more tasks to be created. The test contained inside the class `ProcessAndEventIntegrationTest` creates sequential process instances one after the other. The tests contained inside the class called `ProcessAndEventMultiThreadIntegrationTest` uses multiple threads to run simultaneous processes using the same rules. Check this second example and experiment with it to understand how the same rules can be applied to process instances that are running at the same time. You can try creating your own rules to balance the work load.

Summary

In this chapter, we have covered how Drools Fusion can be integrated with jBPM5 to monitor and influence business processes executions. Drools Fusion can be used in multiple ways to assist and make our business processes more flexible when reacting to scenarios that require event analysis. The following chapter will focus on some tips on integrating processes, rules, and events into a company's infrastructure.

11
Architectural and Integration Tips

Looking at the threads posted in the jBPM5 forums and the Drools mailing lists, we can recognize a set of common questions that come up when people start designing applications. Usually, the answer depends not only on how big and complex these applications are but also on the type of scenario—different scenarios require different answers. This chapter summarizes some of these questions and their answers by recognizing some common patterns that appear in real-life implementations.

We will cover topics such as:

- Different architectural approaches
- Using multiple knowledge sessions inside our applications
- How to define the responsibility for each session
- How to coordinate multiple sessions

Defining our architecture

Depending on the type of application that we are building, we'll need to decide how and where our processes will run. As we know, knowledge sessions are the ones responsible for hosting our processes and rules. They also provide us a runtime environment where our knowledge resources can be executed.

In *Chapter 8, Persistence and Transactions*, we learned how persistent sessions work and what kinds of precautions we need to take if we are planning to use those features. Just as we analyze whether our processes require persistence or whether they can be considered long running processes, we also need to analyze the purpose of our session as a whole.

How we define the application's architecture is based on the problem/scenario that we are trying to solve as well as how much information we need to handle.

Most of the time, we don't exactly know what our application will look like until we start coding and narrowing down its requirements. That's why this section is going to expose some of the decisions that we need to make in order to achieve a successful solution.

If we are trying to integrate the jBPM5 and Drools platform with an already existing application, we will need to analyze how this integration can be carried out as well as where Drools and the jBPM5 runtime will be placed.

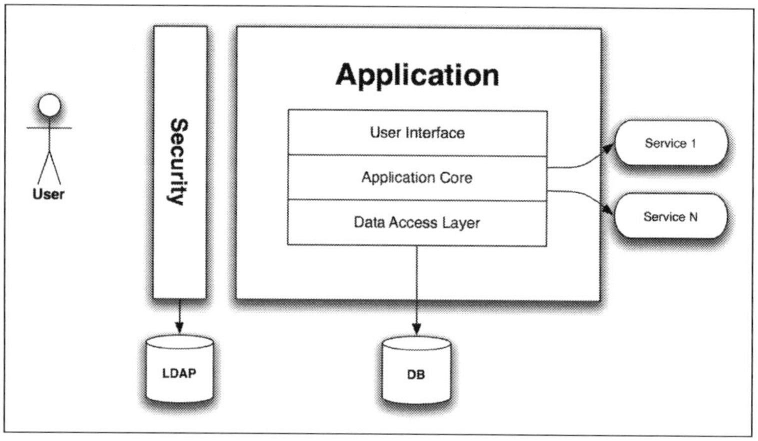

Where can we use the jBPM5 and Drools runtimes in the different application layers proposed in the preceding diagram? Basically, we can embed the jBPM5 runtime in each layer to provide different features, for example:

- **The User Interface layer**: We can include jBPM5 and Drools inside the User Interface layer to build smarter forms or wizards that create or validate the data entered by a user.
- **The Application Core layer**: We can write the application's core logic using rules and processes, or we can coordinate—based on processes and rules—definitions in which external services will need to be called. We can also use rules and processes to collect the information required for calling each of these external services.

- **The Data Access layer**: We can use Drools or jBPM5 to force business restrictions to be applied to the data before persisting it inside our database. Regulations, norms, and standards can be applied and defined using processes and rules.
- **The Security layer**: Inside the security layer, processes can be defined for authorization purposes; rules can also be used to define which resources can be accessed by a certain set of people, based on contextual information.
- **Service layer / services**: Services can be built using processes and rules as part of their internal logic. Our applications will access these services using their exposed interfaces, but internally the logic can be resolved using Drools and the jBPM5 platform.

As you can see, several things can be done with Drools and jBPM5, so when we're deciding where to create our knowledge sessions, we need to choose wisely.

If we think about just one knowledge session—no matter what layer we need it in—there are four things that need to be evaluated:

- How much information we are planning to handle inside our knowledge session
- How many business process instances we are planning to host in the knowledge session
- Whether the knowledge session requires persistence
- Whether the knowledge session is intended to do real-time evaluations for live streams of data

Knowing how much information we are going to maintain within our knowledge session can help us a lot with calculating and deciding the technical requirements. Knowing what kinds of operations we are going to execute inside our session also allows us to recognize some logical problems that may appear.

Basically there are two big categories of restrictions:

- Technical restrictions
- Logical restrictions

Both of them are tied together. Let's start listing some of the most common technical requirements to see how they affect our designs.

The most basic technical restriction is the fact that a knowledge session cannot be divided to run on multiple JVMs. This means that when we create a knowledge session, that session will live in only one JVM instance. Using persistence mechanisms, we can migrate a session from one JVM instance to another, but the runtime will be contained inside the running JVM process. This restriction is related to how the rule engine builds an undividable network that analyzes all the facts in an efficient way. Up to now, there have been experiments on how to distribute a **RETE** network (the core of the rule engine) on multiple machines, but there is nothing that is officially released or stable enough to be used. Because of this restriction, the knowledge session shares all of the same restrictions that a single JVM has:

- **Memory restrictions**: Each JVM process has a finite amount of memory to allocate. This limit defines the amount of information that we will be able to host in our knowledge session. If our JVM is configured to access 4 GB of RAM and we want to host 8 GB of domain objects, we cannot expect good performance for obvious reasons.
- **CPU restrictions**: The operating system will decide when the JVM has priority over other processes running on that machine.
- **Performance restrictions**: Our knowledge session will be tied to the JVM performance as well as to the number of other applications running inside the same JVM.

These technical restrictions related to the JVM need to be taken into account when we insert information into our knowledge sessions. How much time it will take for the JVM to create the object's structure that will be handled by the session depends on how and where we obtain the information that will be handled by the session. A common example of this restriction is when we want to insert a lot of data from a database to a knowledge session. With these requirements, we especially need to be careful while detecting the possible bottlenecks. If we need to insert several registers from a database into a knowledge session, it's important to measure the object's creation time, examine the latency from the DB (to retrieve the required data), as well as figure out how that process can be improved—but all of this is completely out of the scope of the knowledge session's performance perspective.

From a logical standpoint, the restrictions are a little bit more difficult to see and analyze. Because the rule engine and the process engine allow us to solve an enormous range of problems, it can be difficult to give precise solutions that cover all the possibilities. From a high-level perspective, we can categorize the level or requirements that we will have, based on what we are trying to do with our session.

If we are dealing with processes (as previously discussed in *Chapter 8, Persistence and Transactions*), once we decide whether the persistence mechanism is required, we will start to have a good idea of the behavior and requirements of our session. If we are planning to deal with a mix of in-memory processes and long-running processes, we will need to start measuring how easy/hard it is to have them running in the same environment. It's important to understand at this point that running multiple instances of the same process inside the same session is not the same as running multiple instances of different processes in the same session. Whether they can co-exist depends on how our processes are modeled. Most of the time, if processes are completely unrelated and don't have any logical relationship, they are able to run in separated runtime environments. The following section (*Using multiple knowledge sessions*) covers this idea of using multiple knowledge sessions when our scenario allows us to do that.

As you can imagine, when you add rules and event processing to the mix, the analysis becomes even more complicated and dependent on your specific application and performance requirements. When you use a large rule set that evaluates a huge data set, using persistence mechanisms can affect the performance. We need to be aware of the fact that for each insertion/retraction/update that our application executes against the engine, all our facts and the status of the session will be persisted. If we are using rules to evaluate our long-running processes, we will not have a large fact set along with the process instances. For such scenarios, having persistent sessions and rules is not a big deal. When you are planning to do near real-time analysis of incoming streams of events, using the persistence mechanisms is usually not an option. When we have to process incoming streams of events, the amount of information we need to maintain inside our knowledge session depends on how aggressive those streams are.

Something that quickly becomes obvious is the fact that a single knowledge session is not enough if the scenario that we are trying to model requires all the available features of Drools and the jBPM5 platform.

Using multiple knowledge sessions

There is no restriction in Drools and the jBPM5 platform that says you can't use more than one knowledge session in your application. For some reason, this is not often realized by newcomers, who want to do everything inside the same session. If we have only one session, we have just one context that will know about everything, but every time we want to add a piece of new knowledge to the whole, it will gradually become more and more complex to handle.

As introduced in the comparison between old BPMS and jBPM5, it was common practice to use more stateless engines, which could be used to run multiple processes, each one with a very limited context of itself. Just because a knowledge session allows us to run multiple processes within it, it doesn't mean that we always want to do that. Something similar happens with the rule engine; traditional implementations used the rule engine for small and well-defined problems, which were almost always solved by stateless sessions. Now that we have **stateful knowledge sessions**, we tend to think that we can just mix in all our stateless scenarios. I'm not saying that it's impossible, but when we start mixing knowledge (process, rules, and models)—things that were designed to solve different problems inside the same session—we need to make sure that there are no logical or execution conflicts. Depending on the complexity of our environment, doing these coherence checks on our knowledge can become a major task, which can usually be avoided. Having a well-defined set of problems to solve helps us to design and model our domain knowledge in a coherent way.

Next, we'll see from a high-level perspective some patterns that we can use to decide how our knowledge can be distributed between different sessions, according to their execution and logical requirements.

Defining a knowledge context

Let's assume that we are in a big company or organization, such as a hospital for example. Different departments within the hospital have different domain models and different problems or scenarios to solve.

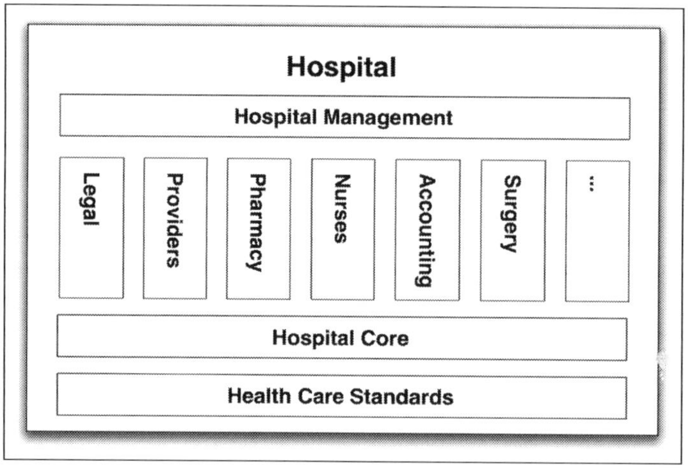

The preceding image shows as vertical boxes some possible subdomains inside a hospital that may or may not share some core hospital concepts (horizontal boxes). As you can imagine, using only a single knowledge session to solve all the hospital problems is not recommended for several reasons:

- Each department handles different information models that may clash with those from other departments. For example, the `Patient` entity could be defined in multiple modules containing information only related to that domain. We may also find similar concepts being handled under different names, so the unification process can get pretty complex.
- Even if we have a hospital-wide unified model, it gets to be a real challenge to write knowledge that solves every specific problem without ending up with extremely complex interactions and dependencies.
- Different problems have different requirements; there is no unified solution for all of them yet.

We could say that a good option for organizing and defining the architecture in this type of scenario is to analyze each department as a separate logical unit. All the things that may be shared between these departments can then be concentrated inside the Hospital Core hub.

If we start noticing that a significant number of departments have shared concerns and similar problems, then new layers can be created to host and share these mechanisms. Topics such as communication between departments, business metrics reports, high-level alerts, and so on can be designed once and used by all of the logical units.

From a high-level perspective, we can say that each department will have its own knowledge context. A top-level department (for example, Hospital Management) can constitute its knowledge context based on information exposed by all the other departments. In other words, each department is isolated so that it has its own knowledge context but still shares information with the rest of the hospital.

One session per knowledge context level

Once we get the big picture of the entire organization and we have the specific requirements of each knowledge context, several subdivisions can be made, depending on the requirements at the department level.

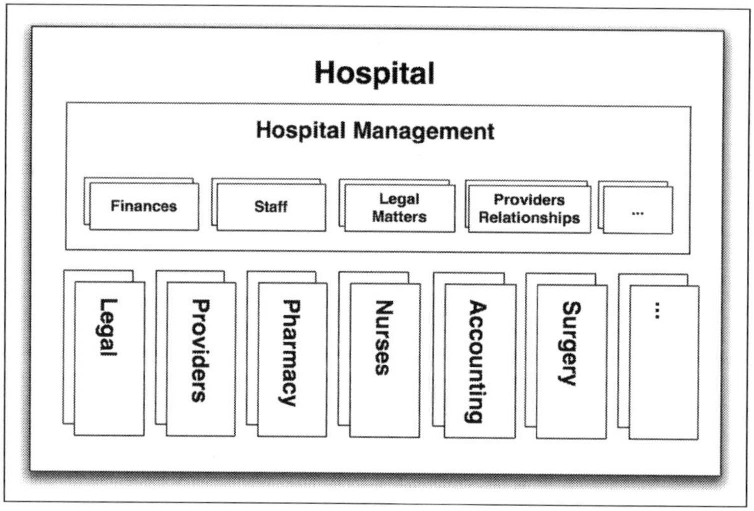

Each knowledge context can be formed by multiple knowledge sessions collaborating together to solve different scenarios within the same context. How many knowledge sessions we will require depends on the variety of problems that we need to solve. The following sections focus on business processes, but similar analysis can be done for rules and complex event processing.

Chances are that you'll usually have to start a project by working in one department (meaning one knowledge context) before having a complete picture of the whole organization, but you will need to apply the same concepts. Remember that to organize and define a realistic architecture, your entire picture should be the department as well as its subdivision of concerns and requirements.

One session per process instance

Business processes share this idea of different layers of abstraction to organize how the work is being done. Where a business process needs to run, as well as its scope, depends on the specifics of the process itself.

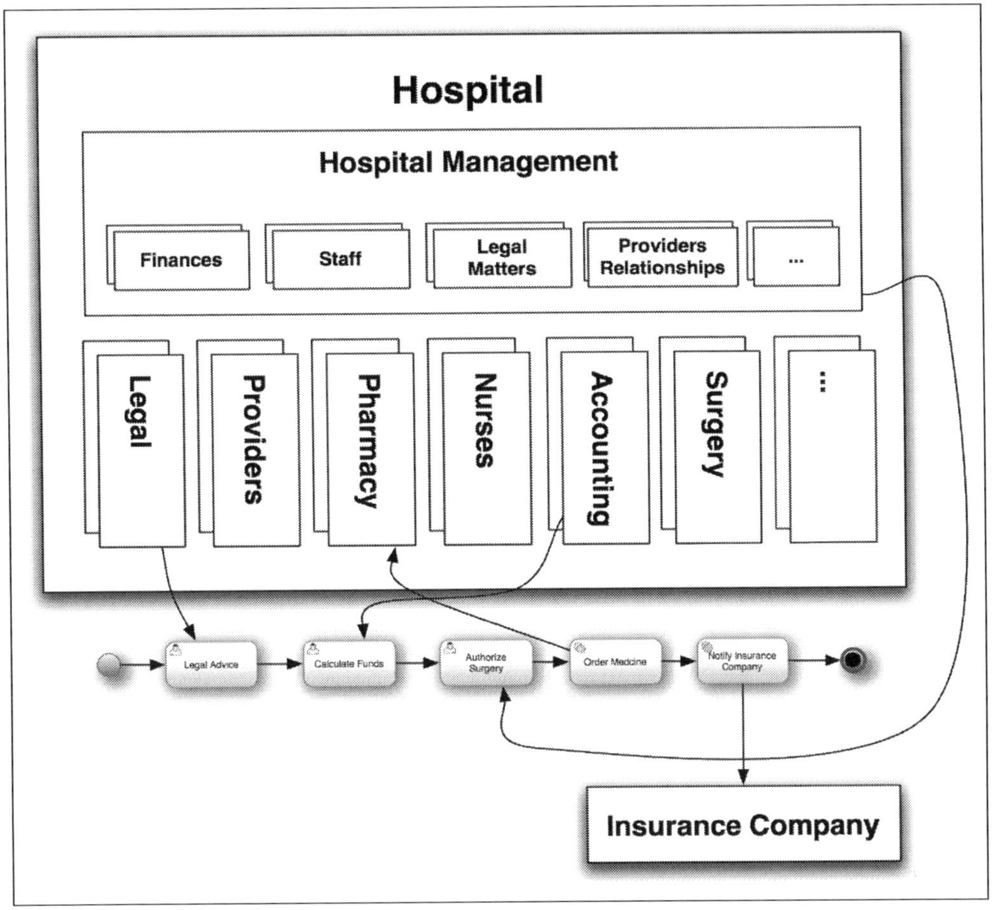

Note that this business process requires interaction from different departments. This is a common situation for high-level, shared processes, so usually we will need to either have a special place to run this process or decide which department is the process owner.

At this point, questions start to appear. How many processes can we run inside a knowledge session? Where will this knowledge session run? Which knowledge context will contain this session? What requirements will this knowledge session have?

The simplest answer for these questions is to have a knowledge session per process instance. This means that we have, inside the session, only the information and knowledge required by that specific process instance. Once the process is over, we will destroy the session and dispose all the information contained in it. This option enables us to run our process with a very limited context. If we have a rich context (for example, a case where information from other departments could influence the process instance behavior), creating one session per process instance is going to be expensive because all of the contextual information will need to be cloned, inserted, and maintained inside the session.

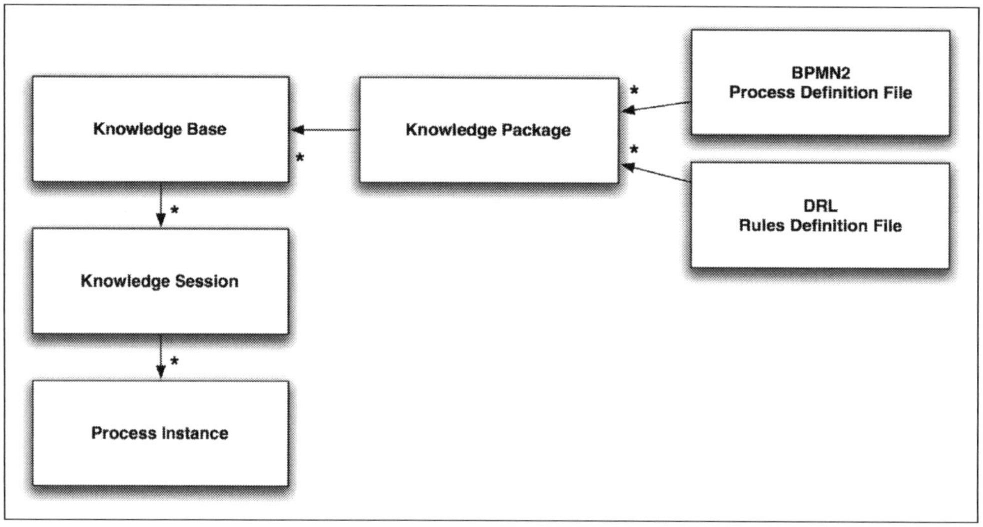

Technically, the cardinality between the components is unlimited, but we will need to think logically when choosing the best option for our scenarios.

You might consider it as good practice to have a knowledge session dedicated to processes such as the one previously introduced, which is long-running and cross-organizational. For that example, here is a list that illustrates good restriction over the proposed cardinalities:

- All long-running and cross-organizational processes can be compiled inside one single knowledge package
- One knowledge base will be created
- One persistent knowledge session will be created
- Multiple process instances from different process definitions will be created inside the knowledge session
- This session needs to be hosted by a runtime that has access to all the services required by the processes

Continue with this approach until you notice that the process definitions can be divided into logical subgroups. If you can divide your processes into smaller logical groups and move them to a new session, you can easily keep their executions under control and track down problems.

Technically speaking, the simplest option is to have a reduced and limited context for executing our business processes. If we define in our architecture that we require a new session per process instance, our process will run without any interference from other knowledge definitions. In such scenarios, the information available for our process is only what we insert into the session (where that process belongs).

The project `jBPM5-Multi-Session-Patterns` contains a set of examples showing these patterns. These tests will show us how we can structure our knowledge assets in different sessions, which will have different responsibilities. The test class called `SingleSessionPatternsTest` contains demos on how to configure our knowledge sessions; it also takes a look at which pieces of extra information will be required and stored as part of the application.

In this section, we will analyze the test method called `singleSessionPerProcessInstance()`, which is about running a long-running process instance inside a knowledge session. So, if we want to create a second process instance, we will need to create another new session.

This test shows the configurations and the steps required to create and start a new process instance:

```
EntityManager em = getEmf().createEntityManager();
UserTransaction ut = (UserTransaction) new InitialContext()
                        .lookup("java:comp/UserTransaction");

Person person = new Person("Salaboy", 29);
Map<String, Object> params1 = new HashMap<String, Object>();
params1.put("person", person);

StatefulKnowledgeSession ksession1 =
            createProcessOneKnowledgeSession(person.getId());
registerWorkItemHandlers(ksession1, person.getId(), em);

int ksession1Id = ksession1.getId();

ksession1.startProcess("com.salaboy.process.AsyncInteractions",
                        params1);
ksession1.dispose();
```

Nothing strange here; we are creating a knowledge session, which contains a process definition, we are registering the Work item handlers required by that process, and finally, we are creating and starting a new process instance.

The `createProcessKnowledgeSession()` method creates a persistent knowledge session for hosting long-running processes. I encourage you to check out the source code to see the configurations.

The `registerWorkItemHandlers(ksession1, person.getId(), em);` line instantiates and registers the relevant work item handlers for the particular process instance that we want to create. For this example, we are using a previously introduced process that contains two human interactions and one external system interaction:

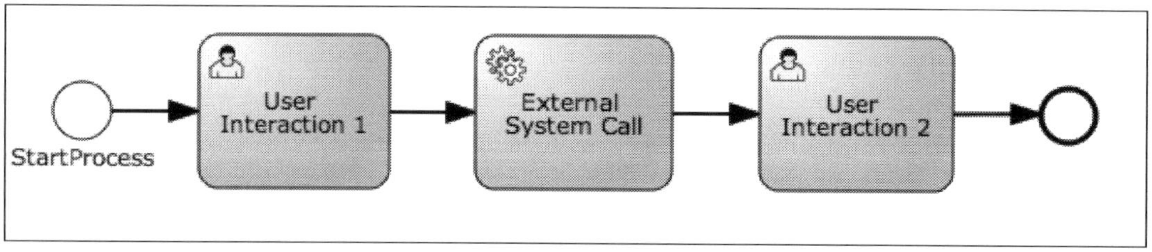

As you can see, we are registering one WorkItemHandler to manage human interactions and another WorkItemHandler to deal with the external system call:

```
protected void registerWorkItemHandlers(
                           StatefulKnowledgeSession ksession,
                           String key, EntityManagerem) {
MockAsyncExternalServiceWorkItemHandler externalHandler =
           newMockAsyncExternalServiceWorkItemHandler(em,
                                         ksession.getId(), key);
ksession.getWorkItemManager().registerWorkItemHandler(
                               "Human Task",
                               mockExternalServiceWorkItemHandler);
ksession.getWorkItemManager().registerWorkItemHandler(
                               "External Service Call",
                               mockExternalServiceWorkItemHandler);
}
```

Notice that both work item handlers receive the session ID and business key in their constructors.

Both interactions will be asynchronous—a fact that requires us to keep track of the session running the process so that we'll be able to reload it when an external interaction is completed.

In this simplified example, we are using a mock handler for the human interactions, so you can see how the internal mechanisms work.

If you take a look at the `MockAsyncExternalServiceWorkItemHandler` class, you will notice that this handler is in charge of keeping the following information in persistent storage:

- Business key
- Session ID
- Process instance ID
- Work item ID

As soon as the interaction is completed, we'll use this information to locate the corresponding knowledge session that was hosting the process so that we can continue the execution. The `businessKey` entity for this example is shown in the following code:

```
@Entity
public class BusinessEntity {
  @Id
  @GeneratedValue
  private Long id;
  private int sessionId;
  private long processId;
  private long workItemId;
  private String businessKey;
  private boolean active = true;
    // Include any other relevant information about the
    //  process or session
    // Like for example the interaction owner or information
    //  that is unique for this relationship
  public BusinessEntity() {
  }
  public BusinessEntity(intsessionId, long processId,
                        long workItemId, String businessKey) {
    this.sessionId = sessionId;
    this.processId = processId;
    this.workItemId = workItemId;
    this.businessKey = businessKey;
  }
   // Getters and Setters omitted
}
```

This entity contains the basic parts required to locate the knowledge session and process instance where the interaction was created. Most of the time, this entity also contains application-specific information. As you can see, the work item ID (which uniquely represents the interaction) is stored on the process engine side, but if you are interacting with an external service, any information that the external service gives you to represent that interaction can be stored inside this entity.

Let's analyze the `MockAsyncExternalServiceWorkItemHandler` implementation:

```
public void executeWorkItem(WorkItemwi, WorkItemManagerwim) {
  long workItemId = wi.getId();
  long processInstanceId = wi.getProcessInstanceId();
  if (businessKey == null || businessKey.equals("")) {
    businessKey = UUID.randomUUID().toString();
  }
  BusinessEntity businessEntity =
               new BusinessEntity(sessionId,
                                  processInstanceId,
                                  workItemId, businessKey);
  em.joinTransaction();
  em.persist(businessEntity);
}
```

As you can see, before scheduling an external interaction, the work item handler is in charge of persisting this relationship. Because the interactions inside the work item handlers are outside the scope of the process engine, this information is usually stored in the application that is creating the new process instance. For this example, we are using an entity manager, but you can use whatever persistence mechanism is available. This business entity will represent the process owner, and it is able to contain all of the necessary domain information that we want to store in order to be able to locate the process instance when needed. For this example, the business key is the Person ID, which is associated with the process instance. **Business keys** must be unique, so if you have to start more than one process per person, remember to add more information to the business key.

Depending on the external service is whether we can get an interaction key. For example, the Task ID that was created in the Human Task Module or a confirmation message from a web service can also be stored as part of the business key.

When we want to complete the external interaction, we will need to locate the correct session and pending work item ID by querying the business key to proceed with the execution:

```
List<BusinessEntity> activeBusinessEntities =
                     getActiveBusinessEntities(em);
```

```
ksession2 = loadKnowldgeSession(businessEntity.getSessionId(),
                            businessEntity.getBusinessKey(), em);
registerWorkItemHandlers(ksession2,
                         businessEntity.getBusinessKey(), em);
try {
  ut.begin();
  ksession2.getWorkItemManager()
        .completeWorkItem(businessEntity.getWorkItemId(), null);
  markBusinessEntityAsCompleted(businessEntity.getId(), em);
  ut.commit();
} catch (Exception e) {
  System.out.println("Rolling back because of: " +
                     e.getMessage());
  ut.rollback();
}
```

In this example, we're using the business key to locate the knowledge session that contains the process instance related to that specific person. For different scenarios, different pieces of information can be used to locate the specific runtime required.

Once we locate the correct session ID (in this case, the one contained inside the `businessKey` entity), we can use the `JPAKnowledgeService.loadStatefulKnowledgeSession(...)` method to restore the session. Some important things to notice here are:

- We need to reload the session because another thread/application may have been interacting with it
- The knowledge bases can be cached or recreated as long as they contain the same resources
- The environment can be cached or recreated as long as it contains the same configurations
- The execution can happen in a different thread to a different application

> If two or more threads want to load and interact with the same session concurrently, only one of them will persist the changes, while the others will need to retry the operation. This fact forces us to think about the limitation of running multiple process and rules in the same session. As soon as we keep the knowledge inside the session coherent with a set of functional requirements, we will be able to measure the potential number of concurrent access attempts to a session. If we create a session containing a wide range of knowledge, the potential number of clients will grow, causing this concurrent access to occur more frequently.

When we are done with the interaction and complete the corresponding work item, we should mark our business entity as inactive, avoiding future queries being able to retrieve a completed interaction. Notice that this must happen in the same transaction to avoid storing incoherent states.

The following sections use the same mechanisms to describe different patterns of usage.

One session per process category

For the previous example, I suggested using a single knowledge session to run all of the long-running and cross-organizational processes. Most of the time, this categorization can also be done for internal department business processes. Inside a department, business processes can be divided based on different levels of abstraction. Technical processes can be placed together in the Bottom Layer, regulation and domain standard processes in the Middle Layer, and processes sharing information with other departments (for example, management) in the Top Layer:

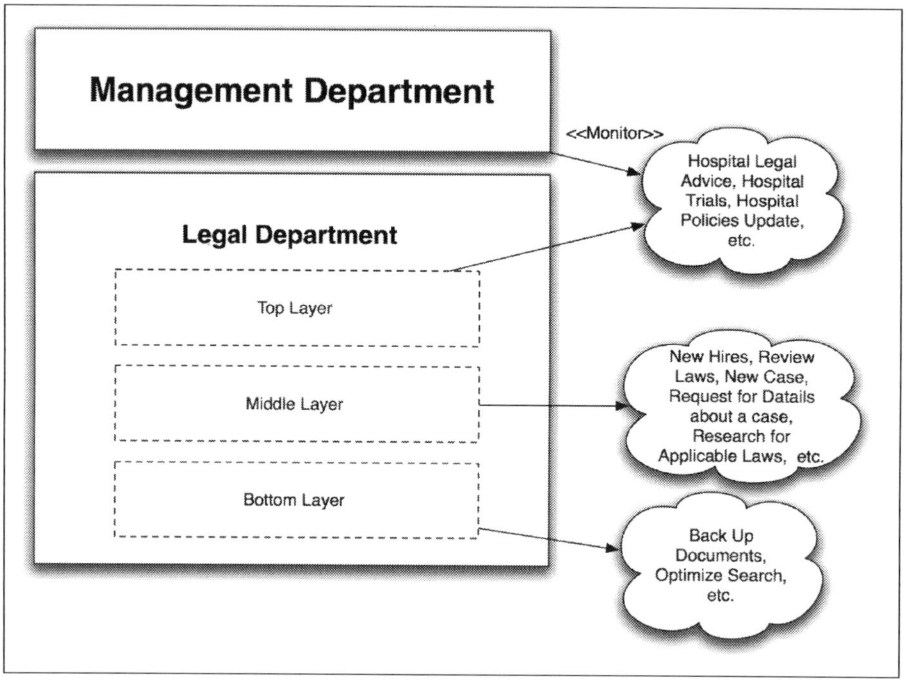

As you may notice, how you divide the layers is entirely up to you, but some way or another, you need to make a clear distinction about where to place each process. Defining these layers will help you to explain where each knowledge session belongs and the scope of the knowledge contained inside it. Knowledge packages can then be related and built according to these layers' definitions. Once you have this logical division, you can use the technical requirements to define exactly how many sessions will be required, and what information needs to be shared between them.

Here is where we start categorizing our processes based on which layer they fit in as well as on their technical requirements:

- Is persistence required? If so, long-running or in-memory?
- Do we need a department context to be filled or can it run in an isolated context?
- Do we have a set of rules that evaluates a group of process instances together? Do we have a set of rules that decides when to start our processes?

Based on the answers to these questions, we'll create buckets that represent which processes will need to run together, which ones can be isolated, and which ones have logic dependencies that need to be taken into account when we define our architecture.

The process definitions and knowledge that belong to the same knowledge context, and share similar runtime requirements can be made to share the same knowledge session.

The test called `singleSessionPerProcessDefinition()` shows this concept in action. The same mechanisms used in the previous example are now being used in this test as well. The only difference is that now we are sharing the session between different process instances, so multiple different people can be associated with each process inside our session. For this particular test, the business key is autogenerated inside the work item, which contains a token (unique ID) provided by the external application.

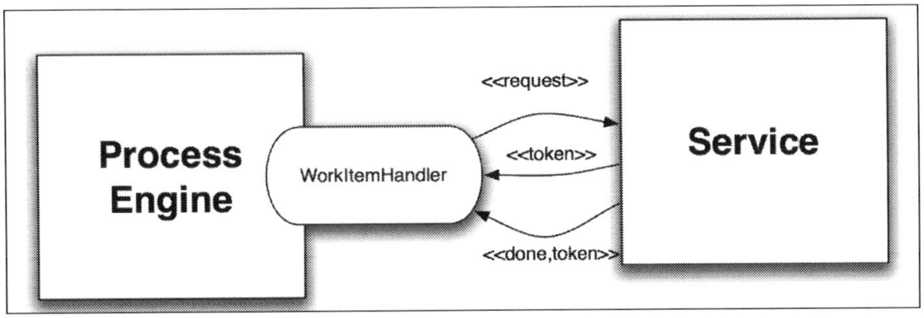

Usually, when we use this kind of business key, the external application is in charge of notifying when the interaction has been finished. Using the provided token, it finds the correct session and propagates the execution to the next activity.

In contrast to the process engine perspective, we can always use the process ID (process instance ID) or the work item ID to locate the session and complete the external interaction. The queries inside the test are done by the process ID and work item ID, since we don't know the generated token from the process perspective. We can run these queries because we are in a controlled scenario; remember though, that it's up to you to implement the mechanisms that correlate an interaction token with a specific session or process instance ID.

Multiple sessions' coordination

When we start having multiple sessions spread around our application, we will encounter some situations where we want to communicate information from one of the sessions to another. This can be achieved in several ways, but here we will see an example of how we can implement a simple mechanism to coordinate multiple sessions.

We know that we can store information about our current sessions using the business entity. In this example, the external interaction from our process will look up another session and insert a fact notifying of this request. To show that we can share information with a different session, the example inserts the generated business entity into a session that only contains rules.

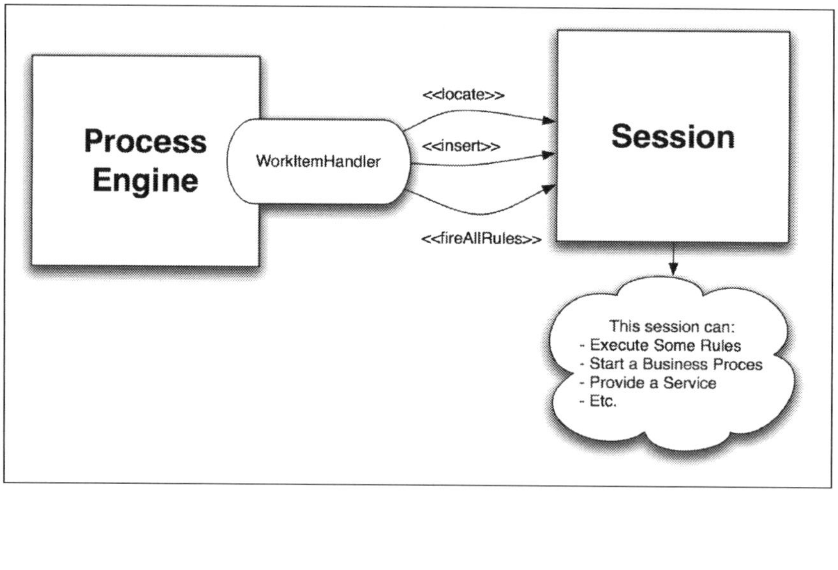

Our work item can contact any service available, and using the business entity, we can locate any session. Once we do that, we can make use of that session the way we want to; it's a technique that allows us to decouple the session's responsibility.

We can go one step further and insert an identifier into the other session to locate the session that contains the process and work item.

If you open the test class called `MultiSessionsPatternsTest`, you will find an example of how we can implement these interactions. As you can see, the WorkItemHandler will insert the business entity (generated by the interaction) into a specific session. This entity will contain the session ID and the work item ID that were used in that interaction.

The test also defines another session that contains rules defining when and how that interaction must be completed.

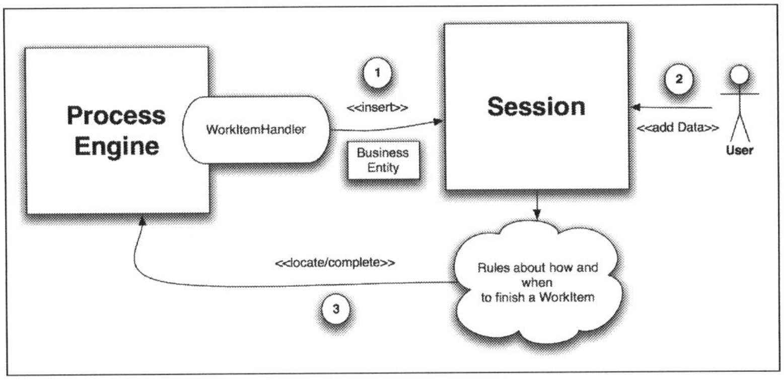

Note that in the previous figure, the rules evaluate the existence of a Business Entity as well as some business data that a user must add. When everything is in place, a rule will be activated and fired, causing the completion of the work item (which was pending), and the business process will be moved forward.

```
rule "Complete Interaction When We Receive Data"
when
    $be: BusinessEntity(active == true)
    $data: Data()
then
  StatefulKnowledgeSessionksession =
  ksessionSupport.loadKnowldgeSession(
                              $be.getSessionId(),
                              $be.getBusinessKey(),
                              em);
  ksessionSupport.completeInteraction(ksession,em,
                                  $be, $data.getDataMap());
end
```

As you can see, the left-hand side of the rule is simple and clear. If we have a business entity and the expected data, this rule will be activated and eligible to fire. The right-hand side of the rule contains all the boilerplate code required to locate a session (based on the business entity-provided IDs) and complete a work item within that session.

Take a look at the method `completeInteraction(..)` inside the `SessionsPatternsTestsBase` class, which is a helper to only be used inside the rules, to complete a work item, and mark the business entity as completed:

```
public void completeInteraction(
             StatefulKnowledgeSession ksession,
             EntityManager em,
             BusinessEntity entity,
             Map<String, Object> results) throws Exception {
  ksession.getWorkItemManager()
          .completeWorkItem(entity.getWorkItemId(), results);
  markBusinessEntityAsCompleted(entity.getId(), em);
}
```

I strongly recommend that you take a look at the `README` file provided with the chapter and at the comments inside the test classes. There are more tests than the ones described in this chapter, so feel free to review them in order to understand more advanced patterns.

Summary

In this chapter, we have covered important patterns that we need to know in order to define our architectures. How we mix and match these patterns depends on the size of the scenario that we are trying to represent. To see how the patterns presented in this chapter can be extended and adapted to cover your business situations, I encourage you to analyze real-life scenarios to mix and match the topics described in this chapter.

I strongly suggest that you join the community after reading this book; it is by far the best way to learn about the project state and future directions. This book will be used as a foundation to write more advanced articles describing topics that weren't covered by the book, so keep an eye on Esteban's blog (`http://ilesteban.wordpress.com`) and my blog (`http://salaboy.com`). Feel free to contact us by commenting on our blogs or by using the community channels, such as the jBPM forum or IRC channels. We hope to have guided you on your first step with jBPM or given you an in-depth perspective of the project components and designs. jBPM and Drools are such big projects that it is almost impossible to cover all of them in just one book. For that reason, we strongly believe that we have set the starting point for iteratively creating more content that helps us to spread the word about these great projects. As you may notice, the second half of this book was about rules and events, where we are definitely extending the BPM system capabilities for more advanced scenarios. Help us to spread the word about this BPMS evolution and if you are interested in contributing back, drop us a line or contact any other project member, as we are always willing to help and guide people to contribute with bug fixes, new features, improvements, documentation, and so on. So don't be shy, and stay in touch!

Index

A

abortWorkItem() method 171, 173
abstract task 75
Abstract Task, task nodes 143
activationCreated( ) method 273
ActiveMQ
  URL 210
ActorId attribute 104
Actors property 141
addService() method 41
addTask() method 213
AdHoc property 135
afterProcessStarted( ) method 273
antinstall.demo command 96
Apache Ant 1.8.X
  URL 94
Apache Mina
  URL 210
application core layer 310
architecture 309, 310
Archive Manager panel 129
Archive option 129
artifacts 74
Assignments property 140-145
asynchronous interactions
  about 176, 177
  executor component 178, 179
  executor service, implementing 180-184
  executor service internals 185, 186
Audit/History Logs module
  about 46
  data analysis tool 47
  data mining tool 47
  real-time dashboards 47
automagicDataInputSet variable 146

B

Background property 137
BAM 46
BasicExecutorBaseTest class 183
before and after temporal operators 294-296
Bitronix 241
BLiP 93
Border Color property 137
BPM
  about 7, 8, 16
  activities, coordinating 23, 24
  activities, orchestrating 23, 24
  business activities, sequence 12, 13
  business entity model 21, 22
  business goal, achieving 15
  business process 11
  business processes, discovering 17-19
  conceptual background 10
  improvements stage 25
  monitoring stage 24, 25
  new processes, formalizing 19, 20
  process 10
  runtime stage 23, 24
  technical assets, implementing 21
BPMN2 34
BPMN 2.0
  about 66
  business scenarios, modelling 77
  common executable Conformance 67
  hospital emergency scenario 77-80
  hospital emergency scenario, technical overview 81-85
  process modelling conformance 66
  task 168, 169

BPMN elements
about 67
artifacts 74
data associations 73
data inputs 73
data objects 72
data stores 72
flow objects 68
grouping elements 73
objects, connecting 71
properties 73
URL 67
BPMS
about 26
check list 26, 27
core 32
key components 31, 32
BPMS core
process engine 33, 34
process engine execution, mechanisms 37, 38
process instance structures 37
semantic module 33
BPM system
and rule engine, integration 60, 61
Business Activity Monitoring. *See* BAM
businessKey entity 321
Business keys 322
Business Logic integration Platform. *See* BLiP
business process 11
Business Process Management. *See* BPM
Business Process Management System. *See* BPMS
Business Process using the BPMN2 Standard (BPMN2) 50
Business Rule Engine (BRE) 76
business rule task 75, 76
Business Rule task, task nodes 142
By Category option 128
By Status option 128

C

Callback (callbacksInput) 191
CDI/WELD 178
CEP 289
CHANGE_SET 51
coincides temporal operator 296, 297
CommandBasedKnowledgeSession instance 238
Command (commandInput) 191
CommandContext object 182
CommandContext parameter 179
Comment property 142
common executable conformance 67
Compiled Package (PKG) 50
complete() method 213
CompleteWorkItemCallback callback 191
CompleteWorkItemCallback class 191
completeWorkItem() method 174
Complex event processing. *See* CEP
Complex Event Processing Features (CEP Features) 48
complex gateway 70, 71
conditional section. *See* LHS
conditional sequence flow 71
Condition expression language property 139
Condition Expression property 139
Contact Customer for Follow Up task 221
CPU restrictions 312
Create new option 126
createProcessKnowledgeSession() method 320
createTaskService() method 247

D

data access layer 311
data analysis tool 47
data associations 73
dataInputAssociation tag 90
dataInput mapping 191
data inputs 73
DataInputSet property 140-143
data mining tool 47
data objects 72
DataOutputAssociation property 138, 156
dataOutputAssociation tag 90
DataOutput property 138, 156
Data Output set editor 144
DataOutputSet property 140-143
data stores 72

Decision Table (DTABLE) 50
Default gate property 150
default sequence flow 71
delayed activation 296
display name section, work Item definition editor 161
documentation property 135
Domain-specific Language Mapping (DSL) 50
domain-specific tasks, Web Process Designer 160
Downloads section 95
Drools Business Rule File (BRL) 51
Drools Flow (DRF) 50
Drools Fusion
  about 290
  before and after temporal operators 294-296
  capabilities 290-292
  coincides temporal operator 296, 297
  event definitions 290-292
  events life cycle management 299, 300
  in action 300, 301
  sliding window, support 298
  system clocks 293
  temporal operators 294
Drools Guvnor
  about 98, 114
  and web process designer 114-118
Drools Rule Engine
  about 259
  declarative approaches and imperative approaches, differences 260
  documentation, URL 260
  example 263, 264
Drools Rule Language (DRL) 50

E

Eclipse BPMN 2.0 plugin 125
Eclipse IDE 101
EDA 287, 288, 61-64
edition canvas section, Web Process Designer 132
Emergency Bed Request Process First Design
  about 134
  End Event node, configuring 148
  process definition, testing 148
  process properties, configuring 135, 136
  sequence flow elements, configuring 138, 139
  Start Event node, configuring 137, 138
  task nodes, configuring 139-143
Emergency Bed Request Process V2
  about 149
  End Event nodes, configuring 154
  Exclusive Gateway node, configuring 150
  process definition, testing 154
  process properties, configuring 150
  Sequence Flow elements, configuring 151, 152
  task nodes, configuring 153
Emergency Bed Request Process V3
  about 154, 155
  Intermediate Signal events, configuring 156
  process definition, testing 157
  process modeling, summary 158
  process properties, configuring 155
  Terminate End events, configuring 156, 157
enabledToDrive attribute 264
End Event node, Emergency Bed Request Process First Design
  configuring 148
End Event nodes, Emergency Bed Request Process V2
  configuring 154
end events 69
Enterprise Service Bus. *See* **ESB**
environment
  setting up 94
ESB 56-58
event
  about 284
  characteristics 285, 286
  interval events 292
  point-in-time events 292
event channels 287
event consumer 287, 288
event definitions, Drools Fusion 290-292
Event Driven Architecture. *See* EDA
event processing agents 287
event producers 287
events life cycle management 299, 300

exclusive gateway 70
Exclusive Gateway node, Emergency Bed Request Process V2
configuring 150
Default gate property 150
Gateway type property 150
X-Marker visible property 150
XOR type property 150
executable property 135
executeWorkItem() method 171, 173, 177
executionResults 191
executor service
about 179
implementing 180-184
internals 185, 186
external service, interactions
about 186-188
context, monitoring 196, 197
data flow 195, 196
execution flow 193-195
executor service 189-193

F

F.A.Q.s 109-113, 119, 120
fireAllRules() method 234, 266
flow objects, BPMN elements
about 68
activities 69
end events 69
events 68
gateways 70, 71
intermediate events 68
start events 68
subprocess activity 69
Font Color property 137
Font Size property 138
footer section, Web Process Designer 133
Frequently asked questions 252-255

G

Gateway conditions
about 269
Java-based conditions 269, 270
Rule-based conditions 271-274
Gateway type property 150
getFactHandle() method 277
GetPatientDataCommand class 191
getPatientData() method 188
getTask() method 213
GitHub repository
URL 215
globals property 135
GroupID property 141
groups 74
Group task lists 219
Guvnor BRMS
about 126
existing processes, accessing 128
existing processes, deleting 129
existing processes, modifying 128, 129
new processes, creating 126, 127
Guvnor's global area 127

H

hospital emergency scenario
about 77-80
simple process data, adding 85-91
technical overview 81-85
HR (Human Resources) 216
Human interactions
about 199
and business processes interaction 207
inside processes 200
Human Task Component entity
about 44
APIs 45
audit/history logs 47
Audit/History logs module 46
identity component 45, 46
Identity component 44
life cycle 45
human task component, jBPM5
about 208-210
HT work item handler, example 215, 216
Human task service APIs 210-213
Human task service APIs, example 210
UserGroupCallback, example 215, 216
user/group callbacks 215
work item handler 214
Human task service APIs
example 210-213
Human tasks life cycle 205-207

HumanTasksLifecycleAPITest test class 210, 211
Human tasks service APIs
about 203-205
external identity component, integration 207
Human tasks life cycle 205-207

I

Identity component 44
ID property 135
if statement 261
imports property 135
inclusive gateway 70
in-memory processes 230
insert() method 234, 265
InsuranceServiceImpl class 187
integration patterns 258
Interface property 141
intermediate events 68
Intermediate Signal Catch event 85
Intermediate Signal events, Emergency Bed Request Process V3
configuring 156
DataOutputAssociation property 156
DataOutput property 156
SignalRef property 156
internalTrigger() method 41
interval events 292
interval parameter 180

J

Java-based conditions 269, 270
javaBasedDecisionTest() method 270
Java Content Repository (JCR) 98
Java Persistence API (JPA) 208
JBoss application server 97
jBPM5
advanced persistence and transactions, configuring 248, 249
components 48
domain-specific behavior 169, 171
persistence 233-235
persistence and transactions, configuring 240-247
robustness, need for 250, 251
synchronous interactions 173
work item handler interface 171, 172
JBPM5 Eclipse plugin 122, 123
jBPM5-GOP-NodeInstance project 34, 35
jBPM5 GWT console 99
jBPM5 installer
default installed tools 97
downloading 94-96
running 96
jBPM5 installer, default installed tools
Drools Guvnor 98
Eclipse IDE 101-106
JBoss application server 97
jBPM5 GWT console 99
jBPM5 process server 99
jBPM GWT console 107, 108
Web process designer 100, 101
jBPM5 official page
URL 94
jBPM5-Process-Events-Patterns project 302
jBPM5 process server 99
jBPM GWT console
summary 113
JDK 6
URL 94
JMS via HornetQ
URL 210
JPAKnowledgeService helper class 235
JPAKnowledgeService. loadStatefulKnowledgeSession( ) method 323

K

kbuilder.getKnowledgePackages() method 51
Knowledge Base 51
Knowledge Builder 50
KnowledgeBuilder.add() method 50
Knowledge-centric APIs
about 49
Knowledge Base 51
Knowledge Builder 50
Knowledge Session 51
Knowledge Session
stateful sessions 52
stateless sessions 52
ksession.getId() method 235

L

LdapUserGroupCallback 216
Left-Hand-Side. *See* **LHS**
length sliding windows 298
LHS 59
loadStatefulKnowledgeSession(...) method 235
LocalHTWorkItemHandler 214
LocalHTWorkItemHandler subclass 216
logical restriction 311
long-running processes
about 230
persisting 232, 233

M

Maven
URL 119
memory restrictions 312
MessageRef property 140
MockAsyncExternalServiceWorkItemHandler class 321
multiple knowledge sessions
coordination 326-328
knowledge context, defining 314, 315
one session per knowledge context level 316
one session per process category 324, 325
one session per process instance 316-319
using, inside application 313, 314
MultiProcessEvaluationTest class 276
multi process instance
evaluations 274-277
MultiSessionsPatternsTest 327

N

name property 135
name section, work Item definition editor 161
New BPMN2 Process option 127
newStatefulKnowledgeSession() method 235
node instance based approach 38-41
NodeInstance object 41

O

On Entry Action property 140-143
one session per knowledge context level 316
one session per process category 324, 325
one session per process instance 316-319
On Exit Action property 140-143
Open button 128
Operation property 141
Oryx 123
over 18 enabled to drive rule 263

P

package property 136
parallel gateway 70
parameters section, work Item definition editor 161
performance restrictions 312
persistence mechanisms
need for 229
states, persisting 231
Persistence & Transactions mechanisms 49
PersistentProcessTest class 243
PM (Project Managers) 216
point-in-time events 292
Predictive Model Markup Language (PMML) 51
Priority property 142
process
about 10
Multi process instance, evaluation 275
Rule-based process, selecting 278-280
ProcessAndHumanTasksTest test class 216
process definition, Emergency Bed Request Process First Design
testing 148
process definition, Emergency Bed Request Process V2
testing 154
process definition, Emergency Bed Request Process V3
testing 157
ProcessDefinitionImpl class 35
ProcessDefinition interface 35

process definitions, Web Process Designer
importing 158, 159
process engine
about 33
components, summary 47
execution, mechanisms 37
process definition structures 34-36
process engine, execution
node instance based approach 38-41
persistence 42, 43
token based approach 38
transactions 42, 43
ProcessEventListener instance 302
ProcessEventListener method 302
ProcessInstance interface 37, 38
processInstancesAndLocalHTTest() 245
ProcessInstance structure
about 39
starting, steps for 39
process modeling conformance 66, 67
process modeling, Emergency Bed Request Process V3
summary 158
process properties, Emergency Bed Request Process First Design
AdHoc property 135
documentation property 135
executable property 135
globals property 135
ID property 135
imports property 135
name property 135
package property 136
Target Namespace property 136
Type Language property 136
Variable Definitions property 136
version property 136
process properties, Emergency Bed Request Process V2
configuring 150
process properties, Emergency Bed Request Process V3
configuring 155
properties 73
properties panel section, Web Process Designer 133
Protobuf
URL 234

R

real-time dashboards 47
Receive task, task nodes 140
regularFlowTest() method 212
Resources class 275
restrictions
CPU restrictions 312
logical restriction 311
memory restrictions 312
performance restrictions 312
technical restriction 311
results section, work Item definition editor 161
RETE network 312
retract() method 234, 266
retries parameter 180
Review Translated Document task form 222, 224
RHS 59
Right-Hand-Side. *See* **RHS**
robustness
need for 250-252
Rule-based conditions 271-274
Rule-based process
selecting 278-280
rule engine
about 59
and BPM system, integration 60
Ruleflow group 144
Ruleflow Group property 142
Rules using Domain-specific Languages (DSLR) 50

S

safe point state 232
safe state 232
Save and close option 128
Save changes option 128
scheduleRequest() method 181
Script Language property 143
Script property 143
script task 76

ScriptTaskNodeInstance object 40
Script task, task nodes 143
security layer 311
semantic module, BPMS core 33
Send task, task nodes 140
sequenceFlow element 84
sequence flow elements, Emergency Bed Request Process First Design
Condition expression language property 139
Condition Expression property 139
configuring 138, 139
sequence flow elements, Emergency Bed Request Process V2
configuring 151, 152
sequence flows 71
service layer 311
service-oriented architecture. *See* **SOA**
service repository
about 163
and Web Process Designer, integrating 163, 164
services 311
Services Human Task. *See* **WS-HT**
services orchestration 54, 55
service task 75
Service task, task nodes 141
SessionsPatternsTestsBase class 328
setUp() method 211
shape repository section, Web Process Designer 131, 132
SignalRef property 156
SimpleProcessExecutionTest.java class 35
singleSessionPerProcessDefinition() test 325
singleSessionPerProcessInstance() method 319
Skippable property 142
sliding window, Drools Fusion
about 298
length sliding windows 298
time sliding windows 298
SOA 53, 54
Start Event node, Emergency Bed Request Process First Design
Background property 137
Border Color property 137
configuring 137, 138
DataOutput property 138
Font Color property 137
Font Size property 138
start events 68
start() method 40, 213
StartProcessCommand execution 240
startProcess() method 175-177, 194, 239
StatefulKnowledgeSession instance 52, 268
StatefulKnowledgeSession interface 235-237
stateful knowledge sessions 314
stateful sessions 52
stateless sessions 52
Subject Matter Experts (SMEs) 284
subprocess activity 69
synchronous interactions 173-175
system clocks, Drools Fusion 293

T

Target Namespace property 136
Task forms
about 220
examples 221-223
requisites 220
Review Translated Document task form 224
Task list oriented user interfaces
about 217
Group task lists 219, 220
Task forms 220-223
Task lists 217, 218
Task lists
about 217
Creation date 218
Description 218
Due date 218
Last update 218
Priority 218
Task name 218
taskName attribute 172
Task Name property 142, 143, 146
task nodes, Emergency Bed Request Process First Design
Actors property 141
Assignments property 140-143

Comment property 142
configuring 139, 140
DataInputSet property 140-143
DataOutputSet property 140-143
GroupID property 141
Interface property 141
MessageRef property 140
On Entry Action property 140-143
On Exit Action property 140-143
Operation property 141
Priority property 142
Ruleflow Group property 142
Script Language property 143
Script property 143
Skippable property 142
Task Name property 142, 143
task nodes, Emergency Bed Request Process V2
configuring 153
TaskService interface 206
taskSpeed.getAmount() method 304
TaskType property 144
task types
abstract task 75
business rule task 75, 76
script task 75, 76
service task 75
user task 75, 76
technical restriction 311
temporal operators, Drools Fusion
about 294
Before and After temporal operators 294-296
Coincides temporal operator 296, 297
summary 297
types 294
Terminate End events, Emergency Bed Request Process V3
configuring 156, 157
testMultiProcessEvaluation() method 276
testProcessCreationDelegation() 279
testSimpleRulesDecision() method 271
text Annotations 74
Then part. *See* **LHS**
threadPoolSize parameter 180
Thread.sleep( ) method 272
time sliding windows 298
tns$taskName attribute 172
token based approach 38
toolbar section, Web Process Designer 131
transaction.manager_lookup_class property 241
transaction mechanism
need for 237-240
Type Language property 136

U

uncontrolled sequence flow 71
update() method 234, 266
UserGroupCallback interface 215, 216
User Interface layer 310
user interfaces
building 225-228
user task 76
userTask instance 88
User task, task nodes 141, 142

V

Variable Definitions property 136
version property 136
visual process validation, Web Process Designer 159

W

wait state 232
WaitTillComplete (waitTillCompleteInput) parameter 191
WebDav
URL 98
Web Process Designer
about 100, 101, 123, 124, 130, 158
and service repository, integrating 163, 164
domain-specific tasks 160
edition canvas section 132
footer section 133
instance 131
process definitions, importing 158, 159
properties panel section 133
service repository 163
shape repository section 131, 132
toolbar section 131

visual process validation 159
work Item definition editor 161
work Item definition editor, using 162, 163
Web Process editor
about 126
existing processes, accessing 128
existing processes, deleting 129
existing processes, modifying 128, 129
new processes, creating 126, 127
Web Service Human Tasks. *See* **WS-HT**
Web Services Business Process Execution Language. *See* **WS-BPEL**
Web Services Human Task. *See* **WS-HT**
when keyword 261
When part. *See* **LHS**
work Item definition editor, Web Process Designer
about 161
display name section 161
icon section 162
name section 161
parameters section 161
results section 161
using 162, 163
work item handler, human task 214
work item handler interface 171, 172
WS-BPEL 54, 55
WS-HT
about 199
Human tasks service APIs 203-205
specification 201, 202
specification in PDF format, URL 200
WS-HTabout 29, 45

X

X-Marker visible property 150
XML Drools Rule Language (XDRL) 50
XOR Exclusive Diverging gateway 84
XOR type property 150

Thank you for buying

jBPM5 Developer Guide

About Packt Publishing

Packt, pronounced 'packed', published its first book "*Mastering phpMyAdmin for Effective MySQL Management*" in April 2004 and subsequently continued to specialize in publishing highly focused books on specific technologies and solutions.

Our books and publications share the experiences of your fellow IT professionals in adapting and customizing today's systems, applications, and frameworks. Our solution based books give you the knowledge and power to customize the software and technologies you're using to get the job done. Packt books are more specific and less general than the IT books you have seen in the past. Our unique business model allows us to bring you more focused information, giving you more of what you need to know, and less of what you don't.

Packt is a modern, yet unique publishing company, which focuses on producing quality, cutting-edge books for communities of developers, administrators, and newbies alike. For more information, please visit our website: `www.packtpub.com`.

About Packt Open Source

In 2010, Packt launched two new brands, Packt Open Source and Packt Enterprise, in order to continue its focus on specialization. This book is part of the Packt Open Source brand, home to books published on software built around Open Source licences, and offering information to anybody from advanced developers to budding web designers. The Open Source brand also runs Packt's Open Source Royalty Scheme, by which Packt gives a royalty to each Open Source project about whose software a book is sold.

Writing for Packt

We welcome all inquiries from people who are interested in authoring. Book proposals should be sent to author@packtpub.com. If your book idea is still at an early stage and you would like to discuss it first before writing a formal book proposal, contact us; one of our commissioning editors will get in touch with you.

We're not just looking for published authors; if you have strong technical skills but no writing experience, our experienced editors can help you develop a writing career, or simply get some additional reward for your expertise.

2818240R00194

Printed in Great Britain
by Amazon.co.uk, Ltd.,
Marston Gate.